INQUISITION AND SOCIETY
IN THE KINGDOM OF
VALENCIA,
1478–1834

INQUISITION AND SOCIETY IN THE KINGDOM OF VALENCIA, 1478–1834

STEPHEN HALICZER

UNIVERSITY OF CALIFORNIA PRESS
BERKELEY   LOS ANGELES   OXFORD

The publisher wishes to acknowledge the generous assistance of the
Program for Cultural Cooperation between Spain's Ministry of Culture and
United States Universities in the publication of this book.

University of California Press
Berkeley and Los Angeles, California

University of California Press
Oxford, England

Library of Congress Cataloging-in-Publication Data

Haliczer, Stephen, 1942–
     Inquisition and society in the kingdom of Valencia, 1478–1834 /
Stephen Haliczer.
         p.   cm.
     Includes bibliographical references.
     ISBN 0-520-06729-0 (alk. paper)   26258706
     1. Inquisition—Spain—Valencia (Province)—History.   2. Valencia
(Spain : Province)—Church history.   I. Title.
     BX1735.H355   1990
     272'.2'0946763—dc20

89-48935
CIP

Printed in the United States of America

1   2   3   4   5   6   7   8   9

The paper used in this publication meets the minimum requirements
of American National Standard for Information Sciences—Permanence
of Paper for Printed Library Materials, ANSI Z39.48-1984 ∞

For Deborah and Elena

Contents

Acknowledgments

During the years of research and writing that went into this book, the author has benefited, directly or indirectly, from the advice and inspiration of various friends and colleagues. Jean-Pierre Dedieu was kind enough to give me a general orientation to the Inquisition records contained in the Archivo Histórico Nacional when I first started my research. Jaime Contreras, Virgilio Pinto Crespo, and José Martínez Millán were also helpful at various times as the research went forward. The author also remembers with great appreciation stimulating conversations with Rafael de Leca García about mutual research concerns. John Elliott read through a late draft of the manuscript, and his excellent suggestions helped me to put it in its final and publishable form. I am also indebted to William Beik, my colleague in early modern history, for his stimulating critique of the manuscript.

I would also like to thank Karen Blaser who, along with her assistants at the Manuscript Services Center, typed the manuscript on several occasions. Eve Simonson of the NIU Computing Information Center was extremely helpful with the computer analysis of my data. The maps and table were prepared at the NIU Art-Photo Laboratory.

Financial support for the project came from the U.S.-Spanish Joint Committee for Cultural and Educational Cooperation. The author was also helped by a grant from the NIU Graduate School. Finally, this project would not have come to fruition without the unflagging support, advice, and intellectual companionship of my wife, Deborah Haliczer.

Abbreviations

AGS: Archivo General de Simancas

AHN: Archivo Histórico Nacional

AMV: Archivo Municipal de Valencia

ARV: Archivo del Reyno de Valencia

BNM: Biblioteca Nacional de Madrid

Note on Spelling and Usage

To maintain uniformity, I have decided to use the Castilian rather than the Valencian or Catalan form of proper names. In the case of institutions and currency denominations, however, I have preserved the original Valencian. Place-names have been rendered in Castilian throughout.

Introduction

From the earliest years of its existence to the present, the Spanish Inquisition has been a controversial institution. Its first victims, the converted Jews, accused it of being far more interested in the money it could make from confiscations than in religious heresy. It was a Spanish Protestant, writing under the name of Reginaldo González Montano, who gave the Spanish Inquisition its reputation as barbarous, arbitrary, and cruel which remains embedded in the public mind to this very day. Montano's book, which was first published in Latin in 1567 and later translated into English, French, Dutch, and German, strongly influenced later Protestant writers like Limborch, Foxe, and Dugdale. An opposing view was presented by Catholic authors like Caesare Carena and Luis de Paramo who depicted the Holy Office as a bulwark of orthodoxy that operated in accordance with widely accepted judicial procedures.[1]

During the eighteenth century, Enlightenment opinion blamed the Inquisition for Spain's intellectual backwardness relative to the rest of Western Europe.[2] Furthermore, judicial reformers demanding a more rational system of justice with clearly defined crimes and appropriately proportioned punishments were outraged by inquisitorial procedure and especially by the auto de fé where "they chant, say mass and kill" all at the same time. So barbarous was this spectacle that if an Asiatic were present, it was alleged that he would not be able to tell whether he had stumbled across "a religious festival, a sacrifice or a slaughterhouse."[3]

Modern Inquisition scholarship really began with the work of

Juan Antonio Llorente, former secretary of Madrid's Corte tribunal, who was put in charge of the archives of the Holy Office after Napoleon abolished the Inquisition in 1808. Using the wealth of material at his disposal, Llorente produced a four-volume history of the Spanish Inquisition first published in French in 1817 and then translated into most of the major European languages. Llorente's position as a prominent supporter of Joseph I's French-imposed government and his criticism of an institution that became the darling of nineteenth-century right-wing opinion made him a controversial figure, and his book had little influence on the future development of Inquisition studies.[4]

Henry Charles Lea, the American publisher and historian, also used an impressive number of copies of original documents, rare books of early modern jurisprudence, and other original materials to compose his *A History of the Inquisition in Spain* (1906–07). This work, which represents the finest flowering of that wave of nineteenth-century American fascination with Spain and her empire was little known in Spain and was only translated into Spanish in 1982.[5]

Except for the publication of a few worthwhile works on specialized subjects, Inquisition scholarship languished from the turn of the century to the early 1960s. But beginning in the mid-1960s, powerful forces that were changing the history profession began to revive interest in the archives of the Holy Office.

For one thing, historians began to realize that the achievements of kings, princes, and statesmen were not the whole of history or the whole of human activity. A growing number attempted to write history from the standpoint of the ordinary person, but in doing so, they had to explore nontraditional sources. It was soon realized that judicial records were among the most valuable of these sources because they were rich in sociological data about accused and accusers. Italian historian Carlo Ginzburg was one of the first to make use of Inquisition records to write social history in his *I Benandanti*, first published in 1966 and translated under the title *The Night Battles* in 1983. This period also marks the beginning of the use of the computer by historians to analyze masses of data that had defied earlier generations. Among the first to apply computer analysis to Inquisition records were Gustav Henningsen and Jaime Contreras, whose work with the case summaries that provincial tribunals sent to Madrid has inspired a generation of Inquisition scholars.[6]

Another important element in the changing historical perspective of the 1960s and 1970s was the growing impact of the Annales school on Spanish historical writing. The emphasis placed by the Annales on the importance of detailed local and regional studies was particularly important to a historical tradition always excessively concerned with the accomplishments and tribulations of central government. The best of these studies, like Bartolomé Bennassar's *Valladolid au siècle d'or* (1967) or Angel García Sanz, *Desarrollo y crisis del antiguo régimen en Castilla la Vieja* (1977), are comprehensive, dealing with all aspects of the life of a particular region—geography, demography, social structure, mental attitudes—to create a rich composite picture.

Directly or indirectly, the influence of the Annales on Inquisition scholarship has been to inspire a number of historians to work on the history of provincial tribunals. Contreras's *El Santo Oficio de la Inquisición de Galicia* (1982), like Bennassar's book on Valladolid, deals with all aspects of the tribunal and attempts to place it firmly within a specific local and regional context. Jean-Pierre Dedieu has recently published a study of the Toledo tribunal, and Rafael de Leca García is working on the tribunal of Granada. Valuable work on the tribunal of Sicily is being done by Agostino Borromeo and on the American tribunals by Richard Greenleaf and Bartolomé Escandell Bonet.[7]

The choice of the Valencia tribunal for my own study was based on the comparative richness of the sources. Unlike certain other tribunals (Barcelona, Córdoba), Valencia's archives preserve book after book of letters to and from the Supreme Council (Suprema). Valencia is also extremely rich in the genealogical records of those who served the tribunal as inquisitors or officials. It has a particularly large collection of the genealogies of familiares, those lay assistants who, I felt, played a far more important role in the history of the Holy Office than historians have given them credit for. Furthermore, while the archives of important tribunals like Valladolid or Seville lack a significant run of case summaries and preserve few original ones, Valencia preserves case summaries from 1560 to the 1720s as well as a significant number of cases. In addition to this material, which may be found in the Archivo Histórico Nacional in

Madrid, the researcher can also find valuable documents in Valencia's local archives, the Archivo del Reyno de Valencia and the Archivo Municipal.

When I began my work on the Valencia tribunal in 1977–78, I was aware of the publication of the first volume of what eventually became a two-volume study of the Valencia tribunal by Ricardo García Cárcel. While I recognize the value of this pioneering effort, my book differs radically from that of García Cárcel in both approach and interpretation.

In the first place, García Cárcel's study stops with the expulsion of the Moriscos and its immediate aftermath, while I have extended my own right down to the end of the tribunal's existence as an institution in the 1820s. I have done this deliberately because I believe that a longer time frame allows me to evaluate trends and tendencies apparent in the early or middle years of the tribunal's history in the light of later developments.

By stopping in the early seventeenth century, for example, García Cárcel comes to the conclusion that the tribunal never had to deal with the problem of illuminism. As I demonstrate, however, the tribunal encountered an important group of illuminists in the later seventeenth century just when the same problem had assumed increased importance in several other districts.[8] García Cárcel's shorter time frame also gives the reader the impression that Judaizing was no longer a major issue for the tribunal after the mid-sixteenth century since the number of cases in this category declines sharply after 1550. Nevertheless, Valencia's inquisitors did remain extremely vigilant against any sign of Judaizing and participated eagerly in the massive attack on prominent New Christian families which involved several tribunals during the 1720s and 1730s.

I have replaced García Cárcel's system of categories for the offenses tried by the tribunal and have adopted one that is as close as possible to the working definitions in use by the tribunal itself. García Cárcel places all of the tribunal's activity under three major headings: counterculture, including the converted Jews, Moriscos, and witchcraft/superstition; sexual crimes, including bigamy, solicitation, simple fornication, sodomy, and bestiality; and crimes of thought and expression. Attempting to force all of the activity of the Holy Office into these rather arbitrary categories (which were never used by the Inquisition itself) is to do violence to the nature of the offense as understood by contemporaries and obscure the reasons the Inquisition became concerned with it. Bigamy and solicitation in the confessional came under the jurisdiction of the Holy Office because of the disrespect for the sacraments of holy matrimony and penance implied in these offenses and not because of their sexual content. In the case of bigamy, the Inquisition did not even deal with the sexual aspects of the case because ecclesiastical courts were left to rule on the question of which of the marriages was valid. The Inquisition's jurisdiction over solicitation was initially confined only to acts or expressions during auricular confession itself, carefully skirting the issue of any wider sexual activity by the accused.

A second major difficulty with García Cárcel's broad categories is that they make it difficult to come to grips with the issue of the social and religious differences among the accused. Not all of the converted Jews, for example, formed part of a religious or social counterculture. Many who were tried by the Inquisition considered themselves devout Catholics, and many others did not experience any significant discrimination on racial grounds and became well integrated into Valencian society. By the same token, the solid citizens who formed partnerships so as to find and release enchanted treasure would have been shocked to find themselves classed with countercultural elements even though they were engaging in superstitious practices.

Finally, I have approached the study of the Valencia tribunal not only by making use of a much larger percentage of the available documentation but by making more intense use of what other historians have skimmed over. More work with the books of letters, for example, might have saved García Cárcel from one of his most grievous errors—the assertion in Book I (only partially corrected in Book II) that the tribunal did not have commissioners.[9] I have also made intensive use of the genealogical records of those who served the tribunal, a category of document that García Cárcel has barely consulted. In dealing with the case summaries, I have gone considerably further than Henningsen and Contreras in gleaning sociological data not only about the accused but also about the way in which trials were conducted and punishments handed out.

To those familiar with García Cárcel's work, my first chapter will appear as a complex refutation of his interpretation of the political history of the tribunal. Where García Cárcel mentions isolated incidents of conflict with other local institutions, I trace a coherent pattern of change and evolution in which a once-powerful tribunal suffers a series of defeats beginning in the early 1550s and finally stabilizes at a much lower level of prestige and political authority.

Furthermore, I cannot accept García Cárcel's interpretation of the role of Valencia's inquisitors as the docile clients and servants of the Inquisitor-Generals who appointed them.[10] Once in Valencia, the inquisitors were far from the reproving eye of inquisitor-general or Suprema, and each man tended to interpret for himself the role of provincial inquisitor. I have chosen to illustrate this point by telling the stories of several of the inquisitors who served on the tribunal at different stages of its history, because it is only by recounting the stories themselves that I can demonstrate to—and evoke for—readers the extent to which inquisitors responded to the needs and opportunities offered by local conditions.

As I stated above, one of the things that drew me to study the Valencia tribunal in the first place was the relative abundance of material about familiares. By making use of a far greater number and variety of documents, I can offer a much fuller account of the evolution of the corps of familiares than García Cárcel, who relies mainly on two censuses, one of them incomplete. Furthermore, I am able to document the political importance of the familiares in giving the tribunal critical support in the rural areas of the district—an issue that García Cárcel entirely ignores.

In these and many other ways, I have sought not to rewrite or even to revise what others have said about the Valencia tribunal or the Kingdom of Valencia itself but to recount an entirely different story. This story involves the inexorable transformation of a once-alien institution into one much more closely identified with the Valencian scene. It is to be hoped that studies of tribunals like this one will eventually result in a new synthesis in which a better balance will be achieved between center and periphery and the role of regional interests in shaping the overall history of the Spanish Inquisition will be given its proper place.

The Kingdom of Valencia, which with a few villages along the Catalan border and the Teruel region of Aragon formed the tribunal's district, had been overrun by the Catalans and Aragonese under James the Conqueror in just sixteen years, from 1229 to

1245.[11] Christian resettlement left mainly Catalan speakers along the coast and Castilian speakers in upland regions, but both were immersed in an Islamic sea as the population remained largely Moorish for many generations.[12] By the time the Valencia tribunal began its operations, the Moors had been pushed out of coastal regions and reduced as a percentage of the population. But, as Moriscos (after 1525), they formed a substantial minority of proto-Moslems who were to provide the tribunal with a large number of its victims.

Geographically, the region is one of sharp contrasts between the lush coastal plains of Castellón or Alicante and the tortuous mountain ranges of the interior. Agriculture, which was the mainstay of the economy, followed the geographic pattern with dry farming in the upland areas and intensive irrigation-based cultivation in the densely populated huerta districts near the Mediterranean coast.[13]

At the time of the Reconquest, Valencia joined Catalonia and Aragon as the third major component of the Crown of Aragon. Ruled by a Catalan dynasty and inspired by Catalan political thought, the monarchy developed a series of unique institutions based on a notion of reciprocity between ruler and ruled. This contractual idea, which set limits to royal power in each of the states, left the Kingdom of Valencia with its own distinct form of government that was to endure until 1707 when it was abolished by order of Philip V.[14]

By the early Hapsburg period, administrative and judicial responsibilities were shared between the viceroy, who represented the king, and the Audiencia (founded in 1506) staffed by Valencian judges. The Audiencia acted as the viceroy's advisory council and functioned as a high court of appeal in both civil and criminal cases.[15]

Like the other states forming the Crown of Aragon, the Kingdom of Valencia had its own individual Cortes, composed of representatives of the clergy, nobility, and towns. The Diputació was a subcommittee of the Cortes responsible for collecting the subsidies granted to the crown. Unlike its counterparts in Catalonia and Aragon, however, the Valencian Diputació never developed into a full-fledged constitutional watchdog able to check the encroachments of overzealous royal officials against the kingdom's traditional contractual constitution.[16]

In spite of an increasing cultural Castilianization, the kingdom was far from easy to govern. Valencia's traditional legal code (furs), which went all the way back to the Reconquest, continued to form the basis for the relationship between king and subject. Violations of the furs by overzealous royal officials would lead to immediate protests by the Cortes, which could assemble whenever it wished.[17]

On two occasions during the life of the tribunal, the tensions that were always just beneath the surface of Valencian society boiled over into violent social upheavals (the first and second Germanías of 1519–1522 and 1693). In 1705–06, the kingdom demonstrated its disloyalty to the Bourbon Philip V by supporting his rival, Charles III. As the demonstrations and processions in support of the sainthood of Padre Francisco Simón were to demonstrate in the period 1612 to 1619, even Audiencia judges could place regional pride above their loyalty to the crown.

The Inquisition in Valencia was founded at a supreme moment of religious fanaticism and strong centralization. As a new and weak institution, it needed and received strong royal protection. By the middle of the sixteenth century, however, local forces were reasserting themselves. After sustaining a series of defeats in conflicts with the cathedral chapter, the jurats, and other institutions, the tribunal found itself largely abandoned by the crown and the Suprema. The tribunal's gradual evolution into a primarily Valencian institution was, therefore, motivated by necessity, the necessity of survival in a world where regional interests had become paramount.

I

Between Monarchy and Kingdom: The Tribunal in Regional Politics

The Spanish Inquisition was not an institution that sprang fully formed from the minds of Ferdinand and Isabella, even though they were responsible for bringing the modern institution into existence and molding its early structure and development. During the early history of the church, the ferreting out of heretics was the responsibility of each bishop, and cases of heresy were heard in the episcopal courts.[1] In the late twelfth and early thirteenth centuries, successive popes began appointing individuals with special powers to investigate and see to the punishment of heretics, in part because of the manifest failure of local bishops to cope with the Albigensian movement in southwestern France and in part out of a desire to further extend direct papal control over the church.[2] By the mid-thirteenth century, the Dominican order was becoming more and more closely associated with these papal efforts to extirpate heresy, and by 1232, when the papal Inquisition came to Spain, the bishops were clearly taking second place to the Dominican friars whose monasteries had the right to name inquisitors from among their own brethren.[3]

Among the states of the Iberian peninsula, the Crown of Aragon appears to have had a much stronger medieval Inquisition than Castile or Portugal, perhaps because it was linked geographically and culturally to areas of France affected by the Albigensian heresy.[4]

The Crown of Aragon had Dominican inquisitors almost continu-
ously throughout much of the fourteenth and fifteenth centuries,
including Inquisitor-General Nicolás Eymerich whose celebrated
work on legal procedures written in the fourteenth century had a
profound effect on the development of the modern Inquisition.[5]

In Castile, the inquisitorial tradition appears to have been much
weaker. Although the Dominican provincial of Castile had the
power to name inquisitors for the province, there is little evidence
that this was ever done, and prosecution of heretics remained
largely in the hands of bishops. So far was Castile from having a
regularly constituted Inquisition like that of the Crown of Aragon
that in 1460, when the reformed Franciscans complained to Henry
IV concerning the religious practices of the converted Jews, he
referred them to Archbishop Carrillo of Toledo.[6]

Several factors combined to alter this situation and endow Castile with the most formidable inquisitorial apparatus in Europe. For
one thing, the converted Jews themselves were becoming the objects of popular hostility, and their unpopularity was being used by
their enemies to exclude them from desirable positions on city
councils and cathedral chapters.[7] To end this mob violence and
deflect the hatred that Old Christians were expressing for all converts regardless of their sincerity, certain converso intellectuals
came to favor the establishment of an institutionalized way of discovering and punishing Judaizing. In this way, the stubborn and
irreconcilable could be justly punished and an example could be
set for the larger number of the confused, uninstructed, and unde-
cided.[8] Converso influence, or the suggestions of conversos like
Alonso de Espina, may have induced Henry IV to attempt to establish an Inquisition under royal control in 1461.[9]

If the idea of an inquisition was the subject of a certain amount of
discussion in the 1460s and 1470s, it took the marriage of Ferdinand
and Isabella and their firm establishment on the Castilian throne
after the end of the first part of the War of Succession to create the
appropriate climate for its creation. Castile and Aragon were linked
politically by this marriage, and while they remained separate king-
doms, a channel had been created through Ferdinand for the migration of certain Aragonese institutions, whose worth had been proven
not only in governing a far-flung Mediterranean empire but internally in the political control of a kingdom that was really a confedera-

tion of provinces. Whether in the area of industrial regulation, as in the greater official toleration accorded to industrial guilds, or in commerce with the establishment of the mercantile Consulate of Burgos in imitation of the Barcelona Consulate of the Sea, or in administration with use by Castile of the viceroy, an Aragonese invention created to deal with the problem of long royal absences, Aragonese influence was very strong throughout the last quarter of the fifteenth century and during the first years of the sixteenth century.[10] The Inquisition was still another Aragonese institution that the Crown of Aragon had used so long and so successfully to prevent the infiltration of unorthodox ideas from France.

Certainly, anyone who has worked extensively in the Inquisition archives is forced to concur with Lea's observation that the Spanish Inquisition in both Castile and Aragon remained firmly under Ferdinand's direction throughout the joint reign.[11] Ferdinand's strong interest in the Inquisition was very much in the tradition of the Aragonese monarchs, who had always been active partisans and sponsors of the Dominican-controlled Inquisition in their dominions.[12]

The papal bull of November 1, 1478, however, which founded the "modern" Inquisition in the Crown of Castile, provided for the establishment of an institution that differed in some very important respects from its medieval Aragonese predecessor. The Dominican-controlled Inquisition in the Crown of Aragon had always depended very much on the goodwill and support of the bishops, who themselves continued their role in the suppression of heresy and formulated cases against heretics in their own courts. At most, the Dominicans had a parallel responsibility for the suppression of heresy, but episcopal jurisdiction was never wholly superseded.[13] In Castile, of course, whatever inquisitorial activity there was, was carried out entirely by the bishops. The kings of Aragon had little or no control over the institution; the inquisitors were appointed directly by the pope. The papal bull of 1478, however, gave the Castilian sovereigns full powers to name inquisitors who would enjoy the same powers and jurisdiction as the bishops and papal inquisitors. The only vestige of papal control over appointments which remained was the right to formally appoint the royal nominees.[14] Ferdinand and Isabella moved quickly to take advantage of their new powers, and by the end of

1481, the first provincial tribunal was operating in Seville. The careers of the two Dominican monks named as Castile's first inquisitors strongly indicate the essential unity of royal policy toward the church. Both Juan de San Martín and Miguel de Morillo were hardened veterans of the early struggles of the monastic reform movement in the Dominican order, and Morillo had just been appointed provincial of the reformed Dominicans of Aragon.[15] In early 1479, just a few months after the papal bull founding the Castilian Inquisition was issued, an embassy was sent to Rome to request many of the same powers over monastic reform that the crown had already obtained over judicial inquiry into heresy, especially the right to appoint prelates who would carry on the reformation of all the kingdom's monasteries.[16] Like the Inquisition, the visitation and reform of monasteries was an exclusively ecclesiastical (and papal) function before the reign of Ferdinand and Isabella, and, like the Inquisition, that function and the power and patronage it represented were eventually taken over by the state with only nominal papal intervention.[17] After a brief experiment with a papal/Dominican Inquisition when Sixtus revoked the 1478 bull and appointed seven Dominican friars to act as inquisitors for Castile, the Castilian Inquisition was firmly reestablished by spring 1483 and began to spread to other parts of the kingdom.

Ferdinand's eagerness to establish an Inquisition under royal control in his own kingdom of Aragon is demonstrated by his attempt to bring the institution into being in advance of the papal response. On Ferdinand's instigation, the general of the Dominican order in Aragon appointed Gaspar Jutglar inquisitor-general of Aragon with the power to appoint subdelegates, and on September 18, 1481, Ferdinand issued writs confirming the appointments of Jutglar and his two nominees, Juan Orts and Juan Cristóbal de Gualbes, who began their work in Valencia in December 1481.[18] In spite of papal reluctance to approve Ferdinand's original request and the revocation of the powers that had been granted to Jutglar by the Dominican general, there is no evidence that they ceased their activities. The papal bull reestablishing the medieval Inquisition in the Crown of Aragon was dated April 18, 1482. But in May of that year, Orts and Gualbes had proclaimed an edict of faith, and eleven individuals presented themselves for reconciliation.[19] By early 1493, overt papal resistance had been brought to an end, and on October 17, Fray Tomás de Torquemada, the royal nominee, was named inquisitor-general of the Crown of Aragon.[20]

Torquemada's nomination as inquisitor-general marks the real beginning of the modern Inquisition in that kingdom as a centralized agency distinct from the Dominican and papal institution that had been in operation during the fifteenth century. Even though Ferdinand failed in his repeated attempts to obtain a papal bull that would extend to Aragon the same absolute powers of appointment and dismissal that he had in Castile, he proceeded as if he had obtained it, naming inquisitors for Aragon, Catalonia, and Valencia in April–May 1484.[21]

In Aragon, however, resistance to the new institution was tenacious, even violent, and the Inquisition required constant royal support to ensure its survival. In Teruel, on the Aragonese-Valencian border, the converso community was powerful and well entrenched within the local oligarchy, so that when inquisitors were sent there at about the same time as the establishment of the Zaragoza tribunal, they found the city gates closed against them and were forced to retire to Cella, a village on the outskirts.[22] From charges brought against the city council by fiscal Juan Jiménez de las Cuevas, it appears that the members of the council and other municipal officials had systematically intimidated all those who openly voiced support for the establishment of the Inquisition, even going so far as to set up a stake in the central plaza and threatening to use it to stone anyone who entered carrying orders from the inquisitors. Alonso de Santángel and other prominent conversos threatened to kill the inquisitors if they disturbed the graves of their ancestors, and the entire city council openly declared that the city would never receive the Inquisition because it would violate its liberties.[23] From their refuge in Cella, the inquisitors responded by fulminating a ban of excommunication against Teruel, but local authorities responded by seizing and imprisoning jurado Fernando de Logroño, who brought a copy of the ban to the city, and by threatening to punish Cella for its support of the inquisitors.[24]

Given the tenacity of Teruel's resistance to the Inquisition, only direct intervention by Ferdinand himself could break the deadlock. Ferdinand needed no urging from the inquisitors and proceeded to resolve the crisis by calling on the Aragonese nobility to mobilize their forces to invade the city. While there is no evidence that such an attack ever took place, the threat of armed action was sufficient to force local authorities to yield and admit the Inquisition, which proceeded to punish several members of the city council for their role in the resistance.[25] The tradition of resistance to the Inquisition died hard in Teruel, and even after it was absorbed by the Valencia tribunal and a subtribunal established there in 1517, there was constant friction between subtribunal officials and local citizens.[26]

In Valencia, the opposition was less violent but more united, taking the form of a series of complaints and demands for reform made by the branches of the Valencian Cortes and then further elaborated in an embassy sent to the king in October–December 1484. These demands, some of which were repeated at the Cortes of Monzón in 1510–1512, would have drastically modified the structure and procedures of the Valencian tribunal and made it a much less dangerous institution. In the first place, the deputies protested against the use of outsiders, that is, non-Valencians, as inquisitors and officials of the court. The Cortes protest was especially directed against Inquisitor Juan Epila, a Dominican monk who was a native of Aragon. The deputies demanded that only Valencians be employed as inquisitors and that these should work without pay.[27]

Proposals to reform the actual procedures used by the tribunal centered around two themes: a lessening of the economic impact of confiscations on the families of the convicted heretic and the concealment of the names of witnesses. Regarding confiscation, the deputies demanded that it should be limited only to property acquired from the day of sentencing and not from when the crime had been committed. To further protect the heretic's family, it was requested that the inquisitorial receiver automatically return the dowry of his wife as long as it could be demonstrated that it had been fully paid over to him. Cortes ambassador Juan Ruiz de Eliori also made a point of criticizing the use of secret testimony on the grounds that such testimony encouraged denunciations motivated by a desire for vengeance rather than by an eagerness to punish heretics.[28]

Superficially, at least, Valencia's leading classes seemed to be supportive of the Inquisition, with the Cortes delegates protesting in their 1484 list of demands that they were not putting them forward in order to prevent the Inquisition from operating effectively.[29] Acceptance of these demands, however, especially the ones voiced at the Cortes of 1484, would have severely handicapped the tribunal. Revealing the names of witnesses would undoubtedly have discouraged denunciations, especially among the tightly knit converso community with its many intricate family connections, while making confiscations date from the day of sentence would have greatly reduced the tribunal's chief economic base.

Complaints from the Cortes about violations of the traditional liberties of the kingdom had little impact on Ferdinand, who was eager to use the new institution as a tool of centralization and who reveled in the fact that he had helped to create a legal institution that could operate free of such constraints. Ferdinand's obstinate refusal to reform the tribunal was accompanied by a concerted effort to defend its independence and authority from both the local oligarchy and the royal officials in the kingdom alike. In response to the series of complaints issued by the Cortes in 1484, Ferdinand ordered his governor to discover the identities of those "malicious" persons who were "threatening" the inquisitors.[30]

Undaunted by Ferdinand's firm support for the tribunal, authorities in Valencia city in collaboration with local notaries concocted a scheme to paralyze it by depriving its notarial staff of the right to certify legal documents such as those pertaining to confiscated property. Supported by the jurats, Valencia's municipal councillors, the chief of Valencia's notaries brought suit to prevent inquisitorial notary Juan Pérez from practicing in the city on the grounds that he was not a member of the notarial college. After the tribunal had apprised him of the situation, Ferdinand acted immediately, writing to the viceroy to order him to take the Inquisition's notaries under his personal protection. At the same time, he addressed himself directly to the head of the notarial college, ordering him to desist from any attempt to prevent the notaries from carrying out their functions and ordering suspension of the case that had been brought against Juan Pérez in the court of the racional.[31]

One of the most consistent demands voiced by local authorities during this early period was that the inquisitors should show them their powers before beginning to exercise their office. If the inquisitors could be forced to do this, then a clear subordination to local authority and local law would be implied and objections could legitimately be put forward to any "irregular" appointments. This demand was first made with respect to the Aragonese Juan Epila whom Ferdinand had appointed to serve as inquisitor in Valencia. Ferdinand, who wished to retain total freedom of action with regard to the new tribunal, had no intention of permitting this, and in 1485, he issued a rather cynical statement justifying his position in which he declared that the officials of the Inquisition occupied ecclesiastical offices instituted by the pope and were therefore not subject to the furs or subordinate to local justices. This royal recognition of papal authority over the Inquisition would have been welcomed by Pope Sixtus IV, from whom Ferdinand had been trying unsuccessfully to obtain full powers of appointment since 1481–82.[32] Regardless of this anomaly, however, it was perfectly consistent with Ferdinand's policy of unlimited support for the Inquisition that the inquisitors should refuse to show their powers to the jurats or to other representatives of local authority and that Ferdinand should support them in their refusal. Later, when this demand was renewed by the jurats, Inquisitors Juan de Monestario and Rodrigo Sanz de Mercado refused, while Ferdinand wrote angrily to the jurats telling them that they had no right to make such a demand and congratulated the inquisitors on their firmness.[33]

If Ferdinand was concerned to prevent local authorities from gaining any measure of control over the tribunal, he was equally concerned to protect and enhance the autonomy of its legal jurisdiction, especially in the area of confiscated property. In 1499, when the governor, jurats, racional, and other local authorities attempted to prevent the tribunal from carrying out a certain confiscation, Ferdinand brusquely ordered them to desist from issuing any further legal requisitions and stated that the only proper way to appeal against anything that was done by the tribunal was to go before its own superior—the Suprema.[34] It was probably as a result of Ferdinand's constant and unremitting support that on June 28, 1500, the Valencia tribunal felt itself strong enough to call all local officials into its presence and demand an oath of loyalty and obedience.[35] From then on, such oaths were routinely demanded and acceded to by the jurats and other local officials.[36] The day was long past when local authorities could demand that inquisitors like Juan Epila present their powers for verification; instead of making the tribunal subordinate to local authority, the chief representatives of local authority were becoming subservient to the tribunal.

One result of constant royal intervention on behalf of the tribunal was to make it dependent on the crown and open the way for Ferdinand to intervene in every aspect of its operations. In spite of Ferdinand's insistence that the authority of the inquisitorial court be maintained inviolate, he himself had no compunction in interceding on behalf of certain individuals if he felt it to be necessary. After learning that the tribunal's receiver was confiscating the property of a group of conversos who thought they had an agreement that protected them from such seizures, Ferdinand ordered further confiscations to cease. Several months later, however, instead of making the tribunal restore the already confiscated property, he ordered it held by the receiver so that part of it could be used to pay the debts owed by this group to certain condemned heretics whose property was already forfeit.[37]

In general, Ferdinand encouraged the zeal of the inquisitors even when the tribunal's actions were of a questionable legality. Certainly, when that zeal seemed to flag, Ferdinand could be caustic in his criticism. The discovery of a secret synagogue concealed in the home of Salvador Vives Valeriola in 1500, long after the tribunal had commenced its operations against the converted Jews, provoked Ferdinand to write an angry letter in which he accused the tribunal of being "lazy and negligent" because of its tardy discovery of a synagogue where Jewish ceremonies were being "openly performed." Ferdinand went on to castigate the tribunal for its failure to obtain an accurate inventory of the property of the accused in this case at the time of their arrest. As a result, a great deal of property that should have been confiscated for the royal treasury was being retained by third parties.[38]

During the reign of Charles V, the Spanish crown continued to provide the Inquisition with strong political support, but where Ferdinand had sought to exercise close control over the institution's operations, especially in the areas of personnel and finance, Charles, who resided in Spain less than 16 years out of his nearly 40-year reign, moved to grant it greater autonomy. In September 1520, Cardinal Adrian of Utrecht, who had already been appointed sole inquisitor-general for Castile and Aragon, was granted full powers of appointment for both inquisitors and officials.[39] Gone were the days when Ferdinand intervened freely to appoint and dismiss inquisitors like Valencia's Juan de Monestario, who after nine years of faithful service was abruptly ordered to pack his bags for Seville.[40]

Finance was another area in which the Inquisition gradually acquired a large measure of autonomy. Just before leaving Spain on May 20, 1520, Charles gave Adrian full authority to issue payment orders; this was confirmed by a September 12 cedula sent to the receivers of all the tribunals.[41] The lengths to which the crown was now prepared to go in abrogating any direct control over inquisitorial finances was demonstrated by an extraordinary royal cedula in which Charles gave the Inquisition permission to ignore any royal orders making grants from confiscated property unless they were countersigned by the members of the Suprema.[42]

Given this general background of firm and unwavering royal support plus the advent of a series of viceroys who tended to perceive the Inquisition as an agent of centralization in a kingdom overly jealous of its privileges, the Valencia tribunal was able to carve out a preeminent position for itself and for all those associated with it. If this preeminence did not outlast the early part of the reign of Philip II, the tribunal's success in combating other local authorities and winning special privileges for its friends enabled it to build up enough political capital to sustain itself even in a later period when its principal function, the pursuit of religious heretics, had been much reduced in importance.

Perhaps the most formidable weapon that the tribunal could wield in its innumerable conflicts with other authorities was its power to lay down a sentence of excommunication that could only be removed by the pope or by the Holy Office itself.[43] The weapon was especially formidable against the mainly secular authorities (Audiencia, jurats, financial agencies) with which the tribunal tended to have the majority of its disputes, since they could not counterattack effectively and were left to appeal to the king for relief. Even if the king was willing to intervene, it was always by the gracious permission of the Holy Office that the ban was lifted, so that the secular tribunal was always placed in a position of inferiority.

The frequency with which the Valencia tribunal used this formidable weapon against the Audiencia is attested by the Concordia of May 11, 1554. In this earliest of all the agreements by which the crown attempted to mitigate the worst abuses of inquisitorial jurisdiction over its own officials and familiares, the Valencia tribunal was ordered to exercise the utmost restraint in using the censure of excommunication against the officers of royal justice, particularly the recently established Audiencia.[44]

The tribunal, however, had no intention of obeying the spirit of the Concordia, as testimony received during the visitation of 1566 clearly indicated. According to the tribunal's judge of the civil cases of familiares, Inquisitor Aguilera had frequently used ecclesiastical censures against the Audiencia judges and other royal officials as well as against the Cortes without attempting any prior conciliation of the subject under dispute. The indiscriminate use of ecclesiastical censures as well as the frequent arrest and incarceration of constables connected with the Audiencia had made the Inquisition "hated in the entire republic."[45]

By the late 1560s, when inquisitorial abuses had become so serious that the other royal courts were in danger of becoming discredited, it was decided to dispatch a member of the Supreme Council itself to make a special visitation to the tribunal. While in Valencia, this official was presented with a long memorial by the judges of the Audiencia which complained bitterly of the recent use of ecclesiastical censures excommunicating them along with the agents of the royal treasury and prominent private individuals. According to the memorial, these censures had been issued for matters of little importance, and their unceasing use was "ruining the respect" that was due the Audiencia and the royal treasury as representatives of the king's authority in the Kingdom of Valencia.[46]

Another very powerful device that the tribunal could use to intimidate its enemies was to accuse them of creating obstacles to the free exercise of the Holy Office. Eymerich's manual for inquisitors states that any such person was to be excommunicated with the proviso that if the ban was not lifted within one year, they were automatically considered heretics. In the sixteenth century, several papal bulls further refined the definition of the crime of obstructing the Holy Office and provided that anyone threatening the person of an inquisitor or preventing the Inquisition from carrying out its responsibilities was to be relaxed to the secular arm.[47] The importance of preventing opposition to the Holy Office was made known to the general public by equating "impeders of the Holy Office" with heretics in the oath to support the Inquisition that was sworn by all present at the annual proclamation of the Edict of Faith.[48]

Given the Valencia tribunal's eagerness to enhance its power and authority, it quickly recognized the value of being able to formulate what amounted to a heresy case against its political opponents whose opposition could be equated with attempting to prevent the Inquisition from carrying out its proper duties. In 1528, the tribunal was presented with an excellent opportunity to demonstrate the power of this particular weapon. The seizure of Onofre Centellas, an important Valencian noble, for aiding two of his in-laws in resisting arrest by the Inquisition aroused a storm of indignation among the greater and lesser Valencian nobility. Two well-known Valencian lawyers, Damián Andrés and Melchor Mont, but especially the latter, played a leading role in organizing this opposition. Andrés and Mont organized an emergency meeting of the Valencian estates at the cathedral, while Mont drew up a petition for presentation to the viceroy. It was all very well for the Inquisition to exercise its authority over the converted Jews, the protest declared, but its extension to "other persons and cases," especially, it may be presumed, cases involving the Valencian nobility, was denounced as a usurpation of "imperial jurisdiction." After drawing up his petition, Mont went on to loudly support a proposal that the delegates arm themselves and march on the Inquisition to demand Centellas's release and even proposed that the tribunal's prosecuting attorney be seized as a hostage.

Fortunately for the tribunal, Fernando de Aragón, Duke of Calabria, was one of those early sixteenth-century viceroys whose policy was characterized by firm and unwavering support for the Inquisition. On receiving Mont's petition, the duke wrote immediately to Inquisitor-General Alfonso Manrique to apprise him of the situation, and Manrique in turn ordered the immediate arrest of Mont and Andrés. On January 28, 1528, the two men were placed under house arrest in spite of Mont's attempt to claim the archbishop's protection by taking sanctuary in the cathedral, and fiscal Juan González de Munebrega formally accused them of "obstructing the exercise of this Holy Office." After being tried and found guilty, both were publicly humiliated in such a way as to serve as a warning to other members of Valencia's ruling elite who might have similar ideas. The two men were forced to hear mass in the cathedral bareheaded and holding lighted candles and then to swear obedience to the commandments of the church and to fully support the jurisdiction of the Holy Office; they were also deprived of the right to plead before the Audiencia until the inquisitor-general should decide to lift the ban. Even though Manrique acted quickly to release the men and lift the restriction on their practice of law, the point had been made. The Valencia tribunal was prepared to intervene against its political opponents on the grounds that they were "obstructing" its work, and henceforth even the highest ranking nobles could not consider themselves immune from prosecution.[49]

One area of great and consuming interest to everyone connected with the Valencia tribunal was the issue of obtaining tax exemptions. Since royal policy was far from consistent, the degree of exemption became the subject of a power struggle between the Inquisition, on the one hand, and the representatives of the various taxing bodies, on the other. In the Kingdom of Valencia, the Diputació was a committee of the Cortes empowered to collect and administer the taxes that were used to defend the kingdom. The major source of income was derived from customs duties payable by everyone carrying merchandise across Valencia's land borders, but according to a letter sent to Charles by the Cortes deputies in 1525, Valencia's inquisitors were regularly issuing licenses stating that exported items were destined for the Suprema and were therefore under inquisitorial protection. While theoretically the several tribunals had the right to send items that were for the exclusive personal use of the members of the Suprema free of customs duties, the Valencia tribunal was abusing this privilege and carrying on a lucrative trade in contraband merchandise. All that the deputies received for their pains was a letter from Ugo de Urríes, a secretary of the Suprema, blandly assuring them that the matter would be handled to everyone's satisfaction, but when they sent several delegates to court to make further remonstrations, they were arrested by order of the inquisitor-general.[50]

The Valencia tribunal's successful assertion of its right to avoid paying the customs duties levied by the Diputació was matched by a similar attitude toward the Peatge and Quema, which were customs duties forming part of the royal patrimony and levied by the Bailía General, the royal treasury of the kingdom.[51] Licenses protecting cargoes from inspection were a sore point with the Bailía collectors who were always looking for a way to assert their jurisdiction. An inadvertent declaration of part of a cargo that was being exported under the guidance of one of the officials of a Valencian subtribunal seemed to establish just the sort of precedent that the royal collectors were looking for, and high officials of the Bailía were quick to instruct their agents to levy duties on all merchandise being exported under license of the Inquisition. Confronted with this threat to what they had come to consider their rights, the Valencian inquisitors reacted immediately by excommunicating the entire staff of the royal treasury.[52]

One of the most delicate issues in the relations between the Spanish regions revolved around the export of grain from regions of relative plenty to areas of relative dearth. The needs of importing regions like Valencia, which was never self-sufficient in grains, were met in part by imports from grain-producing areas of the Crown of Aragon, but such imports clashed with that kingdom's natural desire to retain as much as possible against the possibility of poor harvests. The Valencia tribunal and its agents had a real opportunity to profit by the kingdom's perennial need for imported grain because two Aragonese grain-producing regions, Teruel and Albarracín, were included in the inquisitorial district and therefore subject to its authority. In Teruel, the opportunity was even greater because there was a subtribunal in residence. Ostensibly, only small amounts of grain were to be exported from the Aragonese part of the district to meet the specific needs of the judges and salaried members of the Valencia tribunal. Constant complaints by the Council of Aragon of exports far in excess of these requirements finally forced the tribunal itself to undertake an investigation and bring criminal charges against its own lieutenant-inquisitor in Teruel, canon Pablo Guillem. During the course of his trial, Guillem was accused of issuing inquisitorial export licenses broadcast to members of his own family, local familiares, and other officials of the subtribunal and of personally leading raids on royal customs officials who had confiscated contraband grain and other items.[53] Guillem was sentenced to be suspended from serving on the subtribunal for four years, but the evidence suggests that the pattern of illegal grain export from the Aragonese parts of the district continued well into the latter part of the sixteenth century. Even after the subtribunals had been abolished and replaced by comisarios, the lure of quick profits to be made from grain exports to Valencia proved irresistible, and the comisarios continued issuing licenses to local familiares in spite of the fact that the Concordia of 1568 had specifically denied them that right.[54]

The sweeping exemption from customs duties, whether levied by royal or provincial taxing bodies, was of considerable benefit to everyone connected with the tribunal, from inquisitors and officials down to familiares. If licenses issued by the tribunal could be used to avoid the ubiquitous transit taxes levied in early modern Spain, then those who could obtain them would have an inestimable advantage over any potential business rival.

Of course, customs duties were not the only taxes paid by citizens of the kingdom, and the licensing system could only benefit a relatively few officials and familiares. For the larger group who did not engage in the export trade, exemption from local excise taxes and protection from creditors was far more important. On the whole, and in spite of the protests voiced at the Cortes of 1510, the tribunal was able to win complete tax exemption for titled officials from at least 1514.[55] The Concordia of 1568 specifically freed inquisitors and officials from payment of municipal taxes, while in 1570, an agreement between the viceroy and the local tax farmers which provided for excluding titled officials from the tax rolls indicates that such tax exemptions had become routine.[56]

As far as the familiares were concerned, the Concordia of 1554 specifically denied them any tax exemptions from royal or municipal taxes.[57] As we have already seen, however, many familiares were able to exempt themselves and their merchandise from customs duties by making use of inquisitorial licenses. On a municipal level, the Inquisition's protection was less effective, but in some parts of the district, familiares were able to secure a measure of exemption from local taxation. In other respects, the Inquisition could and did extend its protection in ways that were beneficial to the familiares. Prohibitions listed in the 1568 Concordia clearly indicate that the tribunal had made a practice of interposing its authority to protect artisans and merchants who were familiares when they cheated their customers and familiares who were tax-farmers when they defrauded the Diputació treasury.[58]

Familiares could also count on exemptions from quartering troops or members of the royal court. That this exemption had been fully observed during much of the sixteenth century is clear in testimony taken by the tribunal from certain of its longest-serving officials and familiares in 1575 when the viceroy made an effort to test the exemption by lodging a soldier in the home of a familiar. According to testimony received from familiar Alejo Castellano de Aguirre, who at age 66 had served the tribunal for forty years, his own exemption had been tested when Charles V visited Valencia in December 1542. On being asked by the viceroy's lieutenant to house several imperial halberdiers, Aguirre refused, alleging an exemption on the grounds of his familiatura, and the soldiers were billeted on someone else.[59] Testimony taken a few days earlier from an official, Alcalde Juan de Oñate, indicates that the tribunal had always tenaciously defended this exception, using its favorite weapon—the ecclesiastical censure—when necessary against royal captains who attempted to lodge their troops at homes of familiares or officials.[60]

By far the most significant benefits that were brought to the lives of those associated with the Inquisition came because they, their families, servants, and even slaves, all formed a distinct corporate group enjoying a fuero, or separate legal status, of their own. Like the members of the Order of Montesa in Valencia or of other military orders in the rest of Spain, these privileged persons could not be tried on civil or criminal charges before the ordinary courts but had the right to a trial before their own court, in this case, that of the Inquisition.[61]

It was during the early period of the Inquisition's existence, when Ferdinand was struggling to protect the fledgling institution from its numerous enemies, that the principle of the Inquisition's right to exercise complete jurisdiction over the civil and criminal cases of officials and familiares was first stated.[62] Widespread abuses, however, gave rise to a chorus of complaints, so the 1498 Instructions sharply limited inquisitorial jurisdiction by disallowing any cognizance over civil cases and by limiting jurisdiction in criminal cases to officials only.[63] But accepting the limitations imposed by the 1498 Instructions would have undermined the basis of the alliance between the Inquisition and the growing body of familiares who were providing it with increasingly effective political support. In Valencia, where the corps of familiares was larger and more important than anywhere else in Spain, the tribunal had no intention of observing the restrictions imposed by the 1498 Instructions. Familiares and officials were accorded the fullest possible protection, and even the well-established legal principle that the plaintiff had to seek the court of the defendant was ignored. Familiares and officials were routinely accorded the active fuero, being allowed to bring accusations before the inquisitorial court in both civil and criminal cases in spite of constant protests from the regent of the Audiencia.[64] In their zeal to cement their alliance with the familiares by extending the fuero, the Valencia inquisitors even went so far as to issue edicts containing ecclesiastical censures against persons suspected of robbing them and intervening to force their debtors to pay what they owed.[65]

To further enhance its authority and increase its income from hearing ordinary cases, the tribunal extended its fuero to as many people as possible. The 1568 Concordia allowed the fuero to be extended not only to the wives and families of officials and familiares but also to those commonly forming part of their household.[66] In 1589, testimony received by the tribunal from Francisco Baziero, its longtime notary of civil cases, revealed that for the entire twenty-five years that he had spent in the tribunal's service, his court had even heard civil cases brought by reconciled persons since they too "enjoyed the fuero." In his testimony, Baziero also gave a list of persons who had successfully invoked the tribunal's jurisdiction to collect debts owed to them.[67]

Another very important privilege that the tribunal was able to gain for its familiares was the right to bear arms of all sorts whenever they chose, including the feared flintlocks. In the 1554 Concordia, Prince Philip turned a blind eye to any potential abuses of this privilege in vendetta-ridden Valencia with the bland statement that since familiares were to be chosen from among the most "peace-loving" segment of the population and were committed to the royal service, there was no need whatever to limit their right to carry arms. Of course, this generous demonstration of royal support flew in the face of another royal policy, enunciated by successive viceroys and enforced by the royal Audiencia, which was to limit the number of weapons in circulation and eliminate the flintlock entirely. Efforts by the Audiencia to enforce successive vice-regal prohibitions, however, entailed a head-on clash with the Holy Office on each of the many occasions when a familiar was arrested carrying prohibited arms. One of the most bitter complaints voiced by the Audiencia in the list that it prepared for visitor Francisco de

Soto Salazar in 1567 was that the tribunal had never been willing to cooperate informally to reduce the number of flintlocks in the hands of its familiares and whenever the royal constables detained a familiar for possession of a prohibited weapon, the inquisitors had intervened to place the constables themselves under arrest.[68]

Confident of automatic royal support or at least tolerance of its activities and eager to build up a political clientele throughout the kingdom, the Valencia tribunal was quite willing to intervene in local disputes even though such intervention went far beyond its stated responsibilities. During the 1560s, Tortosa was divided between the Molinar and Despuche factions. Juan Molinar was a familiar and could count on the support of Tortosa's Lieutenant-Inquisitor Pedro Boteller and his alguacil, Cosme Castellar. Castellar, in turn, enjoyed a warm relationship with the man who had appointed him, the tribunal's chief constable Francisco de Hermosa. Whenever Castellar would come to Valencia, he would stay with Hermosa, and Hermosa was not above accepting valuable presents and favors from the Molinar group. In their struggle with the Despuche faction, the Molinar family enjoyed some very significant advantages as a result of their close ties with the Inquisition. As an official of the Holy Office, Lieutenant-Inquisitor Boteller was protected by the fuero from having to allow any royal constable to enter his home. As a result, whenever the Molinar gang returned from one of its violent forays, they would take refuge with Boteller and thumb their noses at any constable who came to arrest them. Boteller would also use his considerable political influence on behalf of the Molinar group. On one occasion, when Molinar wished to rid himself of Juan Pérez Morena, a member of the opposing faction, he had him denounced for murder, whereupon he was duly arrested by the royal constables and brought to trial. Since the charges against Morena were obviously false, he was acquitted and was on the point of being released when Boteller intervened, forcing the royal officials to continue his detention.[69]

For their part, the Despuche faction bitterly resented the role that the members of the subtribunal were playing in their conflict with the Molinar, and they were determined to strike back. In February 1565, they attacked and burned Castellar's home. This direct attack on a member of the subtribunal, whatever its provocation, was considered an effort to "obstruct" the operations of the Holy

Office by the tribunal in Valencia, and Castellar's friend, Francisco de Hermosa, came to Tortosa to arrest the three leading members of the rival faction and to conduct them back to Valencia.[70]

Fully confident of the complaisance of a series of tolerant viceroys, the tribunal felt little need to show any outward respect for or cooperate with other institutions, whether royal (the Audiencia) or ecclesiastical. During the early 1560s, the Suprema received several letters from both the Audiencia and the archbishop's court complaining of a lack of even elementary cooperation by the tribunal. The Audiencia was particularly angry because the tribunal would frequently remove prisoners from the royal prison where they were awaiting trial, try them for some minor offense, and then let them go free without returning them. Since this practice was becoming well known among the criminal element, it was increasingly common for some dangerous criminal awaiting trial for murder to utter a blasphemy in his cell, where he would be overheard by other prisoners and then denounced to the Inquisition. Since the penalty for blasphemy was usually rather mild and the offender could count on being set free afterward, serious crimes were left "without punishment" to the "great detriment of the administration of justice."[71]

As jurists and veterans of the imperial bureaucracy, the Valencian inquisitors were well aware of the importance of seizing and holding positions of preeminence at public ceremonies or in places where others who could lay claim to similar status were present. By permitting and seeming to approve of, or at least acquiesce in, conspicuous displays of status by the inquisitors, their peers among the social and political elite implicitly validated these claims, while the general public, which witnessed the inquisitors occupying such exalted positions, could not fail to be awed by the general respect in which their persons and the institution that they represented seemed to be held.

Naturally, the inquisitors played a leading role in the great public autos de fé and the procession that preceded them, but high visibility on other occasions or in other places not directly connected with the Inquisition was necessary if the tribunal was to attain the sort of prestige that it desired. At ordinary religious processions such as Corpus Christi, therefore, the members of the tribunal insisted on marching in a position of the greatest honor even if it meant displacing several canons of the cathedral. In the cathedral itself, the inquisitors were able to obtain control over the two most prestigious stalls in the choir, much to the dismay of the canons.[72] The inquisitors were also frequently present at other public spectacles such as civic processions and bullfights. As spectators, they made it their business to use the most magnificent cushions and to place themselves in a conspicuous position at the windows to the inquisitorial palace so that everyone would notice them.[73]

Quite apart from its frequently rather high-handed relations with other institutions, the tribunal could behave in an aggressive manner toward private citizens in ordinary matters that had nothing to do with its area of responsibility. Typical of this aggressive attitude was the way that the tribunal forced notary Berengario Serra to leave the house he had been renting near the inquisitorial palace. The tribunal wanted the house for Nicolás Verdun, one of its notaries, who had himself been displaced because the owner of the house he was renting had returned to Valencia and Serra's house was cheaper and closer to the tribunal than any other.[74]

Throughout the last years of the reign of Ferdinand the Catholic and during most of the reign of his successor, Charles V, the Spanish Inquisition in general and the Valencia tribunal in particular had enjoyed a golden age. Basking in the glow of royal favor and approval, the Holy Office was openly disdainful of the other institutions of royal justice and arrogant in its relations with the representatives of clergy or local government.

Several years before the reign of Philip II officially began in 1556, the climate in which the Inquisition had flourished so remarkably had begun to change. Philip's attitude—as prince and regent and, later, king—toward the Inquisition was very much in line with his general policy, which was to endeavor to bring the rather chaotic administration that he had inherited from his father under firmer central control and to reduce the scope for private profit and abuse of power by those connected with state service.

In the case of the Inquisition, Philip's unwavering support for its role in preserving a Catholic Spain was never in doubt, but to allow it to assume a position of superiority in areas outside its area of competence was to undermine the principle of royal control and damage the credibility of the ordinary courts whose operations were the most visible and continuous manifestation of royal sovereignty. Given the general orientation of his policies, therefore, Philip was highly receptive to complaints from Audiencia judges that the Inquisition was abusing its authority over officials and familiares to the detriment of royal justice. Typical of these complaints was a letter from the regent of Audiencia of the Valencian Audiencia complaining of the excessively large number of familiares in the kingdom and of the use of the active and passive fuero in both civil and criminal cases.[75] Similar protests from Castile had already moved Philip to suspend the provisions of the July 15, 1518, cedula by which his father had granted the criminal fuero to the familiares of the Castilian tribunals.[76]

Alarmed by the complaints reaching him from the Audiencia and other sources, Philip decided to replace his lieutenant-viceroy, Juan Lorenzo de Villarrasa, with a new viceroy who would be given full powers to investigate the situation and make recommendations for reform.[77] Already suspicious of the Inquisition because of the mandate that he had been given to investigate its abuses, the new viceroy, Bernardino de Cárdenas, lost no time in becoming involved in a bitter dispute over a familiar. Cárdenas's arrest of Mateo Juan on suspicion of murder forced the tribunal to issue a ban of excommunication against him and destroyed any opportunity that it might have had to create a more amicable relationship with him during his term of office. Viceregal interference with the fuero, however, prompted considerable soul searching by the tribunal and a recognition that its activities were creating many enemies among the politically influential.[78]

In April 1553, the viceroy filed a report with Philip in which he charged that familiares were committing "many crimes" under the tribunal's protection and warned of the dangers to royal jurisdiction that abuses of the fuero might entail.[79] But the viceroy's real opportunity to launch an attack on the tribunal was provided by a resolution taken at the Cortes of Monzón, which called for limitations on the fuero and a reduction in the number of familiares. This rather timid resolution, which was only supported by two of the three estates, might have easily been ignored, and the fact that it was not is an indication that the crown was now serious about reform.[80]

Taking their cue from the resolution passed at the Cortes, Valencia's jurats were quick to present a petition to the viceroy filled with specific complaints about abuses of the inquisitorial fuero and the excessive number of familiares and echoing the viceroy's warnings about potential damage to royal jurisdiction. For once, the normally feuding representatives of municipal and royal authority were in concert, and the regent of the Audiencia was instructed by Viceroy Cárdenas to undertake an investigation of the charges presented in the jurats' petition. What followed was a dramatic series of hearings held before the judges of the Audiencia, with a parade of witnesses drawn primarily from notaries and officials of agencies with a history of frequent conflict with the tribunal. To no one's surprise, the testimony was uniformly unfavorable to the fuero and detailed abuses calculated to anger Philip, such as armed resistance offered by familiares to royal constables. The tribunal had clearly miscalculated the degree to which its enemies could coordinate their efforts, and its response to the challenge posed by the Audiencia hearings was so slow that it was a full fifteen days before it was even aware that they were being held.[81]

The most important result of this campaign was the Concordia of May 11, 1554, which was drawn up at a joint meeting of the Suprema and the Council of Aragon. In this agreement, which was the first of the four Concordias regulating the Inquisition in the Crown of Aragon, limits were placed on the number of familiares that each town and village could have, wives and children were excluded from the protection of the fuero, and the scope of the fuero in civil cases was limited only to cases where familiares were defendants.[82] The Concordia also excluded use of the fuero in cases of commercial fraud and stated specifically that familiares were subject to all royal and provincial taxes.[83]

That Philip himself intended the Concordia to be interpreted so that ambiguous cases would be tried by the ordinary courts was made clear by his intervention in the case of Francisco Juan Vergonoys, a familiar from Barcelona who was caught attempting to export oil without paying the duties levied by the Diputació. When consulted by the tribunal after Vergonoys was arrested by local officials, the Suprema stated that the tribunal had a right to take cognizance of the case since the 1554 Concordia said nothing about jurisdiction over cases involving tax evasion. But Philip had a different interpretation, and on July 12, 1560, he ordered the tribunal to surrender the case to the ordinary civil courts.[84]

The need to further define those areas of civil law where the fuero would not be extended was one of the most important reasons for issuing a new Concordia in 1568. In this document, the ordinary civil courts were given jurisdiction over familiares who attempted to avoid payment of duties levied by the Diputació or who committed frauds while acting as collectors for that institution or for the city itself. Familiares who violated ordinances that set limits on the amount of timber that could be imported and sold, or regulated the planting of rice, could also no longer expect protection. In criminal matters, the tribunal was not permitted to use ecclesiastical censures to force those who had robbed officials, consultores, or familiares to reveal themselves or force debtors to pay their debts.[85]

Another important provision of the 1568 Concordia dealt with the issue of the subtribunals. The corruption and abuses of the subtribunals and their officials formed a large part of the evidence taken during the visitations of 1560 and 1567, while the illegal export of grain from those areas of the district that really belonged to the Crown of Aragon were a sore point with the Aragonese authorities. Philip's anger about this situation came to a head in 1567 when he insisted that the Suprema order the arrest of the tribunal's lieutenant-inquisitor and lieutenant alcalde in Teruel because they had issued numerous licenses for illegal grain exports.[86] The Concordia provided for the elimination of the subtribunals and their replacement by comisarios. In matters of heresy, the comisario would only be able to receive information that he would then forward to the tribunal, and he would only be able to carry out arrests when he believed that the suspect was about to escape. Comisarios were strictly forbidden to issue licenses to individuals wishing to transport wheat or other commodities.[87]

In practice, however, the comisarios made use of their powers to do a brisk business in the sale of export licenses in spite of the growing opposition of royal financial officials and the Aragonese Cortes. Finally, it was the Suprema itself, alarmed at the growing chorus of complaints from the king, the Council of Aragon, and the Cortes that intervened to halt this practice. When Philip relayed information that had reached him concerning the illegal issuing of licenses by canon Camarena, the tribunal's comisario in Teruel, the Suprema cracked down, threatening him with severe punishment

if these practices continued. The practice of issuing excessive numbers of export licenses had clearly become a political liability at
court and was embroiling the Suprema in an embarrassing series of
conflicts from which it could only emerge with dishonor. In 1607–
08 when the deputies to the Cortes of Aragon flatly refused to
tolerate any further licenses for the export of grain from the kingdom and complained directly to the king about the activities of the
Valencia tribunal, the Suprema ordered the Valencia tribunal to
abstain from any further attempts to ship grain from Aragon without special permission.[88]

Philip was also concerned to regulate the relations between the
tribunal and the Audiencia. Noisy disputes and the public excommunication of royal officials were hardly conducive to maintaining
public respect for the institutions of royal government, and constant feuding among the royal courts distracted them from carrying
out their primary responsibilities. One step in the direction of
promoting better relations among the various courts was to order
the Inquisition to cease its practice of removing individuals from
the criminal jails on suspicion of a crime against the faith and then
releasing them when their trial was concluded. It was also made
mandatory for the Holy Office to at least notify a royal court of a
disagreement before resorting to ecclesiastical censures. Finally, an
elaborate procedure was instituted which was designed to provide
for the settlement of jurisdictional disputes. If the tribunal found
itself to be in disagreement with the Audiencia as to the disposition
of a case, the oldest inquisitor and the regent of the Audiencia were
to meet and attempt to settle the dispute. If this effort were to fail,
then the case should be suspended and each tribunal would forward a copy of the case to its respective superior, the Council of
Aragon for the Audiencia and the Suprema for the tribunal, with a
panel drawn from both councils making the final decision.[89]

The Concordias of 1554 and 1568 represented a moderate and
reasonable approach toward making the legal machinery of the
state function more smoothly and with fewer acrimonious public
disputes. But the very fact that, for the first time, specific limits
were being placed on the extent of the jurisdiction that the Holy
Office could exercise over familiares and officiales gave the Audiencia a priceless opportunity to expand its jurisdiction at the Inquisition's expense. This was especially true because the Concordias

reduced the effectiveness of the Inquisition's most formidable weapon, the immediate imposition of ecclesiastical censures. In fact, even before the 1568 Concordias in which these curbs were initiated, the Suprema, no doubt painfully aware of the changing climate at court, had introduced its own restrictions on the use of such censures. After 1560, local tribunals could no longer automatically impose them and were forced to send details of the dispute to the Suprema, which would make the final decision.[90]

Far from stabilizing the boundaries of the respective jurisdictions, therefore, the Concordias put the Inquisition on the defensive and marked the beginning of the Audiencia's long and ultimately successful struggle to reduce or eradicate the special position that the tribunal and those associated with it had made for themselves. That the Suprema itself was nervous about the new climate is revealed by a symbolic marshaling of the documents that conferred special status on the Inquisition. Symbolic because its request to the tribunal to forward a summary of all the papal bulls and even the cartas acordadas, which demonstrated "how favored" were the things of the Holy Office and "how its jurisdiction had been amplified and extended by popes and kings," was unnecessary as the Suprema had copies of most of these items in its own files. Even if the Suprema genuinely lacked some of these documents, the underlying reason for its request and the tribunal's resulting dispatch of the desired summary was a search for reassurance and an effort at mutual encouragement by the officials of an institution sensing the beginning of decline. This was the first in a long series of frantic searches through tribunal records for evidence that would support the Inquisition's pretensions. While the searches and the institutional insecurity were part of the process that led to the organization of the inquisitorial archive and greatly benefited future investigators, the endless regurgitation of the same material provides an ironic counterpoint to the decline of a once-formidable institution.[91]

The Audiencia's efforts to undercut the provisions favorable to the Inquisition in the Concordia began with the yearly oath by which Audiencia judges and municipal officeholders alike promised to support the Holy Office. In the 1554 Concordia, the oath was required of all officeholders, but the Audiencia judges and other royal officers dragged their feet on compliance until they openly refused in 1563 on the grounds that as they had not sworn the oath every year since

1554, the demand that they take it now was an "innovation." Almost one year later, the regent and judges agreed to take the oath but in a modified form, leaving out words such as "preeminence" which seemed to make the ordinary royal courts subservient to the tribunal.[92] The tribunal had won a Pyrrhic victory in the matter of the oath, but the Audiencia's strategy of seeking to establish precedents that would support its long-term effort to undercut the tribunal's position had become firmly established.

One rather peculiar aspect of the inquisitorial fuero was its extension to cover reconciled persons. Whatever their punishment, the reconciled had, in effect, become "clients" of the Holy Office, which claimed full jurisdiction over both criminal and civil cases involving them. This unreasonable extension of the fuero, which was clearly just a way for the Inquisition to tap a lucrative source of legal business, was the subject of a bitter complaint in the Audiencia's memorial presented to visitor Francisco de Soto Salazar in 1567. This aspect of the fuero was ignored in the 1568 Concordia, and according to testimony received from Jerónimo Almenara, an Audiencia notary, later in the century, the tribunal had tried all civil and criminal cases involving reconciled persons during the entire time that he had been associated with that body.

The fact that the tribunal's jurisdiction over these individuals was neither confirmed nor denied in the Concordia, however, placed the whole issue in an unregulated zone where matters were resolved by a struggle between the two tribunals, both using every means at their disposal. In 1582, the Audiencia felt strong enough to contest the tribunal's uninterrupted enjoyment of the right to try reconciled persons by ordering the arrest and trial of Luis Picote, who was accused of rape after his reconciliation by the Holy Office. It also sought to create a precedent for the reconciled to appeal directly to it by inducing Juan Corsi, a reconciled Morisco, to denounce certain persons who assaulted him before the Audiencia instead of before the tribunal.[93]

In dealing with the Inquisition's clear and unambiguous right to try the criminal cases of officials and familiares, the tactics employed by the Audiencia were subtler. Instead of making a direct assault on the tribunal's criminal jurisdiction, the Audiencia sought to use other provisions of the Concordias or other ordinances relating to familiares to undermine its authority in specific cases and to assert its own key role in the enforcement of viceregal pragmaticas and royal laws to override the criminal fuero in others. If the Audiencia could actually try a familiar for violating any of these laws, a precedent would be established and the entire fuero would become vulnerable to attack.

In the 1568 Concordia, there were a number of specific provisions aimed at moulding the corps of familiares in such a way as to make it more tractable, uniform, and obedient. One of these provisions was that familiares should be chosen from among commoners and that men with authority over others should be excluded. The tribunal was naturally alarmed at the potential loss of politically influential elements and so sought by a variety of means to retain as many nobles as possible. The Audiencia was very well aware of the fact that this violation of the Concordia presented it with a golden opportunity to break the criminal fuero. When the tribunal arrested Pedro Asensio Romero, a familiar who collected seigneurial dues and exercised lesser jurisdiction in a small village, the Audiencia demanded the case on the grounds that as a baron, Romero had been given his license as familiar in violation of the Concordia and could therefore not enjoy its privileges.[94]

Another of the qualifications that candidates for the familiatura were expected to have was to be either married or a widower.[95] This qualification was frequently waived by the Suprema, especially if the candidate was wealthy or had powerful connections, but unmarried familiares were also vulnerable to attack by the Audiencia since they did not meet the technical qualifications for the office. Vicente Millán, a young Valencian knight who had managed to run through a rather considerable inheritance in just a few years, found this out to his cost after his attempts to coerce a wealthy widow into marrying him went too far and he was arrested by order of the viceroy. In this instance, the tribunal's attempt to claim him was halted by a royal order that he be stripped of his familiatura and turned over to the Audiencia on the grounds that he was unmarried and therefore should not have been granted the title in the first place.[96]

Alleged violations of viceregal ordinances and royal laws were undoubtedly the most fertile source of jurisdictional disputes between the Inquisition and the Audiencia during the last decades of the sixteenth century. In one instance, Francisco Jover, a familiar of

Castellón de la Plana, was arrested for not removing his hat when the lieutenant-governor passed him on a public street. The tribunal stepped in immediately and secured Jover's release to the custody of the comisario of Castellón, but he was promptly rearrested, brought to Valencia, and incarcerated in the ordinary criminal prison by royal constables acting under orders from the Audiencia, which claimed that all cases of disrespect for royal officials fell under its jurisdiction.[97]

Not unnaturally, the Audiencia's attitude toward the Inquisition and everyone connected with it was perceived as one of constant and relentless hostility by observers at the turn of the sixteenth century. During hearings held by the tribunal into the problems that notary Jerónimo Sans was having in attempting to work for the Audiencia and the tribunal simultaneously, one witness commented that "there is no greater antagonism in the world than that between the royal Audiencia and the Inquisition."[98] In 1589, a familiar testified before the tribunal concerning the Audiencia's general hostility to all familiares. At Audiencia instigation, royal constables would arrest and harass familiares and would make their imprisonment even more rigorous when they proclaimed their rights under the fuero. As the tribunal stated ruefully, if a familiar "takes a stroll in the sun they regard it as a serious crime."[99]

Another part of the fuero that became a prime target for the Audiencia was the tribunal's jurisdiction over compacts designed to promote harmony among warring families. According to testimony taken from Ramón Bernet, one of the Audiencia's own constables, successive regents had encouraged familiares to take these agreements before the tribunal even when the signatories were not familiares.[100] This cooperative attitude changed abruptly in the early 1550s. When Mateo Juan indicated his desire to sign an agreement with several persons whom he suspected of being accessories to the murder of one of his relatives, Judge Roca attempted to persuade him to sign it before the Audiencia. When Juan refused, pointing to the tradition of familiares signing such agreements before the tribunal, Roca ordered his arrest. After being imprisoned for nine days and repeatedly threatened with the garrote, Juan renounced his familiatura and signed the articles of concord before the Audiencia. He was then released, but only after being fined twenty reales for costs.[101]

By holding hearings in which a number of Audiencia officials and constables testified that compacts involving familiares had always been signed before it, the tribunal was able to stop the Audiencia's offensive, but the Audiencia continued its efforts to establish a legal precedent that would enable it to gain the upper hand. In the early seventeenth century, the Suprema unwisely permitted an agreement drawn up between a familiar and a knight of Montesa to be signed before the Audiencia on what was supposed to be a one-time-only basis. From then on, according to Inquisitor Ambrosio Roche, "on every occasion that presents itself they try the same thing." In each case, Audiencia notaries would carefully record the day and person who signed agreements before them to more fully establish their claim to jurisdiction. Finally, in a letter to the inquisitor-general which summarized the whole frustrating experience of the tribunal's dealings with the Audiencia from the mid-1550s, Roche declared that "even though these matters appear to be of little account, they serve as steppingstones for other, more serious demands which Your Eminence must not agree to."[102]

In its efforts to whittle down and eventually destroy the Inquisition's special privileges, the Audiencia had no more formidable ally than the viceroy, its nominal president. These powerful officials were mostly appointed for three-year terms and were therefore quite dependent on the Audiencia judges who formed their council of advisors. In spite of this dependence and the fact that both viceroy and Audiencia were representatives of royal jurisdiction, the Inquisition enjoyed good rapport with the viceroys up to the early 1570s. The one exception came in 1553 when the duke of Maqueda collaborated closely with the Audiencia and the estates in their campaign against the tribunal, but the duke was operating under explicit orders from Prince Philip and not out of any strong sympathy for the Audiencia or local interests. Indeed, in the late 1560s and early 1570s, the tribunal enjoyed excellent relations with both Viceroy Antonio Alfonso Pimentel de Herrera, count of Benavente, and his lieutenant, Luis Ferrer. The count strongly supported the proposed subsidy that the Morisco community was to pay the Inquisition so as to obtain immunity from confiscation in spite of strong opposition from the estates. In 1570, the tribunal wrote the Suprema in glowing terms to praise "the enthusiasm and good will that he shows in all matters touching this Inquisition."[103]

From the mid-1570s, however, the relations between viceroy and tribunal were transformed, until by 1600, Viceroy Juan Alfonso Pimentel de Herrera considered himself an open ally of the Audiencia in its efforts to undermine the fuero. As the most direct representatives of royal authority in the kingdom, viceroys were naturally highly sensitive to any institution or body of officials whose prestige and authority seemed to rival their own. Ostentatious display by inquisitors and officials both at public ceremonies and processions and in the cathedral provoked the ire of Viceroy Pedro Manrique de Lara, duke of Nájera, who declared that he would no longer tolerate the inquisitors' custom of observing public spectacles at the windows of the inquisitorial palace seated on cushions more magnificent than his own. The duke also demanded that the inquisitors stop their practice of placing special chairs for themselves in front of the congregation in the cathedral on important religious occasions.[104] By 1619, the tribunal's inability to come to terms with its reduced importance by accepting a lesser place on public occasions caused it to drastically reduce its visibility and abstain from witnessing or participating in them as much as possible.[105]

Viceregal efforts to restrain an alarming increase in urban violence by enforcing ordinances against persons carrying prohibited arms and circulating within the city without carrying lanterns provided a firm basis for the growth of a tactical alliance between the viceroy and the Audiencia which was aimed at undermining the inquisitorial fuero. The first serious efforts to prohibit the use of the flintlock in Valencia were undertaken during the viceroyalty of the count of Aytona (1581–1594). These efforts culminated in Philip II's draconian royal ordinance of January 21, 1584, which was aimed at obliterating "even the memory" of flintlocks.[106] It was the viceroy's responsibility to enforce the ordinance, while cognizance of violations was vested in the Audiencia. Rule making during the early modern period was always subject to exceptions for special interest groups. In practice, the officials and constabulary of the Diputació, royal customs, captain-general, and crusade administration were exempt as was a large percentage of the local clergy.[107] Familiares, however, found it almost impossible to obtain viceregal licenses even when many of their neighbors had done so. As familiar Martín Hinoga of Guadasuar explained to the tribunal in a petition concerning this matter, the fact that familiares could not obtain licenses to carry flintlocks put them at a grave disadvantage in the constant violence, "with daily danger to their persons and possessions."[108] Nevertheless, in 1613, when the royal ordinance was reissued by the marquis of Caracena, the tribunal acceded and issued its own edict making familiares subject to its provisions.[109]

On October 6, 1575, shortly after he assumed office, Viceroy Vespasiano Gonzaga issued an ordinance aimed at reducing the wave of violent assault plaguing Valencia by forcing everyone circulating after curfew to carry a lantern.[110] This ordinance was very strictly enforced, even for knights and other privileged individuals, under Gonzaga's administration and that of his successor, the duke of Nájera, who reissued it in September 1578. The one group, apart from the royal constables themselves, that was able to enjoy an exemption from the ordinance were the familiares who merely had to show their licenses to escape arrest.[111]

Under the administration of Archbishop Juan de Ribera, who served as viceroy from 1602 to 1604, the ordinance was issued again, but this time familiares were specifically included under its provisions since he considered many of them to be "troublemakers."[112] The tribunal's reaction to this fresh attempt to reduce the familiares' special privileges was cynical and shortsighted. A large protest meeting was held involving more than three hundred persons, including salaried officials, but privately the tribunal assured the Suprema that it was quite willing to tolerate the ordinance as long as officials were exempt and cases involving familiares were placed squarely within its jurisdiction.[113]

Loss of privileged status might make the familiatura less attractive for some, but in the short term, familiares' increased vulnerability to arrest and prosecution would swell revenue from fines, while by issuing a special edict of its own ordering familiares not to carry prohibited arms, the Inquisition could lay claim to exclusive cognizance and still protect familiares with the fuero. The scheme was a failure. The Audiencia advanced its claim to try all of these cases based on its preeminence in the enforcement of royal law. Moreover, with strong viceregal support, it insisted on trying familiares whom royal constables caught carrying prohibited weapons or circulating after curfew without lanterns, and the tribunal was forced to recognize the Audiencia's jurisdiction by allowing bail to be posted in the name of both courts.[114] Finally, in 1613, a royal ordinance gave the Audiencia explicit authority to try all persons enjoying special fueros who were arrested carrying prohibited arms.[115] Beset by dozens of jurisdictional disputes over this issue and fearing still wider assaults on the Inquisition's criminal jurisdiction if it continued to resist, the Suprema agreed that the final disposition of the cases of familiares presently being held by royal justices for possession of prohibited arms be determined by the Council of Aragon exclusively, which meant conceding most of them to the Audiencia.[116]

Confronted by a tacit alliance between a powerful and aggressive Audiencia and several viceroys who were concerned about the threat that familiares posed to public order and were committed to reducing its prerogatives, the tribunal was thrown increasingly on the defensive around the turn of the century. It took a direct confrontation with Viceroy Juan Alfonso Pimentel de Herrera, however, to demonstrate just how far the tribunal's prestige had fallen from the period of splendor before 1550.

On August 7, 1600, three familiares who were also city notaries were arrested on suspicion of having defrauded the public in the exercise of their functions and incarcerated in the royal criminal prison at Serranos gate. On the following day, the three prisoners sent a message to the tribunal asking that it intervene to have them transferred to its own prison, since as familiares they enjoyed the fuero and were therefore under inquisitorial, not royal, jurisdiction. Following normal procedures in such cases, the tribunal ordered Pedro Juan Vidal, one of the secretaries, to present himself before the viceroy with this request. Vidal went to the viceroy twice. The first time he received a courteous but evasive reply, the viceroy merely telling him that he would contact the inquisitor-general about the case himself.

Several days later, Inquisitors Honorato Figuerola and Antonio Canseco de Quiñones decided to try again, and Vidal returned to the viceregal palace with yet another note asking that the three familiares be sent to the Holy Office along with the evidence of their wrongdoing so that it could begin proceedings against them. It was at this meeting that Viceroy Pimentel de Herrera demonstrated his complete contempt for the Holy Office by treating its representatives in a manner that would have been utterly inconceivable just twenty-five years earlier. Brushing aside the tribunal's request for custody, the viceroy demanded that no further requests be made, and when asked by a now-bareheaded and trembling Pedro Vidal what formal reply he should make to his masters, the viceroy replied, "You can give them this for a reply; that I said not to send me any more such requests because I'll send them (the inquisitors) to Madrid aboard some cross-eyed pack mules and throw the person who comes to present it to me out this window. Now get along with you, get along with you and give them this reply and let them be grateful that I don't send them to Madrid on some cross-eyed mules."[117]

The tribunal did not learn of the viceroy's next move until three days after it happened, when the inquisitors had one of their secretaries translate a notarial document written in Valencian by which the three *familiares* formally renounced the fuero and submitted themselves to the judgment of the royal Audiencia.[118] The new tactic was completely successful, and when the regent came to the tribunal to discuss the case, Inquisitor Figuerola had to concede that he had lost all authority over the three men.[119]

In the gloomy assessment of the situation that they sent to the Suprema on August 21, Inquisitors Figuerola and Quiñones made no effort to conceal the fact that the tribunal had sustained a major defeat. While it was true that *familiares* accused of violating the public trust while holding royal offices were to be tried by the ordinary courts, the fact that the viceroy had previously arrested several other notaries on charges of malfeasance and then released them without trial after they had renounced their *familiaturas* demonstrates clearly that he was less interested in purifying the notarial college than in destroying the inquisitorial fuero.[120] The previous arrest and release of notaries after they had renounced the use of the fuero persuaded the three *familiares* to follow their example. Moreover, the wide publicity given to the viceroy's humiliating treatment of Pedro Juan Vidal and his insolent reply to the inquisitors' messages hurt the tribunal's prestige, leaving it "without authority so that if a remedy is not provided we will see ourselves in greater difficulty every day."[121]

By 1600, the Valencia tribunal that had once excommunicated virtually every royal officer in the kingdom watched helplessly as its criminal jurisdiction was steadily eroded through the joint action of viceroy and Audiencia. *Familiares* who insisted on claiming the protections of the fuero were regularly harassed and feelings ran high, even breaking out in violence during a confrontation between the viceregal guard and a group of familiares who provided the inquisitors with an escort when they came to the palace to give the viceroy their annual Christmas greeting.[122] The tribunal was still a powerful institution with important allies, but the tone of its relations with the kingdom's viceroys had changed. No longer able to count on automatic support from these powerful officials, the tribunal found it safer to approach them with "fair words and circumspection," to quote Figuerola and Canseco de Quiñones, and behave diplomatically even in the face of insulting behavior.[123] Even more inauspicious for the future of the tribunal, however, was the fact that the weakness of its relationship with the viceroy and friction with the Audiencia encouraged other anti-inquisitorial forces in the kingdom to attempt to recover some of the authority and prestige that they had lost during the heyday of the tribunal before 1550.

Without doubt, the institution that lost the most with the development and extension of the modern Inquisition was the church, specifically, the bishops, whose authority over religious and moral offenses had been sharply reduced. Even though a representative of the bishop acted as consultor in all trials of individuals from his diocese, his vote was only one among several, and if he disagreed with the inquisitors, the most that would happen was that the case would go to the Suprema for review.[124] Frustration over the Inquisition's exclusive and expanding jurisdiction over matters of faith and morality, which were normally within the purview of the ecclesiastical courts, was probably responsible for an edict issued in 1552 by Archbishop Tomás de Villanueva in which he demanded that all those with knowledge of heresy should denounce it before him.[125] In 1576, Archbishop Juan de Ribera published another such edict that was equally unsuccessful but subtler than that of his predecessor. Ribera called on those with knowledge of heresy to denounce it before his court so that his officials could, in turn, inform the Inquisition, but he reserved moral offenses like bigamy and blasphemy, over which the tribunal also claimed jurisdiction, for his own court.[126]

The tribunal's problems with the haughty and unpopular Archbishop Ribera did not end with his attempt to limit its jurisdiction over moral offenses. Ribera wanted to put himself forward, even if only symbolically, as the chief protector of orthodoxy in Valencia, and since the Inquisition had long since established its predominant role in this area, he, at least, wanted to make it seem that this was being done under his authority. To create that impression, he demanded a preeminent seat at the public auto de fé even if it meant displacing the oldest inquisitor and was offended by the fact that the tribunal's cross, rather than his own, was carried in the most outstanding place in the procession of the faith. In the end, Ribera's demands were refused by the Suprema, but he took his revenge on the tribunal after he became viceroy.[127]

Relations with Valencia's powerful cathedral chapter also took a turn for the worse in the 1560s, and here the tribunal sustained a decisive defeat from which its prestige and authority never fully recovered. In spite of the fact that the tribunal regularly employed cathedral canons as consultores and notaries, there were certain issues that tended to poison relations between the two institutions. For one thing, the cathedral chapter, and the income of the canons themselves, depended on the collection of tithes and mortgage interest. The great increase in the tribunal's activity against the Moriscos in the 1560s and the wholesale confiscation of their property threatened to reduce the canons' income, which depended, in part, on Morisco villages. In 1566, Inquisitor Aguilera wrote the Suprema warning of a memorial that had been sent to court by the cathedral chapter to protest his recent visitation to certain Morisco villages in the district.[128] On December 21, 1568, the council of canons even went so far as to defy royal and viceregal orders and flatly refused to name a canon to assist Inquisitor-General de Miranda in publishing the Edict of Faith in Morisco villages surrounding the capital.[129] In June of that same year, Jerónimo Carroz, canon and sacristan of the cathedral, led a delegation from the Estates to formally protest confiscation of Morisco property as a violation of a royal order that had been issued by Charles V on December 24, 1533, prohibiting such confiscations for the crime of heresy.[130] The embassy demanded that the tribunal suspend the confiscations ordered at the auto de fé of June 7, 1568, but licentiate Moyano, the tribunal's prosecuting attorney, replied by denying the validity of the royal order itself on the grounds that Charles could not possibly have granted such sweeping concessions to those guilty of such "grievous and wicked" crimes.[131] In spite of this inquisitorial bluster, the political pressure exerted by the canons during winter 1568 had its effect, and in January 1569, the tribunal began negotiations for a subsidy to be paid by the Morisco community in lieu of confiscations.[132]

The canons' concern over the possible effects of the campaign against the Moriscos paled in significance beside their resentment over the way in which the inquisitors had made a privileged position for themselves in the cathedral by displacing two canons from their places in the principal choir and freely using its pulpit for all kinds of inquisitorial functions. Encouraged by the poor relations between the tribunal and then Archbishop Francisco de Navarra, canons decided that the time was ripe for a bold stroke to recover their prerogatives.[133] When Inquisitor Francisco Ramírez arrived to take his accustomed seat in the choir on December 11, 1561, he found it occupied by its actual proprietor, the archdeacon mayor. There was a violent scuffle in which Inquisitor Ramírez managed to force the archdeacon out of his seat with the assistance of the tribunal's alcalde mayor, but the cabildo was quick to enlist the support of Archbishop Navarra who ordered the inquisitors not to return to the cathedral.[134]

In its account of the incident, which was sent to court a few days later, the cabildo cleverly managed to throw all the blame on the inquisitors while insinuating that the crown's political interests were being compromised by the insolent behavior of the tribunal. According to the canons, the inquisitors had taken to claiming places in the choir as their right instead of accepting them as a mark of courtesy that could be withdrawn at any time. They warned that forcible ejection of the archdeacon might have done the crown's political interests lasting damage because he belonged to one of the king's principal families.[135] Since the deputies from Valencia's cathedral chapter were the only group to be largely immune from royal control in the Ecclesiastical Estate of the Cortes, this was a powerful argument. As a result of the cabildo's protests, the inquisitors made no further attempt to claim their seats in the cathedral choir, and the Suprema recognized that the position had been lost by ordering them to bring their own chairs to the cathedral when the Edict of Faith was to be read so as not to disturb the canons' prerogatives.[136]

If the defense or acquisition of individual honor and prestige was the real source of both private vengeance and judicial duels in the early modern period, institutions and collectivities were also engaged in a constant struggle for that same elusive quality. To seize and control a coveted position or to upstage representatives of an opposing or competing institution before a public that was extremely sensitive to the nuances of place was an accepted way of altering the balance of prestige and distinction, and with these reduced, a decline in the public deference paid to the institution and its officials could not be far behind. The sudden absence of the two inquisitors from their accustomed seats in the principal choir of the cathedral caused a sensation among the people of Valencia, and as Inquisitor Ramírez ruefully commented in a letter to the Suprema, the tribunal's prestige and reputation had suffered severe, perhaps irreparable damage as a result.[137] A few years later, the council of canons denied the tribunal the right to use its pulpit for reading routine orders and announcements, and in 1674, the canons completed the process of ejecting the tribunal from the cathedral by receiving royal permission to prevent the reading there of both the Edict of Faith and the Anathema.[138]

There were several interlocking factors in the conflict between Valencia's city council and the tribunal which only broke into the open at the end of the sixteenth century. The jurats, as leading members of the kingdom's local political elite, had always bitterly resented the yearly oath of loyalty that they were obliged to take by which they swore to support the Inquisition and uphold the privileges of its officials. The Inquisition, after all, was a Castilian institution that had been imposed on the kingdom against its will, and to be forced to swear a special oath of loyalty to a "foreign" institution whose presence they resented seemed particularly galling. The city's extensive financial responsibilities also made the jurats extremely sensitive to the tax exemptions claimed by the tribunal's officials, and they made several unsuccessful attempts to force them to pay the sises majors, the taxes on foodstuffs that constituted the basis of municipal revenues.[139]

In practice, however, the jurats had to tread warily in any confrontation with a powerful institution like the Inquisition because, on the one hand, they could not risk offending the monarch who drew up the list of candidates from which jurats were selected, and, on the other, they had to be careful to obtain the support of the sometimes turbulent Consell General, or local assembly.[140] In the decisive conflict, when it did come, the jurats were able to move with the tacit encouragement of the viceroy and gain the enthusiastic support of the members of the assembly by waving the flag of civic patriotism.

Once again, the dispute centered around a question of place and position in one of the public spectacles that played such an important role in the life of early modern Valencia. But, unlike the canons, the jurats chose to confront the Inquisition on its own territory, during the course of the procession that brought penitents to the auto de fé. The very fact that the tribunal could be so confronted, not in the cathedral where the canons were the acknowledged masters and the inquisitors the interlopers but in this procession where the Inquisition had always dominated, provided a sensational example of just how far the tribunal had slipped from its former ascendancy.

On July 15, 1591, just as the procession had formed to proceed to the scaffolding that had been erected for the public auto, the municipal constables, as if by prearrangement, shouldered their way forward to a position alongside and in front of the standard of the Inquisition. This was deliberate provocation, since such lowly persons could never hope to claim such an exalted position, and it quickly achieved its purpose by eliciting a violent reaction from the supporters of the Inquisition. Several familiares and unsalaried officials forcibly ejected the constables from their position and Inquisitor Girón ordered them back to their assigned place. But this did not end the incident, because after the auto was over and the inquisitors were waiting in front of the scaffolding for the customary return procession to form, they were advised that the jurats and constables had left before them. Moreover, as testimony taken in the tribunal's chambers two days after the event revealed, the jurats had not acted entirely on their own. Before deciding on this unprecedented step, they sent an emissary to Viceroy Francisco de Moncada to advise him of their intentions, declaring that they were willing to accompany the Inquisition "if he so ordered." While expressing a certain caution, the viceroy merely said that they could do "what they wished," which in effect meant condoning the jurats' intended action.[141]

A few days later, while the tribunal was still taking testimony about the events of September 15, the jurats moved to gain the support of the popular classes who were represented in the assembly. Before a joint meeting of the jurats and the Consell, jurat Antonio Matheu presented an account of the incident that was carefully calculated to stir up popular passions. According to Matheu, the municipal constables were peacefully occupying their accustomed place near the jurats when they were attacked and forcibly ejected by several familiares and unsalaried officials (although why they should wish to do this was not made clear). Foremost in this attack were several familiares, including Alonso de Borja and Felipe de Cardona and three unsalaried officials, Dr. Pedro Asensio, a calificador, Dr. José Requart, physician to the tribunal, and Dr. Francisco Burgos, abogado de presos. Nothing could be done to the two familiares since they were members of powerful noble families, but the city could revenge itself on the three unsalaried officials since they held posts over which the city exercised control. Incensed by the seemingly unprovoked attack on the municipal constables, the assembly voted to strip the three of their positions (Asensio and Requart both taught at the university), elect others in their place, and send representatives to court to protest before the king and the inquisitor-general.[142]

Friends of the tribunal, many of whom had faithfully attended the public autos de fé for many years, were astounded by the jurats' failure to accompany the inquisitors on their return to the palace. Fray Rodrigo Ximenez, the vicar-general of the order of minors (minimos), told the tribunal that the monks of his monastery were "scandalized" by the jurats' action. Another witness, Juan de la Tonda, a parish priest from the district, also expressed amazement and declared that in his forty years of attending these processions he had never seen the municipal constables attempt to occupy a different position.[143]

The tribunal had been publicly insulted in front of some of its most avid supporters from all over the district, but the opportunity to capitalize on the sense of public outrage to launch strong protests or ecclesiastical censures against the jurats was missed, probably because the inquisitors realized that it was not politically expedient to do so. While lamenting the "disastrous outcome," the inquisitors told the Suprema that "for our part, we have done nothing more than receive testimony about these events."[144] The tribunal's perceptions of the situation were probably correct, as in his final orders to Vice-

roy Moncada regarding the resolution of this conflict, Philip II wrote
that he should intervene with the jurats to restore the university
posts and censos that had been seized from the officials but that he
should also rebuke the tribunal for having "overstepped the modesty
and reserve that it should have observed on that day."[145] Philip II
clearly preferred the city council's version of the events of September 15, not because it was correct but because of the importance of
maintaining good relations with the Valencian oligarchy. If the count
of Aytona's efforts to eradicate violent crime in the city of Valencia
through a campaign of forced deportation had already stirred protests from the Braç Real, overt royal support for the Inquisition
could only inflame center-periphery reactions still further and de-
tract from the main lines of royal policy in the kingdom.[146]

Even after the royal letter of September 26, 1592, the Suprema
found it had to intervene directly to make sure that the city
returned the university posts and the censos that it had confiscated from the unsalaried officials.[147] By the end of October, there
is evidence that the city had done so, but not before leveling
another blow at the tribunal by passing a new municipal ordinance that prohibited lawyers practicing in the municipal courts
from serving the Inquisition.[148] According to a letter from the
tribunal to the Suprema, this ordinance was motivated solely "by
hatred for this tribunal and its ministers," and by forcing local
attorneys to choose between well-compensated work in the ordinary courts and the poorly paid work at the tribunal it threatened
to deprive the tribunal of defense attorneys and therefore make
trials more difficult.[149]

Hostility and suspicion marked relations between the city council and the tribunal throughout the 1590s, but a second open confrontation between the two institutions did not occur until the
viceroyalty of Juan de Ribera in 1603. During this conflict, the
tribunal was placed in the uncomfortable position of seeming to
interfere with the legitimate exercise of municipal jurisdiction over
local markets and was confronted by the united opposition of viceroy, Audiencia, and city council.

According to an account prepared for presentation to the Duke
of Lerma by the city's special ambassador, Gaspar de Monsoriu, the
city had received many complaints about certain fishmongers in
the plaza del mercat who placed their fish tuns on two rows of

tables set up far outside the legal limits. Finally, on June 7, 1603, the jurats ordered the municipal almotacen (the official in charge of the market) to tour the plaza and force the fishmongers to remove the tables that protruded farthest into the square. Everyone obeyed the order except Antonio Ruis, whose tables were in front of a house he rented from the Inquisition. Confiscated from a Judaizer early in the previous century, the house had long been rented by fishmongers who had taken advantage of the protection of the tribunal's judge of confiscated property to flout the authority of the almotacen. On this occasion, when asked to remove his tables, Ruis mocked the official and claimed that he had no authority over him because his tables were in front of property owned by the Holy Office. The almotacen then fined Ruis, but the tribunal's judge of confiscated property ordered the fine returned. When the almotacen refused, he sent the tribunal's alguacil to his home to obtain property worth a comparable amount. After Viceroy Ribera had assured them of his support by denying that the tribunal had "any authority over matters concerning the city," the jurats ordered municipal constables to burn the offending tables and place Ruis, his wife, and his servants under arrest for his slander of a municipal official.[150] The Ruis family was quickly released by order of Viceroy Ribera, but the jurats delivered the coup de grâce by stripping them of their citizenship and forcing them to leave the city.[151]

The tribunal's reaction to this attack was completely ineffective. Refusing to join the Audiencia in a formal jurisdictional dispute over the issue, it demanded that the jurats replace the tables they had ordered destroyed on pain of excommunication. The old threats had lost their potency, however, and in the face of a strong reaction by the jurats and the estates, the threat of ecclesiastical censures was removed and the tribunal was forced to accept a fait accompli.[152] Several years later, the city completed its move against the fishmongers by ordering the demolition of the remaining tables and the sluices that carried water away from the area. On May 13, 1609, when the city constables dismantled the tables, a near riot was caused when the tribunal arrested two constables and when the jurats ordered the seizure of Nuncio Vidal Criado. Prisoners were released by order of the viceroy, but the tables were gone nonetheless, and the jurats took harsh vengeance on Jaime Juan Sevillan, a familiar who had been particularly forward in his support of the tribunal, by stripping him of his citizenship and refusing payment of the censos he held on municipal revenues.[153]

By the end of the sixteenth century, the Valencia tribunal was being forced to operate in a much less favorable political climate than it had enjoyed before 1550, and growing cooperation among its enemies was demonstrated by the crisis over the fishmongers' tables. Poor relations with successive viceroys ensured viceregal support for the position taken by the jurats, while the endemic conflict with the Audiencia over the fuero meant that that powerful body would automatically support any effort to diminish the tribunal's prestige.

Another element in the equation, already hinted at in the testimony of Nuncio Miguel Juan during the hearings that the tribunal held in 1553, was that of the antagonism felt by certain powerful individuals for the Holy Office.[154] As testimony taken about the events surrounding the incident in the plaza del mercat indicated, several of the men who authorized the burning of the tables had no great love for the tribunal. The almotacen himself was a member of the confraternity of San Lorenzo and resented the presence of the Inquisition in the parish, which meant that familiares were given precedence over members of the confraternity in church functions. Leading jurats like Francisco March were members of converso families whose ancestors had been punished by the Inquisition. In March's case, his own grandparents had been reconciled and lashed publicly, and many other members of the family had been reconciled and relaxed during the early, anti-Semitic period of the tribunal's activities. Relatives of other men involved had also suffered at the hands of the tribunal. Gaspar Daqui, the brother of former jurat Juan Bautista Daqui, had spent two years in the inquisitorial prison.[155] While it would be misleading to suggest that persons with individual grievances were orchestrating the anti-inquisitorial campaign, the evidence does indicate that the tribunal had made many enemies who could lend their weight to such a campaign once it got started. Besides, memories were long in a kingdom dominated by powerful families, and the tribunal had good reason to be apprehensive about influential conversos like the March family, whose wealth and political influence had greatly increased in spite of the prosecution of their grandparents for Judaizing.

Confronted by a powerful and aggressive Audiencia, acrimonious relations with successive incumbents of the viceregal palace, and a city council determined to avenge the slights it had suffered at its hands, the Valencia tribunal had been thrown increasingly on the defensive in the last half of the sixteenth century. At the same time, however, this period also saw a significant expansion of inquisitorial jurisdiction over matters of faith and the exercise of greater responsibility in other more strictly political matters. Quite apart from the increasing importance of the tribunal's role in the repression of the Moriscos and its involvement in the effort to enforce the new post-Tridentine morality, the Inquisition remained the one Valencian institution that maintained a high degree of independence from local political influence and could be counted on to represent the interests of the Spanish monarchy. In recognition of this fact, Philip II never pushed his campaign to reduce the authority of the Holy Office so far as to undermine its authority and usefulness.

Certainly, for inquisitors like Bernardino de Aguilera, the authority of the Holy Office and the crown were so closely linked as to be almost interdependent. He once wrote in a memorial to the Suprema, "Increasing the authority of the Holy Office is what is most in the service of God and the king because without it his Majesty could not carry out his will in this kingdom because of the many fueros and privileges that it enjoys."[156] In Teruel, where the Valencia tribunal frequently came into conflict with local officials who accused it of violating the fueros, it proved itself a firm enemy of Aragonese autonomy. When agents of the Justicia of Aragon removed Antonio Gamir from the custody of its comisario, the tribunal arrested and punished those involved, including the alcalde and Juan Pérez, the Justicia's notary who was condemned to 300 lashes and 12 years in the galleys.[157]

One of the most potentially dangerous clashes between the interests of the Spanish monarchy and Valencian regionalism was the movement that took place in support of the canonization of a benefice holder in the parish church of San Andrés, Padre Francisco Simón, and that continued, with varying degrees of intensity, from his death on April 25, 1612, to about 1620. When he died at thirty-three, Padre Simón left behind a formidable reputation as a priest who claimed to be able to invoke the powers of the supernatural in a unique and personal way. On one occasion, when Ana Llopis's brother began a violent argument with him about his illicit relationship with her, he promised that if he would accept Simón's assurances that nothing sinful had taken place between them, he would give him a signed warrant that would allow him to pass straight to paradise after his death.[158]

On May 19, 1612, another such warrant was brought to the tribunal by a worried Fray Juan Catalan, one of its calificadores and a very strong supporter of Padre Simón. In this document, Simón assured the faithful that if they would "pray for the drops of blood that fell from Christ's body during the crucifixion for fifteen years," they would gain as much merit as if they had "died as a martyr for the faith and that Our Lord, the Virgin Mary, and the entire heavenly host would come to receive their souls after their death." Believing that the paper contained serious doctrinal errors, Catalan had come to the tribunal not to defame Simón's memory but to ask that all copies be confiscated to protect his reputation.[159] Simón's bold claims to control over supernatural forces must have made a profound impression in a city where the ability to use them to advantage was a topic of constant concern, and it no doubt explains his close relations with Angela and Inés Pérez, who were both reputed sorceresses. The Pérez sisters and Luis Colomer, who was also suspected of superstitious practices, played a significant role in creating popular support for Simón's canonization by going from house to house calling him a saint and organizing processions and demonstrations in his favor.[160]

For their part, the parish clergy of San Andrés, lured by the prospect of an income from alms that would, in the words of one benefice holder, "make benefices in San Andrés as valuable as a canonry in the cathedral," promoted the cult by every means at their disposal. Word that a saint had just died was shouted to passersby as the parish clergy busied themselves dressing the corpse and surrounding it with roses. Priests from other parishes were brought into the cult, and they led their faithful to San Andrés, which was soon inundated by a "great multitude of people."[161] By the third day, most of Valencia's governing elite had been drawn in; the jurats came in full regalia to pay him honor, mass was said by Tomás de Spinosa and attended by all the cathedral canons, and the viceroy himself came to visit the tomb accompanied by his entire guard.[162]

The cult was spread throughout the rest of the kingdom and even into parts of Murcia and Aragon by preachers drawn from the parish clergy, and within the city itself, devotion to Padre Simón was reaching into all classes. Great processions marked the first anniversary of his death in 1613; those marching included members of craft guilds and many citizens, nobles, and clergy. Almost the entire city was illuminated in his honor, and more than 1,000 altars were set up to venerate him.[163] At the second anniversary celebration, even greater numbers participated in the processions and the city ordered twelve cannons to be fired in his honor.[164] During this period, many members of the kingdom's judicial elite became closely identified with the movement, including the regent of the Audiencia and two judges, Ramón Sans and Dr. Pedro Juan Rejuale, and some of the Valencian members of the Council of Aragon including its prosecuting attorney, Dr. Jerónimo de Léon.[165]

The reaction of the authorities in Madrid, meanwhile, was one of growing alarm. For one thing, any movement involving very large numbers of people, especially from the lower classes, conjured up visions of earlier popular movements that had always ended by endangering royal authority. For another, the fact that many of the men the crown had regarded as key political supporters were so closely identified with a movement inspired by a specifically Valencian religious hero had disturbing implications for Madrid.

For the crown as well as the Vatican, the whole question of beatification and canonization resolved itself into a question of time, money, and political influence. A larger number of Spanish saints would increase the country's prestige, but such negotiations should be handled at the highest levels and mediated through the central government, not by local political chiefs backed by mass demonstrations. The crown, therefore, turned to the Inquisition as its only reliable agent in the kingdom, and the tribunal was instructed by the Suprema to dampen the movement by every means at its disposal. Under constant prodding by the Suprema, the tribunal began to pressure the provincials of the various religious orders to prohibit their monks from mentioning Simón in their sermons, and when the Jesuit Padre Sotello stated in a sermon that the Suprema had reviewed Padre Simón's case and pronounced in his favor, the tribunal forced him to make a public retraction.[166] Following the Suprema's orders, the tribunal then prohibited the public exhibition of Padre

Simón's portrait and ordered the confiscation of a book recently printed in Segorbe detailing his life and miracles.[167] Later that summer, the Vatican's attitude toward the cult was demonstrated when Cardinal D'Este visited the city in August and never came to pay his respects at Simón's chapel in San Andrés in spite of urging by the jurats and "much to the disgust of the populace."[168]

By this time, the inquisitorial prohibitions had had their desired effect, and public celebration of the cult was beginning to decline. Some members of the local elite, like the marquis of Cocentaina, had publicly opposed it. In 1615, no public ceremony marked the anniversary of Simón's death.[169]

With political support for the cult beginning to wane, it only remained for the crown to eliminate the remaining focal points of intense observance for the process of canonization to return to the well-trodden paths of diplomacy. After a consulta held with the Suprema on July 12, 1618, had concluded that the total elimination of public worship was necessary so as not to hinder the canonization process and cause further resentment in Rome, the king issued an edict ordering that all images of Simón be removed within thirty days.[170]

But all those involved in these decisions had seriously miscalculated the mood in Valencia, and when Antonio Calafat, one of the tribunal's secretaries, attempted to read out the decree in the cathedral, there were cries of fury from the congregation and he was compelled to descend from the pulpit. Two nights of rioting followed during which the windows of the archbishop's palace were smashed and mobs roamed the streets crying "Victory to Padre Simón." The new viceroy, Antonio Pimentel y Toledo, marquis of Tavera, was forced to voice approval of the illumination of buildings in favor of Simón, while large groups of people were continually presenting themselves at San Andrés to worship at his tomb.[171]

At the same time, the local political interests, whose earlier support for the cult had helped it to flourish, seized their chance to ingratiate themselves still further with the masses at the expense of Madrid by making the defense of Padre Simón a matter of national pride. Both the jurats and the Noble Estate sent embassies to protest against any effort to interfere with the cult. The representative of the Noble Estate, Baltasar de Blanes, even succeeded in having Pedro Cabeças, a Valencian who had attacked the cult before the pope and in memorials to Philip II, arrested and incarcerated by the vicar-general of the See of Toledo. In his point by point refutation of Cabeças's statement made before that official, Blanes took a strongly regionalist line, stressing that Cabeças deserved punishment "as an imposter who bore false witness against such a pious man of God, such faithful vassals of the king our lord, and against a kingdom as pious as it is illustrious."[172]

The new viceroy, however, was made of sterner stuff than his predecessor, and undaunted by the rioting, he soon reverted to the crown's original policy of reducing the cult by ordering the removal of the images of Padre Simón that had been set up on the street running from San Salvador to San Andrés.[173] The authorities were also fortunate in that popular attention was being distracted from Padre Simón by the recent beatification of another Valencian religious figure of a much more acceptable kind, former Archbishop Tomás de Villanueva. There only remained the main focal point of the cult in the parish church of San Andrés, and here the tribunal was supposed to use its influence with the rector and lay officials of the parish to remove the votive lamps around the tomb.

This council's intention "is to remove the abuses in this affair," proclaimed the Suprema in a letter to the tribunal on May 27, 1619.[174] But in spite of this show of determination, neither the tribunal nor the Suprema was very anxious to become deeply involved in any new confrontation with the supporters of the cult. Although repeatedly urging the tribunal to take action in the matter of the votive lamps, the Suprema also advised it to ignore the fact that the parish clergy were still collecting alms to promote Simón's canonization.[175] For its part, the tribunal made only half-hearted efforts to convince the parish clergy to remove the lamps. Its lack of enthusiasm earned it a surprisingly mild rebuke from the Suprema on July 22.[176] By August, the Suprema had abandoned any effort to prod the tribunal into action and was openly urging caution even in the matter of the lamps. The tribunal was told to allow the viceroy to take the lead in repressing the cult and confine itself to gathering information about those who took a leading role in supporting it.[177] Even after Juan Selma, one of the instigators of the March 2 and 3 rioting, was arrested in Zaragoza, the Suprema decided it would be safer to try him there than return him to Valencia where his presence might be the cause of another riot.[178]

The wavering or outright disloyalty of many members of Valencia's political and judicial elite over the issue of Padre Simón brought the crown once again to realize the value of maintaining a thoroughly Castilian institution in a kingdom where even religious issues could take on a violently regionalist tinge. But by 1619, the Inquisition was no longer in a position to openly confront local political interests, and the rioting of March 2 and 3 proved that it could easily become the first target of any movement directed against Madrid. Nevertheless, the tribunal's loyalty in this crisis earned it approval at court and was no doubt influential in winning it very favorable treatment in the financial settlement that followed the expulsion of the Moriscos. Moreover, royal and papal approval meant a further increase in inquisitorial jurisdiction. In 1624, the pope charged Inquisitor-General Andrés Pacheco with the responsibility for the investigation into Padre Simón's worthiness to receive beatification, and in 1634, papal recognition of the dangers of unrecognized saint cults led Urban VIII to give the Inquisition power to repress them.[179]

Another reason the decline in the prestige and authority of the Holy Office in Valencia was only relative but not absolute was that even though the agents of the central government in Valencia competed among themselves, these very same institutions were obliged to understand one another and reach a modus vivendi. Therefore, in spite of all of its ingenious attempts to whittle down the fuero, the Audiencia never attempted to eliminate it entirely because it represented a fundamental constitutional principle that had become an integral part of the social and political system of the Hispanic world. Just as the Hapsburg rulers continued to recognize the political and constitutional autonomy of the several states that constituted their dominions, so they created special corporate bodies among their subjects as a way of dividing them and tying them more closely to the crown.

In obedience to the concordias and other pieces of royal legislation, the Audiencia and the tribunal found themselves collaborating on cases involving familiares. When familiar Antonio Calvo was arrested by royal constables on a charge of carrying prohibited arms and threatening to murder someone, both tribunals agreed that the Inquisition should have cognizance and that the criminal case should be tried before a civil case pending against Calvo in the Audiencia.[180]

An even more striking example of the pattern of cooperation between Audiencia and tribunal is that both were involved in the protection of bandit leaders during much of the seventeenth century. When the violence threatened to get out of hand, as it did in 1636, the crown called on both Audiencia and tribunal to collaborate in restoring order by, in effect, restraining their followers.[181] Again, in December 1659, when Francisco Berenger de Blanes Valterra, a familiar and brother-in-law to José Valterra, an infamous bandit, came to the tribunal for protection, it was quick to send an emissary to the Audiencia offering its mediation between royal officials and the Valterra family to "end these conflicts through some form of compromise."[182]

Whatever their disagreement with it, Valencia's archbishops could also rely on the tribunal, since in the last analysis they represented the principles of authority, orthodoxy, and hierarchy that the Inquisition was established to uphold. When Archbishop Ribera's heavy-handed campaign against the university theology faculty and in favor of the Jesuit college of San Pablo resulted in hostile lampoons being posted in the city, the tribunal intervened to arrest the protestors in spite of its view that it would be better for the archbishop himself if the issue was forgotten.[183] The tribunal and the archbishop also found themselves on the same side in the Padre Simón affair. For six years, Archbishop Aliaga was unable to carry out a visitation because he was afraid of being confronted by manifestations of the cult, while during the rioting of March 2 and 3, 1619, the windows of both the inquisitorial and archdiocesan palaces were broken by angry mobs.[184]

When it began its operations in the Kingdom of Valencia, the Holy Office encountered powerful local opposition and needed strong and consistent royal support to overcome it. Encouraged by this, and virtually immune to any serious scrutiny from royal officials during the reign of Charles V, the tribunal became arrogant and abused its power, seriously alienating the local interests on whose support royal and viceregal authority rested. Even before he became king in 1556, Philip II was determined to bring imperial administration under more effective control and prevent any one unit from becoming overly powerful. Ironically, Philip's successful drive to curb the excesses of the Valencia tribunal provided its enemies with the opening they needed to diminish its authority.

The Concordias of the 1550s and 1560s marked the opening of a conflict with the Audiencia that lasted for generations. At the same time, powerful local interests interpreted the change in the crown's attitude as an opportunity for a counterattack of their own.

After the first decades of the seventeenth century, the tribunal's worst excesses had been curbed, and it remained the crown's first line of defense against religious heresy. Conflict with the Audiencia continued, but the two institutions also needed to collaborate to maintain public order and political stability. However, both the Suprema and the tribunal had learned a hard lesson from the sharp confrontations of the early seventeenth century. If the remaining privileges of the Valencia tribunal were to be preserved for the enjoyment of its officials, Valencia's local political elite, whatever its ethnic origins or current reputation, had to be brought to regard the Holy Office more positively. The stage was set, therefore, for a gradual but significant policy shift, one that involved accommodation and conciliation of powerful local families, soft peddling traditional anti-Semitism, and an effort to avoid direct confrontation. During the later seventeenth and eighteenth century, "circumspection and prudence" became the watchwords of a tribunal that had once relentlessly pursued its enemies.

II

Judicial Procedures and Financial Structure

As an institution established in spite of strong local opposition, the Inquisition had to employ a judicious combination of mercy, terror, and public education to generate confessions and denunciations and to break down the hostility to outside interference that protected the tight-knit local communities and interlocking families that made up Valencian society from the encroachment of alien, central authority. In the early years of the Inquisition, the tribunals moved from place to place. Its arrival in a given town or village would immediately be followed by a reading of the "edict of grace," which listed a series of heresies and invited those with something on their conscience to confess during a term of grace.[1] Voluntary confession during this period, which varied from three to six months in Valencia, would entitle the individual to receive reconciliation without confiscation of property, although the inquisitor himself could impose some monetary penance.[2]

By offering an opportunity for reconciliation to the church without incurring harsh penalties, the edicts of grace appeared to be a reasonable and moderate solution to the persistence of Judaic practices among the converted Jews. In fact, however, the edicts contained a trap for the unwary in the shape of a demand for complete and full confession of all Judaic practices that they had ever engaged in at any point in their lives as well as the names of others whom they knew performed the same acts. Any concealment, even of acts that took place many years earlier or in childhood, rendered the confession void and placed the would-be penitent in the dangerous category of a *diminuto* whose presumably deliberate concealment of apostasy demonstrated that he was really still a heretic. Since Torquemada's 1484 instructions call for the *diminuto* to be prosecuted if later evidence demonstrates that he has concealed anything, the hundreds of confessions taken during the grace period and carefully preserved by the tribunal really provided it with its first file of clients. During the first years of the Valencia tribunal, only twelve percent of those presenting themselves during the period of grace escaped later persecution.[3]

We must presume that the duplicitous character of the edicts of grace became well known in the converso community. The declining numbers of those willing to come forward led to their partial abandonment after 1500 and the substitution of a new device called the Edict of Faith, which omitted the grace period.[4] The Edict of Faith, which was proclaimed yearly in the seats of the tribunals and in district villages and towns on the arrival of an inquisitor, was a recitation of heretical practices and offenses against orthodox Catholicism and an invitation to the entire population to confess those that they may have engaged in or to denounce those of which they had knowledge.[5] On the third Sunday after the proclamation of the edict, an anathema against heretics and those who sought to conceal them was pronounced in the principal church. This reading of the anathema was preceded and followed by a rather impressive procession of the local clergy accompanied by the tolling of bells.[6] In its detailed reply to the series of objections to the use of the anathema which were raised in 1587 by the cathedral chapter, the Valencia tribunal stated that the anathema was desirable to inject a greater element of "terror" into the ceremonial surrounding the proclamation of the Edict of Faith.[7]

From the standpoint of the Inquisition, the edicts had the effect of advertising the details of heretical acts and causing people to search their memories for instances in which they had heard or seen them performed. Moreover, like the public execution where the presence of the masses was a way of "invoking the vengeance of the people to become a . . . part of the vengeance of the sovereign," the edict involved the entire population in the Inquisition's task of ferreting out and punishing offenders against the faith.[8] Use of the edicts, and their regular annual recitation before the assembled population, had the effect of clearly advertising the existence of specific boundaries of accepted behavior, although the general conservatism that characterized all early modern institutions meant that a mature edict such as the one preached in Valencia on March 16, 1642, was both a catalog of errors and a museum piece in that it included certain items, like practice of the Islamic faith, that no longer posed a threat to Spanish society or formed a significant part of inquisitorial activity.[9]

Periods of grace and Edicts of Faith were only two of a number of devices that allowed the Inquisition to accumulate evidence that could form the basis for the prosecution of offenders. One of the most interesting of these devices was taking of an actual census of suspect groups. In Valencia, the tribunal compiled a list of converted Jews in 1506. This census, of which we only have fragments, lists converso families by parish and street and includes an impressive amount of detail about the situation of each family, including the occupation of the head of the household and his father, ages of the husband and wife, number of children, and the family "criminal" record of persons reconciled or relaxed.[10] The tribunal was also interested in compiling information about Morisco settlement. In 1568, Inquisitor Miranda, then carrying out a visitation in Morisco areas in the northern part of the district, carefully recorded the names of all the new Christians (Moriscos) of Castellón de la Plana.[11]

In accumulating the evidence needed to undertake prosecution, the Inquisition could count on important outside support. In the first place, parish priests were always a faithful auxiliary. The division of the 1506 census of conversos by parish indicates the key role they must have played in formulating it. As confessors, moreover, the parish priests were in an ideal position to receive confidences, and when these concerned heretical practices they were required to refuse to grant absolution unless their penitents agreed to appear before the Inquisition.[12] In 1654, for example, the Valencia tribunal received a visit from Basilia Ferrer, who had been urged to come by her parish priest after he had confessed to having learned certain love magic from Esperanza Badía. Basilia later appeared as a witness against Esperanza in the latter's trial on charges of superstition, and her testimony was important in obtaining the conviction of her erstwhile friend.[13]

The tribunal could also count on the active support of the network of familiares scattered throughout the district. When inquisitors toured the district on the periodic visitas, familiares would come forward to testify to any suspicious behavior they had observed or heard about. Comisarios, who were the tribunal's representatives in the major towns, were frequently given information by local familiares. In 1570, for example, Canon López de Camarena, the Valencia tribunal's comisario in Teruel, wrote to inform the tribunal that he had received information from a familiar from the village of Galve concerning acts of bestiality committed by a married man in the village.[14]

One of the most effective ways of obtaining denunciations against suspected heretics was sending inquisitors to tour the district. The presence of an inquisitor was an open invitation for people to search their memories for heretical acts and naturally served to focus local animosities by allowing individuals to denounce their neighbors for a variety of motives.

Visitation to the district was among the most important responsibilities of inquisitors as detailed on the earliest instructions for the Holy Office, those of Torquemada (1498) and Deza (1500).[15] By 1517, the visitation had become regularized, with each of the two inquisitors going to a different part of the district every four months.[16] Before the instructions of 1561 were issued, the visitation was an impressive affair in which the inquisitor made use of his authority to arrest suspects and carry out all kinds of trials on the spot. The danger of allowing inquisitors so much discretion was revealed during the visitation to the Valencia tribunal which took place in 1560. As a result of this visitation, Inquisitor Gregorio de Miranda was charged with abusing his powers and violating procedural rules during his visitations to Játiva and Teruel in 1557. Among other things, Miranda was accused of ordering heavy punishments without sufficient proof, putting minors on trial without providing them with a guardian as specified in the ordinances regulating inquisitorial procedure, and totally ignoring the judge of the episcopal court.[17]

After the reforms of 1561, the inquisitors tended to proceed more carefully when on visitation, dispatching the less important cases on the spot but sending evidence concerning graver matters back to the tribunal for decision. By the later sixteenth century, the visitation had become more and more an occasion for gathering accusations to be included with those already in the tribunal's file. To some degree, one can even refer to a certain specific targeting of the visitations to areas where denunciations had already accumulated and only a little more evidence was needed to trigger a series of trials. Certainly that is the impression one gains from reviewing the visitation by Inquisitor Pedro Girón to Gandía in 1590. In his memorial of the visitation, Girón stated that he went there because there were already a number of denunciations from that city so that if additional evidence could be garnered during the visitation, the suspects could be arrested.[18]

Evidence derived from the results of visitations or from the Inquisition's network of informers was always less important as a source of prosecutions than the evidence provided by the accused themselves when in the course of their interrogations they were forced to reveal fully not only their direct accomplices but anyone else engaging in heretical acts. Inquisitorial procedures in this respect were a good deal stricter than in the ordinary criminal courts, where the accused were not even expected to be asked about their accomplices except in crimes such as sodomy where an accomplice was necessary to commit the act.[19] In what must have been something of a record for a number of persons implicated in the testimony of a single accused, Francisco Caffor, a Morisco, testified against some 964 individuals in the course of his trial for Islamic practices.[20] Sometimes the case against an individual could be made considerably more serious by testimony given at another trial. Evidence given against Francisco Sebastián, a Morisco of Teruel, by Luis Caminero was sufficient to doom Sebastián to relaxation (execution by burning) after Inquisitor Juan de Llano de Vargas changed his vote.[21]

Perhaps the most remarkable tribute to the Inquisition's hold on the popular imagination was the steady stream of individuals who came forward spontaneously to confess their errors. Of course, some "spontaneous" confessions were only motivated by the fear of imminent arrest or by the knowledge that one had already been denounced. Such was the case of Dr. Gaspar Jornet, who came to the tribunal to confess his homosexual relations with José Castello, a student at the law faculty. When Jornet came to the tribunal on January 13, 1687, he must have been aware that Castello had come before it to confess only four days earlier.[22] Fear of denunciation was behind the confession of Fray Anselmo de Gracia, guardian of the monastery of San Antonio of Mora, who was engaged in a strenuous effort to reform the monastery in the face of opposition from many of his fellow monks. Fray Anselmo admitted that at a moment of supreme frustration he had exclaimed in the hearing of other monks that if some are given a crown in heaven for their travail on earth, he would have to be given three. Although this was perhaps not a very serious matter, he had been advised that some of his enemies among the monks intended to denounce him to the Inquisition and to distort his statement to make it appear like a heretical proposition. To prevent this, he felt it was necessary to appear before the tribunal on his own.[23]

Another clear motivation was the feeling on the part of the individual, which was shared by the Inquisition's defense attorneys, that self-confession could lead to a reduction in penalties. This was certainly true of Fray Augustin Cabades, whose spontaneous confession of soliciting sexual favors from his female penitents in the confessional was cited by his defense attorney as exceptionally full and truthful in his plea that his client be sentenced in private to prevent damage to his reputation. The tribunal was evidently sympathetic to the argument and agreed that Cabades should be sentenced and admonished within the tribunal's own chambers and in the presence of only three outside witnesses.[24] It was by no means certain, however, that the tribunal would always react the same way, as another solicitante, Dr. Juan Bautista Catalá, rector of the village of Yátova, found in 1764. Even though Catalá's defense attorney, Dr. Joaquín Solsona, argued that his client's spontaneous confession indicated his "contrition and sincere repentance," the tribunal turned a deaf ear, and while it did permit the sentence to be read out within the audience chamber, as was customary in this sort of case, it insisted on the presence of eighteen confessors drawn from the secular and regular clergy and sentenced Catalá to four years of exile and one year of indoctrination in a monastery. The trial record indicates that the tribunal took spontaneous confession into account as only one aspect of the case and that leniency would be shown only if other factors did not mitigate against it. As far as Catalá was concerned, the number of witnesses and the fact that they included several of the wealthiest farmers of the village indicated that he could no longer effectively serve his office and made exile from the village a foregone conclusion. Moreover, his amorous pursuit of village women had come to the attention of several Franciscan friars as well as a Jesuit on mission, and this made it necessary to call in a representative group of confessors so that Catalá could serve as an example.[25]

The number of those making spontaneous confessions tended to vary widely with the particular group. The Moriscos, for example, accounted for very few because of the strong pattern of group solidarity they had managed to maintain. Of all the groups subject to inquisitorial jurisdiction, it was Old Christians, especially rather simple people who were afraid that they had uttered some blasphemy, who were most apt to present themselves at the tribunal. A typical representative of this group was the illiterate silk worker Jerónimo Mevin who came all the way from Caspe to denounce himself before the tribunal before having said, while playing ball, "I deny God and his saints." The remorseful young man explained that he had been angry at losing the ball game when he uttered those words, that he had no real intention to blaspheme, and that "he was deeply sorry."[26]

For certain persons, the very fact of the Inquisition's existence was vastly reassuring as it was the obvious and accepted place to unburden one's conscience regarding certain acts or statements. In 1678, one of the porters of the Diputació came to the tribunal to declare that fifteen years earlier he had practiced anal intercourse with a woman named Jerónima Brunet. Confessing with his parish priest did not seem to offer more than temporary solace, and he was never able to "achieve peace of mind until he came to the Holy Office."[27]

The clergy, both secular and regular, were also well indoctrinated and regarded the Inquisition as the place to take their religious doubts and receive absolution. In 1691, Fray José Marti, a Carmelite, came to the tribunal to denounce himself for a certain statement that he had made during a sermon which might have been heretical. In the same year, Fray Silverio Garcerón, a reader in philosophy at the academy of the monastery of La Merced in Elche, came to denounce himself for certain positions that he had defended during the course of his oral examination for the post of reader of theology.[28]

Inner wavering as to the truth or value of Catholicism was also felt to be something that should be brought to the Inquisition before the individual fell into graver doubt. When Juan Montalva, priest and benefice holder in the parish of San Martín, came to the tribunal to confess his growing skepticism about whether Catholicism was the only correct religion, he stated he had learned when he was a seminary student that the Inquisition was the proper place to come for such matters.[29]

Once evidence had been accumulated from whatever source, the tribunal's response to it was governed by the rules of evidence followed in inquisitorial procedure modified by its own experience. In Western Europe, inquisitorial procedure was the product of a long historical tradition reaching back to the last half of the twelfth century when criticism of the ordeal as a method of proof and the growing centralization of governments, both papal and monarchial, provided the means for the development of more rational alternatives based on specialized legal procedures.[30] The chief characteristic of Inquisition procedure was that the central power (state or papacy) asserted the public interest in the punishment of crime and that a government agency undertook all aspects of a criminal proceeding, from initial investigation to establishing the proof necessary for punishment.[31]

In general, it was the medieval church that took the lead in establishing inquisitorial procedure, largely because it needed a more effective means to combat the rising tide of heresy. The ordeal could hardly help to reveal inner thoughts and feelings, and in the heresy trial, it was the mind and not the body that chiefly concerned the judges. Only a group of experts using sophisticated legal methods could hope to discover offenders and bring them to confess and abjure their sins.[32]

The fact that inquisitorial procedure was first developed to defend the faith against heretics lent to it an arbitrary quality that would have probably been absent from a body of criminal law designed to punish more ordinary offenders. The heretic, according to Eymerich, was one who had deliberately chosen error and had therefore placed himself outside of and in opposition to the community of believers.[33]

For Eymerich's sixteenth-century editor, Francisco Peña, the heretic was particularly odious because he believes and actively

teaches things contrary to the faith of Christ. Terrible consequences would follow for nations that tolerated heretics in their
midst since sedition would be inevitable and would result in the
destruction of public order and prosperity.[34] This concept of the
religious heretic as an especially dangerous and hateful individual
whose crime had placed him automatically outside of and in opposition to the religious community and the social body is of key importance in understanding the emergence of a form of jurisprudence so
heavily weighted in favor of the prosecution.[35]

Taking its departure from the urgent need to stamp out such
vicious criminals, the Inquisition tended to accept evidence from
any sort of witness, however discreditable. In answer to the question
of whether criminals, known perjurers, or persons of infamous reputation should be allowed to testify for the prosecution, Eymerich
answered in the affirmative because "the crime of heresy is of such
gravity." The only exception to this rule was in the case of mortal
enemies of the accused.[36] In practice, however, the accused's protection against ill-wishers and malicious denunciation was wholly dependent on his ability to name his enemies specifically, because the
inquisitors themselves made little effort to cross-examine witnesses
to find out if their testimony was based on fact. It was not uncommon
for persons to be arrested and incarcerated on the basis of the flimsi-
est of accusations by a single witness of dubious reliability and only
saved from condemnation when the witness confessed the falsity of
the charge to a third party who came to the tribunal with the information. In 1565, for example, the Valencia tribunal arrested thirteen
Moriscos who were accused by Angela Michaela of having been
involved in the desecration and burial of a cross but was forced to
release all of them after her confessor came to the tribunal to declare
that she had sought absolution for having lied to the tribunal to cover
up for some of her relatives.[37] Interestingly, the arrest and trial of
these Moriscos on the basis of the testimony of a single and not very
reliable witness figured among the charges brought against Inquisitor Bernardino de Aguilera during the visitation of 1566–67.[38] The
inquisitor defended himself by simply reminding the Suprema that
it had been fully informed about the case from the beginning and had
specifically authorized the arrests.[39]

A standard item in Inquisition procedure as practiced on the
Continent was the requirement of two eyewitnesses for conviction.

Frequently, however, this rigorous standard was of little help to the accused because one eyewitness was sufficient to permit the inquisitor to use torture to extort the remaining measure of "truth."[40] Insufficient evidence was not considered grounds for presuming innocence, but it had the effect of leaving the accused "semiguilty" and exposed to the next link in the chain of judicial procedures, which was itself a form of punishment.[41]

In accordance with the general secrecy of proceedings, witnesses' names were not divulged to the accused. The reason for this policy, which dates from the medieval Inquisition, was that informers would be in danger from the friends and relatives of the accused. Certainly, by making it easy and safe to testify in an inquisitorial court, confidentiality had the effect of ensuring a continuous flow of denunciations.[42]

After sufficient evidence had been accumulated, an arrest was ordered at the request of the prosecuting attorney. Once brought to the prison by the alguacil mayor or, as happened frequently, by several familiares, the prisoner was made to declare all his property, which was then sequestered and placed in the hands of a factor appointed by the tribunal. This property would be returned if the prisoner was found innocent, but in the meanwhile, portions of it were sold to pay the costs of imprisonment. There was nothing especially unusual about sequestration in a judicial system that depended for its support on revenues from its victims or clients, and Villadiego tells us that the same procedure of sequestration and inventory of property was used in the ordinary courts.[43] When a prisoner had no property, the tribunal undertook to feed and clothe him out of its own resources, although this was only a part of the tribunal's judicial function and should not be taken as an indication of any softness toward the poor.

Ideally, the "secret prison" into which the accused was conducted after his arrest was to be characterized by a political economy of silence and isolation. This, at least, was the intention of the Suprema, which even wrote to the tribunals demanding that the patios by which prisoners could communicate with one another be closed off. Removed from the world and each other, the prisoners were to be well fed, with meat at least every other day, while the prison itself was to receive regular visits from the inquisitors, who were to pay careful attention to any complaints or special requests.[44]

During the early years of the Valencia tribunal, the ideal could not be realized because the Inquisition did not have its own quarters and prisoners were housed in the ordinary city jail for common criminals. Somewhat later, as part of the process whereby the Inquisition acquired its own precincts, the prisoners were removed to separate quarters near the Trinity Gate.[45] Silence and lack of communication among prisoners do not seem to have been characteristic of Valencia's secret prison even after this early period. For one thing, prisoners were hardly ever placed in single cells, and usually had at least one, and sometimes as many as four, cell mates. A statement taken from Judaizer Brianda Gacente during the long period of imprisonment before the conclusion of her trial revealed that she was originally placed in a cell with four other women prisoners and that she frequently had conversations with the jailer about her case.[46]

In spite of the violation of the ideal internal economy of the inquisitorial prison, the tribunal found it useful to continue the practice of placing several prisoners together since cell mates could report conversations that they had with one another and could serve as witnesses to shore up an otherwise shaky case with additional charges. When Juan Casanyosas, a French silk winder living in Valencia, was brought to prison on October 12, 1564, on a charge of Lutheranism, there was only one witness against him. Casanyosas made the fatal mistake of deriding Catholicism repeatedly in arguments with his cell mate, a priest named Jerónimo Biosa. After several such arguments in which Casanyosas declared that miracles were the invention of the devil and that he did not believe in purgatory, Biosa asked for a special audience with the inquisitors to testify about what he had heard and to plead for a change of cell so that he would no longer have to listen to these "heresies." Apart from his confession under torture and the one outside witness, the only evidence against Casanyosas was the testimony of two fellow prisoners, Biosa and José Esquerdon, who overheard the two quarreling.[47]

After repeated complaints by officials of the tribunal about the inadequacy and discomfort of the prison and at least one plan of reform that was never implemented for lack of funds, Inquisitor-

General Quiroga sent his own chaplain to investigate the situation. It is to his report that we owe a detailed description of the precincts occupied by the Valencia tribunal toward the end of the sixteenth century.[48] According to him, the Inquisition formed an "island" all to itself in which were contained the audience chambers and secret archive as well as the residences of the two inquisitors and the alcalde of the prison. What is the most striking about the layout of the inquisitorial enclave is the physical closeness of judges and prisoners. The prisoners' cells were not only right alongside one another so that prisoners could easily communicate but they shared a wall with the second inquisitor's bedroom through which he could hear them speaking to one another "in loud voices" at night. The prison had a total of nineteen cells for men and five cells for women located in a separate loft area above the audience chamber and archive. All the cells were no more than 15 to 15½ feet square and were frequently overcrowded with prisoners awaiting the auto de fé. Since the prison was too small to accommodate the desired number of suspects, this had the effect of reducing the scope of inquisitorial activity.[49] In light of this situation, the chaplain proposed the expansion of the prison space into the houses occupied by the second inquisitor and alcalde. Although this plan would not be very costly, the composition of the precinct out of a diverse group of buildings constructed at different times and of varying quality meant that several would have to be rebuilt; poor construction had already allowed many prisoners to escape.[50] In spite of the reforms made later in the century, there is every indication that many of the problems indicated in the visitor's report remained unresolved.[51]

As far as the prisoners themselves are concerned, the record seems to be one of generally moderate treatment marred by sporadic abuse and exploitation rather than one of systematic ill-treatment. During the visitation of 1528, Alcalde Juan Velásquez, who apparently was an active silk manufacturer, was accused of forcing the women prisoners to work up silk and paying them less than the going rate. And prisoners were not fed properly because Velásquez was off tending to his business.[52] In 1566 testimony concerning Vicente Corboran, who was responsible for actually cooking and serving the prisoners' food, revealed that he was in the habit of withholding one-third of the ordinary ration (which he sold privately), and he consistently refused to purchase any special items even when given money to do so.[53]

However, the inquisitors of Valencia did carry out their obligation to visit the prisoners at regular intervals, and there seems to have been little systematic abuse or cruelty (beating of prisoners by guards, etc.). If anything, the prison seems to have lacked sufficient security. The guards, such as they were, were in more danger from the prisoners than a danger to them. In 1605, the alcalde mentioned several deadly assaults on his assistants in a letter to the Suprema.[54]

One pathetic example of the way criminals with experience of both the ordinary criminal jails and those of the Inquisition viewed the latter comes from a request by Pedro Adel for transfer to the inquisitorial prison in 1575. Adel, who had been tried by the Inquisition and sentenced to a term of galley service, was so decrepit that the galley captain would not accept him, and he was sent back to Valencia where, blind and impoverished, he was thrown into the municipal prison. He pleaded for a transfer to the inquisitorial prison where he would be properly "fed and taken care of." The tribunal referred his request to the Suprema, which would have nothing to do with him and ordered him to be given two hundred lashes and permanently exiled.[55]

The relatively favorable view of the Inquisition's prison among offenders and the harrowing description of the ordinary criminal jails of Valencia city by Dr. Tomás Cerdan de Tallada, a late-sixteenth-century defense attorney, would seem to support Lea's conclusion that "the secret prisons of the Inquisition were less intolerable places of abode than the episcopal and public gaols."[56]

If prisoners in the "secret prison" were not subject to systematic abuse by guards and workers, they were frequently forced to wait long periods before their cases were concluded. A survey of all the prisoners being held on July 18, 1566, reveals widely varying periods of incarceration before all stages of the trial process were concluded, ranging from a few months to as long as two-and-one-half years.[57] In general, prisoners were not exposed to such long periods of imprisonment; however, the average stay before sentencing was around three months.[58] It was the numerous exceptions to this general rule and the psychological impact that long incarceration had on certain individuals which sometimes drove them to mad-ness or suicide that the Suprema must have had in mind when it wrote the tribunal reminding it of the October 22, 1610, carta acordada (administrative order) that ordered speedy trials to prevent "the misfortunes that have occurred when prisoners become desperate as a result of the long delay in concluding their cases."[59]

Once incarcerated and interrogated concerning his property, the prisoner was not at first informed of the charges against him but was brought instead before the inquisitors who admonished him to confess any heretical acts that he had committed or heard about. Left in ignorance of the charges against him and denied benefit of defense counsel at this stage of the proceedings, the accused might confess immediately even to things the Inquisition was unaware of at the time of his arrest.[60] Even if the prisoner did not confess, he was left in an agony of doubt about what the Inquisition actually knew about his case and what sort of evidence had been brought against him. It was during the first three audiences with the prisoner that the inquisitors obtained the detailed sociological and biographical information that affords the historian fascinating insights into the mental state of the accused. This included the standard information requested of prisoners in the ordinary courts (age, marital status, occupation, and place of residence) but went far beyond it to probe the prisoners' personal history and knowledge of Catholic dogma and ritual.

Another interesting aspect of interrogation at this stage of the proceedings was the effort made by the inquisitors to trap prisoners into admitting their guilt or to at least say things that would support the allegations of the witnesses. Peña's sixteenth-century comments on Eymerich reveal the emergence of much more sophisticated procedures, perhaps under the influence of the ordinary criminal courts. Peña notes that the prisoner should be put at a psychological disadvantage immediately by being placed on a chair that was "lower and humbler" than that of the inquisitors themselves. In questioning the prisoner, the inquisitor should be careful not to "irritate" or provoke him, for this would only get him angry and make him more difficult to deal with. Instead, the inquisitor should be subtle, never indicating or suggesting to the prisoner what exactly was wanted from him, first questioning him in general terms about any heretical acts he had seen or committed, then "by degrees" moving to the chief indictment itself.[61] One example of just how effective this questioning could be comes from a bigamy case tried before the tribunal in 1659. In this instance, Valencia's inquisitors were successful in trapping the accused into admitting that he had knowingly committed bigamy by going to live with his third wife while his second wife was still alive.[62] Casanyosas, the convicted French Lutheran, commented ruefully on the brutal effectiveness of the questioning that he had been subjected to by Inquisitor Bernardino de Aguilera. According to him, Aguilera "had a virtuous face but was really a villain because having imprisoned men he makes them take an oath and forces them to admit to things they neither did nor imagined."[63]

At the end of the first three audiences, the charges against the prisoner were presented to the inquisitors by the prosecuting attorney or fiscal. The interposition of this official between judge and accused was a refinement and modification of traditional inquisitorial procedure in the sense that the inquisitors themselves could now preserve a formal impartiality, even though they had played the major role in creating the case against the accused.[64] The prosecuting attorney also represented the emerging idea that the crime was an offense to the public and should be prosecuted even in the absence of a private complaint.[65]

There was frequently a good deal of hearsay evidence presented in the prosecutor's arraignment, even though it was largely superfluous to proving the crime and often amounted to little more than one individual swearing that he had heard one of the principal witnesses state that the accused was guilty of heresy. In spite of the expense and time involved in interviewing these witnesses, the purpose was to make the amount of evidence against the accused seem greater than it really was and to buttress what was frequently a slender case at the start of the trial.[66] Rhetorical flourishes were also not uncommon, with some fiscales making an effort to make the crime appear more deliberate and more serious than it really was. The prosecuting attorney in the case of Brianda Gacenta, who was accused of Judaizing and specifically of participating in the lashing of a cross with Christ's figure on it, claimed that those present "took great delight in the cruel passion and torment that the Jews inflicted on his sacred person and proclaimed a strong desire to have been present at the passion." None of the rather flimsy and inconsistent evidence about the alleged incident as presented at the trial indicated any such glorying in the torture inflicted on Christ by the Jews of biblical times, and the prosecutor's statement was obviously meant to inflate the importance and significance of the heretical acts attributed to Gacente.[67] After the accusation was presented to him by the tribunal's secretaries, the accused was required to answer each item on the spot. After this, he was permitted to choose defense counsel.[68]

At the end of the arraignment, the prosecutor would frequently ask that the accused be made to undergo torture until he should admit the truth of the allegations made against him. In practice, however, torture was not decided on until after the prosecution and defense had concluded their arguments. If the case was still in doubt, the matter would be discussed by the members of the consulta de fé, and it was this body that would make a recommendation regarding torture if the evidence was insufficient for condemnation.[69]

After the choice of a defense attorney had been made, the case was formally received to proof, beginning with the ratification of the testimony of the original witnesses on which the original arraignment was based. Generally, ratification involved calling back the original witnesses to repeat their testimony before the inquisitors. And, according to the rules, no evidence could be used unless it was ratified. While a rigorous system of ratification involving careful reinterrogation of witnesses by the inquisitors could have been an effective protection for the accused, few inquisitors ever put themselves to so much trouble, and ratification was limited to mere repetition of the original testimony. Moreover, witnesses could ask to have their original statements read over to them to refresh their memories and even add material to their original testimony.[70]

At the sixth audience, the summary of evidence was drawn up, carefully omitting the names of witnesses, and presented to the accused who was required to answer every allegation immediately. After cross-examination by the inquisitors, the defense counsel was called in and given the summary of the witnesses' testimony along with the replies of the accused, although in fact those accused before the Valencia tribunal were not always assured of a formal defense until the mid-1540s.[71]

In the Spanish Inquisition, the defense labored under some very particular constraints that made the preparation of an effective case extremely difficult even if the court had not been biased in favor of the prosecution from the very start. For one thing, there was the ambiguous, even dangerous, position of the defense attorney himself. As a recognized, if minor, official of the court, the defense attorney would naturally want to retain the respect and approval of the inquisitors, especially if he wished to continue practicing before the tribunal. Under the circumstances, many defense attorneys were tempted to do little more than advise their clients to confess and to offer only a very perfunctory defense even if a more vigorous one were possible.

Another inhibiting factor for defense attorneys was that their role was ambiguous. An individual who presented too strong a case for his client might be seen as a protector of heretics and thus liable to suspicion. In Peña's commentary, he stresses that such protectors of heretics may "act with or without arms, during or after the trial." Since anyone who "opposed" or obstructed the work of the Holy Office in any way whatever could be considered a protector of heretics, a conscientious defense attorney had to walk a narrow line between presenting an adequate defense and avoiding the impression that he supported his client's erroneous beliefs. Torquemada's instructions of 1484 contain a clear reference to this linkage between defense attorneys and the "defenders of heretics" when they are warned not to undertake the defense of any part of the case where they know their client is guilty and not to impose "captious objections or malicious delay" on the trial, which must have inhibited them from deploying the full range of their legal talents on their client's behalf.[72] When the defense attorney agreed to undertake the defense, he had to swear to defend his client but also to "undeceive him" if he did not have justice on his side.[73]

Some defense attorneys took their status as officials of the Holy Office and defenders of the faith so seriously that they were unwilling to carry out their responsibilities to their clients. When Abdella Alcaxet, a Valencian Morisco turned Barbary pirate, was captured and brought to the tribunal, Luis Sarcola was assigned to defend him. Going beyond the usual admonition to confess and receive mercy, Sarcola remonstrated openly with his client and urged him to convert to Catholicism. Alcaxet remained obdurate, saying that he wanted to live as a Moor and die in the Islamic faith. On hearing this, Sarcola said he would have nothing more to do with the defense. Since Alcaxet was impenitent, the tribunal apparently did not feel it needed to provide him with anyone to replace Sarcola, and so no defense plea was entered and the case was closed. Clearly, in the case of someone like Alcaxet who boasted openly of his corsair activities against Christian shipping and of his landings on the Valencian coast to pick up groups of Moriscos who wanted to escape to Algeria, all pretense of fairness broke down. Alcaxet was an avowed enemy of Catholic Spain, and it would have taken a far better developed sense of the rights of the accused than that possessed by the Spanish Inquisition for him to have been afforded procedural safeguards that he himself probably did not expect.[74]

Quite apart from the difficulties presented by the awkward position of the defense attorney himself, the defense labored under a series of disabilities imposed by the nature of the procedures followed by the Inquisition. The best known of all of these disabilities was the Inquisition's refusal to divulge the names of the witnesses for the prosecution or any particulars that might allow the accused to discover them. As stated earlier, the accused was supposed to be protected from having the evil-intentioned testimony of his mortal enemies used against him, but to make use of this protection he would have to separate his mortal enemies from the other witnesses using the deliberately vague summary given to him by the inquisitors. Just how useless the rule barring the testimony of enemies was to a prisoner who was unable to guess the names of the witnesses against him is demonstrated by the case of Pedro Matheo, a Valencian velvet worker who was accused of Judaizing in 1521. Out of twelve witnesses against him, Matheo was only able to name one (his wife) as a mortal enemy and was therefore convicted and sentenced to perpetual imprisonment.[75]

If a defendant was to formulate a case, he would need witnesses who could help him disable opposing testimony by proving enmity or demonstrate good character. The sorts of witnesses admissible for the defense, however, were much more restricted than those allowed the prosecution, which could even call criminals or excommunicates.[76] When a list of defense witnesses was presented to the inquisitors, they were also given a series of questions to be put to them. Even here, conscious bias against the defendant may be seen in the fact that the inquisitors did not have to accept either witnesses or questions in their entirety, and it was not uncommon for some defense questions to be set aside as "impertinent."[77]

In spite of these obvious problems, some defense attorneys labored conscientiously on behalf of their clients. Dr. Ramos, who represented Matheo in his Judaizing case, presented what may almost be called an ideal defense. After establishing Matheo's reputation as a good Catholic who went to mass regularly and accepted everything as taught by the Roman Catholic church, Ramos went on to impugn the testimony of his wife with whom he was always quarreling. To buttress the testimony of the mainly converso witnesses who testified to his frequent attendance at mass, Ramos brought forward Yolante Martínez, an Old Christian, who had lived and worked in Matheo's home for several months. Martínez testified that she had seen Matheo attend mass in San Lorenzo "many times" and that work did not cease in his house on Friday nights and Saturdays, when Judaic law dictated that no work be performed. This testimony should have impressed the inquisitors as they frequently attempted to ascertain whether converso families would alter household routines to celebrate the Jewish Sabbath.

Ramos then expertly dismantled the prosecution's case. He began by pointing out that all the prosecution witnesses were "singular," that is, the specific incidences of Judaizing or blasphemy that they testified to were not corroborated by any of the others. Even though Matheo had performed certain Judaic ceremonies, the circumstances under which they had been performed did not indicate any pattern of criminal behavior. As a young apprentice, when he committed certain of the acts in question, Matheo would naturally have felt compelled to conform to the customs of the household, but mere conformity did not indicate conviction.

Matheo was sentenced to perpetual imprisonment in the house of another velvet worker in spite of the fiscal's demand for relaxation and during a period when converted Jews were being routinely sentenced to death, and while it would be difficult to ascribe this relative leniency wholly to Ramos's defense, there is no question that in this instance a defense attorney did well by his client.[78] Procedural disabilities notwithstanding, it is clear that conscientious defense attorneys were able to present a successful and coherent defense that might well have been convincing in a modern court of law. Unfortunately, the Inquisition was not a modern court, and although it was willing to go further in the formal protection of accused than the French or English criminal courts of the period which did not even permit defense attorneys, the bias of inquisitorial procedure favored the prosecution, and the efforts by defense attorneys could too easily be dismissed as placing unwarranted delays in the way of just punishment.[79] Moreover, efforts by defense attorneys to remove some of the difficulties under which they labored proved unavailing in the face of the prosecutorial bias of the Holy Office. When Dr. Montaner, an abogado de presos of the Barcelona tribunal, petitioned the Suprema to allow names of prosecution witnesses to be revealed to the defense, he and the other attorneys signing the petition were threatened with arrest.[80]

After the prosecution and defense had concluded their presentations, the trial itself was terminated and ready for sentencing. It was at this point that the trial became open, as it were, to influence from other centers of judicial authority, since the inquisitors could not sentence alone and had to form a committee, called the consulta de fé, with a representative of the bishop of the diocese in which the accused as well as a judge of the chancery court lived.[81] The group responsible for voting on the sentence of Esperanza Badía, for example, included three inquisitors as well as Dr. Francisco Fenollet, dean of the cathedral chapter acting for the archbishop of Valencia, and Dr. Basilio Esteve, a judge from the Audiencia.[82] Although there was a certain controversy among jurists about whether the vote of the consultores was decisive, when the bishop's representative and the inquisitors disagreed, the case was generally referred to the Suprema. Later in the history of the Inquisition, when the tribunals were forced to refer most of their verdicts to the Suprema anyway, the consulta served as little more than a means for debating the issues in a case, while the Suprema, which made the decisive judgment, was under no obligation to take its deliberations into account.[83]

If there was sufficient evidence, the consulta could then sentence the accused directly or could vote for torture on the grounds that although strong proof existed, the entire truth was not yet known; therefore, a last effort to obtain a confession from the accused must be attempted, whatever the risk to the prosecution case. To the contemporary mind, judicial torture is perhaps the most repugnant aspect of inquisitorial procedure, yet it must be seen as a necessary element in a judicial system whose major goal was to obtain the confession of the accused. Confession was vital because of the high and often impossible standard of proof (two independent eyewitnesses) necessary for complete certainty of guilt. The frequent failure to produce two eyewitnesses led to a whole legal "arithmetic" of partial proofs and to a considerable degree of uncertainty in sentencing, while the absence of any empirical method of evaluating circumstantial evidence made it very difficult to supplement denunciations with any other proofs. If the accused could be induced to confess, the court could resolve all of these issues and the prosecution's case would be automatically validated.[84]

Judicial torture as practiced in early modern courts had a strong connection to the trials and ordeals of an older, more primitive legal tradition. As a real test of the veracity of the accused's assertions of innocence, it could not be unlimited and beyond endurance because the accused would obviously have to have a chance to prove his innocence by passing the ordeal successfully. This notion of torture as a "test" emerges clearly from Peña's disparaging comments about certain judges who had invented new forms of torture, an activity that smacked more "of the work of the hangman" than of the "theologians and jurists" who made up the inquisitorial tribunals.[85]

In practice, the Spanish Inquisition used forms of torture that were common to the entire judicial system and was undoubtedly more careful than the secular courts in applying it.[86] Moreover, in spite of the considerable discretion given to judges in the 1561 Instructions, the repetition of torture was extremely unusual even where the victim had revoked an earlier confession. In only 0.8 percent of the cases for which trial details are available was torture repeated.[87] However, the Inquisition, like the secular courts, resorted to torture because of the difficulty of producing the requisite two witnesses to the same act.[88]

Confessions obtained under torture, unlike those given freely during interrogation, implied the failure of the entire effort to make the accused "play the role of voluntary partner in the procedure" and thereby to validate the politicoreligious role of the Inquisition.[89] Since the ritual of acceptance and repentance could not be valid without a strong element of voluntarism, the accused who confessed under torture had to be brought back within 24 hours to confirm the confession that he had made.

At the conclusion of the trial, the consulta de fé was required to recommend sentencing. There were a number of possible sentences that could be handed down by the tribunal. Of course, the accused could be acquitted, but outright acquittal was rather uncommon in the Inquisition because it constituted an admission that the tribunal was wrong to prosecute the case, and given the inquisitors' sensitivity to their honor and reputation, they were extremely unwilling to lay themselves open to such an inference. Between 1478 and 1530, the Valencia tribunal only handed down 12 absolutions out of 1,862 sentences.[90]

Simple suspension of a case was far more common than outright acquittal, since suspension saved the Inquisition's reputation for infallibility and left the accused under a permanent cloud of suspicion. Suspended cases, moreover, could always be reopened if any fresh evidence presented itself. Suspensions formed an increasingly large number of the sentences handed down by the Valencia tribunal from the mid-sixteenth century and continued to increase as a percentage of all sentences through the eighteenth century.[91] Those who were penanced were required to "abjure" heresy, specifically, the heresy of which they were guilty. There were two forms of abjuration: *de levi,* for a minor offense, and *de vehementi,* for a more serious one.[92]

Exile was another punishment that was frequently imposed by the Inquisition.[93] Normally, a sentence of exile would simply be a blanket prohibition to enter a certain place or places and their vicinity for a period of years. During the seventeenth century, the royal court (which really meant Madrid and its vicinity) was included in the sentence regardless of any other places mentioned. Sometimes the tribunal would go further in trying to make the sentence appropriate to the situation and proclivities of the criminal. Cristóbal de Centelles, one of the Valencian nobles who was arrested during the tribunal's crackdown on Old Christian lords of Morisco vassals in the 1560s and 1570s, was found not only to have permitted his vassals to freely practice their traditional customs and rituals but to have engaged in illicit sexual practices with certain Morisco women. Centelles was fined 600 ducats and permanently forbidden from living in places with a predominantly

Morisco population, which meant, in effect, that he could not live on his own estates.[94]

Spiritual penance, which could range from actual incarceration in a monastery to religious instruction and the performance of certain observances, was widely used, especially for the two privileged classes, nobility and clergy, and for persons convicted of lesser crimes like blasphemy. Reclusion in a monastery along with religious indoctrination, and deprivation of the right to celebrate mass or hear confession, was a punishment used in the solicitation cases that became such an important part of the business of the tribunal in the seventeenth and eighteenth centuries.[95] Occasionally, the tribunal would even specify the nature of the religious instruction that it wished the penitent to have while in reclusion. On December 17, 1764, the tribunal sentenced Dr. Juan Batista Catalá, the rector of the village of Yátova north of Buñol who had been convicted of solicitation and "evil doctrine" because of certain statements he made to one of his female penitents, to one year of exile in a monastery and instructed him to read the works of Fray Luis de Granada.[96]

A certain percentage of the sentences handed down by the tribuanl called for scourging. Usually between 100 and 200 lashes were laid on by the public executioner as the penitent rode through the streets mounted on a mule the day after he had been reconciled.[97]

Public disgrace, which was administered by leading the criminal through the streets on an ass, carrying the insignia of his offense, could be considered one of the lightest penalties administered by the tribunal. In a reputation-conscious society, however, such a penalty could have a fatal impact on the social standing of the victim and his family.[98]

In 1567, at the beginning of the great naval buildup that led to the battle of Lepanto, the Suprema ordered that all penitents sentenced to perpetual imprisonment and the habit should have their sentences changed to at least three years of galley service.[99] In reality, what the Suprema was doing was falling into line with what had already been done by the ordinary criminal courts in response to a series of royal pragmáticas issued between 1552 and 1556 when Philip II began taking control of the Spanish galley fleet from the private contractors who had run it under Charles V. These laws changed the ordinary penalties for thieves, vagabonds, and perjurers to galley service, which varied from several years for the first offense to life for the second.[100] Direct administration and the rapidly increasing size of crews of the Spanish galley fleet required ever greater numbers of men, so that in 1573, the Suprema, under considerable royal pressure, ordered that even the so-called buen confitente who confessed early and was normally given a light sentence should be sent to the galleys for a three-year term.[101]

Given the harsh conditions of the service, it was hardly surprising that many of the wealthier prisoners sought to reduce their term in the galleys through a monetary payment. By the late sixteenth century, this commerce in reduced sentences had become so regularized that a standard price of 300 ducats and the purchase of a slave who would serve the oars in perpetuity was established. In 1593, several of the thirty-eight Moriscos from Valencia's inquisitorial district then serving in the galleys petitioned for a reduction of their term through attorney Francisco Fuster, claiming that their relatives would help them to pay the necessary fee. These requests for remission of galley service usually became the subject of an individual dossier, that is, the meritos de reos, which included a brief summary of the case and details of the comportment of each prisoner during the term of his sentence. It was the Suprema that decided on the prisoner's merits, but normally it would agree to commute the sentence as long as the monetary payment was forthcoming, even though such early release ran contrary to royal policy and the navy's need for manpower.[102] In the mid-eighteenth century, galley service for all crimes was eliminated, and those who would have received it were sentenced to hard labor in the Almadén mines or the North African fortresses, where they were frequently worse off than they would have been in the galleys.[103]

In canon law, perpetual imprisonment was the ordinary punishment imposed on the reconciled heretic, and the Spanish Inquisition in both its medieval and modern forms frequently handed down such sentences.[104] During the early years of the modern Inquisition, the tribunals frequently did not have perpetual prisons and were forced to use the ordinary prisons, as in Valencia, or make do with other expedients. Around the middle of the sixteenth century, the Valencia tribunal established its own prison, but the need to find some way to support the prisoners without placing an undue burden on its resources meant that the number of persons actually in the perpetual prison at any one time tended to be small. Testimony taken during the visitation of 1566 indicated that there were only four people serving their terms in the prison, while many others sentenced to perpetual imprisonment were living in their own homes and freely practicing their trades with little or no supervision.[105]

There was also a tendency to reduce the term of perpetual imprisonment, usually for a money payment. Peña's 1578 commentary on Eymerich's discussion of imprisonment, which reflected current practice in the Spanish Inquisition, makes the point that these sentences were generally commuted to a term of from three to eight years, and in Valencia it was rare to have anyone serve more than one year during much of the sixteenth century.[106]

The sanbenito, a penitential garment made of yellow cloth (green in Valencia) emblazoned with two oblique crosses, was always worn by those sentenced to prison during the term of their imprisonment and even after their release. This garment was also the key element in perpetuating the infamy of those convicted of heresy and their families. Penitential garments worn by the reconciled were displayed prominently in local churches when they were removed either after the auto de fé or when they had served their term of imprisonment; garments worn by the relaxed were displayed immediately after the auto.[107] Using the sanbenito to perpetuate the memory of those convicted of heresy and apostasy was consistent with the effort to bar the descendants of the convicted heretic from holding public office, carrying on honorable trades or professions, or entering an ecclesiastical career.[108] Transmission of the penalty was a logical consequence of the hereditary nature of sin, a concept defended by such sixteenth-century writers as Gregorio López or Diego Covarrubias de Leyva and applied by them to treason both "human" and "divine."[109]

The Spanish Inquisition, which condemned many individuals to the stake, did not actually carry out the executions itself. The supreme penalty was incurred by heretics after they were in effect "cut off from the church" and left to the secular authorities to deal with. The secular authorities, for their part, had little choice since canon law provided the penalty of excommunication for those officials who failed to punish heretics given to them by the Inquisition.[110] In fact, the secular authorities needed no urging to carry out executions.

Several different outcomes of a case could result in the death penalty. The obstinate heretic who persisted in defending his beliefs in spite of all attempts to reason with him was judged pertinacious and condemned to the stake. The negativo, an individual who continued to deny his guilt in the face of what was felt to be overwhelming evidence against him, was considered an unrepentant heretic and also condemned to be executed. Even if an accused heretic confessed during the course of his trial, he could still be given the death penalty if his confession was judged to be incomplete. Imperfect confessions were regarded as false; they implied obstinacy and therefore placed the individual in the same position as the pertinacious heretic. A confession could be regarded as incomplete or mendacious for two principal reasons: failure to mention the names of accomplices or confession of heretical acts but denial of the intention to actually commit heresy.[111]

Finally, the relapsed heretic was liable to the supreme penalty. This was a potentially fruitful source of condemnations because any return to former practices or even former associates could indicate that the individual was impenitent and that his conversion was false. In actual fact, however, even during the early years of the Valencia tribunal, most relapsed persons were not condemned to be executed but were given other penalties.[112]

Between 1817 and 1818, Juan Antonio Llorente, the last secretary of the Corte (Madrid) tribunal, published the first major study of the Spanish Inquisition to be based on extensive archival materials. Llorente's work was the real beginning of modern Inquisition scholarship, but whatever its value in other respects, Llorente can justly be accused of greatly exaggerating the number of persons actually executed. In light of current research, it is difficult to accept Llorente's figure of more than 30,000 deaths. What is apparent from the figures for the Valencia tribunal is that the ferocity of the early years was succeeded by a long period of declining severity. During the forty-six years from 1484 to 1530, some 754 individuals, or 37.7 percent of the total of those whose penalty is known, were sentenced to death. By 1530, the incidence of death sentences had fallen sharply, with 81 percent of all the executions decreed before 1592 having already taken place.[113] During the later history of the tribunal, both the number of executions and the percentage of death sentences handed down had fallen dramatically. Between 1580 and 1820, only 1.4 percent of those tried by the Valencia tribunal were condemned to death, and only half were actually executed.[114]

Even when the death sentence had been imposed, the tribunals did their utmost to bring about conversion and confession so that a lesser penalty could be substituted. Monks, theologians used as consultants by the tribunal, and others worked feverishly to bring about an eleventh-hour conversion to reconcile the heretic with the church, and their opportunity was made even greater when the Suprema ordered that prisoners were to be notified of sentences of relaxation a full three days before the auto de fé itself.[115]

The auto de fé, at which prisoners' sentences were announced before a vast crowd, was one of those great public spectacles that played so large a part in the politicoreligious life of early modern Europe. Early autos were relatively simple ceremonies, with condemned persons being unceremoniously marched to the central plaza where their sentences were briefly read out before they were taken away to be executed.[116]

The auto de fé became much more elaborate later in the sixteenth century as Spain emerged as the leader of the Counter-Reformation and the struggle against Islam and as the state therefore became more involved in asserting its power over heretics. As heresy became equated with treason against the ruler, it was necessary to arrange a ceremony by which "injured sovereignty" could be reconstituted and in which "an empathic affirmation of political power" could be arranged for the edification of the public. Moreover, such a ceremony, through the presence of troops and local authorities and then the public burning of victims that took place later, could provide a "terrific example" of princely power while advertising openly the limits of socially acceptable behavior.[117]

In Valencia, the autos took place on the average of one per year. In many ways, it can be said that preparation for this event set the pace for the tribunal's life through much of the sixteenth and seventeenth centuries. After a sufficient number of convictions had been obtained, permission was requested from the Suprema to proceed with the auto. The ceremony took place before a large crowd as well as before the viceroy, president, and judges of the Audiencia, the archbishop, and the canons of the cathedral. After the sentences were read out, those sentenced to death were burned by the public executioner at a location near the present site of the botanical gardens.[118] By the end of the seventeenth century, the public auto de fé had been largely superseded by smaller, cheaper ceremonies held in one of Valencia's parish churches.

Significant gaps in the records, particularly between 1540 and 1570 and for several years in the seventeenth century, will probably make it impossible to know the exact number of cases tried by the Valencia tribunal. Combining the figures compiled by García Cárcel and Henningsen and Contreras for the period before 1700 with my own computations for 1700–1820, I arrive at a total of 11,458 cases, which probably understates the true figure by several thousand. (See table 1.)

In general, the tribunal's activity may be divided into three distinct periods of unequal duration. The first of these, from 1481 to 1530, was the period of intense prosecution of converted Jews who accounted for 2,160 of the 2,354 cases. The second period, 1560 to 1614, was dominated by activity against the Moriscos who comprised 2,465 of the 3,366 cases, or 73.2 percent. During the next, and much longer period, 1615 to 1820, the Inquisition concentrated on the majority Old Christian population for a variety of offenses, primarily infringing post-Tridentine moral and religious ideals.[119]

One of the principal differences between the medieval and Spanish inquisitions was the subordination of all of Spain's provincial tribunals to a central authority vested in the Council of the Inquisition (the Suprema) headed by the inquisitor-general. Like the Spanish monarchy's other governing councils, the Suprema had considerable autonomy and carried on the day-to-day business of the Inquisition with a minimum of outside interference.

In the early years of the sixteenth century, the Suprema's intervention in matters of faith was limited primarily to appeals and to the minority of cases where voting revealed disagreement among the local inquisitors and the ordinary. Where unanimity had been achieved, the Suprema was usually content to let well enough alone and was even reluctant to offer advice when the tribunal requested it. This extreme reticence was shown when, in 1512, the Suprema refused even to offer its advice about a case springing

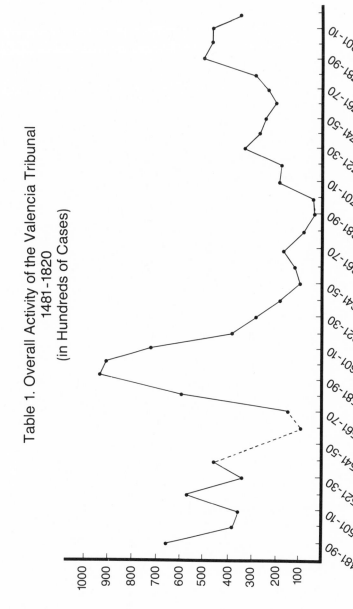

Table 1. Overall Activity of the Valencia Tribunal
1481-1820
(in Hundreds of Cases)

Note: The substantial lacunae in the relaciones de causas, especially between 1541 and 1570, and the dispersal of those records in the Archivo Histórico Nacional make it impossible to ever arrive at an accurate count of cases for the 1481–1700 period. For 1701–1820, I used a document (Clero 161) drawn up at the Valencia tribunal when its archive was still intact. Activity in this later period, however, had less and less concrete results as convictions became rare and most offenders were let off with a trivial fine or a warning.

from the murder of familiar Bartolomé Molner and returned it to the Valencia tribunal without comment.[120]

During the 1540s and 1550s, however, there is evidence of growing interference by the Suprema, with an increasing number of cases being submitted to it for comment and modification by the Valencia tribunal.[121] At this stage, though, the Suprema's advice was not always followed automatically. In 1556, when the Moriscos of Valencia seemed particularly restive, the Suprema wrote the tribunal ordering the suspension of several cases that were being formulated against certain Morisco tagarinos (Moriscos reared among Christians whose orthodox Catholicism had suddenly been questioned). In compliance with these orders, the tribunal released the Moriscos on bond, but when several of them used the opportunity to flee the kingdom, those remaining were rearrested, tried, and punished. To the Suprema's complaint that its express orders were being violated, Valencia's inquisitors replied that they had handled the matter in such a way as to "best satisfy their own consciences."[122]

This pattern of sporadic and sometimes ineffective intervention began to be replaced by a more rigorous central control with the Valdés Instructions of 1561, where prior consultation with the Suprema was mandated before an order to arrest persons of quality could be carried into effect.[123] That this order was being obeyed by the tribunal with not entirely satisfactory results from its own point of view is demonstrated by the case of Gaspar Centelles, a Valencian noble suspected of Protestant sympathies. After forwarding the depositions of two witnesses to the Suprema and urging a quick decision, the tribunal had to wait a full seven months before it received a reply from the Suprema allowing it to proceed.[124]

Ten years after its dilatory intervention in the Centelles case, the Suprema was presented with another opportunity to deal with an important Valencian noble, but this time the scope of its intervention had broadened considerably. Pedro Luis de Borja, grandmaster of Valencia's own military order of Montesa, was half brother to the duke of Gandía, Francisco de Borja, and himself a grandee of Spain so that his arrest on sodomy charges in 1572 was a major national event. In this case, the Suprema had not only ordered the arrest (after consultation with the king) but guided every stage of the conduct of the case itself, including his living accommodations while on trial, questions to be asked the accused, and a review of the sentence handed down by the tribunal.[125] By 1566, when the visitations that had been carried out into the proceedings of the Aragonese tribunals revealed a disturbing pattern of arbitrary behavior and gross violation of procedural norms that contrasted sharply with Philip II's personal commitment to a fair and impartial judicial system, the stage was set for an even greater reduction in the autonomy of the local tribunals.[126] In June 1568, a carta acordada (administrative order) mandated that all death sentences should be submitted to the Suprema even if they were voted unanimously.[127] Earlier that spring, another carta acordada brought the Suprema even more directly into trials of Moriscos when it ordered that all cases involving Morisco religious teachers (alfaquis) should be referred to it.[128] During the early seventeenth century, the last vestiges of the provincial tribunal's autonomy in matters of faith were removed when a carta acordada of August 2, 1625, mandated that the records of trials that resulted in sentences of galleys, penance, or lashing should be submitted to the Suprema before sentence was carried out.[129]

The process of judicial centralization, whereby provincial tribunals were required to submit their proceedings for review by higher courts, had become a part of seventeenth-century jurisprudence all over the Continent. In Spain, Villadiego informs us that ordinary criminal judges were required to consult their superiors before proceeding in all serious cases.[130] In 1624, the Parlement of Paris, France's high court of appeals, ordered that all serious cases of sorcery that involved torture, sentences of death, or other corporal punishment must be referred to it regardless of whether the accused had requested an appeal.[131]

In the case of the Spanish Inquisition, continuous oversight of procedure in matters of faith was facilitated by requiring that the tribunals send summaries of all cases tried by them to the Suprema regardless of type or punishment. These relaciones de causas began in a tentative way in the 1540s, but by the 1560s, continuous series began to appear. By 1610, the Suprema began to insist on details such as the date of incarceration and the date when the accusation was presented which would permit it to monitor the entire trial.[132] In 1632, the Suprema increased its supervision still further by ordering monthly reports on cases pending before the tribunal.[133]

Comments scrawled in the margins of the relaciones de causas or relayed to the tribunal by the carta acordada are characteristically terse and confined to procedural matters, while virtually ignoring questions of precedent or underlying legal philosophy. Such issues were addressed by the Suprema itself in the body of Instructions that it drew up to guide provincial inquisitors, especially those of 1561. But Spanish Inquisition law also evolved through the work of such distinguished canonists as Bishop Diego de Simancas or Francisco Peña, whose new edition of Eymerich's *Manual* with marginal notes based on the experience of the Spanish tribunals went through several editions. There were also a certain number of Spanish inquisitors like Juan de Rojas who addressed themselves to procedural issues.[134]

It is in the area of sentencing that the real influence of the Suprema on the tribunal may be discerned, since it became common practice to refer sentences to the Suprema after they were voted on by the tribunal's junta de fé. The Suprema's impact on sentencing was twofold: in supplying the details of the punishment that the offender would have to undergo and in altering that punishment both before sentence was actually pronounced and later when it could consider reducing terms of imprisonment, galley service, or exile.

The Suprema could also generally be counted on to intervene on the side of greater leniency, frequently reducing the term of imprisonment or exile suggested by the consulta de fé. In 1647–48, when the tribunal sentenced several women to greatly extended periods of exile for having violated the provisions of their original sentences, the Suprema responded either by demanding to see the original trial record or by drastically reducing the sentence. In general, the Suprema was about two-and-one-half times more likely to decrease a sentence as it was to increase its severity.[135]

Sentences could be further reduced after the culprit had already begun serving them for a certain period, although this would frequently depend on the receipt of favorable reports on the way in which the individual was serving his or her sentence. Thus, the Suprema ignored Fray Pablo Cenedo's first request for relief from the remainder of his term of confinement in a monastery and only accepted his second request after receiving detailed information on his behavior from the tribunal.[136] In the case of Fray Tomás de los

Arcos who was condemned as a *solicitante* in 1677, sentence was lifted but only after the Suprema had received many testimonials concerning his exemplary conduct in the monastery to which he had been confined.[137]

There can be little doubt that a pattern of greater leniency imposed by a superior court could signal changed perceptions of certain social groups or the greater acceptance or tolerance of certain sorts of behavior by the authorities. Thus it was by modifying sentences in the direction of greater leniency rather than through elaborate disquisitions on cases that the Suprema indicated the path it wished the provincial tribunals to take. As in every other respect, however, the penal practice of the Valencia tribunal was not a passive response to the demands of the Suprema. By the early seventeenth century, for example, the tribunal had taken on itself jettisoning the harsh provisions of Valencian law that mandated the death penalty for convicted sodomites and was following a new and more lenient policy.[138]

The structure of the earliest inquisitorial courts was extremely simple, with a minimal number of officials. In 1483, according to a memorial by Ferdinand the Catholic, each tribunal in the Crown of Aragon was to be composed of two inquisitors, a trained jurist to act as legal assessor, a prosecuting attorney (fiscal), a scribe, a constable to carry out arrests, and a porter.[139] Within a few decades, however, the number of officials and the cost of maintaining them had increased dramatically.[140] A letter to the Suprema by Valencia's Inquisitor Martín Pérez de Arteaga in 1553 complaining of excessive staff mentions five nuncios along with two barber surgeons and a doctor, all this in the face of increasingly inadequate funding.[141] As early as 1534, the Valencia tribunal was regularly staffed by three inquisitors, a fiscal, and four (later five) secretaries as well as chaplains and stewards, although by that time inquisitors were all trained jurists and the post of assessor had been eliminated.[142]

During its early years, the new Spanish National Inquisition shared with its medieval predecessor the quality of not having any fixed revenue base. The medieval Inquisition in the Crown of Aragon had always depended on the somewhat grudging support of the bishops and had supplemented what they chose to provide with erratic income from the sale of confiscated property and fines levied against convicted heretics.[143] When it was first established, the modern Spanish Inquisition depended on the crown, which controlled absolutely all inquisitorial finances, receiving all income and paying expenses through the royal treasury until well into the reign of Charles V. By the 1550s, however, the principle of royal control was gradually abandoned, and, in 1561, we find the Suprema ordering the provincial tribunals to stop sending information to the crown about confiscations. Instead, this information was to be sent to the Suprema, which would decide what if anything should be told to the officials of the treasury.[144]

The Suprema used a variety of methods to gain a greater measure of control over the income and expenditure of local tribunals. To regulate the activities of receivers or treasurers, a finance committee (junta de hacienda) was established in 1569.[145] This committee, which consisted of the inquisitors, the receiver, the notary of sequestrations, and the judge of confiscations, met each month to decide financial issues and to review the activities of the receiver who was required to present his accounts and to declare how much of the funds he had collected had actually been deposited in the tribunal treasury.[146] By the 1570s, the deliberations of the junta de hacienda were being reported to the Suprema on a regular basis, and by the 1620s, it was insisting on a full status report on all financial cases being tried before the tribunal.[147] Once the receivers' accounts were drawn up, they were audited yearly by the Contador-General of the Suprema.[148]

The Suprema also showed no compunction about using the information provided by the receivers to tax the wealthier tribunals for the benefit of its own treasury.[149] That this practice continued right down to the final years of the institution is demonstrated by the series of urgent payment orders sent to the Valencia tribunal between September 1806 and April 15, 1807, in which it was required to send the Suprema a total of 300,000 reales and 470 bolts of cloth.[150]

In spite of these constraints, however, notorious laxity in the face of official malpractice emboldened local receivers and other financial officials to defy the Suprema and flagrantly disregard the safeguards that had been designed to prevent embezzlement.[151] Distrust of the accounts rendered by receivers led to a struggle between the Suprema on one side and the local tribunal on the other, but the Suprema's unwillingness to punish the receivers or challenge the control that a few families exercised over that office meant that its efforts were doomed in advance and that receivers could continue their peculations unmolested until such time as the tribunal's own poverty made further profiteering impossible.

The Suprema's tenderness toward receivers and its reluctance to interrupt the comfortable nepotism that had come to dominate the office is perfectly illustrated in the case of receiver Carlos Albornoz. After experiencing difficulties in obtaining his accounts for 1723 and several other years, the Suprema permitted him to resign in favor of his son in 1727. At this point, he was forced to render his final accounts and disgorge some 6,000 reales that he still owed the treasury. After his account was audited, however, it was found that he still owed the treasury some 6,248 lliures besides censals collected from several towns but not entered on his books. Efforts to collect these not inconsiderable sums continued until 1734, producing an extensive correspondence and consuming much time and energy. Throughout this seven-year period, no thought was given to punishing him or to ordering the sale of his property so as to cover the debt he owed the treasury, and his son continued to peacefully serve his office.[152]

According to regulations laid down by the Suprema, receivers were supposed to render their accounts every year so that they could be reviewed by the auditor-general. Receivers were always dilatory about this responsibility, but by 1800, the Suprema seemed to have lost control completely and was forced to engage in a protracted struggle with the Valencia tribunal and its receiver, Francisco Antonio Polop, to obtain his accounts and those of his predecessors dating back to 1785. In the end, Polop flatly refused to forward his own accounts and sent only those of his two predecessors, which occasioned an outburst from the auditor-general who accused Polop of "bad faith" and demanded that he produce the accounts within two months.[153]

During the early period, the Inquisition derived its income largely from three principal sources: compositions, rehabilitations, and confiscations. Compositions were agreements whereby an individual convicted of heresy, which normally meant the confiscation of his property, could satisfy treasury claims by paying only a certain proportion. Sometimes these agreements were arrived at by the offender himself or sometimes by his heirs, as in the case of Dr.

Luis Esparça who arranged to pay the royal treasury 9,000 lliures in return for which the Inquisition agreed to drop its efforts to seize the property of his brother Manuel, a convicted heretic.[154] There were also agreements of a more inclusive nature such as the one arrived at between Ferdinand and the children of the condemned heretics of the Crown of Aragon whereby they could enjoy all the property of the condemned in return for a 5,000 ducat servicio.[155] In Valencia, compositions tended to diminish in importance after 1500, in part because the conversos themselves had learned to distrust the local tribunal, which frequently violated composition agreements by confiscating the property of those listed on them.[156]

For the large number of reconciled persons, one of the most fearsome penalties for themselves and their families was deprivation of the right to hold honorable offices. This penalty was the cause of numerous petitions to the pope by the affected individuals and their families and resulted in a series of battles over jurisdiction, until Alexander VI conceded the right to rehabilitate exclusively to the inquisitor-general of Spain.[157] Rehabilitations then became a fertile source of revenue for the Inquisition.

By far the most significant source of income enjoyed by the Valencia tribunal during its early years was derived from confiscations. The Furs of Valencia followed canon law and medieval custom in prescribing death and confiscation of property as the penalty for heresy, and the early Spanish Inquisition placed heavy emphasis on efforts to seize the property of convicted heretics.[158] When an individual was arrested, his property was subject to immediate sequestration, and he was expected to cooperate in making an accurate inventory, which was drawn up by the receiver and the notary of sequestration. This list was to be exhaustive, including such things as the amounts he was owed, any dowry he had given or received, even the slaves he owned and their purchase price.[159] A verdict of innocence would of course involve the return of the sequestered property, but such verdicts were rare, and in many cases sequestration became the equivalent of confiscation because as long as the case continued, the Inquisition obtained the funds it needed to support the prisoner in captivity from the sale of his property. When the almost inevitable verdict of guilty was reached, the sequestered property was usually sold at public auction.

While confiscation was the chief source of revenue enjoyed by the Valencia tribunal during its early years, there was always a considerable gap between the amounts stated in the inventory and the actual collections. The main problem here was the inability of the Inquisition to collect the debts owed to the accused. The Inquisition could not proceed arbitrarily against the property of third parties, and it not infrequently lost cases brought before its own judge of confiscated property.[160]

Concealment of property, the uncertainty and expense of attempting to collect debts owed to converso merchants, and, above all, the decline in the number of cases involving conversos made revenues from confiscations an increasingly unreliable source of support for the Inquisition in the 1530s and 1540s. From 1487 to 1530, the Inquisition received a total of 6,431,517 sueldos primarily from confiscations, but revenues fell drastically from 1529, and from 1530 to 1544, the tribunal collected only 737,188 sueldos.[161] After 1579, moreover, revenues from confiscations dropped to practically nothing.[162]

Sharply decreasing income from confiscations meant that the Valencia tribunal was in serious financial trouble from the late 1550s. With conversos no longer comprising even a significant minority of the accused, the tribunal was left with a largely Morisco clientele, some of whom were so poor that the tribunal spent more to feed them while they were in prison than it could hope to recover from the sale of their property. This situation prompted the Suprema to issue an order to the effect that impecunious prisoners were to be dealt with promptly without waiting for an auto de fé in order to avoid the costs of imprisoning them for long periods.[163]

The situation had changed radically from the halcyon days earlier in the century. According to a letter to the Suprema written by receiver Amador de Aliaga in May 1556, virtually nothing had been received from confiscations recently.[164] The steep decline in revenues from fines and confiscations plus the heavy burden of indigent Morisco prisoners meant that the tribunal could not even meet its most essential expenses. In August 1556, Aliaga drew up a list showing that the tribunal was behind anywhere from eight months to three years in its salary payments to officials, and he was being forced to loan them money out of his own pocket so that they could feed themselves and their families.[165] This situation continued into the early and mid-1560s when the new receiver, Bernardino Gutiérrez, reported that the tribunal still owed its inquisitors and officials 5,300 escudos.[166] There seems little reason to doubt this estimate since it was confirmed in a letter concerning the tribunal's financial situation written by the visitors who were carrying on a general investigation into the tribunal's affairs at that time. In their analysis of the reasons for this unfortunate situation, the visitors seem to be echoing the words of Amador de Aliaga several years before. After having carefully reviewed the tribunal's register of autos de fé, the visitors concluded that the sorts of cases that the tribunal was trying were generally of "poca calidad" and that little income could be expected from them. Of the eleven prisoners presently in the "secret prison" (mainly for Lutheranism), all were very poor and had to be supported by the Holy Office.[167] In light of its manifest poverty, the eagerness with which the tribunal greeted the prospect of seizing the extensive property of Gaspar de Centelles, who was relaxed at the auto of September 17, 1564, is hardly surprising.[168]

The ultimate solution to the Inquisition's financial problems had already been perceived by Charles V in October 1519 when he urged the tribunals to invest their funds in such a way as to yield a steady source of income. The first steps toward providing the Inquisition with a fixed endowment date from its early years when rental houses as well as long-term loans (censals) were confiscated from wealthy conversos. From 1528, the Valencia tribunal also absorbed the revenues of the former mosques and began purchasing new censals situated on Morisco and Old Christian villages.[169] The arrival of Inquisitor-General Fernando de Valdés in 1547 marked a watershed in inquisitorial finance, and his determination to give the Inquisition a firm basis for its existence and make it independent of the royal treasury led him to throw his full support behind the policy of acquiring new censals. This policy was followed by his successors who repeatedly insisted on the reinvestment of any monies derived from the redemption of censals.[170] Under this prodding, the tribunal greatly increased its holdings, especially at the end of the sixteenth century and during the first years of the seventeenth century. By the beginning of the seventeenth century, this policy was paying off handsomely, and the average income from censals in 1604 was at a level more than four times greater than it had been in 1529.[171]

The other important new revenue source that was, at least in part, a product of Fernando de Valdés's efforts on behalf of the institution that he headed was the setting aside of the income of one canonry in each cathedral or collegiate church in favor of the Inquisition. A papal bull issued by the compliant Pope Alexander VI in 1501 had already permitted the Inquisition this right, but successive popes refused to confirm it. It was not until Philip II came to the throne, and the discovery of Protestant elements in Spain itself pointed to the need for a more powerful Inquisition, that Pope Paul IV could be induced to issue the briefs that would allow for the implementation of this policy.[172] In January 1559, Paul ordered that the first canonry in each metropolitan church, cathedral, or collegiate church to become vacant should be suppressed in favor of the Inquisition. In spite of tenacious resistance by some cabildos in its district, the Valencia tribunal was able to boast of receiving the income from benefices in the five most important churches in the district by November 1566.[173]

The third major change in the tribunal's finances was the result of an agreement with representatives of the Morisco community which provided the tribunal with a substantial subsidy in return for abstaining from confiscating Morisco property. This agreement, which was signed in 1571, had a long gestation period going back to the tribunal's frustration with the comparative poverty of convicted Morisco heretics in the 1550s and 1560s and opposition to the policy of confiscation that had been voiced by cathedral canons and other members of Valencia's ruling elite. By 1563–64, Inquisitors Sotomayor and Aguilera were petitioning the Suprema for its support for a substantial subsidy from the Morisco community.[174] Several years of negotiations followed during which the tribunal found itself embroiled with the nobility and the aristocratic estate in the Cortes before the issue was finally resolved in its favor. The agreement, which provided a subsidy of some 2,500 lliures, was less than the tribunal had originally sought but still gave it 42.7 percent of its income in the late sixteenth century.[175]

Greatly aided by these important new revenue sources, the tribunal's balance sheet improved drastically after 1565. By 1566, collection of the canonries in Valencia, Játiva, and Teruel allowed the tribunal to bring all salary payments up to date.

By the late 1580s, the Inquisition's new financial policy seemed to have paid off handsomely. The account of receiver Benito Sanguino for 1587–88 shows a favorable balance of 100,663 sueldos, with all salaries paid in full through August 1588.[176] No longer dependent on the unstable income from confiscations, the tribunal's finances seemed solidly based on assured revenues that would have been the envy of any local rentier. In one respect, however, the new revenue base was more precarious than the old since the Inquisition's economic health was now heavily dependent on the general prosperity of the Valencian economy as a whole and on the survival of the Moriscos whose cheap labor was one of its strongest elements. Even as the income from the Morisco subsidy, canonries, and censals grew during the 1570s and 1580s, declining agricultural and industrial production and the increasing political and social pressure against the Moriscos were threatening to undermine the whole basis of the new system.[177]

Given the tribunal's dependence on the economy and its increasing investments in censals paid by nobles like the duke of Gandía who was himself heavily dependent on his Morisco vassals, the expulsion of the Moriscos could hardly fail to have a severe financial impact. The most immediate effect was the loss of revenues directly connected with the Morisco presence: subsidies, fines, and the censals paid by Morisco villages. The tribunal's financial problems were further exacerbated by the crown's policy of protecting the Valencian nobility from its creditors. In a report filed on October 26, 1615, the Suprema's prosecuting attorney painted a gloomy picture of the tribunal's situation and noted that royal protection was preventing it from foreclosing on several censals owed by the duke of Gandía.[178] The reduction in the interest paid on censals was a further blow to large censal holders and elicited widespread but ineffectual protests from lenders, including the Inquisition.[179]

In the last analysis, Philip III's government was not prepared to sacrifice the Inquisition even in the interest of its local aristocratic allies. In a step that mirrored previous royal policies of bailing out the Holy Office with revenues drawn from the Spanish church, the crown interceded with the Pope to obtain 3,158 lliures in additional income for the tribunal, drawn from the endowment of the now-defunct Morisco colleges. The colleges, which were originally set up by Archbishop Juan de Ribera, enjoyed an endowment drawn from censals owned by the archbishopric. These censals were turned over to the Inquisition in exchange for a group of now-worthless censals owned by the tribunal and situated on several Morisco villages.[180] Bowing to further pressure from the tribunal, Philip III also moved to indemnify it for its losses by making it a substantial grant drawn from the proceeds of sales of ex-Morisco property located in the royal patrimony. Finally, under the new administration of Philip IV, the crown partially reversed its previous policies regarding aristocratic debtors and ordered the duke of Gandía's estate to repay some 6,949 lliures in principal and 2,200 lliures in accumulated interest to the Holy Office.[181]

Royal largess and the extremely favorable treatment accorded the Inquisition in the matter of aristocratic debt made for a rapid recovery after the financial uncertainties of the immediate postexpulsion period. Favorable balances and the redemption of censals in the 1620s and 1630s also allowed the tribunal to acquire new censals.[182] But income from censals and canonries, which had become the financial mainstay of the tribunal, depended heavily on Valencian agriculture, which had been undermined by the expulsion of the Moriscos. By the 1660s, income had fallen to one quarter of its peak in 1608–09, and by 1687, revenues had fallen to their lowest level of the century.[183] The widespread economic disruption that was caused by the War of Succession and the invasion of the kingdom by foreign troops in 1706 only confirmed the tribunal's financial decadence.[184]

Rising population and the recovery of the Valencian economy after the War of Succession, however, brought an improvement in the financial condition of all institutions whose income depended largely on agricultural rent. The Valencia tribunal was one of these beneficiaries, and the mid-eighteenth century ushered in a "golden age" of financial plenty that was to last until the wars of the 1790s brought on the final crisis of the Spanish Old Regime.

If, during its early years, the Spanish Inquisition can be said to have resembled its medieval predecessor in more than a few respects, by the 1560s, it had evolved into a substantially different institution. No longer dependent on traditional sources of financial support, it had acquired its own revenue base derived from investments in censals, real estate, and canonries. Morever, as Peña's marginal notes to his 1578 edition of Eymerich's *Directorium inquisitorum* indicate, the Holy Office had evolved its own procedures that were derived from its experience with a deviant population far larger and more complex than that encountered by the medieval tribunal. By the mid-sixteenth century, the prestige of the Inquisition as a judicial institution had never stood higher, so much so that it frequently received testimony from persons who came to denounce themselves. Fear of persecution and an oppressive and pervasive system of informants had something to do with this, of course, but so too did public esteem for an institution that had successfully established itself as a strong defender of the faith, the monarchy, and the established order.

III

Inquisitors and Officials

In a remarkable and suggestive book of essays published in 1970, Julio Caro Baroja identified one of the most significant lacunae in our knowledge of the Spanish Inquisition when he pointed out that while frequent references to the lives and careers of inquisitors-general may be found in the literature, we know very little about the average inquisitor. This individual, at once the occupant of a middle-ranking judgeship on one of the many royal tribunals and representative of a centuries-old tradition of uncompromising defense of the Catholic faith, remains an enigma whose outlines are obscured rather than revealed by what we know about the political activities of a great ecclesiastical politician like Fernando de Valdés, a religious fanatic like Tomás de Torquemada, or the romantic portrait of the Grand Inquisitor sketched by Dostoevski in *The Brothers Karamazov.* Yet, as Caro Baroja has indicated, "for several centuries and up until recently ordinary inquisitors walked the streets of Toledo, Seville, Granada, and Cuenca and could be seen talking with canons and letrados, caballeros and hidalgos, as well as people who were humbler or more presumptuous."[1] Caro Baroja's basic question remains unanswered: who were the inquisitors? What can we find out about their origins, education, and careers? If the psychological and ideological gulf between the first inquisitor-general, Tomás de Torquemada, who was appointed in 1483, and the afrancesado, Ramón Josef de Arce y Reynoso, who ruled the Inquisition in the first years of the nineteenth century and died in Paris in 1814, is vast and almost incomprehensible, so too the gulf between the earliest inquisitors of Valencia, Fray Juan de Gualbes or Fray Juan Epila, and those who sat on the tribunal in the seventeenth century or the early nineteenth century is similarly vast.

Certainly, the specialist leafing through the pages of Lea's four-volume work on the Spanish Inquisition in the hope of obtaining such information about provincial inquisitors would be sorely disappointed. In volume 1, Lea's entire discussion of these matters takes up a scant four pages and confines itself to generalities about the formal requirements for sitting on a tribunal.[2] Even though other information on these topics is scattered throughout the work, it would be nearly impossible to reach any accurate conclusions from these references, and in this instance, one would be forced to agree with Caro Baroja's observation that Lea's critical apparatus appears more complete than it really is.[3]

The task of gathering information about the judges who sat on the Valencia tribunal is made easier because the Inquisition required extensive genealogical investigations of all those applying for official posts. Analysis of seventy genealogies (out of 134 judges who sat on the tribunal of Valencia between 1481 and 1818) reveals much about their social origins, personal characteristics, education, and careers and should serve to at least partially remove some of the mystery that still surrounds the figure of the ordinary provincial inquisitor.

One of the series of reforms that followed the Comunero Revolution of 1520–21 was the reservation of places on the councils and other institutions comprising the Castilian central administration for subjects of the Crown of Castile.[4] While this policy did not extend itself to the Council of Aragon, all of whose members (with the exception of the treasurer-general) were Aragonese subjects, it did have the effect of ensuring an overwhelming preponderance of Castilians on the Valencia tribunal, which represented the Spanish National Inquisition in the kingdom. Of the 62 judges whose place of birth is mentioned in their genealogies, 50, or 80.6 percent, came from the Crown of Castile.

Within the Crown of Castile itself, moreover, the northern part of the kingdom, including Navarre, Galicia, León, and Old Castile (especially Burgos and its district), maintained a clear predominance throughout the period under review. Overall, some 48.3 percent of the inquisitors whose place of birth is known came from these northern regions, and of the 50 who were born in the kingdom of Castile, 30 were from the north.

There is no doubt that the predominant position of letrados drawn from the northern part of the Crown of Castile in recruitment to the Hapsburg bureaucracy can be explained principally by two factors: the geographic distribution of the lesser nobility from whose ranks most letrado bureaucrats were drawn and the greater availability of educational opportunities at both a secondary and university level. The de facto exclusion of Aragonese subjects from serving on the tribunal was only strictly observed until the end of the sixteenth century. Under the later Hapsburgs and Bourbons, it began to receive a few Aragonese judges. The numbers remained modest, however, with only twelve Aragonese subjects serving on the tribunal in the 207 years between 1602 and 1809. Moreover, since nine of these were either from the kingdom of Valencia or from Teruel, which was within the inquisitorial district, the tribunal's belated move to recruit local judges can be related to the critical need to reinforce its local political base to counter the unrelenting hostility of the jurats and the Audiencia rather than any desire to promote equalization of employment opportunities among the regions.[5]

One of its greatest successes in this campaign was the appointment of Dr. Honorato Figuerola as inquisitor of Valencia in 1598. Figuerola was one of the very few canons of Valencia's cathedral ever recruited for a judgeship. He came from an extremely influential Valencian family whose political support would be highly beneficial to the tribunal. As early as 1506, Juan Figuerola, Honorato's paternal great-grandfather, had enjoyed the status of ciutadà ("citizen" with rentier status) and held the key post of treasurer of the city of Valencia to which he was reelected in 1511.[6] Honorato's paternal grandfather had served as jurat of Valencia, while his brother Melchor Figuerola, a wealthy cavaller who owned property in Valencia and wheat fields in the countryside, had served as one of the Estament Militar's two deputies on the Diputació, the kingdom's chief revenue-collecting body.[7] Dr. Honorato Figuerola's service as inquisitor, although brief (he left in 1600), was the beginning of a long and fruitful involvement of the Figuerola and their connections with the tribunal, which would continue right down to the mid-eighteenth century and bring such notables as Bernardo Boyl, lord of Manesis, into the ranks of the familiares.[8]

If the tribunal was concerned with the additional political support it could obtain by awarding judgeships to the members of politically useful families, it was also compelled to reward at least some individuals whose families had served the tribunal for long periods, often in an unpaid capacity. Dr. Juan Joseph Martínez Rubio, who served as inquisitor of Valencia from 1619 to 1625, was himself rather typical in that he held an advanced degree in canon law and had served as an official of the archbishopric, but what distinguished him as a candidate for the judgeship was his family's loyal support for the tribunal in the remote and mountainous eastern part of the district. Both his father, Pedro Martínez Rubio, and his paternal grandfather had served the tribunal as familiares in the isolated village of Ródenas in the Sierra Menera where Juan Joseph Martínez Rubio himself had served as rector of the parish before moving to Valencia.[9]

Abdón Exea, at 64 the oldest person ever to begin his service on the tribunal, came from Albalat de la Ribera on the estates of the duke of Gandía, where he had served as rector of the parish and two of his brothers were familiares, which was far from easy given ducal resentment of any outside authority.[10] Normally, even this family tradition of service in a difficult and dangerous area (which was the scene of a violent feud between the Timors and the Talons during the early sixteenth century) would not have been enough to give Exea a post on the tribunal, given his complete lack of proper educational qualifications.[11] In their commentary on his genealogy, Inquisitors Ambrosio Roche and Herrera y Guzmán noted that "he has not followed any course of instruction at the university nor is it known that he has improved himself by study."[12] Since posts on inquisitorial courts, like other high posts in the letrado hierarchy, were reserved exclusively for university graduates holding advanced degrees, Exea's success in gaining a judgeship can only be attributed to his long service in the church, which eventually brought him an influential canonry in Valencia's cathedral, and his devotion to the tribunal, which he served as comisario and calificador.

In the Aragonese town of Teruel, where the Inquisition had been established despite stubborn resistance, the tribunal needed important political allies to overcome strong local resentment about Aragonese subjects being placed under the control of a Valencian-based institution.[13] Given the tribunal's shaky authority in Teruel, the only possible strategy was to establish close and durable relations with a few of the town's most influential families. A deep and lasting involvement with the Inquisition on many levels would serve to flatter these families' sense of importance and permit them to join the national bureaucratic elite, while at the same time a place on the tribunal itself would underscore their political support for its continued presence in Teruel.

One of the most distinguished and influential families in Teruel during the period of the later Hapsburgs and Bourbons was the Campillo, the family of Doctor Francisco Antonio Campillo y Tarín, who served as inquisitor of Valencia between 1762 and 1780. This family of hidalgos was so wealthy and influential that throughout the seventeenth century, successive Campillos had housed the Hapsburg rulers when they passed through Teruel, while Francisco Antonio's father, Juan Antonio Campillo, not only housed Philip V but was chosen to swear allegiance to him in the city's name. The family's direct involvement with the Inquisition really began with Francisco Antonio's brother, Dr. Joaquín Ramón Campillo y Tarín, who served as secretary of the Santiago tribunal beginning in 1753.[14] Francisco Antonio himself made his early career in the church as a canon of his native Teruel and as an official of the see of Albarracín and Teruel. In the latter post, he served with distinction and impressed his bishop, Francisco Pérez de Prado y Cuesta, so much so that when Prado y Cuesta was appointed inquisitor-general in 1746 he entrusted Francisco Antonio with the care of the bishopric. Scion of a distinguished and politically influential Teruel family and faithful servant of the inquisitor-general, Francisco Antonio could not fail to be an attractive candidate to serve on the Valencia tribunal, to which he was duly appointed after serving as fiscal in Murcia.[15]

One interesting result of my analysis of the social origins of Valencia's inquisitors is the discovery of several judges who were only one or two generations removed from the peasantry. Although the numbers involved are small, totaling no more than eight inquisitors, it does appear to indicate that the several inquisitorial tribunals scattered around the country may well have provided ambitious commoners with an important path to upward social mobility. If the Inquisition was genuinely popular among the vast majority of Spaniards, it was not only because of its "decisively Old Christian ideology" but because it was perceived as an institution that welcomed persons of humble social origins into the ranks and, in some instances, onto the tribunal itself.[16]

Although the details offered by the genealogies concerning the humblest ancestors of prospective inquisitorial officials are typically scanty, they do provide some interesting insights into the forms taken by social mobility during the Spanish Old Regime. In the case of Miguel Fernandez, a labrador in the province of Toledo who was Inquisitor Pedro Cifontes de Loarte's maternal grandfather, upward social mobility really began with a favorable marriage. Miguel Fernandez, who lived in the señorial village of Pinto, was able to marry Catalina de Cifontes, the daughter, of his lord's steward, Rodrigo de Cifontes. Catalina de Cifontes, their daughter, was given her mother's name in preference to her father's because of her maternal grandfather's superior social status, and the inquisitor himself was known by that name.[17]

Of course, it is to be presumed that our small group of inquisitors of peasant origin came from only the wealthiest segment of Spain's large and diverse peasant community. Certainly, the great mass of impoverished landless laborers, who numbered almost as many as all peasant proprietors and tenant farmers combined in the census of 1797, were totally excluded from even the possibility of social mobility.[18] Excluded also were those peasant landowners or tenants who farmed miserable plots of land too small to give them much more than a bare subsistence. Such individuals were always at grave risk of being forced to abandon their holding to become mere day laborers.[19] On the other side of the picture are families like the Bertrán, who came from the village of Sierra Engarcerán and had connections throughout the grain-producing region that stretched from Morella to the sea. These Spanish versions of the "coq du village" would seek to profit by withholding their grain from market when prices were low, obtain tax exemptions for their land, and oppress their neighbors by obtaining a stranglehold over village government.[20] The Bertrán were typical representatives of this sector of the peasantry. Described by a witness in Sierra Engarcerán as "the most highly respected of all the property owners of this village," they had frequently acted as bailiffs and chief constables, while one member of the family had been parish priest for more than seventy years. Pedro Juan Bertrán's son, Felipe

Bertrán, after a long and distinguished career in the church that culminated when he was made bishop of Salamanca, was appointed inquisitor-general in December 1774 after the resignation of Manuel Quintano Bonifaz. During his period in office, which lasted until 1783, Felipe used his influence to place four of his nephews in important posts in the Inquisition, including Dr. Mathias Bertrán, who entered as an official in 1780 and served as inquisitor of Valencia from 1784 to 1809.[21]

Whatever else we may conclude about the social composition of Valencia's inquisitors, and in spite of a significant minority who came from peasant backgrounds, there is no doubt that the vast majority (66%) were drawn from the aristocracy. Throughout the early modern period, the Spanish aristocracy was the most numerous in Western Europe, comprising a full 10.2 percent of the Castilian population in the incomplete census of 1591, while in other societies of the period, no more than 2 to 3 percent could claim this status.[22] Apart from the fact that the population of entire provinces (Vizcaya and Guipúzcoa) in the north claimed noble rank, the enormous size of the Spanish nobility resulted from the large number of hidalgos, that untitled lesser nobility for which there is no real equivalent in other parts of Western Europe.

During the fifteenth century, hidalgo status belonged above all to those with three generations of noble ancestors in the paternal line enjoying exemption from ordinary taxes (pechos) and leading a certain life-style that excluded any "base occupations." The purity of blood statutes, which had become all-pervasive by the mid-sixteenth century, appeared to indicate a closing off of opportunities to enter the ranks of the hidalgos by erecting a formal barrier in the shape of a heritable quality without which it would be impossible to claim noble rank.[23] This new barrier was made explicit by the existence of genealogical investigations governing entrance to colleges, cathedral chapters, and other honorable corporations. At the same time, the growth and increasing prestige of the royal courts made it acceptable for them to resolve doubtful claims to noble status by hearing the so-called pleitos de hidalguía, which would usually begin when a village or town included on its tax rolls an individual claiming exemption from ordinary taxes.[24] The result of these two developments was, paradoxically, to open hidalgo status more and more to those with money because only they could pay the costs of the genealogical investigations that were indispensible if one wished to enter honorable corporations normally associated with a noble rank or "prove" nobility in the salas de hijosdalgos. The length (frequently up to 20 years) and excessive costs of such litigation had the effect of making it easier for the wealthy plebeian to prove a dishonest claim than for a poor but genuine hidalgo to validate a legitimate one. By the sixteenth century, a noble could no longer be made, and nobility was considered a product of certain heritable qualities (lineage and race) whose validity was paradoxically wholly dependent on the reputation that one's family possessed in the community. By the end of the sixteenth century, then, the Spanish nobility had become a porous structure, open, in spite of its impressive and seemingly exhaustive genealogical investigations, to those capable of forging royal documents, bribing witnesses, or influencing local officials to act in their favor.

At the apex of the Spanish aristocracy stood the tiny elite of titled nobility (titulos), each of whom possessed an important seigneurial estate as well as a fully accepted claim to hidalgo status.[25] Such titles were frequently granted for extraordinary services such as raising troops at one's own expense, membership on the Council of Castile or other important councils, or simple monetary payment.[26] Within the group of titulos, there was a still smaller group of grandees composed of the leading noble families in Spain, many of whom were related to the royal house.[27] While the number of titulos remained small relative to the Spanish aristocracy as a whole throughout the early modern period, the absolute numbers tended to increase especially after the outright sale of titulos became accepted in the seventeenth century. By 1627, the 120 titulos of 1600 had increased to 168, of which 41 were grandees. By 1787, the number of titulos had grown to 654, including 119 grandees.[28]

Of the three Valencian inquisitors who came from titled families, one, Dr. Pablo Acedo Rico, was the son of Juan Acedo Rico whose title of count of La Cañada was one of the many conceded by the Bourbons in the late eighteenth century.[29] The other two, licentiates Philippe de Haro and Pedro Pacheco Portocarrero, were the illegitimate sons of two brothers, Luis Mendez de Haro, a member of the Cámara de Castilla, and Juan Pacheco de Córdoba, a judge on the Chancillería of Valladolid. Haro and Córdoba were younger sons of a titled father, Luis Mendez de Haro, marquis of El Carpio.

With the prestige of the family at stake, the two illegitimate children could be neither disowned nor abandoned. Philippe de Haro was brought up in part by his aunt, Beatriz de Haro, on her estate of Lúque in the province of Córdoba and in part by his uncle, Diego López de Haro, marquis of El Carpio, and then sent to the University of Salamanca where he became a colegial of the Colegio Mayor of Cuenca.[30] Pacheco Puertocarrero was raised by his two uncles and then attended the University of Salamanca where his father had gone before him and became fiscal on the tribunal of Granada before coming to Valencia as inquisitor in 1613.[31]

Some 25 out of the 40 judges for whom information about the social status of parents or relatives is available can be classed as members of the nobility, but fully 22 of these pertained to the middle and lesser nobility of caballeros and hidalgos. Given the lack of clear legal definitions and the confusion in the popular mind about who exactly should be considered noble and what that status should entail, it is difficult to define exactly the differences between these two classes of nobles. In general, however, the caballeros may be distinguished by their greater wealth but more particularly by the greater prestige attached to the functions they performed. In certain regions, for example, caballeros had a virtual stranglehold on city councils from which they could gain easy access to the Councils of State and other agencies of government.[32] To distinguish themselves from the mass of hidalgos still further, these men sought to become members of one of the three great military orders. Receiving a hábito meant nothing in material terms and few could hope to obtain one of the lucrative commanderies, but membership in a military order meant that the caballero had been able to meet rigorous entrance requirements that were a guarantee of both impeccable aristocratic origins and purity of blood.[33] So popular had the military orders become among Spain's middle-ranking nobility that in 1625, there were 1,459 knights distributed among the three orders, with Santiago alone numbering 957—up sharply from 221 in 1572.[34]

A firm grasp on positions in local government and hábitos and the ability to establish themselves on the highest councils of state were all characteristics of the caballero families among this group of inquisitors. Iñigo Ortíz de la Peña, who was inquisitor from 1744 to 1763, came from a family that was closely associated with the elite "twelve families" of Soria, a special group of knightly lineages who, with their allies, dominated local government and monopolized positions on the city council. Ortíz de la Peña's father was a regidor, and both his father and grandfather were Cortes deputies representing the nobility of the town. His brother, Joseph Ortíz, was perpetual city councillor and acting Cortes representative, while another brother, Francisco Ortíz de la Peña, was dean of Soria's cathedral.[35]

Dr. Alonso de Hoces was another inquisitor who came from a family that was firmly established within one of Castile's local oligarchies. Alonso's father and maternal grandfather were both veinticuatros (city councilors) of Córdoba. Local distinction was not enough to satisfy the members of this ambitious family. Both Alonso's father and his brother became members of military orders, as did two cousins, one of whom, Lope de Hoces y Córdoba, count of Hornachuelos, served on the Council of the Indies between 1637 and 1639.[36]

In sharp contrast to the group of caballero families, the hidalgo families could not boast of membership in the military orders, and when they served the crown, it was in lesser capacities. Dr. Tomás de Soto Calderón came of an old-line hidalgo family originally from the north which became established in Seville in the lifetime of Soto Calderón's grandparents. His father, licentiate Alonso de Soto Calderón, was an advocate and was appointed one of the three criminal justices in Seville's new Audiencia.[37] Antonio de Canseco de Quiñones also came of a family with a tradition of practicing law. Canseco de Quiñones's maternal grandfather, Juan Ochoa de Urquixu, was one of that large number of Basques who migrated to Old Castile in search of better economic opportunities during the sixteenth century. A successful attorney in his adopted city of Valladolid, he eventually became one of the thirty licensed to practice before the chancillería. His father, Gabriel de Canseco, practiced before the Inquisition and gained the rank of hidalgo.[38]

This general pattern of failure to join the prestigious military orders or obtain positions on the leading institutions of state (chancillerías, councils) holds true even for the Campillo y Tarín, easily the most distinguished hidalgo family in our sample. Even though Dr. Francisco Antonio Campillo y Tarín's father, grandfather, and great grandfather had greeted visiting monarchs in the name of the city of Teruel and dominated city offices, they were still very much a family of local and regional, not national, importance, and there is no evidence that the family had either hábitos or high state offices to its credit.[39]

Interestingly, the social group that was substantially underrepresented among Valencia's inquisitors was the middle strata, or what might be termed the bourgeoisie.[40] Of all the inquisitors in my sample, there were only three whose parents were professionals without hidalgo status. One of these, Diego García de Trasmiera, came from the elite of this group since his father was a royal financial officer.[41] The other two inquisitors of bourgeois origin were drawn from the ranks of lawyers and notaries. Merchants and shopkeepers, generally agreed to be the lowest-ranking members of the bourgeoisie, were entirely absent from the tribunal. It may be assumed that the exclusion of merchants from the prestigious judgeships reflected in part the bias of Spanish society against trade, which was reflected in the preferences of a social and political elite whose wealth and social standing was based on landholding and income from mortgages and annuities.[42] Of course, this social preference was greatly accentuated by the identification of commerce with converted Jews and New Christians. In a society in which honor and "purity of blood" were becoming inextricably linked, the activities of merchants and traders could not fail to be suspect, especially when the discovery of Judaizers among the Portuguese merchants and financiers who flocked to Spain after 1600 reinforced old prejudices.[43]

Among Valencia's inquisitors, the tendency toward aristocratization that was characteristic of the Spanish bureaucracy as a whole becomes evident from a comparison of the social origins of parents and grandparents. As far as peasant origin is concerned, slightly less than one-quarter of grandparents but only 7.6 percent of the parents of inquisitors came from this social stratum. Apart from a sharp decline in the number of peasants, the higher social status of parents as opposed to grandparents can be measured by the larger percentage of parents who counted themselves among the nobility. Altogether, some 62.5 percent of the parents of Valencia's inquisitors were either titulos or enjoyed lesser noble status, as compared to only 51 percent of grandparents.

Throughout the entire Spanish Old Regime, even during the

eighteenth century when the traditional educational system was coming under attack from reformers, university training, especially from the law faculties, remained the essential qualification for entry and preferment in the letrado hierarchy. The Inquisition was no exception to this rule, even though many of the early inquisitors were actually theologians and not lawyers. The Spanish Inquisition, in common with other criminal courts of the period, used Roman canon process, whose complicated procedures and detailed trial records required a professional judiciary.[44] Thus, by 1545, Spanish practice had altered definitively, and Diego de Simancas could remark that Spanish experience indicated that it was "more useful to select jurists rather than theologians as inquisitors."[45]

In common with other aspiring letrados, future inquisitors tended to flock to Salamanca, Valladolid, or Alcalá de Henares, Castile's most prestigious universities, because of the greater employment opportunities enjoyed by graduates.[46] Information drawn from the responses to a 1666 request from the newly installed inquisitor-general, Father Juan Nithard, for information concerning the careers of inquisitors and officials then serving on the provincial tribunals indicates that of the 38 inquisitors whose university affiliation is indicated, 33, or 86.8 percent, had attended one of the three major universities.[47] On the Inquisition of Valencia, the percentages are similar if somewhat lower, with 72 percent of the judges having attended one of the three institutions. Among the three elite institutions, moreover, there was a clear preference for the University of Salamanca, with 26 out of the 38 inquisitors of 1666 attending and 16 out of the 33 Valencian inquisitors whose university affiliation is known. The reasons for this preference are not hard to find as Salamanca had long been both the most prestigious and the largest of the universities in the Iberian peninsula. It enrolled nearly twice as many students as the University of Alcalá, its closest competitor in the sixteenth century.[48] Prestige and numbers meant that there were more Salamanca graduates occupying coveted university lectureships, which in turn led to important appointments in the letrado hierarchy.[49] Preference for the "imperial" universities did not, however, preclude attendance at lesser ones. The increasing costs of taking advanced degrees at the three major institutions made it common practice to transfer to one of the newer, less prestigious institutions.[50] A bachelor from Salamanca,

Alcalá, or Valladolid could take an advanced degree at Irache, Sigüenza, Oñate, or Ávila far more quickly and at much less expense than he could at his home institution. Judging by the results of the 1666 survey, taking an advanced degree from a lesser institution was quite common in the seventeenth century and did not present any obstacle to advancement in the letrado hierarchy. Of the 33 inquisitors who attended one of the three major institutions, 15 took their advanced degrees at lesser ones.[51]

Within Castile's great universities were a number of semiautonomous colleges mostly founded under ecclesiastical auspices during the fifteenth and sixteenth centuries. Outstanding among these colleges were the six Colegios Mayores, which were distinguished from the others by their requirement of a baccalaureate for admission and the right to select their own members after rigorous examination of their academic ability and purity of blood.[52]

Among Valencia's inquisitors, 54.5 percent of those whose university affiliation is known attended one of the six Colegios Mayores, while among the inquisitors of 1666, 42 percent had a Colegio Mayor affiliation, although some did not actually take advanced degrees while in residence at their colleges. In light of the generally declining prestige of the Inquisition after the end of the sixteenth century, it is significant that more of Valencia's inquisitors attended the relatively less prestigious Colegio Mayor of Santa Cruz at the University of Valladolid than any other college, while San Bartolomé, the oldest and most distinguished, enrolled the fewest.[53]

Early in the history of the letrado hierarchy, during the reign of Ferdinand and Isabella, students holding the bachelor's degree were frequently appointed to important positions on the courts or the councils of the realm. During succeeding centuries, however, the advanced degree became the norm, and those holding the licentiate and doctorate enjoyed a virtual monopoly of office.[54] As time went on, even the licentiate suffered a loss of prestige, and only the doctorate remained valuable, especially for ambitious students who were unable to enter the Colegios Mayores (manteistas) but who still wished to compete with colegiales for official posts. Of the 65 inquisitors on the Valencia tribunal whose degree status appears before their name in their genealogy, 36 were licentiates and 27 had doctorates, but of that group fully 22 were taken by individuals joining the tribunal after 1600. This marked preference for the doctorate by Valencia's inquisitors appears to confirm the increased importance of that degree in the later history of the letrado hierarchy.

Up to the end of their graduate training, there seems to be little to distinguish those whose letrado careers were to be confined mainly to the Inquisition and those who were to enter the broader field of the secular bureaucracy. At this point, however, the career patterns and experiences of future inquisitors diverge from those of other letrados, and that divergence tended to make inquisitors less attractive as candidates for positions on the councils or in other areas of the secular bureaucracy.

Law graduates whose careers would take them to one of the top-ranked secular councils like the Council of the Indies or the Council of Castile tended to prefer their first job to be on one of the two chancillerías of Valladolid or Granada or on the prestigious Audiencias of Seville or Galicia. Failing a judgeship on one of these tribunals, they would accept a somewhat lesser post like fiscal (prosecuting attorney) or alcalde de los hijosdalgo which would almost inevitably lead to a judgeship after a few years.[55] A rapid glance at the actual functions of the chancillerías reveals that service on them would give a letrado excellent training for a career on the Council of Castile. Like the Council of Castile or the Council of the Indies, the chancillería acted as an appeals court in cases involving town councils, nobles, or royal officials as well as in tax disputes and claims to hidalgo status.[56] Furthermore, a young letrado serving as prosecuting attorney or judge on the chancillería of Valladolid would have the advantage of experience in ordinary criminal cases as that body was court of first instance for certain crimes committed within the city of Valladolid and five leagues around it. This experience was useful training for service in the chamber of the alcaldes de casa y corte of the Council of Castile, which had jurisdiction over criminal cases in Madrid and its immediate surroundings.[57] Service as an alcalde generally provided an excellent stepping-stone to membership on the Council of Castile.

Other letrados would seek to avoid service as alcaldes (always dangerous and unpopular) and go directly to another council. The Councils of Finance, Indies, and Military Orders provided the Council of Castile with the bulk of its recruits, while the Councils of the Inquisition, Aragon, and the Crusade were the least important.[58] A letrado with service on the Council of the Indies, for example, was six times as likely as a member of the Suprema to be selected for a post on the Council of Castile, while a member of the Council of Finance was more than seven times as likely.

To explain the seeming inability of the Inquisition to place its judges on the empire's most important council, it will be necessary to consider certain peculiarities in the careers of inquisitors after they left the university. In the first place, all of Valencia's inquisitors took at least minor clerical orders just before or soon after graduation. Unlike most other law graduates who sought posts on the chancillerías or Audiencias, provincial inquisitors tended to begin their service with a post in the ecclesiastical bureaucracy, usually as chief judge of an episcopal court or as governor of a diocese.[59] Of the 58 judges of the Valencia tribunal for whom information about previous positions is available 36, or 65 percent, had held a post in the ecclesiastical court system or in episcopal administration before beginning their service with the Inquisition.

The jurisdiction of the ecclesiastical court system, even though somewhat reduced in scope by the expanding royal courts and by the coming of the Inquisition, still encompassed many offenses against public morality (like concubinage or sodomy) and religion (like the failure to go to confession or attend mass).[60] These offenses were closer in nature and origin to the sorts of things the Inquisition dealt with, some of which (like sodomy) had formerly been under the exclusive control of the ecclesiastical courts. An even more direct connection between service as an ecclesiastical court judge and service on an inquisitorial tribunal was formed in certain cases when the provisor, or chief judge, of the episcopal court was called to sit in judgment with the inquisitors of that district when they were dealing with cases involving individuals residing within their diocese. In certain instances, regular service with a provincial tribunal led directly to an appointment with the Inquisition. A case in point is that of licentiate Luis Benito de Oliver, inquisitor of Seville in 1666, who, while serving as provisor in the bishoprics of Córdoba and Cuenca, sat regularly with the judges of the inquisitorial tribunals as inquisitor ordinario and was then appointed to the post of fiscal on the Valencia tribunal. After four years of service in that post, Oliver was then promoted to the tribunal of Seville as inquisitor in 1661.[61]

In a society in which the prince considered himself "the most competent defender of the church," relations between church and state could not fail to be very close.[62] Bishops and many other lesser clergy were chosen for their posts by the Cámara de Castilla (which controlled all positions in the royal bureaucracy except those on the Inquisition), and bishops were expected to act as loyal agents of the monarchy in their diocese when they were not working directly for the crown in some administrative capacity.[63]

However, there were serious problems in church-state relations under both Hapsburgs and Bourbons and none thornier than defining the extent and limits of ecclesiastical jurisdiction over both laymen and priests. Spokesmen for the church like the Franciscan Miguel Agia demanded ample powers for the ecclesiastical courts to judge offenses against Christian morality, even including such things as usury, dancing on holy days, and excessive display of luxurious clothing and other items. Defenders of civil jurisdiction replied by denying the ecclesiastical courts any such powers, and in the Nueva Recopilación, such courts were specifically prohibited from imprisoning laymen or sequestering their property on their own authority. In spite of this prohibition, the church courts continued to do exactly that, and the boundary between the jurisdiction of the royal and ecclesiastical court systems was never firmly delineated.[64]

In the conflict between the royal and ecclesiastical courts, the institutional and political history of the Inquisition placed it in an ambiguous position. Founded by the Catholic sovereigns but instituted by a papal bull and enjoying a considerable measure of autonomy in financial and personnel matters, the Inquisition could and did act as an instrument of regalism but could also abandon that position and become the most fervent defender of ecclesiastical jurisdiction.[65] The Inquisition's use of regalism and ecclesiastical immunity as alternative flags of convenience could not fail to stir the suspicion and enmity of the members of the secular bureaucracy whose interests wedded them to a strong regalist position. This suspicion was greatly increased by the jurisdictional conflicts that pitted the inquisitorial tribunals against the royal court system. Given this political background, it is hardly surprising that a letrado with several decades of experience as an ecclesiastical court judge and provincial inquisitor would be too closely linked with a different and rival judicial system to pass easily onto one of the secular councils of state.[66]

Quite apart from the suspicion with which they were regarded by the members of the secular bureaucracy, inquisitors seeking positions on the councils of state would also be at a disadvantage because their experience on the provincial tribunals or the Suprema would have given them far less training in the kind of cases that came before institutions like the Council of Castile than if they had served as a judge on one of the chancillerías or Audiencias. While it is true that provincial inquisitors would have some experience with civil and criminal cases involving officials and familiares, this experience was necessarily limited by the small number of persons included within the tribunals' ordinary jurisdiction and by the fact that at least some of these cases would be lost to the Audiencias after the inevitable competencia suit was decided. In financial matters, the provincial inquisitor's experience was limited by the fact that disputes involving confiscated property were decided by a collateral court headed by a special judge. By the mid-seventeenth century, this position had been suppressed in most places and responsibility for those cases vested in one of the inquisitors, but confiscations—and therefore the disputes arising from them—had fallen off dramatically from their sixteenth-century levels. Service with the Holy Office or other ecclesiastical courts would provide little, if any, experience in the disputes over land, water rights, or pasturage that were the stock-in-trade of the Audiencias and chancillerías and were frequently appealed to the highest councillor level.

Thus, confronted with the suspicious attitude of many members of the secular bureaucracy and partially disqualified for service on the councils of state by the narrow range of judicial experience afforded by their service on the ecclesiastical courts and provincial tribunals, letrados who had taken service with the Inquisition made their careers largely or entirely within that institution. Of the 58 inquisitors of Valencia for whom information about previous positions is given in their genealogies, 27 had served as prosecuting attorneys for the Inquisition (14 on the Valencia tribunal itself) and 15 had served on other provincial tribunals. After leaving Valencia, options were similarly rather limited, with 20 of the 37 whose future position is known moving on to another provincial tribunal and 10 ending their careers on the Suprema, either going there directly from the Valencia tribunal or serving on other provincial tribunals before their appointment. The Valencia tribunal can also boast two inquisitors-general, Jerónimo Manrique de Lara (1595) and Juan de Cúñiga (1602). When inquisitors left the Inquisition, it was frequently for one of Spain's minor bishoprics for which their previous experience with episcopal administration and undoubted orthodoxy were excellent qualifications.[67]

Even though their career options were rather limited, provincial inquisitors did have ample opportunities to add to their already considerable salaries and living stipends by holding valuable ecclesiastical benefices.[68] When canons or other benefice holders were appointed inquisitors, as they frequently were, they simply continued to collect the revenues from their benefice while serving the Inquisition. The traditional requirement of residence was overcome by a series of papal bulls permitting inquisitors who held ecclesiastical benefices to be considered as present and therefore able to enjoy all the income from their preferment.[69] Fully 55.7 percent of our sample of Valencia's inquisitors were canons, and the vast majority of these were nonresident, as only three held their canonries in Valencia's cathedral, while 60 percent of the provincial inquisitors surveyed in 1666 held a benefice of some sort. The financial benefits derived from these posts were very unevenly distributed. Some inquisitors like licentiate Antonio de Ayala Verganza were veritable collectors of prebends. Ayala Verganza held ten benefices in addition to a canonry in Segovia's cathedral, all of which he occupied before accepting a position as fiscal of Valencia in July 1642. These benefices yielded the fabulous sum of 5,000 ducats annually, or 1,875,000 maravedís (mrs.), which was more than the total salary and living allowance of the inquisitor-general himself.[70] But many other provincial inquisitors had no benefices, and others, like licentiate Carlos de Hoyo of the Zaragoza tribunal, who received only 50 ducats from a patrimonial benefice in Laredo, hardly benefited at all.[71]

Recent investigations into the social history of early modern Europe have pointed up the importance of the phenomenon of endogomy for all social groups but most particularly for members of the magistracy and legal profession.[72] Valencia's inquisitors were no exception to this rule and came of families that could boast long traditions of service to the Inquisition in both salaried and unsalaried capacities.

Royal service performed by the members of our inquisitors' immediate or extended families appears to divide them into two significant groups: a larger one whose service was mainly or entirely to the Inquisition and a much smaller one that seemed able to place its members in a variety of important positions. Family service traditions oriented around one particular court or council do not seem to have been unusual in early modern Spain, and even the Council of Castile, whose prestige and authority should have made it immune from being dominated by particular family networks, was significantly affected.

Material drawn from the genealogies of Valencia's inquisitors reveals very strong traditions of service among certain families, in part because the many unpaid positions (calificador, familiar) presented them with ways to become associated with the institution even without service as salaried officials. After many years, a family would eventually be able to secure a place for one of its members on the tribunal itself and thus found a dynasty of inquisitors that could reach all the way to the Suprema itself.

Slightly over 41 percent of the families of Valencia's inquisitors could boast two or more individuals serving the Inquisition in some capacity. In certain cases, like that of licentiate Pedro de Ochagavia who served on the Valencia tribunal between 1649 and 1660, that association was entirely through the familiatura.[73] In other families, like that of licentiate Antonio de Ayala Verganza, where there was a venerable tradition of intellectual friars, the association was primarily through service as calificador or consultor, even though the family could also boast several familiares among the nine members who had served the Inquisition. Ayala Verganza himself had a very successful career with the Inquisition which included service on the Valencia tribunal (1643–1658) interrupted by a year in Madrid where he worked directly for the Suprema, then promotion to Granada, and finally appointment to the Suprema where he served until his death in 1683.[74]

The fact that 21 out of the 29 families with two or more members serving the Inquisition had no other record of royal service may indicate that the prejudice against inquisitors that we have seen reflected in their inability to move into other areas of the bureaucracy was also directed against their families. It is probably also true that once a family entered the royal service through a particular channel, it continued making progress along the same route as its best and most reliable connections tended to lie in that direction. This was particularly the case as employment opportunities for law graduates tightened at the end of the sixteenth century, placing a premium on personal contacts and influence in the struggle for preferment.

Only a handful of these families, set apart from the others by wealth and social distinction, were able to free themselves from these constraints and place family members wherever they chose in the royal bureaucracy. For this group, a judgeship on a provincial tribunal or even on the Suprema itself was just another remunerative public office among many options that the family could exploit and not, as in the case of so many others, the most they could aspire to after generations of effort. One of these families was that of licentiate Salvador Mateo y Villamayor who served on the Valencia tribunal from 1714 to 1720, first as fiscal and then as inquisitor. Salvador was the youngest son of Dr. Lorenzo Mateo y Sans who served as regent (president) of Valencia's Audiencia and then was posted to Madrid as a member of the Council of Aragon. While in Madrid, he married Mariana de Villamayor, whose father, Francisco de Villamayor, had been royal secretary under Philip IV and whose brother, Jerónimo de Villamayor joined the Council of Castile in 1681.[75] Salvador's younger brother, Lorenzo Mateo y Villamayor, was a knight of Santiago and followed his maternal uncle to the Council of Castile in 1706, while his half brother, Domingo Mateo y Silva, served as a judge on the chancillería of Valladolid.[76]

Finally, there remains the question of just how open the Inquisition was to applicants from marginal groups in Spanish society. This is not a question that can be fully or satisfactorily answered from the genealogies of Valencia's inquisitors, since the inquisitors serving on other tribunals would have to be considered as well as the entire range of lesser offices, both paid and unpaid. Nonetheless, our sample of Valencia's inquisitors, combined with other information, may indicate certain trends.

In the entry requirements for the exclusive military orders as well as in the brief vita et moribus that those who wished to take clerical orders had to file with their superiors, the candidate had to demonstrate legitimate birth.[77] Yet, it does not seem that illegitimacy was a serious barrier to entering the ranks of Spain's honorable corporations, especially if the individual came of an aristocratic family. Some of early modern Spain's most distinguished prelates were illegitimate, including Valencian Archbishops Juan de Ribera, son of the duke of Alcalá, and Antonio Folc de Cardona, the illegitimate son of the admiral of Aragón who served as archbishop of Valencia in 1710.[78] As far as the military orders were concerned, it seems to have been relatively easy, especially from the beginning of the seventeenth century, to obtain a papal dispensation that would allow the applicant to enter the order in spite of his illegitimate birth.[79] Among the inquisitors of Valencia, only two were of illegitimate birth, licentiates Philippe de Haro and Pedro Pacheco Portocarrero.

The other marginal element represented among Valencia's inquisitors were the Judeo-Christians. This group comprised the Inquisition's first victims, but their ambition, abilities, and desire to assimilate brought many of them to seek entrance into honorable corporations in spite of the proliferation of the purity of blood statutes designed to exclude them.[80]

The evolution of a typical converso family from exclusion and discrimination to acceptance and integration may be illustrated by examining the background of Dr. Francisco de Alarcón y Covarrubias, who served on the Valencia tribunal from 1636 to 1638. Francisco de Alarcón's maternal grandfather was none other than licentiate Sebastián de Horozco, the brilliant author of the *Cancionero,* which gives such an incisive portrait of Toledan society in the middle of the sixteenth century.[81] During their lifetimes, Sebastián de Horozco and his two sons, Juan de Horozco y Covarrubias and Sebastián de Covarrubias Horozco, suffered many disappointments and much bitterness as a result of Sebastián de Horozco's well-known Judeo-Christian background. In spite of receiving an excellent legal education at the University of Salamanca when opportunities for letrados were increasing rapidly, Sebastián de Horozco remained a humble attorney practicing law in his native city of Toledo while his fear of the outcome of the required genealogical investigation prevented him from even applying to join the elite confraternities of San Miguel and San Pedro.[82] His son, Sebastián de Covarrubias Horozco, who became canon of Cuenca and one of the royal chaplains, failed when he attempted to become an official of the

Cuenca tribunal in spite of his ability, literary attainments, and zeal for the faith. Sebastián's second son, Juan, who ended his days as bishop of one of Spain's poorest bishoprics (Guadix), had trouble very early in his career when he tried and failed to enter the elite Colegio Mayor of Oviedo. After a second defeat, in 1573, when the commission that was carrying on an investigation into his qualifications for an official post on the tribunal of Toledo suspended its investigations in light of the damaging evidence that had come to light regarding his father, Juan made no further attempt to secure a position requiring a purity of blood examination.[83]

The intense frustration that their blighted career prospects must have caused Juan and Sebastián embittered relations between them and their father. But the next generation of the family was destined to succeed where they had failed. Sebastián de Horozco's daughter, Catalina, was fortunate enough to marry into the family of Sebastián's wife, María Valero de Covarrubias, whose first cousin, Diego, had been president of the Council of Castile. Her husband, Diego Hernando de Alarcón, also joined the Council of Castile after serving as a judge on the chancillería of Valladolid for a number of years. Their eldest son, Fernando de Alarcón, was granted a hábito of Santiago after the personal intervention of King Philip III forced the Council of the Military Orders to reverse its original finding against him and undertake another investigation aimed at obscuring the Horozco connection and playing up the "purity" of the Old Christian Valero.[84] The younger son, Dr. Francisco de Alarcón y Covarrubias, succeeded his uncle Sebastián as canon of Cuenca and in 1624 applied successfully to the Cuenca tribunal for an official post, the very same position that his uncle had failed to obtain in 1606. The genealogy that was executed for him on this occasion notes approvingly that he held "mucha renta eclesiástica" and that his father was a member of the Council of Castile but says not a single word about the Judeo-Christian origins of his grandfather, Sebastián de Horozco.[85]

Insofar as the experiences of the Horozco may be taken as typical of many ambitious and capable converso families who attempted to enter the ecclesiastical or bureaucratic hierarchy, the pattern seems to have been rejection, partial acceptance accompanied by much bitterness and frustration, and then full integration, with the entire process taking three or more generations. Integration took time and a reputation for orthodoxy, which in Sebastián de Horozco's case was gained in part by literary sallies and verbal abuse of other Toledo conversos.[86] But, judging from the families of Valencia's inquisitors, successful integration necessarily implied linkage with families of impeccable Old Christian background. The Old Christian side of the family would have little trouble with genealogical investigations, and their service on courts and councils would confer respectability on the entire family, including its Judeo-Christian element.

As the previous discussion has implied, purity of blood was only one element in making a family acceptable for posts of the highest rank. Other elements were confirmed hidalgo status, a certain level of income, political connections, education, and prior royal service traditions. With its Old Christian element leading the way, a family of mixed Old Christian, New Christian blood would eventually acquire enough of those other elements to outweigh the "impurity" of certain of its members and make the entire family acceptable whatever the degree of consanguinity with a New Christian ancestor. This was certainly the case with the Horozco, whose powerful Covarrubias/Alarcón connections provided the keys to respectability for the family as a whole. Another example of a successful "mixed" family is provided by the Venegas de Figueroa. Dr. Luis Venegas de Figueroa served on the Valencia tribunal from 1636 to 1637 even though his earlier application to become an official of the Córdoba tribunal had been rejected because of the reputed converso origins of his grandmother, Teresa de Córdoba. The Venegas de Figueroa family, however, were solidly Old Christian and related to the dukes of Feria, while a strong tradition of family service to the Inquisition had been established by Antonio Venegas, inquisitor of Granada and member of the Suprema. The power and prestige of these Old Christian relatives were enough to overcome the "impurity" of the Córdoba connection and permit Dr. Luis Venegas de Figueroa to have a career on the Inquisition in spite of the negative testimony contained in his genealogical record.[87]

On the whole, the ability of certain mixed blood families to place family members on the Inquisition or the councils serves to underscore the difficulties rather than illustrate the ease with which conversos could attain high rank themselves. Only six out of the seventy Valencian Inquisitors in my sample were reputed to have Jewish ancestors, and in at least two of the six cases, the evidence is inconclusive. Many conversos, unable or unwilling to face the risks, costs, and potential humiliations of the genealogical investigations that were an indispensable part of rising into the letrado hierarchy may well have decided to content themselves with other careers, more lucrative or more satisfying. Some became distinguished and highly paid lawyers without ever seeking judgeships, some pursued careers as wholesale merchants and financiers, and still others formed a solid group of small merchants and retailers. Such a one was Sebastián de Horozco's good-natured contemporary Baltasar de Toledo, who once declared "others have only one "con"; I have two: confectioner and converted Jew."[88]

United by common social and geographic origins and an education that emphasized rote learning and made use of shopworn ideas, the inquisitors of Valencia formed a small part of the letrado elite that set the tone for Spanish society during the Old Regime. Conformity, both religious and cultural, a strong respect for professional and social hierarchy, and an exclusivism based on racial prejudice were the distinguishing characteristics of this group whose inability to adjust to the sweeping changes going on in the rest of Europe was a major factor in the decline of Spain. Ironically, the letrado hierarchy's very success in largely excluding the Judeo-Christians may have worked to their long-term benefit. Barred from easy access to a political and administrative career by the genealogical investigation, the Judeo-Christians were able to profit from rapidly expanding opportunities in law and international commerce while remaining solidly entrenched in the city councils where they could reap substantial profits from revenue collection and local politics. By the early seventeenth century, of course, the Old Christian letrado hierarchy itself was in deep trouble. Inflation, new and burdensome royal taxes, and forced loans had bitten deeply into salaries, and the administrative class with few exceptions shared in the social and political debacle they had done so much to bring about.[89]

In moving from an analysis of the social origins, education, and careers of Valencia's inquisitors to a discussion of their comportment while serving on the tribunal, one is immediately confronted with the problem first raised by Lea. As he observed, inquisitors, especially in the late fifteenth and early sixteenth centuries, had great power of discretion in judicial proceedings and were the objects of veneration and even fear on the part of the public as a whole. At the same time, there were few restraints on their conduct since it was perfectly true that even those convicted of malfeasance were given what amounted to a slap on the wrist in the form of a fine or suspension followed usually by reappointment to another post.[90]

What, therefore, was to prevent a large number of inquisitors from becoming like the corrupt and odious Diego Rodríguez Lucero, inquisitor of Córdoba, whose excesses are so graphically described by Lea? Part of the answer is provided in my analysis of the lives and careers of a large cross-section of the men who sat on the tribunal of Valencia. It reveals them to be very much like their colleagues in other areas of the "letrado hierarchy," with similar social origins and education generating a similar set of values and producing a body of men whose attitudes toward their official responsibilities were certainly no worse than those of other royal functionaries. Moreover, additional constraints on the behavior of inquisitors were imposed by the instructions that regulated their conduct and by societal expectations that were rather higher for inquisitors than they were for other royal officials precisely because of the importance that contemporaries came to attach to the office and the awe in which they held it. As the jurats of Valencia once said in a memorial to the Suprema, preserving public respect for those serving the Holy Office was of the highest importance since it alone was responsible for "defending the honor of Our Lord."[91]

One of the most remarkable characteristics of the reign of Ferdinand and Isabella (1474–1504) was their effort to control the elaborate public administration that they created through a series of detailed ordinances designed to guide the conduct of royal officials and regulate the activities of government agencies.[92] As an integral part of the new public administration, the Inquisition could hardly be expected to be exempt from this wave of regulation. During the reign of Ferdinand and Isabella alone, three major sets of "instructions" were issued (1484, 1488, 1500) which were designed to regulate the functioning of the provincial tribunals and establish a code of conduct for inquisitors and officials. Of course, it will not be contended here that these instructions and the supplementary regulations and cartas acordadas are an infallible guide to the actual comportment of inquisitors, but they did provide a standard known to the inquisitorial class as a whole against which the behavior of colleagues could be measured.

Given the very wide latitude granted to the early inquisitors with regard to the initiation of cases, and the potential for favoritism, corruption, and abuse of power that the office carried with it, the general thrust of both the early instructions and later cartas acordadas was to attempt to create a body of inquisitors whose contacts with the outside world were sharply limited and confined mainly to members of the official class. Inquisitors and officials were prohibited from accepting gifts of any sort (even food and drink) with a value of one real or more and were required to pay for their food and lodging and to avoid staying in the houses of conversos.[93]

The inquisitors were warned especially to be careful to avoid any public perception of them as biased in favor of or against any individual or family on the basis of their social contacts. One of the major arguments in Valencia's petition against retention of Dr. Honorato Figuerola as inquisitor of Valencia was that as the scion of a powerful local family, he might well ignore accusations against members of his family or their allies and unduly magnify the importance of accusations made against their enemies. Furthermore, as the petition went on to point out, the prestige of the Holy Office depended on the respect in which its inquisitors were held, and to maintain that respect it was essential that they should "not be well known by the entire populace."[94] In recognition of the need to hold the inquisitor aloof so as to increase his reputation for impartiality, a carta acordada of May 25, 1610, ordered provincial inquisitors to sharply curtail their private socializing and confine themselves largely to the customary official visits.[95] If the image that the inquisitor was supposed to present to the outside world was as the aloof, incorruptible defender of the faith within the tribunal itself, he was to act to promote harmony between himself and his colleagues as any major disagreements would reduce the effectiveness of the Holy Office.[96]

In practice, of course, the ideals of behavior set forth in the instructions were modified by broader social values and by human nature itself. As an important representative of royal authority in the kingdom, the inquisitor would be expected to carry on an intense and varied social life and maintain a life-style appropriate to his position. The closest associates of Inquisitor Gregorio de Miranda, for example, included the archbishop of Valencia (with whom he dined lavishly and took promenades through the city), Governor Luis Ferrer, several ciutadans and jurats, canons and benefice holders of the cathedral, and the provincials of the principal monastic orders as well as a group of wealthy local merchants.[97] Apparently, puritanical demands for modesty and sobriety in dress and life-style were far more acceptable to the monks and theologians who manned the tribunals in the early years than to the university-trained letrados who replaced them during the sixteenth century.[98]

The day-to-day conduct of inquisitors was also conditioned by the expectations and anxieties of Valencia's political and social elite, especially those whose involvement with the legal profession brought them into frequent contact with the tribunal. In such sensitive matters as religious heresy or apostasy or in genealogical investigations whose outcome might well affect a family for generations, what was desired above all was fairness and impartiality.[99]

Judging by the results of the two visitations that have come down to us almost intact, harmony among inquisitors and between inquisitors and the fiscal was sometimes difficult to achieve. The 1528 visitation revealed deep divisions between the two inquisitors, licentiate Juan de Churucca and Dr. Arnaldo Alvertín, with the former strongly backing his fiscal, Juan González de Munibrega. The conflict between the two inquisitors came down to a fundamental disagreement over the role of the Inquisition itself. The niceties of legal procedure could safely be ignored if the tribunal's chief responsibility was to struggle against the odious crime of heresy. However, many of the university-trained letrados who sat on the tribunals felt compelled to conduct trials in a juridically respectable manner that should offer some protection to the accused. An inquisitor like Dr. Arnaldo Alvertín, who took his judicial responsibilities seriously, could not fail to come into conflict with a colleague like Churucca, who tended to see himself much more as a prosecutor of religious heresy than an impartial judge. Accused of "weakness" and excessive "scruples and doubts" by Churucca and González de Munibrega, Alvertín was forced to look on helplessly when the fiscal remained present while witnesses verified their testimony in clear violation of the instructions of 1498, browbeat defense witnesses, and subjected accused persons who came to confess their errors to a round of questions designed to trap them into making admissions of a still more damaging nature. In one important case, in which Alvertín had made known his scruples as to the degree of guilt, his colleagues waited until he was away from the city before convening the consulta de fé and passing a death sentence on the accused.[100]

Instructions, ordinances, and cartas acordadas, the expectations of local political elites, and the professional aspirations of the letrado class as a whole provided the essential framework that guided the conduct of the men who sat on the Valencia tribunal. But different individuals would interpret the role differently depending on personality, the possibility of advancement, and the particular circumstances in which the inquisitor found himself at the time of his service on the tribunal. What follows is not an attempt to give the entire range of possible behavior but an attempt to show how three men who served on the tribunal at widely differing periods interpreted the role of provincial inquisitor and thereby shaped the history of the tribunal.

Licentiate Bernardino de Aguilera (1562–1566) was virtually a model inquisitor according to observers both inside and outside the tribunal. A highly competent jurist with a reputation for impartiality, he was proud of his position and would frequently work long hours in the Inquisition's service even when seriously ill.[101] On one occasion, when admonished by one of the tribunal's consultores to take better care of himself, he replied that "God would give him health because he was working in his service in order to strengthen our Holy Catholic Faith."[102]

Aguilera's exalted view of the dignity of the institution that he served frequently meant that familiares who came before him on criminal charges could easily find themselves denied benefit of a confessor and forced to appear in a public auto de fé along with those who had committed crimes against the faith.[103] Pride in his office as inquisitor manifested itself in an insistence on being treated with all the honor and deference that he felt was due someone in his position. So touchy was he on matters of etiquette and the proper forms of address that he once angrily tore up a petition from his own colleague, Gregorio de Miranda, because it did not address him as "Señor" or use other customary civilities, thus "failing to recognize the authority and honor that is owed to my office."[104]

This proud and inflexible man entered the Inquisition's service at one of the most difficult moments in its history. Beset by financial problems, the Inquisition now had to confront a ruler who was far less willing to tolerate its excesses than its predecessor had been.[105] Aguilera's refusal to recognize the changed situation and his insistence on maintaining and even extending the tribunal's authority and privileges in the face of it alienated many of its supporters and led to a disastrous confrontation with royal officials.

Quick to grasp any opportunity to promote the tribunal's judicial business and thereby increase its income from fees and fines during a period of financial stringency, Aguilera appreciated the fact that if the fuero could be extended to cover more people, their quarrels and disputes would soon help to fill its coffers. The tribunal had always had a few artisans attached to its service who would provide essential services (i.e., repair of the jail or of buildings owned by the tribunal) in return for enjoying the protection of the fuero. During the first months of Aguilera's tenure, this handful was increased to several dozen, and they were not only permitted to enjoy the fuero but also to place the seal of the Inquisition above their doors. It was this presumption even more than the potential loss of judicial business that angered Micer Roche, a consultor and judge on the Audiencia, who declared during the visitation of 1566 that "it seemed very wrong for persons holding such vulgar and profane offices to put up the cross of the Holy Office."[106] Even Gregorio de Miranda became incensed over this desecration of the Inquisition's symbols and ordered all the offending parties to remove the crosses.[107]

The mid-sixteenth century was a period of great insecurity for the kingdom because of the constant danger to the coasts posed by Moorish pirates. Raids on Christian settlements occurred frequently, while Christian and Moslem attacked each other's shipping and took prisoners who were either enslaved or held for ransom. The relatives of several officials were caught up in this turbulent situation and had been languishing in captivity in Algiers when Aguilera joined the tribunal in 1564. Determined to do something to help them even in the face of an almost empty treasury, Aguilera adopted what must have seemed to him a fair and reasonable expedient. Wealthy Valencians who were convicted of offenses before the Inquisition were given heavy fines even for such minor crimes as blasphemy with the money to be used to ransom captive members of official families. This policy was very much in accordance with the rough sense of justice that characterized so many of Aguilera's judicial decisions, but it did little to improve the deteriorating relations between the Inquisition and Valencia's political elite and much to reinforce the general impression of arrogance and insensitivity that was creating so much political opposition to the tribunal.[108]

Aguilera's worst defeat, however, occurred when he came into conflict with the officials of the royal treasury in the kingdom. The use of inquisitorial export licenses to send large quantities of goods outside of the kingdom without paying the royal export duty had been tolerated by the officials of Valencia's royal treasury unwillingly and only because the protection that the Inquisition enjoyed at court was so great as to outweigh merely financial considerations. But by the early 1560s, the climate had changed, and Philip II had begun a policy of seeking new revenues and tightening the lax financial administration that he had inherited from his father. Out of this new environment came the dispatch of visitors to the Bailía in December 1565 charged with reviewing the operations of that institution and seeing if the customs could be made to produce more revenue for the crown. It did not take the visitors long to decide that the inquisitorial export license was little more than a particularly flagrant form of smuggling, but there seemed little that could be done about the situation until one of the Inquisition's minor officials mistakenly opened a cargo he was escorting on the request of customs officials. The merchandise was found to be contraband being sent to a private individual, and the Bailía used the incident to demand Peatge y Quema for all cargoes being shipped under inquisitorial license.[109] After attempting unsuccessfully to get this regulation removed by negotiation, Aguilera received orders from the Suprema to defend the Inquisition's rights, so he decided to place an interdict on all the patrimonial officials.[110] In the past, ecclesiastical censures of this sort had proven devastating weapons against a variety of opponents ranging from recalcitrant city councils to royal officials, but this time the treasury officials, encouraged by the court's desire to raise revenues, decided to resist. In a dramatic gesture, which was calculated to have the widest possible impact, they closed down the treasury office entirely, suspending both revenue collection and financial litigation. The repercussions of this move were felt almost immediately in Valencia and at court since the crown began losing tax money as soon as it was introduced and the result was heavy pressure on the Suprema to intervene with the Valencia tribunal. Within fifteen days, Aguilera was forced to remove his interdict, thus accepting the most humiliating defeat ever experienced by the Valencia tribunal in its long struggle to establish its power in the kingdom.[111]

Inquisitor Bernardino de Aguilera came to the Valencia tribunal at one of the most critical moments in its history. Caught up in the severe financial crises of the 1550s and 1560s, the tribunal also faced worsening relations with the powerful royal Audiencia, while a less favorable attitude at court meant that the Suprema could not offer the same degree of political support it had in the past. As if this were not enough, Aguilera's harsh sentences and heavy fines had alienated an important sector of Valencia's local patriciate. When the crisis came, he found himself virtually alone, and his enemies on the Bailía were able to devise an effective strategy with the help of several of their colleagues who had also served as consultores to the Holy Office and were therefore in a position to know the real weakness of Aguilera's position. Aguilera lost his struggle with the Bailía, and the defeat strengthened the tribunal's enemies in the kingdom who were already demanding reform at the Cortes of Monzón in 1564. The result of all this pressure was the 1566 visitation and the Concordia of July 10, 1568, many of whose provisions read like a specific condemnation of Aguilera's policies.[112]

Juan Chacón y Narvaez, who began his service on the Valencia tribunal in 1649 as fiscal and then was promoted to inquisitor in 1651, came from a family with strong aristocratic and military traditions. On his father's side, he was related to the Marquis of los Vélez. His mother was descended from Alonso de Salinas, who served as royal treasurer during the reign of Henry II. His father, Captain Juan Chacón y Narvaez, had served as a squadron commander with the Sicilian galleys and in Flanders, for a total of twenty-four years with the Spanish navy. In this, Juan was following in the footsteps of his grandfather of the same name who had served many years as commissary-general of cavalry in the Flanders army.[113] The family military tradition must have weighed strongly with Chacón y Narvaez himself, and after his own brother was killed in Naples, he threw himself into recruiting activities among the peasants of Toledo where he was serving as vicar-general.

Aristocratic and military connections plus a rather aggressive personality proved beneficial to both Chacón y Narvaez and his superiors after he was appointed fiscal to the Valencia tribunal in 1649. Promoted to inquisitor in 1651, Chacón y Narvaez soon discovered that because of the laxity of his colleagues, the archbishop's ordinary had been allowed to completely usurp jurisdiction over bigamy. Within the first two years of his tenure, he was able to reverse this, and the tribunal was once again trying numerous bigamy cases. He also infused new energy into the tribunal's attempts to recover lost revenue and brought several important financial cases to a successful conclusion with considerable benefit to the treasury. His aristocratic name and contacts also proved highly useful to the tribunal during this period of acute crisis in the Spanish empire when the government's desperate search for money and troops led to the adoption of several expedients (like the media anata) that would have been unthinkable earlier and placed all kinds of privileges in jeopardy. Chacón y Narvaez's intervention with the aristocratic viceroys of Valencia, which was aided by the fact that two of his relatives had recently served in that capacity, was instrumental in preserving intact the privileges and exemptions of both officials and familiares. His interest in, and understanding of, military matters plus his legal training and undoubted patriotism brought him to the attention of Inquisitor-General Diego de Arce y Reynoso, who was always looking for ways to make his inquisitors useful to the government. In 1651, the Castilian campaign to recover Catalonia from the French was in full swing, but the military commanders were hampered in their efforts to obtain reinforcements from the Kingdom of Valencia by laws that prohibited her soldiers from serving outside its borders. It was Chacón y Narvaez who, at the request of the inquisitor-general, intervened with the Estates and got them to place Valencian forces, then being assembled for action against the French-held fortress of Tortosa, at the disposition of the marquis of Mortara who commanded one of the two Castilian armies preparing to enter the principality.[114]

Until 1652, then, Chacón y Narvaez's career closely resembled that of another Valencian inquisitor, Alonso de Salazar Frías, who joined the Inquisition after serving as vicar-general in the diocese of Jáen. Like Chacón y Narvaez, Salazar Frías was marked out as a troubleshooter and given special assignments by the inquisitor-general, but Salazar Frías ended his days on the Suprema while Chacón y Narvaez languished in obscurity on the lowly tribunal of Cuenca.[115] Perhaps the best explanation of this paradox is to be found in the description of Chacón y Narvaez's personality written by his colleague, licentiate Antonio de Ayala Verganza, in December 1653. Ayala Verganza, whose views are especially valuable because they come from a man who became a member of the Suprema and therefore reflect mainstream attitudes about the way that an inquisitor should comport himself, gives us a picture of an individual whose need to emulate his military and aristocratic forebears was so great that he behaved in ways that were inappropriate to his role as letrado and jurist. His exaggerated promises and open partisanship of certain individuals with business before the tribunal undertaken out of a misplaced desire to build an aristocratic-style clientele created problems for the very persons that he was attempting to help, while he himself gained a reputation as a person of dubious character—at once "presumptuous, boastful and crafty."[116]

A number of persons who were taken in by Chacón y Narvaez's promises found later that his grand manner masked a lordly indifference to their fate and that their situation was inevitably made worse, not better, by their involvement with him. Boasting loudly and publicly that "he was the absolute owner" of the Inquisition "and that he could do whatever he pleased with the cases," Chacón y Narvaez soon found himself besieged with requests for help by individuals with business before the Holy Office.[117]

It was his involvement with the Liñan, a wealthy and ambitious family of converso origin, that destroyed his reputation and blighted his once-promising career. In 1653, Dr. Juan Bautista de Liñan, a prominent member of the family and an influential local attorney, applied to become a familiar. The genealogical investigation, which had already begun, promised to be long and difficult and the outcome in doubt because of the family's reputation. Juan Bautista's nephew, Gabriel de Liñan, ciutadan of Valencia, was particularly anxious about his uncle's case because failure would inevitably cast suspicion on the rest of the family and adversely affect his own chances to obtain honorable offices.

Searching for some means of helping his uncle, Gabriel remem-

bered that he had frequently observed Chacón y Narvaez hearing
mass in the chapel of the Carmelite monastery of San Felipe and
decided to approach the prior of the monastery. After giving him a
sympathetic hearing, prior Fray Juan de Espirito Santo introduced
him to Chacón y Narvaez, who professed delight at being able to
assist any fellow devotee of the Carmelites and promised to do
whatever was in his power to bring the genealogical investigation to
a successful conclusion. In the ensuing weeks and months, Chacón
y Narvaez obtained large sums of money from Gabriel de Liñan and
his uncle which he claimed to have dispensed to the inquisitors and
officials of the Zaragoza tribunal who were carrying out part of the
investigation. He also demanded and received a loan of 1,000
reales and received numerous presents from the Liñan family, always using the priors of the Carmelite monastery as his chief intermediaries. In response to increasingly insistent questioning from
Gabriel and his uncle about the progress of the case, Chacón y
Narvaez would declare that it was only "a matter of a few days" or "a
few weeks" until it was successfully resolved.[118] At the same time,
he repeatedly approached Inquisitors Ayala y Verganza and Pedro
de Ochagavia on behalf of Juan Bautista in spite of several warnings
against doing so by his colleagues on the tribunal.

Taken in by the rosy promises, both Gabriel and his uncle were
foolish enough to boast about their future success, thereby publiciz-
ing the fact that Diego was presently undergoing a genealogical
investigation for entrance into the corps of familiares and heighten-
ing the sense of expectation. Meanwhile, Chacón y Narvaez was
flattering his own sense of self-importance by telling anyone who
would listen how much he had already done for the family and how
"difficult the case was." Of course, the effect of all this publicity was
to make it virtually impossible for the inquisitors to decide in favor
of the Liñan, since to do so would have exposed the tribunal to the
charge of favoring a family with known converso ancestry. As Antonio de Ayala Verganza declared when he explained why he had
carried out an especially careful search of the tribunal's registers to
be sure that no member of the Liñan family had been penanced for
heresy, "it was necessary to satisfy the public because of all the
malicious rumours about this case."[119] Inevitably, perhaps, Juan
Bautista's attempt to gain a familiatura was a failure, but, as the
saintly Fray Cristóbal de Liñan told his nephew Gabriel, even if he

had succeeded, the family had already been thoroughly discredited by Chacón y Narvaez's loose talk.[120]

The Liñan family had been taught a hard lesson, but Chacón y Narvaez was not to escape unscathed. Complaints about his conduct had already reached the Suprema and an investigation was ordered under the direction of his colleague, Ayala Verganza. After it was over, Ayala Verganza wrote the inquisitor-general to record his opinion that Chacón was "unfit for our ministry" and to recommend that he be suspended from all inquisitorial functions for four years.[121]

We next encounter Chacón y Narvaez serving as inquisitor on the Barcelona tribunal, a difficult assignment because of the hostility of the stiff-necked Catalans to this distinctively Castilian institution and the notoriously bad relations between the tribunal and successive viceroys. Chastened by his experiences in Valencia, and determined to restore his career to its former luster, Chacón y Narvaez sought every opportunity to improve the tribunal's position. Fortunately, the viceroy at the time was the marquis of Mortara, who had good reason to be grateful to him for his assistance in providing Valencian reinforcements for the army with which he had reconquered the principality five years earlier. To gain additional favor with the marquis, Chacón removed one of the chief irritants in the relationship between the viceregal administration and the tribunal. With full support from Inquisitor-General Diego de Arce y Reynoso, Chacón assisted the viceroy in pacifying the valley of Laret where gangs headed by familiars had gone on a rampage of arson, murder, and robbery.

With the marquis's gratitude now assured, Chacón y Narvaez was able to reach a formal agreement with him which fully guaranteed Catalan familiares exemptions from quartering in time of war and safeguarded their fiscal immunities. This agreement had been eagerly sought by the Barcelona tribunal and went a long way toward reviving the flagging prestige of the familiatura in Catalonia. The marquis's good offices also proved useful when Chacón undertook negotiations with the powerful and traditionally hostile Diputación over payment of the censos that had been allowed to fall into arrears during the rebellion. After protracted negotiations, he was able to reach an agreement that gave the tribunal an immediate payment of 28,000 ducats in principal and back interest and restored interest payments on its remaining censos. He was also able to recover considerable sums owed the tribunal from its investments in ecclesiastical rents, which had also not been paid during the same period. Within a very short time, these measures resulted in the complete economic recovery of a tribunal whose officials had once been so destitute that they had been forced to request aid from their colleagues in Zaragoza.

Chacón y Narvaez's agreement with the viceroy and the success of his negotiations with the Diputación earned him two separate letters of commendation from the inquisitor-general plus an invitation to Madrid. At this point, he must have felt that he had completely rehabilitated himself and that an appointment to a more important and prestigious tribunal like Toledo or Seville was in the offing, followed by promotion to the Suprema itself. He must have been grievously disappointed when, instead, he received 400 ducats and a transfer to Cuenca, undoubtedly the poorest and least prestigious of all the tribunals.[122]

Ambitious and energetic, corrupt yet loyal enough to his "clients" to risk his career on their account, Chacón y Narvaez was surely one of the most complex individuals ever to sit on the Valencia tribunal. His conduct in Valencia and its long-term impact on his career provides an instructive lesson on the effectiveness and significance of institutional constraints as a way of regulating an inquisitor's behavior. At the end of the 1653 investigation, with his guilt in the Liñan case established beyond any doubt, Chacón was given what must seem to the outside observer a rather mild punishment. No effort was made to force him to return the presents or bribes that he had taken (with the exception of a token 30 ducats), and after less than four years' suspension, he received an appointment to the Barcelona tribunal. But, in spite of his obvious energy and loyalty and in spite of his brilliant success in Barcelona, Inquisitor-General Diego de Arce y Reynoso and the members of the Suprema obviously felt that he was unfit for a more important appointment. Only fifty-six in 1666, when a report detailing his career was filed with the Suprema, he had already served the Inquisition for almost twenty years and even from the relative obscurity of Cuenca was able to perform extraordinary and valuable services in discovering a network of thieves among prisoners in Cuenca, Toledo, and Valladolid. Even the confessions of the culprits and the recovery of many thousands of ducats for the treasury were insufficient to gain his superiors' complete confidence. His indiscretion and excessive partisanship for his "clients" during his tenure in Valencia had damned him in the eyes of his mainstream colleagues whose watchwords were discretion and impartiality, and Chacón y Narvaez was destined to remain in the relative obscurity of a minor provincial tribunal while his old nemesis, Antonio de Ayala Verganza, rose to become an important and well-respected member of the Suprema.

One characteristic feature of Spanish Imperial administration as it developed during the sixteenth and seventeenth centuries was the effort to insulate royal officials from the rest of society. By issuing regulations preventing individuals from engaging in business transactions, borrowing or lending money, and establishing strong local ties through marriage, it was hoped that the loyalties and aspirations of lesser officials would be focused on pleasing their superiors on the central councils and getting ahead within the bureaucracy. Even though there were many variations, these regulations continued to be applied to career bureaucrats (with greater or lesser degrees of severity and effectiveness) because they were the only way to guarantee both impartiality in office and loyalty to the crown.[123]

These reflections about the nature of the Spanish bureaucratic ideal have a direct bearing on the unique career of licentiate Ambrosio Roche (also known as Roig). Roche's career was remarkable in part because he spent all of it serving on the Valencia tribunal. Since movement from one post to another was customary within the Spanish bureaucracy and was done to discourage functionaries from developing close relationships with local groups, Roche's unusually long term of service in Valencia indicates his role as a transitional figure whose task was to link the tribunal more closely to politically powerful elements within the kingdom.

During Roche's forty-year term, there was an ongoing process of decentralization and devolution of power throughout Hapsburg Spain paralleling a resurgence of "clan and clientage systems," whether under the patronage of the great nobles, as in the crown of Castile, or lesser men, as in the Kingdom of Valencia. To preserve its power and authority, the tribunal had to align itself with this process since it had already alienated a powerful section of the local elite through its earlier persecution of conversos and more recently by supporting Madrid during the agitation over Padre Simón. As a person with close ties to Valencia's regional political elite, Roche was acutely aware of the tribunal's vulnerability and the critical need to mend fences and build up a clientage system of its own.[124]

The first step in restoring the tribunal's popularity in the kingdom, therefore, was for it to take a less visible role in the suppression of the Padre Simón cult. This was a very serious problem because, as the hearings that were held by the tribunal after the arrival of Alonso de Salazar Frías revealed, neither Governor Ferrer nor any of the judges of the Audiencia had done anything to prevent the rioting of March 3 even though they had received prior warning.[125] The tribunal stood alone and Salazar Frías's aggressive attitude toward members of Valencia's political elite who had supported the cult and failed to aid the Holy Office would not help to mend fences. By March 9, 1620, the tribunal had drawn up a total of twenty-one indictments against leading figures in Valencian political life.[126]

After Salazar Frías's departure in summer 1622, however, Roche let these cases drop, and in the end, the tribunal confined itself to punishing a few small fry who took a prominent part in the rioting. With the cult having died out in most of the kingdom by October, Roche was free to turn his attention to rebuilding the Inquisition's regional political base, even going so far as to ask the Suprema to intervene before the Council of Aragon in favor of Pedro Rejaule, an Audiencia judge who had gotten himself into trouble over his involvement in the riots.[127]

Pedro Rejaule and other prominent supporters of the Padre Simón cult could be of considerable help in improving the tribunal's relations with the provincial elite, but Roche was also well aware of the fact that José del Olmo, one of his own notarios del secreto, was the scion of one of the most powerful and successful families that ever served the tribunal in an official capacity. Del Olmo's wealth, connections, and status as a cavaller enabled him to play a key role in defending the Inquisition's jurisdiction over familiares at the Cortes of 1626.[128] To make even greater use of his influence, Roche supported his request for the Suprema's permission to stand for city office.[129] After having been duly elected jurat, del Olmo was able to intervene effectively with his colleagues to prevent the tribunal's income from censals from being reduced by the city.[130]

Such distinguished services earned him the gratitude of Valencia's inquisitors and commendations from the Suprema, but Roche was well aware that mere gratitude would not be enough to maintain the enthusiasm of an ambitious man like del Olmo. Given the failure of official salaries to keep up with inflation and the limited amount of business performed by the notaries, substantial material rewards could only be made available to del Olmo by allowing him virtually to monopolize genealogical work, which was the real means of livelihood of the tribunal's notaries throughout much of the seventeenth century.[131]

Concerned with the need to maintain good relations with the powerful del Olmo family, Roche went out of his way to throw every bit of lucrative business their way. After receiver Melchor de Mendoza died, del Olmo was permitted to act as interim receiver for nine months until a successor was appointed. This proved a valuable prize because the tribunal's accountant (contador) was extremely slow to audit the tribunal's accounts, and the receivers who served in the 1630s had numerous opportunities to profit by their offices by underreporting income, pretending that certain accounts were uncollectable, and retaining money for use in their business affairs.[132]

While performing their duties at the tribunal, both José del Olmo and his son and successor, José Vicente del Olmo, were permitted to wear hats instead of the berets that were normally prescribed for lay officials. This special mark of distinction was greatly resented by the other notarios del secreto since when they dared to wear their hats to the tribunal they were immediately reprimanded by the inquisitors.[133] Nevertheless, such marks of distinction seemed appropriate for someone like José del Olmo because his political importance in the city was steadily increasing. On February 8, 1636, for example, he was selected for the influential post of justicia civil (head of Valencia city's civil court of first instance).[134]

The period of Roche's tenure on the tribunal (both as fiscal and inquisitor) was a time when many members of distinguished and politically important converso families made their way into the ranks of the familiares or obtained posts as consultor or calificador. Of course, this policy of relative openness to converso families as

far as membership in the corps of familiares was concerned was
received by great hostility by many people in the city and kingdom
who had been nurtured on hatred and disdain for the converted
Jews by the very institution that now seemed so willing to admit
them to honorable positions. As a result, the tribunal's newfound
tolerance drew outraged protests, and several memorials were sent
to the Suprema denouncing the fact that Dr. Onofre Bartolomé
Ginart was now being considered for a familiatura after having been
rejected some years earlier. Of course, as one of the memorialists
declared ruefully, things had changed; years ago, Ginart had been a
mere abogado, while now he had risen to become "one of the most
important members of the royal Audiencia."[135]

The enemies of this new policy, which included people who
were in a position to know about the inner workings of the tribunal,
like notario del secreto Jaime Antonio Calafat, found an ally in
Julián de Palomares, who had been appointed notario del secreto in
December 1625. Palomares, who was soon to become a thorn in
Roche's side, made it his business to search out evidence against
converso applicants.[136]

Palomares's attitude to pretendientes with doubtful claims to
"purity of blood" was certainly not endearing him to Inquisitor
Roche, whose whole program was based on attracting the politically powerful even if he had to turn a blind eye to their obvious
converso origins. Roche's annoyance with Palomares and his eagerness to approve certain powerful converso pretendientes was revealed in his letter to the Suprema of January 28, 1631. Here, he
reported that Palomares had filed objections to several recent candidates for familiaturas and other quasi-official posts, including Pedro
Sanz, a prominent Audiencia judge whom Roche was particularly
eager to attract into the tribunal's service. After making a thorough
search of the tribunal's records, Palomares was able to turn up no
fewer than twenty-seven cases of relaxed or reconciled Judaizers
connected to the judge's family, including eight for the name Sanz.
Fiscal Juan de Espina Velasco (who was later accused by Palomares
of being notably unwilling to give credence to evidence that turned
up against families of pretendientes) reviewed the trial records
himself and gave as his opinion that Palomares's charges were without foundation. Since Inquisitor Roche and his colleagues warmly
concurred with this assessment, they had gone ahead to swear in

Judge Sanz as consultor extraordinario, but they were still faced with the dilemma of whether to include Palomares's extensive memoir in his file. Since the fiscal and inquisitors had already given the judge a clean bill of health, "this would be done only to satisfy Julián de Palomares's objections," so Roche proposed instead that a simple statement be inserted in his genealogy to the effect that "none of the cases alleged against Sanz affected the candidate." Significantly, given Roche's stated convictions about the erroneousness of Palomares's memoir, the Suprema was not prepared to go quite that far and instead suggested that it might be better to say that one of the cases turned up by Palomares "appeared to affect the Sanz family."[137]

But there was an even more direct way to align the tribunal with the new tendencies in Valencian society—to make the jurisdictional fuero and even the cárcel de familiares itself into a safe haven for gang members. In the late 1630s, both Audiencia and viceroy complained repeatedly about the tribunal's consistent refusal to prosecute or properly punish familiares accused of gang-related criminal offenses.[138] A glaring example of the way in which the tribunal would seek to protect certain of the mafia-style gang bosses came when Viceroy Fernando de Borja attempted to expel Jerónimo and Ramón Anglesola from the kingdom because of their involvement in gang warfare. Since both brothers were familiares, the tribunal did everything within its power to prevent the viceroy's order from being carried out. It was not until King Philip IV wrote personally to the inquisitor-general that the impasse was broken and the tribunal was compelled to remove its protection from the two familiares.[139]

But inquisitorial protection of gang members did not end with the use of the fuero. During Roche's tenure as senior inquisitor, the cárcel de familiares itself was transformed into a safe haven for gangsters. In 1635–36, Alcalde Domingo González Carrero and his successor, Melchor Çapata, were arrested and incarcerated after Julián de Palomares and others had complained to the Suprema about their scandalous management of the familiares prison. Several imprisoned familiares were being allowed to carry both offensive and defensive weapons and use the prison as a base of criminal activity, leaving to commit contract murders in the dead of night and then returning to the safety of their cells. For their part, the inquisitors were well aware of at least part of this but did nothing to stop it, even though there were many people who saw the familiares enter and leave their cells.[140]

An even more flagrant example of the way gangster familiares could make use of the Inquisition's precincts occurred in 1659. José de Espinosa, a gang leader who had been threatened with death by his powerful enemy, Audiencia judge Arquer, used a room in the inquisitorial palace itself as a hideout, paying rent as if he were at an inn.[141]

When Roche died in September 1647, leaving a small estate to be administered by his colleague, Pedro de Herrera y Guzmán, the tribunal that he had led for so long had emerged from its early seventeenth-century crisis with its privileges largely intact. The familiatura had been enlarged and had recovered some of its former splendor with the addition of many new cavallers and ciutadans even if their racial purity was somewhat doubtful and Inquisition and Audiencia had reached a new modus vivendi with the inclusion of several judges as consultores.[142] But in terms of Roche's own career, the price that he paid for this success was high. In a bureaucratic system whose ideal was a kind of platonic detachment (however much this ideal might have been violated in practice), he had been forced to become too closely identified with the local elite and its aspirations for power and social distinction. It is this fact, probably more than his often-expressed love for the Kingdom of Valencia, that explains his forty years of service on the tribunal.

One notable fact that emerges is the overwhelming preponderance of Castilians and the small, almost insignificant number drawn from the Kingdom of Valencia. Almost exactly the opposite can be said about the corps of officials, who, with the single exception of the fiscal (probably soon to be promoted to inquisitor) were very largely men drawn from the kingdom and district and, as time went on, from Valencia city itself. In my sample of 28 officials extending from 1578 to 1744, 17 of the 22 whose place of birth is known were born in the inquisitorial district and 13 of these in Valencia city. By the mid-seventeenth century, recruitment of officials had become so concentrated in the capital that residents of the district who wished to enter the corps were almost obligated to marry into an urban family and become established in the city before they could apply. Lorenzo del Mor, who came to the city from Rubielos de Mora, a village near Teruel, around the turn of the sixteenth century, married twice in Valencia city and became a familiar in 1619 some twenty years before he applied for and obtained the post of receiver on the tribunal.[143] Lorenzo's move to Valencia city and his highly responsible position on the tribunal raised his family from the relative obscurity of the village notable. His son, Dr. Carlos del Mor, became an Audiencia judge while strengthening his ties with the tribunal by marrying Fausta Tafalla, whose father, Miguel, was a ciutada and familiar and whose uncle, Calixto, was familiar and depositario de pretendientes. Before attaining his judgeship, Carlos del Mor served as abogado de presos, and his son, José Carlos del Mor, succeeded his grandfather Lorenzo as receiver in 1653.[144]

In spite of the obvious differences in the geographic origins of officials and inquisitors, the social composition of each group appears generally similar—with one important exception. Among the parents of our officials, José de Esplugues y Palavicino, knight of Montesa and baron of Frignestany, whose son Joaquín Palavicino became secretary in 1733, was the only titulo.[145] At the other end of the spectrum, only two officials, Juan del Olmo, who was to become the founder of the tribunal's most powerful official family, and Dr. Onofre Salt came from the sturdy labrador stock that also provided Valencia with a few inquisitors. The overwhelming majority of the remaining officials came from exactly the sort of background as the bulk of the inquisitors: the middling nobility of cavallers and ciutadans. Among the parents of these officials, fully 56 percent were from the middling nobility, although, in part, this was the result of a process of social mobility between the generations. At the same time, the bourgeoisie, so conspicuously lacking among the inquisitors, was well represented among officials, with 37 percent of parents coming from professional and mercantile strata. The fundamental similarity in the social origins of inquisitors and officials gave to the staff of the tribunal as a whole a certain uniformity of outlook that was reflected in the treatment of certain types of deviants or certain classes of prisoners, especially the converted Jews.[146]

In spite of a clause in the 1498 instructions that prohibited the relatives of inquisitors or officials from being appointed to serve on the same tribunal, the hereditary transmission of official posts became acceptable at an early date.[147] In 1558, for example, Juan de Oñate, the tribunal's longtime jailor, requested permission to pass

his office on to his son, Miguel Angel de Oñate. The Suprema duly
approved his request, but in this case at least, the transfer was not
accomplished peacefully as Juan made a remarkable recovery from
the illness that had afflicted him and demanded the office back.
When his son refused to relinquish it, his father conceived such a
violent hatred for him that he attempted to besmirch his reputation
by writing letters to the inquisitors which were sharply critical of
his management of the jail.[148]

Another way in which officials' posts were passed on was by
incorporating them into a dowry. As early as 1554, Pedro Sorell,
who was more than 70 years old, wished to retire after forty-five
years of service as notario del secreto. Since his post was not one of
the plazos de asiento with generous (if seldom used) retirement
provisions, he asked the Suprema to make provision for his old age
by permitting his new son-in-law, Miguel Bellot, a local notary, to
assume his office and live in the house that had been assigned to
him on condition that he remain in the house so that his daughter
could take care of him. Sorell's position was accompanied by a
letter of support from Valencia's inquisitors, who were so confident
the Suprema would grant his request that they were already using
Bellot's services.[149]

Over a period of several generations, the families associated with
the tribunal through officeholding tended to divide themselves
roughly into two kinds: a core group who generation after generation occupy the same official posts and a much larger group whose
connections with the tribunal were less constant but nonetheless
formed an important and respected part of the family tradition. The
fortunes of the core group were very closely associated with the
Inquisition, and they were the first line of defense when the prestige of the Holy Office was at stake or its privileges threatened by
viceroy, Audiencia, or city. The second group, which was no less
important to the survival of the tribunal, provided wider, more
diverse support. Even if a family member had held an official post
in the distant past, the basis for a relationship of mutual trust with
the core families had been laid, and in this tense and often violent
little society, a shared interest in and demonstrated loyalty to the
Inquisition could often provide the basis for business, political, or
marital relations.

The del Olmos were probably the best known of all the Valencia tribunal's core families, both because of their extraordinary record of continuous service and the literary attainments of certain family members.[150] In 1750, when Vicente Salvador y del Olmo sent the Suprema a memorial relating his family history, he was the sixth of his line to occupy the post of secretary and his family had served the Holy Office for 172 years.

As related in the memorial, the saga of the del Olmo family began inauspiciously enough with the arrival of Juan del Olmo from Aragón sometime in the mid-1560s. Juan, who came of humble labrador stock on both sides of the family, was born in Montón, a village near Calatayud. Like Miguel Bellot, Juan del Olmo first attached himself to the Inquisition's service through the practice of allowing serving officials to include their posts in the dowries of their marriageable daughters. In 1578, after marrying sixteen-year-old Madalena Oñate, Juan del Olmo became alcalde de las carceles secretas, a post that had been occupied by her father Miguel Angel de Oñate and her grandfather Juan de Oñate y Churruca since 1540. Not content with the lack of status and the poor salary of the post of jailer, Juan del Olmo must have picked up the rudiments of the notary's trade sometime between 1578 and 1583 when he was appointed notario del secreto.[151]

It was under Juan del Olmo's son and successor, José (from 1609), that the family became firmly established among Valencia's ruling elite. José del Olmo became a cavaller, served repeatedly as jurat for the class of the nobility, represented the city in the Cortes, held the lucrative contract to supply meat to the city, and capped his career in municipal government by becoming justicia civil.

José del Olmo was succeeded by his son, José Vicente del Olmo, in 1629, although he actually continued to serve his office until the late 1630s at least. José Vicente, who served until 1669, was once accused of taking prohibited books out of the secreto to read at home and proved to be the intellectual of the family. It is to José Vicente that we owe one of the best and most complete accounts of an auto de fé (Madrid, 1680) as well as his *Nueva descripción del Orbe*, a work dedicated to King Charles II.[152] By this time the family had become so privileged that José Vicente was paid his full salary from the time he retired until his death in 1696.[153] José Vicente was succeeded by his son, Vicente, whose daughter, Isabel María, carried the office of secretary with her when she married

José Salvador y de León whose great-grandfather, Francisco Jerónimo de León, had been a member of the Council of Aragon.
Finally, the author of the memorial, Vicente Salvador y del Olmo,
succeeded José in 1742 after his father died of a severe illness one
year earlier.[154]

The Salvador y de León were a very good example of one of
these "peripheral" families that were sometimes drawn into a more
direct relationship with the tribunal through marriage into a "core"
family. José Salvador y de León, who became secretario del secreto
in 1719 after his marriage to Isabel María del Olmo, came from
"one of the oldest and most aristocratic" families in San Mateo. At
the time of José's marriage, the Salvador y de León family's connection with the Holy Office was no more recent than José's great-
great grandfather, Francisco Jerónimo de León, who served as consultor when he was a judge on the Audiencia. However tenuous
this connection with the Inquisition may appear, the fact that it
involved a revered ancestor (Francisco Jerónimo de León eventually became a member of the Council of Aragon) was sufficient to
inspire José himself to forge a relationship with a "core" inquisitorial family like the del Olmos and seek a position with the tribunal
in an age when choices about careers and marriage partners tended
to be dictated more by family tradition than individual choice.[155]

The fact that many official posts (even down to the porters)
tended to be held by the same family or group of families for many
generations could make life very difficult for the newcomer, especially if he proved willing to challenge the stranglehold that certain
of the better-established officials had over the more lucrative kinds
of business. It was precisely this sort of situation that led to the
murder of Julián de Palomares.

Appointed notario del secreto in 1625 after several years of service on the tribunal of Cuenca, Palomares arrived at a time when
ordinary officials would need either private means or substantial
additional income from tribunal-related business to support themselves, as special royal taxes, pensions paid to widows of officials,
and the Suprema's own financial problems caused it to be very
difficult to make appointments at full salary.[156] Palomares, therefore, like so many others appointed at the time, only had what
amounted to half the salary and maintenance normally accorded to
someone of his rank. This shortfall in salary plus the need to sup-

port an aged mother and three children made it imperative for him to obtain additional income from performing the lucrative genealogical investigations that were fast becoming the chief business of the tribunal.[157]

Genealogical investigations, and the power and influence that the right to perform them could confer, were a jealously guarded preserve of José del Olmo, whose status as a cavaller and growing influence in the city and the Cortes made him a key figure in Inquisitor Ambrosio Roche's plans to defend the tribunal from its political enemies. In the face of strong opposition by José del Olmo, Palomares's efforts to gain extra income from performing genealogical investigations were of little avail. First, Inquisitor Roche and del Olmo tried to discourage him by forcing him to accept 15 rather than 20 reales per day in living expenses while he was in the field.[158] When this failed, del Olmo, who had charge of paying the other notarios for their work, delayed issuing the payment orders for as long as several months in the hope that Palomares's growing financial problems would force him to resign.[159]

Palomares, however, refused to give in to this pressure and decided to appeal to the Suprema. In response to his letters to Madrid describing the situation and pointing out that on the other Aragonese tribunals genealogical investigations were shared out equally among the notaries, the Suprema responded by demanding that the same policy be instituted in Valencia. Inquisitor Roche chose to ignore this order, however, and sent an ambiguous reply intimating that not all of the tribunal's notaries were "suitable" for genealogical investigations and declaring that such an equal distribution of work would be an innovation. To prevent Palomares from learning about this letter, Roche made sure that it was not copied into the official letter book, which was open to inspection by all officials with access to the secreto.[160] In the meantime, the tribunal continued to ignore the Suprema's demands for equity in the distribution of genealogical work.[161]

Infuriated by his worsening economic circumstances and the stubborn opposition of Roche and del Olmo, Palomares decided to send a detailed memorial to the Suprema which would expose all the corrupt practices on the tribunal, from Roche's protection of his nephew, former receiver Melchor de Mendoza whom he accused of embezzlement, to the theft of prohibited books from the tribunal storehouse. Less than one month later, on November 18, 1636, the Suprema formulated a strongly worded memorandum demanding that the tribunal immediately remedy the most serious problems, particularly the failure to take the accounts of the two previous receivers, Melchor de Mendoza and José del Olmo, the bribery and corruption that was becoming such a strong part of the genealogical investigations, and the inequities surrounding the sharing out of genealogical work among the notaries.[162]

Emboldened by his success with the Suprema, Palomares stepped up his campaign against his two worst enemies on the tribunal, del Olmo and fiscal Juan de Espina Velasco. Sometime in early July 1637, he sent yet another memorial to the Suprema complaining specifically about his problems with Espina Velasco and del Olmo while at the same time moving to block efforts by two of the del Olmos's close associates to obtain familiaturas.

Made desperate by the possible loss of their income from genealogical investigations and already in trouble with the Suprema because of Palomares's earlier memorial, Espina Velasco and del Olmo began to threaten Palomares openly. Palomares, who had already been the victim of one murder attempt in March 1629, was extremely worried about this and had begged the Suprema at the end of his 1636 memorial not to allow anyone on the tribunal to find out about it since "they would have him murdered by the men that are called 'jornalaros.' "[163] Given Palomares's penchant for calling attention to himself and the fact that the other notaries had either been cowed or driven away, it was not difficult for Espina Velasco and del Olmo to figure out who was the author of the memorials. On the morning of July 20, 1637, a violent scene took place between the three men in which the fiscal threatened to smash Palomares's skull with a paperweight and Palomares was forced to draw his sword to escape. Little more than five months later, Julián de Palomares was found murdered, the victim of a conspiracy involving the del Olmos (both José and José Vicente del Olmo were arrested by the Audiencia but later released) and a disgruntled pretendiente closely associated with them.[164]

The Suprema's failure to see that its orders regarding the equal distribution of genealogical business were carried out and its even more glaring failure to order a formal visitation after receiving Palomares's damning memorial must give pause to those who would accept uncritically Lea's dictum that "from a comparatively early period the control assumed by the Suprema over the provincial tribunals was absolute."[165] While this was certainly true with regard to the conduct of heresy trials, it may be argued that the heresy trials themselves were of less and less importance to local officials as their number and the potential income from confiscations decreased. In the seventeenth century, what was really important to the tribunal notaries was the genealogical investigation with its lucrative fee schedule, and here the Suprema failed entirely in its campaign to keep the bulk of these investigations in the hands of local comisarios.[166] In this increasingly important area of the tribunal's activity, at least, the Suprema was the victim of the disaggregation and decentralization that was fast becoming the dominant tendency in Spanish public administration.[167] Certainly, from the hearings into the Palomares case that were held just after his death, the overwhelming impression is of a group of officials who felt that Palomares got what he deserved for having violated the "secrecy" of the tribunal. But the secrecy referred to was not the traditional need to maintain confidentiality about heresy proceedings; it was the all-important need to prevent the Suprema from gaining knowledge about the day-to-day workings of the tribunal. After all, Palomares's worst crime, according to Diego Jerónimo Minuarte, the tribunal's new receiver, was that he "informed Madrid about everything that happened on the tribunal."[168]

The murder of Palomares and the release of José and José Vicente de Olmo, who were briefly imprisoned on suspicion of having perpetrated it, indicates the vast change in the relationship between inquisitors and officials from the early years of the Spanish Inquisition to the seventeenth century. The clerkly bureaucracy, or at least certain of its members, had evidently managed to carve out independent positions for themselves and had become an important part of Valencia's local political elite. For the tribunal, which had been losing ground politically since the mid-sixteenth century, men like del Olmo were essential, and neither provincial inquisitors like Roche nor even the Suprema had the will or the desire to punish them for their misdeeds. Paternalism and protection up and down the chain of command had become the fundamental organizing principles of an institution that had entered into a long and inexorable process of decline.

But paternalism and protection did not lead to rampant corruption or massive abuse of power. Whatever the weakness of the formal constraints on their conduct, inquisitors and officials were part of a bureaucracy that imposed significant social and moral constraints on its members. However much he may have tolerated the dishonesty of others, Ambrosio Roche was never accused of peculation himself, and his career and estate bear all the hallmarks of selfless devotion to the institution he revered. Besides, loyalty and conformity and not honesty or even efficiency were the ideals of the self-serving and self-perpetuating bureaucratic elites of the later Hapsburg era. The inquisitors and officials of the Valencia tribunal were typical members of that bureaucracy, and whatever the conflicts they may have had with one another, they shared a belief in the Holy Office as the first and most important line of defense of the social and religious values common to Spain's Old Christian ruling elite.

IV

The Familiares and Unsalaried Officials

The unpaid lay and clerical assistants—familiares, notarios, and comisarios—spread the influence of the tribunals throughout their sprawling districts, but the role they played in the repression of heresy or other offenses has frequently been misunderstood, and their political importance to an institution that was in constant conflict with powerful enemies has been largely overlooked. The origins of the familiares, like many of the other institutions characteristic of the "modern" Inquisition established by Ferdinand and Isabella, lay with the medieval Inquisition, which permitted its inquisitors to surround themselves with armed guards as they traveled from place to place.[1] During the High Middle Ages, when the Inquisition became established in Aragon, the priors and senior members of the Dominican order who acted as inquisitors made use of young professed monks of the Third Dominican order to assist them in a variety of tasks involving the arrest and transportation of prisoners. As a consequence of their close personal association with the inquisitors, these individuals became known as familiares.[2] In the late fifteenth century, when the modern Spanish Inquisition was established, this title continued to be used even though the group was now composed almost entirely of secular individuals, many of whom never came in direct contact with an inquisitor because they lived in remote areas of one of the inquisitorial districts.

The transformation of the familiares from a small group of young

Dominican monks who were occasionally called on to assist their superiors to a much larger group composed primarily of laymen distributed in hundreds of towns and villages throughout the country involved the beginning of important new social and political responsibilities. But exactly what this new role entailed and how it changed during the course of the Old Regime remains a subject of considerable confusion among Inquisition scholars. Even the number of familiares in a given district cannot easily be established because of the notorious unwillingness of provincial inquisitors to furnish the Suprema, or local authorities, with lists of the familiares.[3] Typical of this obstructionism was the Valencia tribunal's reply to the Suprema's demand for a list of familiares to be drawn up by the district's comisarios in 1630. After claiming that appointments were being made strictly in accordance with regulations, the tribunal declared that complying with the Suprema's request would be a time-consuming and difficult task for only seven commissioners to handle and that an accurate assessment of the tribunal's corps of familiares could only be gained if the commissioners were also charged with providing information about the population of all the places in their area, even those that did not contain familiares.[4] As a result, it was not until 1697, some sixty-seven years later, that the Suprema finally received the comprehensive list it had demanded.

The tribunal's extreme reticence about divulging information concerning the number and distribution of familiares combined with the rudimentary nature of its own record keeping during the first eighty years of its existence make it virtually impossible to estimate the numbers of familiares in the district before the visitation of 1567. What is evident from other sources is that contemporary observers, especially the representatives of the royal administration in the kingdom, felt that the total was too high. As early as February 1551, the president of the royal Audiencia sent a stinging letter to court demanding that the number of familiares be reduced sharply. This letter might well have been ignored, but the atmosphere at court had undergone profound changes since Prince Philip had taken charge of the government of the kingdom, and even Inquisitor-General Valdés could no longer ignore the demand for reform.[5] On March 12, 1551, Valdés brusquely ordered the tribunal to reduce the number of familiares to 100 in Valencia city, with corresponding reductions and limitations in the towns and villages of the district. All commissions were revoked, reappointments were to be made with great care, and new commissions were to carry the signature of both inquisitors and were to be limited in duration with the names to be sent to the Suprema.[6]

Several weeks later, the tribunal vigorously protested Valdés's order, claiming that because of the large number of Moriscos in the kingdom and the protection that was being afforded them by powerful nobles, even 500 would be too few for Valencia city "since without numerous familiares the alguacil would be unable to carry out his orders."[7] Under increasing pressure from Philip, who had taken a personal interest in the wave of complaints about familiares, Valdés could not retreat (much as he might have wanted to), and he insisted that the provisions of his March 12 letter be put into effect without delay. This appears to have been ignored; but finally on March 10, 1552, Valdés wrote again, this time offering to compromise on a figure of 200 familiares for Valencia city.[8] Evidently this was acceptable to the tribunal, because it was the figure agreed on in discussions that were held between Inquisitors Miranda and Arteaga and acting Viceroy Juan Lorenzo de Villarrasa in spring 1552. In his letter to the Suprema informing it of these negotiations (which had been undertaken without its knowledge or permission), Inquisitor Arteaga indicated that the problem of excessive or unmanageable numbers was being taken care of by the two inquisitors themselves on their visitations to the district. His colleague, Gregorio de Miranda, had already regulated the number of familiares in the important Játiva/Alcira area, while Arteaga himself proposed to do the same thing on his upcoming visit to Tortosa.[9] Two hundred appears to have been the number actually serving in Valencia city at this period, since in a letter commenting on a criminal assault in which familiar Antonio Pastor was badly wounded, he was termed "one of those names in the list of 200" that presumably had been furnished the viceroy at the conclusion of the earlier negotiations.[10]

In spite of the evident willingness of Inquisitors Arteaga and Miranda to accommodate themselves to the increasing pressure from court, the situation was still far from satisfactory, and the matter was taken out of their hands when the Suprema and the Council of Aragon together ratified the Concordia of May 11, 1554.[11] According to this agreement, the number of familiares in Valencia city was to be reduced from 200 to a maximum of 180;

towns of more than 1,000 households were to have eight; those of 500 to 1,000 were to have six; and in those of 200 to 500, there could be no more than four unless they were located on the border or had ports, in which case, they could have two additional familiares. Villages with less than 200 households could have a maximum of two familiares.

After 1554, concern over the actual number of familiares in the district seems to have given way to a preoccupation with abuse of the special fuero or jurisdiction that the Holy Office exercised over them. While complaining long and loud about abuses of the fuero, the Cortes of 1563–64 said nothing about the question of numbers, and the Concordia of July 10, 1568, merely called on the tribunal to observe the provisions of the 1544 document, in spite of the fact that the visitation of 1567 had revealed substantial violations.[12] From now on, the number of familiares would depend primarily on demand for the office, and that, in turn, was a function of the economy, the family tradition, the prestige of the tribunal, and the benefits, whether pecuniary or otherwise, that membership in the corps could bring.

Inquisitor Soto-Salazar's 1567 visitation of the district revealed a total of 1,638 familiares, of which some 183 corresponded to the city of Valencia itself.[13] As far as Valencia city is concerned, numbers throughout the latter part of the sixteenth century were at or close to those permitted in the Concordia. In 1575, the account book of the familiares confraternity revealed 178 familiares.[14] In 1591, according to a letter sent to the Suprema some twelve years later, the tribunal could boast 173, with 12 additional applicants making a total of 185, or 5 more than that permitted in the Concordia.[15]

In the seventeenth and eighteenth centuries, official lists are scarce. Thus, to draw any meaningful conclusions about the size of Valencia's corps of familiares, we must rely on a combination of official lists that are available and the names that can be gleaned from the genealogical examinations that were required for new entrants. During the seventeenth century, the picture is one of gradual decline in both the city and the district. I was able to find a total of 1,522 names of familiares serving in the district for the entire century plus some 275 for Valencia city. This is considerably lower than the number serving in the year 1567, but it is only an estimate and probably understates the actual totals by a substantial margin.[16] It would also appear that the number serving during the first half of the century was considerably greater than the number serving at the end. The official list of 1602, which covered only the dioceses of Segorbe and Tortosa in the northern part of the district, indicated that out of 66 places registered, all but 14 had lost familiares, but 9 of the 14 had actually increased their number.[17] In fact, some five years earlier, the governor of one of these places, Castellón de la Plana, had written to the Suprema to complain that there were 15 familiares in his town instead of the 8 permitted by the Concordia.[18] In the city of Valencia, the 1619 list that was furnished to the viceroy contained the names of 161 serving familiares, while the list presented in 1623 had 168 names—only 15 fewer than the census of 1567.[19] As late as 1651, there were still 389 familiares, with 111 in Valencia city, but by the end of the century, numbers had declined substantially, and the official list that the tribunal furnished the Suprema in 1697 indicated a total of only 162 familiares for the entire district with 29 serving in Valencia city.[20]

During the first half of the eighteenth century, there appears to have been a sharp recovery in the numbers of serving familiares, reaching a peak in 1748 with 356. By 1806, however, the number of familiares had fallen to only 157.[21] The tribunal could also rely on a network of priests, who served as notaries, and commissioners who were in many ways more useful to the tribunal because they could interview witnesses and informants. Furthermore, of the 386 notaries in the sample, 201 belong to the eighteenth century, indicating an upswing in interest and support for the Holy Office among the clergy precisely at the time when the corps of familiares was static or declining. This trend is also mirrored in the figures for Valencia city—64 out of 86 notaries served in the eighteenth century. The evolution of the commissioners tended to follow that of the familiares. Of the total of 177, 128 served during the seventeenth century and only 49 during the eighteenth.[22]

One principal goal the architects of the Concordias of 1553–54 attempted to achieve was to create a balanced network of familiares that should cover the entire territory of a district and provide the basis for the policy of "christianization" that was to consume so much of the Inquisition's time and attention during the latter half of the sixteenth century.[23] In reality, however, the geographic distribution of Valencia's familiares corresponded much more to the accidents of geography and climate and the distribution of wealth in the kingdom, since the costs of the genealogical investigations that became a requirement for admission to the corps excluded those without a certain amount of discretionary income.

Taking these factors into account, it is hardly surprising that our map (fig. 1) reveals Valencia's familiares thickly clustered along the coastal lowlands and spread thinly in the interior, especially in the areas that had been the heartland of Morisco Valencia (Sierra de Espadán, Vall de Uxó, Muela de Cortes, Cofrentes), regardless of the ideal distribution pattern as set forth in the Concordia. Concentration in the huerta zone even appears to have increased in the eighteenth century (fig. 2). The nine largest huerta towns, Castellón, Villareal, Burriana, Sagunto, Puzol, Catarroja, Rusafa, Gandía, and Valldigna, had 137 familiares in the seventeenth century sample, or 9 percent of the total, and 125 familiares, or 16.5 percent in the eighteenth century.

Apart from a favored location on the coastal plain, the participation of a town or region in the production and sale of a commercial crop could spell prosperity, even as in the case of Morella, which was located deep in the interior. Morella was called the "granary of the kingdom" in the seventeenth century, and even though the falling prices at the end of the century resulted in a crisis for local landowners, it still had enough wealthy labrador families to provide the tribunal with a total of seventeen familiares.[24] Sagunto, a port town located between Valencia and Castellón de la Plana, was another place that benefited from handling a commercial crop grown in its immediate environs. During the early seventeenth century, wine accounted for almost 50 percent of the value of the harvest.[25] The forty-one familiares, four notaries, and two commissioners included in my sample are much more an indication of the prosperity of the town and its district than of any decision by the tribunal to reinforce its position against the dangers posed by the few foreign ships that touched at the port.

As important as wine was in certain areas, it was silk that took pride of place among the kingdom's commercial crops. Silk cultivation was largely concentrated around several towns in the Júcar Valley, and it is in these towns with their rentiers, merchants, and wealthy peasants that we find another heavy concentration of familiares. The six towns that dominated the zone, Játiva, Alcira,

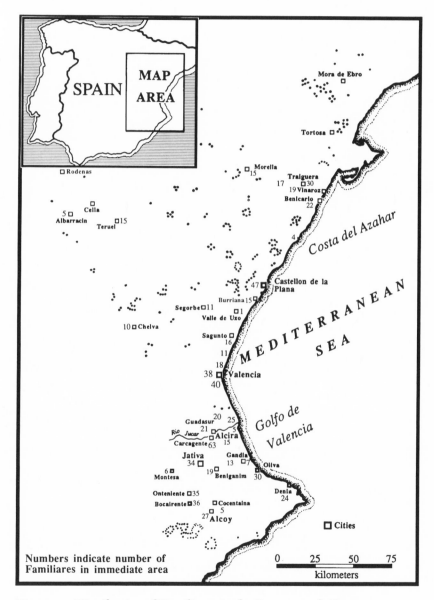

Figure 1. Distribution of Familiares in the Seventeenth Century

Figure 2. Distribution of Familiares in the Eighteenth and Nineteenth
        Centuries

Algemesí, Guadasuar, Carcagente, and Alberique, proved an excellent recruiting ground for the tribunal and account for slightly more than 11 percent of the familiares that I have counted for the seventeenth century. In the eighteenth century, the process of concentration that we have seen above increased the silk towns' share of the corps to well over 14 percent.

But, as a recent study has amply demonstrated, most of the seventeenth century was a period of economic stagnation or decline for the Valencian economy.[26] Periods of economic depression do not, however, spell disaster for everyone as those who already have sufficient capital may be able to benefit from the troubles of the less fortunate. It was precisely this phenomenon, the ability of a relatively few to take advantage of the opportunities offered by hard times, that sustained recruitment into the corps of familiares during the seventeenth century and provided a group of new families that continued to support the Holy Office until well into the next century. In this connection, it is noteworthy that the ten communities whose landholding patterns were surveyed by Casey for the seventeenth and early eighteenth centuries all had a high degree of social and economic inequality, with landholding heavily concentrated in the top 20 percent of the population. Játiva, Gandía, and Castellón, the communities with the greatest concentration of wealth and the worst social inequality, were also places with high concentrations of familiares.[27] Across the two centuries, these communities could boast 259 familiares in my sample, with Castellón de la Plana accounting for 80 and Játiva for 150.

Apart from economic factors, the fact that Valencia's inquisitorial district straddled the borders of the Kingdom of Aragon and the Principality of Catalonia created political problems that affected the number of familiares that could be recruited in those areas. Certainly, the tribunal's punishment of several familiares from the Aragonese town of Teruel for aiding Aragonese authorities in releasing a prisoner from the custody of an alcalde of the Inquisition soured relations between the tribunal and the local elite and sharply reduced the size of the city's once-flourishing corps of familiares.[28]

In spite of the obvious correlation between the concentration of wealth and the distribution of familiares, they were also present in areas devoid of the economic opportunities of the huerta or silk-producing zones. Since these remote villages could hardly be considered hotbeds of heresy, the presence of familiares in them can be explained more by the activity of individual inquisitors or the relationship that the tribunal had with certain nobles than by any plan to cover the kingdom with a dense network of informers.

Sometimes, as in the case of a group of villages in the extreme northern part of the district near Mora de Ebro, the appearance of a large number of familiares where there were few previously can be accounted for by the zeal of an inquisitor. In this case, it was an inquisitorial visitation to the Tortosa/Mora de Ebro region in 1601–02 which resulted in the appointment of familiares in forty-one villages, some as small as twelve households.[29] But the Holy Office could not expect to put down roots in such unpropitious soil, and during the following century, when the corps of familiares tended to be recruited primarily from places with a strong inquisitorial tradition, most of these villages dropped out.

In other remote areas, the Holy Office benefited from the friendship of the local lord who might have encouraged his vassals when they sought titles. It should not be forgotten that most of rural Valencia was under seigneurial jurisdiction and that the majority of the Valencian nobility were far from hostile to the Holy Office. In fact, of the 350 towns where one or more unsalaried officials were present, 133 were seigneurial and only 72 belonged directly to the crown. Certain lords, like the mid-sixteenth-century duke of Segorbe, might have had personal experience of the way familiares could act to defend the social order. In testimony before the tribunal on March 27, 1553, Benito Marco, the alguacil of the Holy Office, recalled how some years earlier he had taken a posse of eighty familiares from Valencia city to certain of the duke's estates to guard against a possible Moorish seaborne assault designed to carry off his Morisco vassals. Ever since that time, the duke had favored the Holy Office and assisted it in carrying out arrests on his estates.[30]

Juan Boil de Arenos, baron of Boil and lord of the village of Alfafar near Montesa, and Jerónimo Girón de Rebolledo, lord of Andilla in the rugged Sierra de Javalambre, were two members of the kingdom's lesser territorial nobility whose strong support of the tribunal translated itself into the consistent recruitment of unpaid officials among their vassals. In 1587, Boil, who was already a familiar in Valencia city, had occasion to learn just how useful his special fuero could be when one of his vassals insulted and threatened him. Boil promptly hauled the man before the bar of the Holy Office, which condemned him to two years exile from Alfafar and a 30 ducat fine.[31] Boil's gratitude to the Holy Office for this and other favors (like maintaining him as a familiar even though he was a baron and therefore ineligible) translated itself into support for the presence of familiares and notaries in Alfafar, a tradition that was maintained by his successors.

The Valencia tribunal also had a firm friend and supporter in Jerónimo Girón de Rebolledo, a familiar who was already acting as lieutenant alguacil of the Holy Office in Liria when he won a court case and became baron of Andilla.[32] In spite of this change in his status, the tribunal insisted on keeping him as a familiar, thereby maintaining good relations with this important gentry family. As a result, he and his successors encouraged certain of their vassals to become associated with the Holy Office, and the tiny and remote village could boast two commissioners and a notary as well as at least four familiares between the late sixteenth and mid-seventeenth century. Without the firm support of the nobility, which controlled most of rural Valencia as well as many important towns (Denia, Sueca, Segorbe), the tribunal would have had much greater difficulty in establishing and maintaining a numerous and widely distributed corps of unpaid officials.[33]

Initially, the formal qualifications that every candidate had to have to become a familiar were relatively straightforward. Candidates had to be of pure Old Christian stock, married or a widower, at least 25 years of age, peaceable and of good moral character, legitimate and of native, not foreign, birth.[34] In addition, after the Concordia of July 10, 1568, familiares could not be drawn from among the powerful (barons and cavallers) but instead had to be plain, ordinary individuals without social pretensions.[35] In practice, however, whenever it seemed financially rewarding or politically expedient, the Valencia tribunal ignored or circumvented these requirements.

It is ironic that during the same period that it unleashed its most ferocious persecution of the converted Jews, the Valencia tribunal should have allowed numerous conversos to become members of the corps of familiares. Although "purity of blood" investigations were apparently being carried on from the 1550s, testimony re-

ceived during the 1566 visitation indicated that the tribunal routinely permitted applicants to present their own list of witnesses, a
practice that was apparently accepted without a murmur by its
official investigators.[36] Such procedural laxity was the cause of a
growing rumor among the public at large that successful candidates
did not have the proper personal and racial qualities.[37]

It would have been difficult, however, for the Holy Office or the
Valencia tribunal to resist the growing pressure for the exclusion of
Judeo-Christians from honorable positions in Spanish society. In
the paranoid atmosphere that prevailed among Spanish ruling circles during the mid-sixteenth century, the hand of Jewry was seen
behind every threat to Catholic Orthodoxy, and more and more of
Spain's premier institutions were adopting statutes excluding those
of Judaic origin. Finally, in the Concordia of July 10, 1568, the
Valencia tribunal was ordered to revoke all the licenses it had
issued and to only reissue them after an official inquiry had been
performed which would encompass not only racial factors but also
the candidate's personal conduct. From these, the tribunal was
supposed to choose the members of a numerically limited but ra-
cially pure corps of familiares comprised of individuals who were
"Old Christians of untarnished lineage."[38] Even though the tribunal was apparently willing to carry out the requisite genealogical
investigations, it balked at actually calling in all its licenses, as this
would make it appear that its critics were right in claiming that
there were many conversos in the corps. Furthermore, the obloquy
that would result might bring the entire corps into ill repute and
could damage the reputations of many families whose members
held titles, even those of the "purest" Old Christian stock. The
stalemate was broken only by the direct intervention of the viceroy
who bluntly refused to recognize the validity of any titles unless
they had first been collected and reexamined as provided in the
Concordia.[39] In the face of pressure from the viceroy and the
Suprema, the tribunal had to abandon its resistance and undertake
the first official series of genealogical investigations in its history,
which were carried out between 1569 and 1571. The results, which
demonstrated that forty-three of Valencia city's familiares and a
large number of their wives lacked the requisite racial qualities,
appeared to underscore the need for rigorous genealogical investigations even though the number of familiares who actually lost

their licenses was rather small because of the danger that massive dismissals would pose to the reputation of the corps as a whole.[40]

The genealogical investigation of familiares and other unpaid officials began when the applicant for a position gave the tribunal a copy of his genealogy and that of his wife, including the names of parents and paternal and maternal grandparents. The tribunal's records would then be searched, and if this failed to turn up any evidence that would disqualify the applicant, then one of the tribunal's secretaries or a commissioner was sent to the places where the family lived to interview witnesses in accordance with a printed questionnaire.[41] Both secretaries and commissioners would normally be accompanied by a notary as witnesses' testimony was taken under oath. In practice, however, the requisite commissioners were frequently not available or were unwilling to undertake journeys far from their homes, and the tribunal would frequently use notaries or even parish priests to carry out all or part of the investigations.[42]

The veracity of the investigations was to be ensured not only by the fact that they were to be "tomados de oficio y no ministrados de parte," that is, using information obtained independently by an official of the Holy Office and not simply furnished by the applicant as formerly, but also because all the officials concerned were supposed to have themselves undergone genealogical examinations. It could be assumed that individuals who had successfully surmounted the genealogical barrier would have a vested interest in maintaining the purity of the corps to which they belonged and that this would outweigh the appeal of any financial advantages offered to them by nervous applicants. In 1630, the Suprema admonished Inquisitor Roche for using a number of commissioners whose own genealogical investigations were not yet complete. His explanation was that they were all the brothers of familiares or the relatives of officials so there seemed to be no harm in the practice.[43]

The actual number of witnesses to be questioned varied substantially. During the late sixteenth and very early seventeenth centuries, when the form that the genealogical investigation was later to follow was not firmly established, the investigators used only six witnesses per location. A change seems to have occurred in 1607, however, when the number "6" is crossed out on the form that was used to investigate one Jaime Amaros and replaced by "12," which was to be the norm in future investigations.[44] However, the investigator's instructions encouraged him to exceed the prescribed number of witnesses whenever there was any doubt or contradiction and to examine as many as he thought necessary. Those carrying out the investigations were well aware of their superiors' bias toward more rather than fewer witnesses, especially in difficult cases. When the Suprema wrote questioning secretary Juan del Olmo's decision to interview only five witnesses in Traiguera, the birthplace of candidate Frances Vidal, where three had testified that the family had Jewish blood, Olmo replied that instead of remaining in Traiguera, he had gone directly on to the birthplace of Vidal's maternal grandmother since the rumors concerned her. There, he had interviewed sixteen witnesses, including three priests and two familiares, all "among the oldest and most honorable in the village."[45] The number of witnesses could mount quickly, lengthening the time of the investigation and sharply increasing its cost. Pedro García Pons, who applied to become a familiar in 1623, had the misfortune to have his parents and grandparents come from three separate towns (Olerida, Flix, and La Granadella), while his wife's maternal grandmother came from the village of Fatarella. In all, the intrepid investigators took testimony from fifty-nine witnesses, and the tribunal ended by rejecting Pons's application anyway, but not before collecting 390 reales in costs.[46]

The instructions gave the investigating official certain minimal but very specific standards for the sort of person that he was to choose to examine. Of course, witnesses were to be natives of the place and of impeccable Old Christian stock. But, more specifically, they were to be chosen from among the oldest inhabitants, were not to have any direct relationship to the candidate (neither relatives, friends, nor enemies), and the local unpaid officials were to be included among them. In practice, investigating officials used their own discretion in deciding when it was appropriate to vary the official format. In my survey of the witnesses called in fifty genealogies of familiares from 1575 to 1801, the average age was just over 60 years old, but the mandate to seek out the oldest inhabitants was frequently not followed by investigating officials. In some places, older people may simply not have been available to interview. This problem was especially acute during the first half of the seventeenth century when disease and economic crises combined to produce sharply higher death rates among the elderly.[47] Moreover, the most important thing about a witness was not age but what that individual knew about the applicant and his family. In the case of Diego Angel, a merchant living in Valencia, secretary Jerónimo Sans, who was carrying out his genealogical investigation, clearly decided that it would be more useful to interview Angel's associates among the other merchants of the city than to seek out the elderly. As a result, the average age of witnesses interviewed in Valencia city was only 44.[48] Investigating officials only made a special point of interviewing the very oldest inhabitants of a place when rumors of some impurity in the applicant's background had surfaced. In such a case, only the testimony of a person whose knowledge of local events went back several generations would suffice. During the investigation that was carried on into the background of Pedro Badía prior to admitting him to the corps of familiares, testimony came from several witnesses that his maternal grandmother, Violante Batallar, was of impure blood. To test the veracity of this testimony, the investigating official turned to what was undoubtedly the oldest inhabitant of the village, a 105-year-old peasant. This individual acknowledged the existence of the rumor but claimed that it was without foundation; that apparently sufficed, as Badía's application was approved without further difficulty.[49]

According to their critics, one of the most deplorable aspects of the purity of blood statutes was their marked egalitarianism. In a society where the statutes were becoming the indispensable passageway to social distinction, the reputations of the wealthy and powerful were being held hostage to the opinions of mere plebeians. In a country where a single ancestor of impure blood could invalidate the purity and orthodoxy of dozens of others, critics charged that the son of the vilest miller or blacksmith could use his status as an Old Christian to hold in contempt the scions of the noblest families in Spain.[50]

Certainly, the results of breaking down the sample of witnesses by social status appears to support the claims made by the critics of the purity of blood examinations. In general, witnesses were drawn from among persons of lower social standing, while there is a striking contrast between the social composition of the corps of familiares and the witnesses in their genealogical examinations. More than 72 percent of witnesses were drawn from the ranks of the peasantry and artisans, while gentry (cavallers) and "citizens" (ciutadà) together comprised only 2.3 percent. Furthermore, there seemed to be little disposition on the part of investigating officials to select members of the local oligarchy, with only a minuscule 0.79 percent (18 individuals) identifying themselves as jurats or other officials of local government. Even the injunction to always interview local familiares or other officials of the Holy Office was seldom obeyed. Only 110 familiares (4.8% of witnesses) were interviewed by investigating officials in spite of the fact that they were ordered to compile a list of the names of local familiares for the tribunal and could, therefore, hardly be unaware of their existence. Even parish priests, who presumably could have given the investigating official a good deal of valuable information about the life and customs of the applicant as well as the frequency of his religious observances, were only represented by 95 individuals (4.1%).

In marked contrast to the procedural laxity of genealogical investigations carried out before the 1570s, seventeenth- and eighteenth-century investigations tended to be characterized by punctilious attention to detail and a willingness to follow up every rumor of impurity of blood no matter how shaky its foundation. Of course, there can be no doubt that the enthusiasm with which the various officials in charge carried out their responsibilities was greatly spurred by the knowledge that their further exertions would be amply rewarded out of the funds the applicant had deposited with the tribunal to cover the costs of his investigation. Miguel José Alapont, who applied to become a familiar in 1726, was unfortunate enough to have maternal grandparents who were both born in different places in Castile, while his mother had been born in Murcia. This unusual situation required investigations to be carried on not only in the Kingdom of Valencia (Valencia city and Alcudia de Carlet, his father's birthplace) but also by the officials of the tribunals of Cuenca, Toledo, and Murcia.[51]

Foreign birth, which was supposed to automatically disqualify a candidate from admission, could be overlooked for exceptional individuals, but the tribunal did feel itself obliged to obtain information about the applicant's family in his country of origin. To do this, it was necessary to obtain the cooperation of foreign ecclesiastical officials who normally proved themselves so eager to help the Spaniards that they carried out their instructions more strictly than they were followed in Spain itself. In the case of Juan Abadia, a merchant who came from the French province of Béarn, the tribunal received authorization from Inquisitor-General Manuel Bonifaz to write to the bishop of Oléron and ask him to carry out a genealogical investigation in the family's native villages. Working from the standard set of instructions given to all officials charged with carrying out such investigations, which told them to find twelve witnesses from among the oldest and most honorable inhabitants, the bishop's agents selected witnesses with an average age of 76 (as opposed to the Spanish Inquisition's norm of 60), including four 80-year-olds and one peasant who claimed to be 95.[52] The tribunal's concern with fulfilling its instructions to the letter was demonstrated when José Ignacio Alama applied to enter the corps in 1740. In this case, the applicant himself was of pure Spanish stock since his family came from Valencia city and the diocese of Tortosa. But his wife's paternal grandfather, Julio Capuz, had come to the kingdom from Genoa, so, inevitably, the Genoese authorities had to be consulted. By the time permission was obtained from the inquisitor-general, letters were dispatched to Genoa and a reply incorporating the results of the Genoese investigation was received; an investigation that should have taken a few months had stretched to three years.[53]

Of course, if the tribunal was prepared to go to such a lot of trouble over the relatively trivial matter of foreign origin, it could be expected to take infinite pains to establish the truth of any allegations of impurity of blood. The fate of Antonio Albert's application to become a familiar in La Ollería is a typical example of the way such rumors could delay the conclusion of an investigation by imposing a need to carry on fresh inquiries in places not originally scheduled. The investigation of Albert's family in La Ollería having been successfully concluded, Commissioner Agustín Vicente López turned his attention to Benigánim, the birthplace of his maternal grandmother, Catalina Moscardó. Here the investigation ran into trouble as several witnesses repeated a rumor that the Moscardós were of Morisco origin. This rumor was strenuously denied by Eugenio Tudela, one of the local familiares, who attributed it to petty jealousy arising from the time when the village of Moscardón (from which the family had come originally) had turned out en masse to repel a Morisco attack, and all the members of the family, even the youngest, had gone on horseback, while many who belonged to the village oligarchy had to go on foot. Even though the testimony of such an important witness as Tudela (just the sort of witness that the commissioner was instructed to seek out) should have ended the matter, the fact that these allegations were being made just at the time of the expulsion of the Moriscos turned a routine investigation into one that would require a great deal more painstaking work before it could be concluded.

After carefully considering the report of its commissioner, the tribunal drew up a special series of instructions designed to track down the ancestors of the original Moscardó who had migrated from that village to Benigánim. The tribunal then appointed canon Martín Rodrigo, its commissioner in Albarracín, to carry out the investigation in Moscardón, which lay a few miles to the south, sending José del Olmo from Valencia to accompany him. Of course, del Olmo's presence was entirely superfluous since the commissioner was perfectly competent to carry out the investigation and could have used a local ecclesiastical notary if he needed one, but the del Olmos were being favored in these matters, and the inquisitors no doubt saw this case as a good opportunity for him to earn a substantial fee. On May 4, 1612, seventeen months after Albert's application had first been received, the two investigators arrived in Moscardón and began to interview witnesses.

In spite of the care that the tribunal took to investigate the origins of the rumors about the family's Morisco origins, however, the outside observer cannot help wondering whether a decision had already been taken in his case even before Rodrigo and del Olmo were dispatched to Moscardón. The majority of the witnesses they interviewed there were probably distant relatives of the candidate, and a subsequent inquiry in Benigánim seemed almost designed to produce a favorable result since it was carried on using a different official and an entirely different set of witnesses. Armed with the "favorable results" of these two investigations, the tribunal felt free to award Albert his title on November 24, 1612, twenty-eight months after Albert had first applied for admission to the corps of familiares.[54] In the case of Albert, as in so many others who applied for familiaturas after the genealogical investigation had been formalized, scrupulous attention to the regulations governing such investigations and a willingness to pursue any rumor of "impure" blood, however farfetched, masked the fact that a decision to admit the candidate had already been taken at a higher level.

Given all the concern over the impact of the purity of blood statutes on Spanish society, it is somewhat surprising to note that only 19, or just 2.6 percent of the 728 applicants whose genealogies I studied, were actually rejected. Below the level of the judges who sat on the tribunal, the imperatives of racial purity gave way to political and financial considerations, so that for essentially honorific positions, such as familiar, there was a built-in predisposition to favor paying applicants—especially those who had some local political power in spite of a family background that should have counted heavily against them. The corps of familiares, therefore, provided a channel for the somewhat grudging integration of the conversos into Old Christian society. Even in this very small sample, however, the fundamental anti-Semitism of the tribunal is revealed as thirteen candidates were rejected because of objections to their Judaic background or that of their wives, but only one was rejected because of his Moorish descent.

Curiously enough, several of the individuals whose applications were rejected came from families that could boast of one or more members serving the tribunal as familiares. Pedro Fargues, for example, who applied in 1639, was rejected by the tribunal after numerous witnesses had denounced both his and his wife's Jewish ancestry. But, at the same time, testimony revealed that the couple was related to no fewer than four individuals who had served or were presently serving as familiares, including two from the Muñoz family, one of those denounced by the witnesses.[55]

In certain cases, the failure of a particular individual to obtain a familiatura should be seen as an isolated misfortune, interrupting but not preventing the process of assimilation. The rejection of Felipe Gaspar Capero of Traiguera in 1603 was one such case, all the more peculiar because his father, Luis, had been a familiar. Gaspar's failure, which can be attributed to the previous removal of his wife's uncle from the corps and to the fact that there were already enough familiares in the town, did not prevent the family from entering the Inquisition as familiares, calificadores, and notaries during the last decades of the seventeenth century.[56]

Finally, a comparison of the social composition of our sample of rejected candidates with the social composition of the familiatura as a whole indicates once again the justice of the charges made by critics of the purity of blood investigations. If the overwhelming majority of familiares in Valencia's district came from the plebeian ranks of the peasantry, presumably less contaminated with Jewish blood than the residents of towns and the upper classes, labradores were underrepresented in the ranks of the rejected, which included such notables as the ciutada Luis Alexandre and Antonio de Cardona, a noble relative of the admirals of Aragon, the Borjas, and other distinguished Valencian families.[57]

Certainly, as far as their marital status was concerned, Valencia's familiares largely conformed to the ideal set forth in the qualifications for admission. Out of the 709 successful applicants in my sample, 615, or 86.7 percent, were married at the time of application, while 10 others were widowers. Moreover, of the 32 bachelors, fully 23 were called "youths" or "minore" in the text of their genealogy, and, with one exception, they were all under 25 years of age. Of course, in these cases, it was virtually certain that most, if not all, of these young bachelors would marry since the social and religious pressure in favor of marriage was so strong. Indeed, even widowers felt obliged to remarry, sometimes with almost indecent haste after the death of their first wife. When Miguel Corachan applied to enter the corps on February 23, 1639, he was married to Madalena Voltes, but less than a year after his title was conferred, his wife died, and he had requested permission from the tribunal to remarry, this time to Esperanza Pujades, a widow whose brother, Miguel Pujades, was a familiar in Campanar.[58]

The fact that the overwhelming majority of Valencia's familiares were married men or were expected to marry within a relatively short time after they joined the corps meant that Valencia's familiares were in substantial conformity with the ideal as set forth in the regulations for admission. The middle-aged man who had never been married or the widower who preferred to remain single so as to carry on freer, less inhibited sexual activity became an object of suspicion and distrust who could even find himself harassed by the local alcaldes if his behavior came to public notice. Confirmed bachelors were rare indeed among Valencia's familiares, but some were clearly acceptable regardless of the prevailing social prejudice. José Juan de Centelles, Marquis of Centelles, was one of these. When the marquis applied for a license in 1699, at the age of

42, the Inquisitor-General was only too happy to dispense with the marital requirement, and in less than three months he was admitted to the corps, in spite of the fact that one of his ancestors had been executed as a Protestant heretic.[59]

In the matter of the age of those accepted into the corps, the Valencia tribunal achieved substantial if not entire compliance with the twenty-five-year rule, with only twenty-two successful applicants under 25 years of age. But, with an average age of 37, the corps of familiares was relatively youthful; fully 62.5 percent of the sample was aged 40 or younger, and only 8.7 percent was between 51 and 60.

Of course, there were exceptions. Twelve applicants out of the sample of 216 were 20 and younger, with the youngest, Agustín Fabregat, only 17 when he was accepted into the corps in 1740.[60] But the Valencian inquisitors had definite reasons for wanting to bend the rules to admit these young men. In some cases, like that of Fabregat, the tribunal wished to reclaim the support of a family whose service had taken place in the distant past.[61] Confronted by an eager youngster who declared that he wanted to "imitate my ancestors," the tribunal could hardly have refused to consider him. In return, Fabregat demonstrated his gratitude by long and faithful service and even married his daughter, Francisca, to Vicente Perciva, another of the familiares of the town.[62]

The case of Dr. Félix Breva illustrates the tribunal's desire to maintain its connections to families with strong and recent ties to the tribunal. Breva's paternal grandfather, Jaime, had served the tribunal as a familiar in the 1630s and 1640s, while his cousin, Luis Breva, had served as inquisitorial notary in Castellón de la Plana since 1682.[63] Later, when Breva went on to become abogado de presos of the Holy Office, two other members of the family, Bautista and Vicente Breva, joined the ranks of Castellón's familiares.[64]

In spite of the fact that both Fabregat and Breva were underaged when appointed to the tribunal, it is difficult to criticize their appointments. They, along with the other underaged candidates, met, and even exceeded, all the other formal requirements, and they and their families were very much the sort of people the tribunal wished to recruit and retain.

Valencia's corps of familiares was almost completely in compliance with the requirement that applicants be natives of Spain. In fact, the corps was not only overwhelmingly Spanish but Valencian, with only eleven individuals identified as being born outside the kingdom and, of these, only six outside Spain. Moreover, several of the Spanish applicants born outside Valencia came of families with long traditions of service to the Holy Office in their home province. One of these men was Juan Diego Aztira, who was born in Zaragoza. In a note attached to his application, Aztira boasted that he was following the footsteps of "many of his relatives and ancestors who have served as officials and familiares." On his father's side, he was distantly related to Dr. Domingo de Aztira, a canon of Zaragoza's cathedral and a former inquisitor, while his uncle, Juan Calvo, had been a familiar in his native village.[65]

Given the generally paranoid atmosphere that gripped Spanish ruling circles during much of the sixteenth century and the fact that most of the Protestant sympathizers arrested in Spain after 1560 were Frenchmen, it is not surprising that the tribunal admitted few foreigners to the corps. In 1575, as if to underscore the importance of caution in this respect, the Suprema even issued a carta acordada requiring that no one of foreign birth should be given a title without express permission from the inquisitor-general and that the tribunals were to send a list of those foreigners already serving as familiares.[66]

Certain individuals of foreign birth made excellent candidates, however, and it would have been foolish and counterproductive not to admit them. Once again, quality and not mechanical compliance with the formal regulations was the norm. Applicants like the prosperous Milanese-born merchant Marco Antonio Muceffi, who had lived in Valencia city for twenty-eight years, or Juan Abadia, who was born in Verdetes (Beaune) and whose Valencian wife Mariana Mulet came of a family with a long tradition of service to the Holy Office, were already so well integrated that no suspicion could attach to them in spite of their foreign birth.[67]

A recent analysis of the social composition of the familiares of Córdoba during the mid-sixteenth century indicates that it was dominated largely by artisans in the leatherworking and textile trades.[68] What is known about the social structure of Valencia's familiares for the same period seems to confirm the existence of a large number of artisans within the corps. Of the 1,219 familiares serving in 1567 whose occupations are known to us, 31 percent were artisans (mainly tailors and textile workers), while only 5.6 percent came from lesser nobility and 4.4 percent from the ranks of the ciutadans. In Valencia city, the predominance of the artisans was even more pronounced, with 46 percent coming from their ranks.[69]

A very different picture, however, is revealed by my sample of 533 familiares drawn from the seventeenth and eighteenth centuries. Here, the percentage of artisans falls to only 2.4 percent, the second lowest of any of the major status/occupation categories. The decline was even more telling in the city of Valencia. My survey of several lists of familiares furnished the viceroy between 1623 and 1628 indicates that of the 186 for whom status/occupation data is available, only 17 individuals (7.5%) can be classed as artisans.

The large number of artisans among Valencia's familiares in the mid-sixteenth century is all the more surprising in light of the massive participation of that group in the Germanía movement of 1519–1521.[70] Given Charles V's general policy of attempting to pacify and coopt the urban classes that fought the crown during the Comunero Revolution in Castile, however, it is tempting to view the social composition of Valencia's mid-sixteenth-century familiares in the same light.[71] By enlisting large numbers of urban artisans in an honorable corporation where they served alongside their social superiors to defend a loyal Catholic Valencia, the Inquisition was providing the government with a way of moderating the social tensions that led to a bloody civil war and imperiled royal authority. This interpretation seems even more convincing when we add to it the fact that at the Cortes of 1528–29, Charles made a deliberate effort to appeal to the disaffected popular masses by accepting a series of proposals that reflected certain of the long-standing complaints of the popular classes of the towns. In Castile, as I have already noted elsewhere, Charles followed a similar policy at the Cortes of 1523, where he attempted to deal with some of the most important proposals for reform that were voiced by rebel leaders during the Comunero Revolution.[72]

The process that would result in considerably reducing the number of artisans in the corps of familiares began as early as the 1550s when changes in the structure of Valencia's textile industry led to the elimination or impoverishment of many small master artisans: this resulted in a market for familiaturas in which certain poor artisans

who held them made them available to wealthy merchants and entre-
preneurs. This process appears to have operated through a series of
intermediaries who were in touch with familiares who wished to sell
and merchants and other wealthy individuals who wished to purchase titles. Testimony taken during the visitation of 1566, for example, reveals that several individuals, including a tavern-keeper and a
familiar, received fees for arranging the transfer of titles. In one
instance, Juan Bautista Miniu, a wealthy merchant, is reported to
have purchased a title from one Armengol, a velvet worker who is
described as "old and poor." In another case, Gabriel Gimeno, a
dyer, called "hombre necesitado" by one witness, sold his title to
another merchant, Antonio Misines. Both of these deals were accomplished through the good offices of one Alejo Botero, a familiar who
received a substantial fee for his services.[73]

The exclusion of artisans from Valencia's corps of familiares,
therefore, was well under way long before the Suprema made it
official policy by issuing its carta acordada of May 9, 1602, which
introduced the requirement of "purity of office" and barred most
artisans from admission.[74] In spite of this ordinance, small numbers
of artisans did apply and were accepted into the corps during the
seventeenth and eighteenth centuries, but the apologetic tone
adopted in certain instances by the applicants and their supporters
indicates an awareness that their applications were unlikely to be
received favorably. Vicente Beltrán, who incautiously listed himself
as a locksmith/labrador on his application, hastened to write the
tribunal again to declare that he only practiced the locksmith's
trade "for his own amusement and not because it is his profession."[75] In 1643, when Jaime Esteve, a pottery maker, applied to
the corps from Traiguera, Dr. Felicio Pellicer, the local inquisitorial
notary, wrote on his behalf to point out that in Traiguera potters
were no ordinary artisans and that they had even been elected to
the town council.[76]

Having established itself in the kingdom despite opposition
from the local elite, the Inquisition was perfectly situated to play a
social role that would allow it to make the corps of familiares into
a bridge between royal government and the popular masses of the
towns. Three well-attended autos de fé were held during the
Germanías, and after the war, the tribunal did not hesitate to
appoint Bernardino Arviso, a prominent former agermanado, lieu-

tenant alcalde, much to the disgust of the cavallers and ciutadans in Valencia city.[77]

By the 1560s, however, the radical, popular phase of the tribunal's activity was at an end. Sustained persecution of the converted Jews had given way to occasional trials, and the tribunal was acquiring its own fixed sources of income, thereby converting itself into just another one of Spain's conservative ecclesiastical/bureaucratic corporations. No longer living precariously on the money from confiscations but dependent on income from censals and tithes like Valencia's elite of nobles and rentiers, the tribunal could no longer afford to identify itself with a class that had once threatened to overturn the established order. After the visitation of 1528, Bernardino de Arviso was removed, and during the 1560s and 1570s, Valencia's inquisitors watched complacently as licenses were transferred from poor artisans to wealthy merchants even if some of them had Jewish blood. By the turn of the century, when the Suprema issued its ukase instituting "purity of office" as a new requirement for admission, the process by which the familiatura was transformed into a monied elite was largely complete, and the corps was taking on the shape that it was to retain for the next two centuries. In the larger towns, it was recruited from a wealthy and conservative rentier class of cavallers and ciutadans solidly entrenched in local politics through the system of insaculació, while in the villages, the familiatura rested firmly on wealthy peasants, the "coqs du village" who dominated village affairs.

Indeed, it may be argued that by forcing the tribunal to perform formal genealogical investigations after the visitation of 1567, the Suprema accelerated the process that was making wealth the sole universal prerequisite for admission to the corps. Genealogical investigations were expensive. The average cost of the investigations in the 206 cases where information is available amounted to 775 reales, or 51.6 Valencian pounds (lliures), in an age when the lower third of the peasantry earned less than 20 lliures per year from the agricultural sector.[78] In fact, many of these investigations were far more expensive, with forty-five (21.8%) costing over 1,000 reales, ten over 2,000 reales, and one a total of 3,306 reales, or 220 lliures, which was more than eleven times the income of a poor peasant in the early eighteenth century.

The wealth barrier became even more difficult to surmount

when, in 1600, the Suprema insisted on substantial sums, usually fixed at 300 reales, that had to be deposited before the investigation could begin.[79] Actually, in ninety-five cases, witnesses even went out of their way to comment approvingly about an applicant's wealth or ability to live off his rents. Given the sharp reduction in the demand for manufactured goods after 1609 and the consequent high unemployment rate among artisans, the cost of the genealogical investigation alone would have been enough to reduce their numbers if social prejudice had not already done so.

Paradoxically enough, the aristocratization of the corps of familiares gained momentum during the late sixteenth century precisely at a time when the Suprema, under heavy pressure from the crown and the Council of Aragon, had agreed to the Concordia of 1568 that specifically excluded caballeros and barons. The goal that was sought by the Council of Aragon as well as by Viceroy Herrera and the delegates to the Cortes of Monzón was to prevent the privileges and special jurisdiction that were granted to familiares from becoming a shield behind which powerful men could defy royal justice. For its part, the tribunal was determined to avoid carrying out this part of the Concordia, because, in an increasingly status-conscious society, the fact that it could no longer enroll the nobility would greatly undermine its prestige. In this effort, it found that it could count on support from the Suprema, which had only agreed to the Concordia under duress and with grave reservations.

The Suprema began by intervening directly with the viceroy and the regent of the Audiencia to reach a compromise by which the tribunal would be allowed to appoint caballeros who were lords of vassals but not titleholders.[80] Accepting even this, however, would have meant that the tribunal would have been cut off from recruiting among Valencia's most influential gentry families. To circumvent this agreement, the tribunal adopted the practice of enrolling the eldest son of titleholders as familiares, with the assurance that these men would eventually inherit their father's title and with the conviction that they would not actually be forced later to renounce their membership in the corps.[81] The most that the Suprema was prepared to do was to make a tactical retreat by ordering the tribunal not to take cognizance of the civil and criminal cases of the count of Buñol, a familiar since 1587. But, as he reminded the tribunal in 1607, his license had never been removed and he remained a familiar in good standing.[82] In fact, as it admitted in 1660, the tribunal had ignored this provision of the Concordia since it could not do without the political support of powerful nobles with votes and influence in the Cortes.[83]

Use of these expedients permitted the tribunal to enroll a respectable number of nobles. Of the 533 men whose occupation/status is listed in their genealogies, 34, or 6.3%, were noble. But most of these men were clearly not drawn from the very top ranks of the Valencian aristocracy. The one exception was the marquis of Centelles, who obtained his license in 1699.[84] At best, the tribunal could expect to enlist certain members of the twenty or so intermediate families who held a lesser title, lived in the kingdom (frequently in Valencia city), and sought a title to enhance their social prestige or to give them added protection from the royal courts. Guillén Carroz y de Artes, who applied in 1639, came of just such a family. His father, Francisco Carroz, was count of Cirat and a holder of one of the thirteen encomiendas of the Order of Montesa. His mother, Teodora Artes de Albanell, was linked to the gentry through her second cousin, Gaspar Artes, who was a familiar and lord of the village of Almàssera, while her brother was a member of the Order of Santiago.[85] Another good example of this group is José Boil, whose father was the marquis of Boil and whose mother, María Figuerola, was related to the former inquisitor of Valencia, Dr. Honorato Figuerola.[86] In certain instances, these men could demonstrate such singular devotion to the Holy Office that membership in the corps of familiares must have meant more to them than the privileges or exemptions that it could provide. The count of Buñol was one of these, and, in a letter begging the tribunal to take cognizance of a particularly delicate civil suit in which he had become involved, he declared that "next to salvation, what he most wanted in this life was the opportunity to employ his person, life and treasure in the service of the Holy Office." That this was not mere rhetoric is indicated by a cover letter written by Valencia's inquisitors when they sent the count's request on to the Suprema. In their letter, the inquisitors attested to the fact that the count had always served the tribunal with "great willingness" and had frequently held one of the ropes attached to the standard that was borne before the inquisitors when they marched in religious processions.[87]

Of course, many of the caballeros who became members of the

corps during the seventeenth and eighteenth centuries belonged to the 129 or so gentry families who held one or two villages and had a relatively modest income from feudal dues which they supplemented with rent from land and houses that they owned.[88] Typical of this group was Carlos de Calatayud, who was lord of the village of Agres with its 200 families.[89]

A far larger number of caballeros were not even lords of vassals but simply held the title of caballeros and derived their income entirely from rent. These were really almost indistinguishable from the citizen rentiers (ciutadans) who were just below them in the social scale. Their presence among Valencia's petty nobility must be accounted for by the fact that in the 1630s it became possible to purchase the status of cavaller for between 250 and 700 lliures, well within the range of the wealthiest 20 percent of Valencia's property-owning class.[90] Typically, these men would also belong to the restricted political elite of the larger towns, which, through the insaculació system, had become virtually self-perpetuating. The insaculats comprised the group of citizens who were eligible to hold municipal offices and were selected for life by their fellows among the officeholding class.[91]

One family that almost perfectly illustrates the combination of rentier and politician so characteristic of the majority of the cavaller families in our sample is the Barberán of Onteniente. Gaspar Barberán and his son Gaspar Jerónimo served together as familiares, the first receiving his title in 1585 and the second in 1629, while Gaspar's nephew José obtained his title in 1632. None of the Barberáns were fiefholders, but Gaspar Jerónimo was reckoned as having more than 12,000 ducats in property. At the same time, they were active in local politics; Gaspar served as justicia of the town at the time of his application, and his nephew was insaculat and had served as justicia and jurat on several occasions. In addition to obtaining titles as familiares, the family was tied in with the Inquisition in other ways. Onofre Barberán, the comisario who served in Onteniente at the time of Gaspar Jerónimo's genealogical investigation, was a relative; Gaspar Barberán's aunt was first cousin to Dr. Miguel Jerónimo Blasco, canon and dean of the cathedral chapter of Valencia and inquisitor of Barcelona.[92]

Rentiers or small fiefholders, politicians and urban dwellers, the petty nobles who entered the ranks of Valencia's familiares represented a very different group from those responsible for the "aristo-cratization" of the corps in Galicia studied by Contreras.[93] Rather than a sturdy feudal class residing on their estates, Valencia's noble familiares formed part of the burgeoning rentier class that took over more and more of the kingdom's wealth after the expulsion of the Moriscos.

Far more representative of this growing rentier class, however, were the ciutadans. Urban based, tied closely to municipal government through the system of insaculació, this group accounted for 24.7 percent of the familiares for whom occupation/status information is available.

Some of these men were very clearly the sons of peasants who had made good and had used their wealth and local political power to propel themselves into the lower ranks of the petty nobility. Bautista Badía, from the village of Sueca, listed himself proudly as a ciutadà on his application but was the descendant of labradores from Sueca and nearby Cullera on both sides of the family.[94] Joaquín Albuixech, who applied from Almusafes in 1762, studiously avoided any reference to his family's social standing in his application, but a letter by the tribunal's special commissioner, Dr. Juan Zapata, reveals that they were wealthy peasants who now had sufficient income so that they no longer needed to cultivate their own land. Apparently, the family had quite a stranglehold on the familiatura in this village of two hundred families, since Joaquín's father and his two grandfathers were all familiares, as were his cousin and several other relatives.[95] At the other extreme were certain individuals who could have fitted easily into the ranks of the cavallers. José Bonet, whose father was lord of the tiny village of Palau, was one of these, and his presence among the ciutadans illustrates the difficulties of making hard and fast distinctions between ciutadans and cavallers.[96]

It is particularly interesting to chart the evolution of the Carbonell family from the important silk-harvesting town of Alcoy since their connection with the Holy Office was maintained throughout their rise to greater social prominence. Ginés Carbonell, the first applicant from the family, was a humble labrador whose application was approved around 1595.[97] By the time his grandson Roque's application was approved in 1631, the family had already achieved ciutadan status. In his application, Roque referred proudly to "the services that his ancestors had rendered to the Holy Office" as his chief reason for applying. His wife, Inés Mayor, came of another family with strong traditions of service on both sides of her family.[98]

In the case of the Feliu family of Benisa and nearby Teulada, the tribunal not only recruited a ciutadan family of exceptional loyalty but also of growing local political importance. By the mid-seventeenth century, when cousins Juan and Miguel Feliu gained entry to the corps, the family had already gained ciutadan status and become very wealthy, with Juan's holdings estimated at more than 9,000 ducats. His cousin, who mentioned the services of his father and grandfather, was related directly or by marriage to no less than thirteen familiares.[99] By the mid-eighteenth century, when Pedro Feliu and his son José applied for entry, the family had attained significant political power, having served as alcaldes, regidores, and governors of both Teulada and Benisa.[100]

The rise of the petty nobility and distinguished citizens in the Valencia of the seventeenth and eighteenth centuries exactly parallels their increasing presence in the corps of familiares, where the tribunal was only too happy to welcome them. But the cavallers and ciutadans who entered the corps, like their counterparts outside it, could hardly be called wealthy. Only 400 lliures in rent was necessary for an individual to become eligible for municipal office in Valencia city during the seventeenth and early eighteenth centuries.[101] The average income of the fourteen nobles and citizens who can be positively identified as familiares or relatives of familiares and who gained insaculó status between 1660 and 1691 was only 582½ lliures. Even this unimpressive total was inflated by just a few individuals—like Felipe Gregorio Alfonso with his two large and prosperous farms in the huerta—who earned far more than most.[102] Of the fourteen, eleven earned less than 500 lliures and two just barely made the minimum of 400. Far more typical was the ciutadan and later familiar, Francisco Ferris, who pieced together his barely qualifying 405 lliures out of the rent of two tiny farms in the huerta, a house in the city, and a butcher stall in the municipal meat market.[103]

Lawyers, notaries, and other professionals constituted the other wing of the nonpeasant sector that had concentrated so much of the kingdom's landed wealth in its hands during the seventeenth and eighteenth centuries.[104] In my sample of genealogies, fifty-six individuals comprising 10.5 percent of those with occupation/status information can be classed as professionals, primarily lawyers and notaries but including a number of distinguished and highly paid physicians. A glimpse at the life-style and activities of familiar Bartolomé Molner, a notary from Castellón de la Plana, where a good deal of litigation was carried on, reveals a busy, prosperous individual with many business interests. Active in both the ecclesiastical and secular courts, Molner was popular with clients and was able to obtain a substantial income from fees. In addition, he did an extensive and lucrative wholesale trade in silk and other textiles. Described at the time of his application as an exceptionally vigorous man of fifty, Molner supported a wife and seven children and had two fine horses, two maids, and several hunting dogs. Unfortunately, he also had enemies, and one day in 1610, three of them crushed his head with a stone when he intervened in a struggle between them and his brother.[105]

Given the increasing importance of lawyers to the life of early modern Spain, incorporating a goodly number of them among the familiares meant, at least in theory, that the tribunal could benefit from their political support. In the always politically difficult city of Teruel, for example, the tribunal enjoyed the firm support of the Ambel family. Jerónimo Ambel was an attorney and a familiar, while his son, Dionisio Ambel, another attorney, had attained ciutadan rank by the time he applied in 1639. Not only did the family connection with the Inquisition go all the way back to the 1560s when Dionisio Ambel's grandfather, Juan, acted as lieutenant receiver to the local inquisitorial subtribunal but he was related to two inquisitors, Jerónimo Gregorio of Barcelona and Francisco Gregorio of Mallorca.[106]

Merchants, who were so poorly represented among the parents of Valencia's inquisitors, accounted for 11 percent of the successful applicants. Having largely excluded themselves from the highly lucrative international export/import trade, Valencian merchants tended to concentrate on local or regional commerce, on exchange with other parts of Spain, or on tax farming, which appeared to offer greater and more secure profits than any commercial endeavor.

Unfortunately, bankruptcy was all too often the fate of Valencia's merchant-familiares, especially in the difficult years around the turn of the sixteenth century. In 1596, Pedro Romero, Juan Lazaro,

Jerónimo Salvador, and Mateo Salvador, all merchants in Valencia city and all familiares, went bankrupt and registered their property with the Holy Office, which had jurisdiction over the suits filed by their creditors.[107] It is little wonder, then, that given the protection that the special inquisitorial fuero offered to familiares, so many merchants sought to obtain titles.

It is reassuring that the percentage of familiares who claimed to be simple labradores is almost the same—43 percent among the familiares whose genealogies I analyzed as in the comprehensive survey of 1567. Indeed, there is little reason to believe that the percentage should have fallen, given the Suprema's marked preference for labradores.[108] Arguably, this preference may be ascribed to the widely held view that peasants were least likely of any social group to have Jewish blood and therefore least likely to contaminate the corps. A far more cogent explanation, however, lies in the sheer economic and political importance of the wealthiest segment of the peasantry—from which our familiares were drawn. With as much right to be called "rentiers" as those with fashionable titles, the wealthy peasants who formed the backbone of the familiatura were frequently ambitious and enterprising men of business.[109] Agustín Balaguer, for example, whose father and grandfather were both familiares, did a substantial trade in silk from the important Júcar Valley town of Carcagente.[110]

Even more important to the tribunal, however, was the fact that wealthy labradores held the key to political power in many of the villages and towns of an overwhelmingly rural kingdom. In a letter that was written by his parish priest at the time of his application, labrador Francisco Pascual Angles was called "regidor primo," while one of the witnesses in his genealogical investigation testified that he was not only one of the heaviest taxpayers in the town but also that he had charge of apportioning taxes among his fellow citizens.[111] Carlos Alabart, who applied from the tiny village of Flix in the diocese of Tortosa, came of a family that had long served as bailiffs and regidores and was able to obtain an impressive series of letters from local notables, including the bishop of Tortosa, in support of his candidacy.[112] One of the most extraordinary examples of the local authority of a labrador was the case of Luis Barrachina who applied from the tiny mountain village of Villamalur. Coming from a family that had long dominated both Villamalur and neighboring Jérica, Barrachina appeared personally—with a notary in tow—to welcome the tribunal's commissioner. Properly impressed by this visit from the local cacique, Ximénez referred to him respectfully as "his honor" in the letter he wrote to the tribunal relating this incident and proceeded to carry out his investigation by concentrating his interviews on witnesses who were related to the applicant.[113]

Politically dominant across much of the kingdom and in a good position to benefit from such economic opportunities as presented themselves during the seventeenth and eighteenth centuries, Valencia's wealthy peasants formed a steady and vital element among the familiares. In return, they received a position of honor and a certification of "purity of blood," which could help them gain higher social standing. Above all, by entering the corps, they had identified themselves with an institution that appeared as the staunchest defender of traditional Catholic Spain, the Spain that had afforded certain members of the peasantry an opportunity to prosper.

The tendency toward endogamy that was such a marked feature of Mediterranean society during the Old Regime was also quite marked among Valencia's familiares. Information contained in the genealogies of the familiares of Valencia reveals that 348 out of the 709 applicants, or 49 percent, had a relative or family member who had served or was serving the Holy Office. In fact, the connection with the corps of familiares was even closer, with fully 26.6 percent having a close family member in the corps, 33.2 percent having one or more relatives, and only 82 applicants, or 11.5 percent, having anyone from their family serving as an official.

The Suprema left the tribunal in little doubt about its preference for applicants from families that already had served in the corps. Sometimes the mere fact that someone from the family was serving would induce the Suprema to waive some particularly onerous and expensive requirement of the genealogical investigation.[114] In other cases, the Suprema would intervene directly to recommend someone to fill a vacant post on the grounds that it had been in the family. As a result, certain families had truly impressive traditions of service. José Barberán, the cavaller who applied in 1633 from the town of Onteniente, could boast a total of eleven familiares in his family in addition to a commissioner.[115] Francisco de Benavent brought his family's tradition of membership in the corps of familiares with him when he moved to Valencia city from Murcia. When he applied in 1641, he could boast of a total of thirteen familiares and four commissioners who had served or were presently serving the Holy Office in the districts of Murcia and Valencia.[116]

The tendency toward endogamy already prevalent among Valencia's familiares was further reinforced by marital choices. Familiares themselves would tend to choose women who came from families with traditions of service to the Holy Office. In the case of Jacinto José Agullo, this choice was made twice as both his first wife, María Cebria, and his second wife, Luisa Aracil, came from families with members serving as familiares, commissioners, and alguaciles.[117]

The inevitable result of this process of intermarriage was to promote the creation of a network of allied families who might dominate the familiatura of a certain region for several generations. In the village of Benisa, near the Costa Blanca south of Valencia city, matrimonial alliances between two sets of cousins brought together the Feliu and Gavila families, who together were to dominate the local familiatura throughout much of the late seventeenth and early eighteenth centuries.[118] Similarly, the marriage between Tomás de Borja, ciutadan and familiar of Játiva, and Anna Gil, of the nearby village of Canals, linked a family that had enjoyed familiaturas for several generations in that town with the Climent family, which had virtually dominated the corps in Canals through Anna Gil's mother, Anna Climent.[119]

One of the features of early modern Spanish society which earned the constant opprobrium of theologians, moralists, and reformers was the effort by the more ambitious and capable members of the popular classes to enter the ranks of the privileged orders. Of course, obtaining a license as a familiar was not the same as becoming a petty noble or ciutada, but with the cost of purchasing such status, never less than 250 lliures, it must have seemed like quite a bargain to pay for a genealogical investigation, the cost of which was 51 lliures. Once that investigation had been successfully concluded, one had achieved formal recognition of "purity of blood," which was the indispensable quality required for attaining noble rank. Such recognition would greatly assist in obtaining membership in one of Spain's prestigious military orders or in helping one's son enter a Colegio Mayor. More important, perhaps, in a land where nobility depended on the ability to successfully assert the right to the privileges accorded to those with noble status, the corps of familiares enjoyed privileges less than but not unlike that of the nobility. It could therefore provide a platform from which to successfully assert noble status in one of the innumerable hidalguía lawsuits by which such claims were frequently decided.

Among Valencia's familiares, this process of using membership in the corps to improve social standing becomes evident if we compare the relative rank of fathers and sons, especially for certain social categories. While the percentage of cavallers does not tend to change very much between the generations, social advancement can be seen in the marked increase in the percentage of ciutadans (11.2% of the fathers as opposed to 24.7% of the sons) and in the dramatic decline of artisans (13.3% to 2.4%) and labradores (49.2% to 43%).

Two of the men whose advancement to the rank of ciutada was clearly bound up with membership in the corps of familiares included Bautista Badía from the village of Sueca and Francisco Bone of Onteniente. The Badía family's involvement with the corps of familiares began when Bautista's father and uncle, who were both wealthy peasants, entered the corps during the early years of the seventeenth century. By the 1630s, his brother and his first cousin Miguel had joined the corps, while his sister had married another familiar from the village. Finally, in 1653, Bautista himself applied, having previously obtained the title of ciutada.[120] In the case of Bone, social advancement was connected not only with his own family's membership in the corps of familiares—both his father and uncle were labradores and familiares—but also with that of his wife, Jesualda Ruescas. Jesualda's father was a merchant, and her maternal grandmother was related to several familiares. In addition, her brother, Melchor Çapata, acted as alcalde of the Valencia tribunal during the visitation of 1566.[121]

Apart from the desire to gain social prestige, which was perhaps best expressed by a peasant from Traiguera who declared that he had applied to the corps to "embellish his person and house with the honorable title of minister of the Holy Office," there were several other personal motives that inspired men to seek the office.[122] The desire to demonstrate a fervent Roman Catholicism was certainly the motive for many who joined the corps in the sixteenth century. Even as late as 1747, a letter concerning Agustín Barrachina, a wealthy peasant from the huerta, attested to his piety and devotion to the church.[123] In many other cases, an application to the corps was simply the result of family tradition. In a society where the family was of overriding importance, and where so many young people were named after their fathers or uncles, we should not be surprised to find many applicants simply declaring that they wanted to "carry on the services rendered by my ancestors."[124]

But, there were other, more tangible advantages to membership in the corps. One of the most important and jealously guarded of the privileges enjoyed by familiares was an exemption from the obligation to quarter the king's soldiers. Although the Kingdom of Valencia was not the scene of major military activities until the War of Succession, and then only briefly, troops did move through the kingdom on their way to Catalonia or occasionally on bandit-hunting expeditions so that the privilege of exemption from quartering was a significant one. Moreover, the very fact that the kingdom was not a theater of war meant that there was less direct pressure from viceroys and quartermasters on the exemption. The privilege, therefore, was much easier to maintain than in a place like Galicia, for example, where the poverty of the region and the exigencies of war forced the crown to suspend it on more than one occasion.[125]

Even so, maintaining the familiares' blanket exemption from quartering was far from easy, especially as most of them were commoners and not normally exempt. A letter to the Suprema, written to obtain its support against the Count of Aytona's attempt to billet troops in familiares' homes in 1583, reveals that both the tribunal and the Suprema had intervened strenuously before Viceroy Vespasiano Gonzaga to prevent him from violating the exemption in the 1570s.[126] Vigilance and a willingness to react quickly when the privilege seemed threatened, however, meant that the exemption privilege was maintained virtually intact through much of the Old Regime.[127]

Less easy to maintain, especially in the critical years of the mid-seventeenth century, was a blanket exemption from military service. The fact that a specific article had to be inserted in the Concordia of 1568 prohibiting the inquisitors from defending familiares who refused to serve their turn guarding the coasts demonstrates that they had been able to lay claim to at least a partial exemption. But by the late 1630s, with the French invasion of Catalonia, Valencia was suddenly thrust closer to the front. As a result, the familiares' military exemptions were suspended, and they were told to be ready for military service whenever called on by the viceroy.[128] During the Catalan Revolt, moreover, when the count of Albalat was put in charge of recruiting soldiers from Valencia, even familiares who were awaiting trial on criminal charges were given inducements to serve.[129]

In the Concordia of 1568, inquisitors were specifically prohibited from attempting to secure tax exemptions for familiares, who were to pay their taxes like any ordinary pechero.[130] In spite of this prohibition, the tribunal and the Suprema were prepared to struggle to protect familiares from the increasing weight of fiscal obligations that bore down on all citizens of the monarchy during the seventeenth century.[131] Given the extent of the financial exigencies facing the monarchy, such efforts could have but limited success. All unsalaried officials, for example, had to pay the new tax on wine that was imposed to fund the donativo general of 1626.[132] In 1639, the Suprema thought it had won a significant victory when it was able to persuade the king to exclude unsalaried officials from the massive forced loan of that year; but pressure on a local level, from corregidores and other officials responsible for raising the money, forced their inclusion.[133] All officials, including inquisitors, were also forced to pay the media anata, a tax of one-half year's salary paid on appointment to office. For familiares and others who collected no salaries, the media anata became an additional fee paid when they received their office.[134] In 1646, however, Philip IV did grant the familiares a small but significant concession by exempting from all special war-related contributions the oldest familiar in each village, the two oldest in towns over 1,000 families, and the four oldest in places over 2,000 families.[135]

Once an individual was accepted into the corps of familiares, the Inquisition exercised jurisdiction over him and would try any civil or criminal offenses he had been accused of. Special statutes that granted certain groups exemption from ordinary royal courts and the right to be tried by judges belonging to that same corporation were an important feature of early modern Spain. The Council of War exercised jurisdiction over cases involving soldiers, ecclesias-

tics were protected by the ecclesiastical statute, and the Council of
the Military Orders was given the right to try criminal cases involving knights in the first instance.[136] Even Valencia's own military
order of Montesa maintained its own jail and tried criminal offenses
committed by the knights.[137]

Placed within the context of the patchwork of statutes comprising the Spanish legal system, the inquisitorial fuero could hardly be
described as unusual. And the actual degree of advantage conferred
by being subject to inquisitorial rather than royal jurisdiction
would depend on the exigencies of the moment and the degree of
competition between the two legal systems. Certainly, as far as
familiares living on seigneurial estates was concerned, the fuero
could provide them with a precious measure of protection from the
arbitrary and abusive behavior of their lords.[138] Indeed, at least in
some instances, use of the fuero may have worked to eliminate or
reduce already existing social inequalities, thereby creating the
basis for a measure of greater social justice. In one instance, Bartolomé de Oviedo, a candlemaker and familiar in Valencia city, went
to the home of cavaller Jaime Roca to collect for some wax that Roca
had purchased. This was not the first time that Oviedo had come to
collect, and almost as soon as the servant had shown him into the
house, Roca began to shout at him, calling him a "Jew," "swindler,"
and "dirty pig." Then, before Oviedo could say anything, Roca
picked up the chair he had been sitting on and hurled it at Oviedo,
injuring him slightly in the arm. In the criminal case that resulted,
the tribunal's decision was favorable to Oviedo, and Roca was
forced to pay his debt and sentenced to two months' exile from the
city.[139]

In the case of *Oviedo vs Roca*, the social distance between an
artisan and a petty noble had been narrowed substantially by the
fact that the former was a familiar and could appeal successfully to
his own jurisdiction to protect his rights. But the fuero could not be
used in such a way as to overtly challenge existing social hierar-
chies, no matter how just the cause. In 1583, Francisco Sanz was a
knight of the Order of Montesa and a commander of Benicarló, but
he was also a gangster whose band of armed thugs terrorized the
village and the surrounding area. Some of these men were captured and imprisoned by local citizens under the leadership of
Pedro Pellicer, a familiar and village councillor. Sanz came to the

village and demanded their immediate release, and, when Pellicer refused, he arranged for a high official of the order to come out from Montesa to brow-beat the villagers. When even this failed and three hundred villagers turned out with their arms to drive the official from the village, Sanz decided to appeal to the Holy Office. Denouncing Pellicer as a rebel, Sanz demanded that the tribunal punish him for persuading the villagers that he could "free them" from the legitimate authority of the order. Memories of the Germanía made any rural uprising, no matter how justified, the terror of Valencia's governing authorities, so the tribunal moved quickly, stripping Pellicer of his title and sentencing him to six years of exile from the village and a 50-ducat fine.[140]

One of the charges most often levied at the Valencia tribunal by viceroys and Audiencia judges alike was that it exercised its criminal jurisdiction in such a way as to shield familiares who had committed crimes from the rigors of royal justice.[141] Even though the source of this view should have invited a certain skepticism, it has been routinely endorsed by modern scholars. Lea, for example, when referring to the Concordia of 1568, which limited the use of the criminal fuero, implies that it was a dead letter as far as the tribunal was concerned, as "the tribunal was not accustomed to be bound by law."[142]

Lea's most glaring error of interpretation has to do with the Suprema's reply to a consulta sent to Philip IV by the Council of Aragon after the murder of Martín Sentis by four familiares in 1632. This consulta incorporated a memorial by the viceroy, the marquis de los Vélez, which repeats many of the traditional charges levied by the enemies of the criminal fuero. Peace and security were impossible to secure because inquisitors never punished familiares harshly enough to deter them from committing crimes. As a result, familiares were the leaders of the criminal gangs that plagued the kingdom, and there was no major crime in which they were not involved.[143] In replying to these charges, the Suprema first ordered the tribunal to work up statistics on the relative severity of the sentences handed down by the criminal chamber of the Audiencia so as to specifically compare the way in which the tribunal dealt with familiares who were guilty of criminal offenses and the way in which the Audiencia dealt with their accomplices. The Suprema then replied formally to the council's memorial denying the charges of excessive leniency and accusing the representatives of royal justice of manifest hostility to familiares. Determined as always to demonstrate the Inquisition's stubborn refusal to accept any limit on its authority, Lea informs us that the statistics gathered by the tribunal "were unsatisfactory" because they were not referred to in the Suprema's reply and that the reply itself was little more than a "passionate outburst, precluding all hope of amendment."[144] But any attempt to assess the relative leniency of the Inquisition in criminal cases involving its familiares must be placed within the context of the operations of the Spanish and Valencian criminal court system. Once this is done, the Suprema's reply and the figures that the tribunal developed for it appear to demonstrate not that the Inquisition was aberrant or unusual for a criminal court of the period but that its procedures and sentencing were, if anything, typical of Spanish criminal justice as a whole.

As the trials and spectacular public executions of bandits and criminals indicate, Valencian criminal justice could be extremely harsh. The marquis of Castelrodrigo (viceroy, 1690–1696), for example, had the executions of several important bandit leaders to his credit.[145] However, as diarist Ignacio Benavent lamented, "pardoning thieves is nothing new in Valencia."[146] Hampered by the constitutional privileges of the kingdom and by the lack of effective police forces, many viceroys found it more expedient to induce bandits to leave, by offering them a pardon in return for a period of military service abroad, than to attempt to hunt them down.[147] In a survey that they carried out on the Suprema's orders, Valencia's inquisitors found that the marquis de los Vélez, the very man who had been complaining so bitterly about the tribunal's excessive leniency, had recently issued twenty-seven pardons for all classes of offenders.[148] The death penalty, which was almost automatically decreed whenever a serious crime had been committed and the offender had fled, was not actually imposed very often. Between January and December 1679, the Audiencia condemned forty-three persons to death, but not one execution actually took place.[149]

As far as any comparison between the Audiencia and the tribunal is concerned, the strong competition for judicial business that characterized the Spanish court system would have made it difficult for one court to be noticeably harsher than another where jurisdictions overlapped. During the seventeenth century, the decline in the number of litigants and the increasing demands on official salaries (media anata, forced loans) sharpened this competition and made both tribunals eager to profit from criminal cases by reducing corporal punishment or imprisonment in favor of fines. The tribunal's increasing dependence on the income from fines in criminal cases is graphically revealed in its reply to one of the many demands for war contributions that were relayed to it by the Suprema. After deploring the fact that some officials were several months behind in their salaries, the inquisitors pointed out that the only way they were able to maintain the financial health of the tribunal was through fines from criminal cases. In the case of this most recent demand—the salaries of four soldiers serving six years—the tribunal declared that the money would only be forthcoming if the Suprema interceded with the king to resolve favorably several jurisdictional disputes in potentially lucrative criminal cases involving familiares.[150]

The military and financial crisis of the seventeenth century also made for delayed salary payments and fiscal difficulties at the top levels of the Spanish administration. In its search for additional revenues, the Suprema made quite a lucrative business out of selling reductions in sentences. The case of Jerónimo Torrelles, who was convicted of attempted murder in 1632, illustrates the way in which both the tribunal and the Suprema were able to profit from a single criminal prosecution. In 1633, after he had been imprisoned for thirteen months, the tribunal sentenced Torrelles to four years exile and a 200-ducat fine. A few months later, on application of Torrelles's attorney, the Suprema agreed to lift his exile in return for a consideration of 50 ducats.[151]

Since the financial pressures on the Bailía General, which paid a large percentage of the salaries of Audiencia judges, were also increasing, the Audiencia also tended to reduce or eliminate corporal punishments in favor of monetary fines. The tribunal was able to turn up several interesting examples of this in its survey of the sentences the Audiencia handed down when it tried the accomplices of familiares whom the tribunal had convicted of murder. Antonio Caballer, who was deeply implicated in the murder of Martín Sentis, was tried by the Audiencia and fined 500 ducats. Caballer's accomplice, familiar Jaime Blau, meanwhile, was tried by the tribunal and sentenced to both a prison term and a fine. Agustín Vidal was sentenced to two years' imprisonment by the Holy Office, but his three accomplices were only given a 70-lliures fine by the Audiencia.

The case of Jerónimo Pitart is a perfect example of the way the representatives of royal justice were willing to trade corporal punishments for heavier monetary fines at the very time they were denouncing the tribunal for excessive leniency in criminal prosecutions. Arrested in 1629 for his complicity in a murder, Pitart was first sentenced to a substantial term in the galleys and a 500-lliures fine. The Audiencia then revoked the galley sentence on appeal, and the viceroy subsequently pardoned Pitart altogether after increasing his fine to 500 ducats.[152]

If competition in the judicial marketplace and the financial difficulties experienced by the entire court system tended to place limits on the severity of judgments in criminal cases, the interest taken in criminal matters by high royal officials worked to prevent the tribunal from being excessively lenient. The struggle between Audiencia and tribunal most often expressed itself in the ubiquitous jurisdictional disputes (competencias) in which the failure of the senior inquisitor and the regent of the Audiencia to agree as to which tribunal should have jurisdiction over a particular case would mean that each would send their version to their respective royal councils. Final decisions would then be made by the king after consultation with councillor representatives. As decisions were taken at the very highest level, they were the subject of intense lobbying. If the tribunal came to be perceived as being excessively lenient, thereby imperiling the maintenance of public order in the kingdom, its entire jurisdiction over familiares would have been in jeopardy. It was this struggle for influence at a higher level that led the marquis de los Vélez to write and send his 1632 memorial to the Council of Aragon, which was then involved in numerous jurisdictional disputes with the Suprema over Valencian familiares.

The impact of this competitive atmosphere on limiting the tribunal's options can be seen quite clearly in the case of Vicente St. German. St. German, a cavaller and familiar in Valencia city, was tried and found guilty of murdering Pedro Jaime and, having fled, was sentenced to death by the Audiencia. Then, after negotiating with the tribunal, which was doubtless eager to have the "business" of such a wealthy criminal, St. German surrendered himself and was placed in the familiares' prison, after having been promised that he would be given only a moderate sentence of three years service in the presidio of Oran.[153]

During the course of his trial, St. German's attorney wrote to the Suprema on his client's behalf asking that he be released on bail. The Suprema then wrote to the tribunal asking for its opinion about this request. In its reply we catch a glimpse of the pressures the tribunal was operating under. Advising the Suprema that it would be best to refuse the request, the tribunal noted the "extreme interest with which the viceroy and the Audiencia are following this case because of their resentment over losing the jurisdictional dispute to the Holy Office." If they saw him let out on bail, the tribunal went on, they would very likely conclude that the "sentence against him would not be carried out and we believe that they would draw up complaints against this tribunal and our mode of procedure."[154] The Audiencia's extreme watchfulness, the possibility that a lenient sentence might provoke a complaint to the crown and weaken the Inquisition's case in future jurisdictional disputes, and greed on the part of both the Suprema and the tribunal all combined to dictate a final sentence far severer than the one St. German was promised when he surrendered. Instead of three years in the presidio of Oran, the tribunal sentenced him to eight years exile from the kingdom, the first six of which were to be served in the presidio of El Peñol, and a 200-lliures fine. Even St. German's appeal to the Suprema misfired since that body sentenced him to ten years forced service in Oran and increased his fine to 300 lliures.[155] Evidently, this sentence was considered at least as severe as any that would have been handed down by the Audiencia in similar cases as it was chosen by the tribunal to substantiate the Suprema's claim, in its response to the Council of Aragon's memorial, that promises of leniency given to familiares so as to induce them to choose the fuero were not always carried out.[156]

One of the most complicated and difficult tasks that the historian faces in discussing the familiares is to evaluate their role in the repression of heterodoxy. We have Lea's dictum that familiares were an obedient army of servants eager to carry out arrests on their own initiative and willing to act as "spies upon their neighbors."[157] More recently, Henry Kamen has challenged this view, denouncing the "exaggerated representation of familiares as a species of secret police" and pointing out that "the majority of denunciations . . . were made by ordinary people."[158] In fact, at least in the Valencia district, the familiar's role in the system of repression appears more complex than it is depicted in either of these interpretations. Spy and arresting officer the familiar certainly was, but more significantly, he could also act as a conduit for vital information that was brought to him because his connection with the Holy Office was known to his neighbors, while the oath that he had sworn and the fact that he was normally a person of some local prominence made him the informant of choice whenever the tribunal needed to find out about local conditions.[159]

If the familiar's role as spy is defined as active information gathering about a certain person or persons which might lead to their conviction on heresy charges, then we must conclude that this role was only occasional and limited primarily to the relatively closed ethnic and religious minorities (Jews, Moriscos, Protestants) whose activities were not likely to become common knowledge. In 1567, for example, after the tribunal had received a report about the existence of a Protestant cell in Teruel, a familiar was sent ahead of Inquisitor Jerónimo Manrique, who was making a visitation in the region, with orders to insinuate himself into the same group of French artisans whose utterances had formed the basis of the report. Earlier that year, the familiares of Teruel were ordered to gather information about a group of men who were suspected of spreading Protestant propaganda while traveling the region disguised as monks.[160]

But it was much less common for familiares to actively gather information than it was for them to relay information they had received through their contacts in the community. Thus, in 1603, when Pedro Linares, a familiar of Villajoyosa, came to the tribunal to report Jaime Lucas de Miguel for harboring Morisco renegades, he was merely passing along information he had been given by the village rector.[161]

In the case of Juan Sala, familiar of Pego, we can catch a glimpse of the activities of a true intermediary between the Holy Office and the community. As a longtime familiar and wealthy labrador, Sala was so well known to his neighbors that they would come to him with information about matters that they felt might pertain to the Inquisition. When Marcos Torres, a young laborer who boarded at Elizabeth Sastre's farm, was observed by Elizabeth's son Jaime having sexual relations with a mule, she went to inform Sala of the incident that very morning.[162] On another occasion, information about an attempt to locate buried treasure by supernatural means was given to Sala by two of the participants in the hope that he would act as their intermediary during the forthcoming visitation by Inquisitor licentiate Hermengildo Jiménez Navarro. With the approval of the two men, therefore, a few days after Jiménez Navarro arrived in the village, Sala came to testify about what he had heard, and the inquisitor then began taking testimony from those implicated in the plot.[163]

If the seemingly effortless accumulation of information by Sala appears to demonstrate the truth of Contreras's assertion that by 1560 familiares and commissioners formed "small and efficient cells" that allowed the Holy Office to enter easily into contact with the population while keeping a close watch over any heterodox tendencies, the way he actually handled the information should warn us against any such generalizations.[164] In the first place, both incidents had occurred from four to five years previously, but Sala made no effort to report them to a nearby commissioner or to inform the tribunal until an inquisitor actually came to Pego on a visitation. Even more remarkable, perhaps, is the fact that the plan to discover buried treasure had long been common knowledge in Pego—and, therefore, could hardly have been unknown to Sala— but he took no official notice of it until it came up directly in a casual conversation with Juan José Ribera, one of the men involved in the scheme, about the general subject of finding hidden treasure. Since this conversation took place in public only one month before the visitation began, the circumstances strongly suggest that it might never have been reported by Sala at all if an inquisitor had not come to the village in person. After all, schemes to locate buried treasure were extremely common in cash-starved rural Valencia during the late seventeenth century, and they involved not only respectable, even distinguished citizens but close relatives of familiares.[165]

As Carlo Ginzburg has already pointed out, the intermediary always plays an active role that "can take different forms, depending on his own social position, attitude towards the culture of his social group, etc." Clearly, an intermediary like the familiar can act entirely in the interest of the elite institution he represents on a local level or he can "attenuate the cultural contents which he transmits."[166]

The fact that it took the tribunal four years to learn about the bestiality incident even though Sala had heard of it the morning after it happened hardly reveals him to be an "efficient" link between the tribunal and the local community. That Ribera could speak openly with Sala about his experiences as a treasure hunter reveals either a complete lack of awareness of Sala's role as familiar or, what is more likely, a feeling that Sala would not report him to the Holy Office because their views on searching for treasure were essentially similar. If an intermediary may be compared to a filter, then, as Ginzburg has stated, "there are no neutral filters."[167] As the example of Sala reveals, the extent and rapidity of the transmission of information by a familiar would depend very much on his own attitudes toward the type of information and the individuals concerned. In the case of ethnic minorities (Moriscos, conversos), information might be transmitted rapidly and without scruple, but in the case of a neighbor and fellow Old Christian like Ribera, the information might be transmitted only under certain special circumstances—like an upcoming visitation—or not at all.

Fortunately for the Holy Office, it did not have to rely exclusively on its familiares for information about what was going on in local communities. Parish priests like Gabriel Riutort of Castell des Castells, who wrote to Inquisitor Jiménez Navarro to report that one of his parishioners had declared that hell did not exist, had a definite interest in maintaining orthodoxy and enforcing the provisions of the Council of Trent regarding respect for sacraments. The case of Barbara Avargues, an ailing spinster who wrote to the inquisitor from Calpe to inform him that Jacinto Balaguer, a labrador of her village, had declared that purgatory was a myth appears to demonstrate the truth of Kamen's dictum that "there was no need to rely on a secret police system because the population as a whole had been taught to recognize the enemy within the gates."[168]

Another and perhaps less ambiguous side of the familiar's role as informant was the tribunal's reliance on him for general information on local conditions. This reliance no doubt reflected the view that his loyalty to the Holy Office would to some degree transcend self-interest and produce more reliable information than any that could be obtained from an ordinary citizen. Thus, in 1575, at a time of increasing concern about possible attempts by Protestants to smuggle quantities of heretical books into Spain, the tribunal called on Miguel Palao, a familiar in Denia, to testify about the activities of the French and British sailors in that port and about what measures could be used to exert greater control over cargoes.[169] Before the expulsion of the Moriscos, familiares living in heavily Morisco areas were the preferred informants when the inquisitors wished to learn about conditions in those places.[170]

Familiares were also used rather extensively to carry out arrests and to convey prisoners to the cells of the Inquisition when they were arrested outside Valencia city. Most often these arrests were carried out at the request of commissioners or officials of the tribunal. As Alcalde Francisco de Hermosa explained when he was asked about this practice during the visitation of 1566, he preferred to use familiares to make arrests even in Valencia city because he was so well known that suspects easily became aware of his approach, while familiares could do the job "con menos escandalo y con mas secreto."[171] During the tribunal's early years, moreover, the frequent use of familiares to carry out arrests of suspected Judaizers had the effect of actively involving them in the tribunal's anti-Semitic campaign. In hearings held in 1553, familiar Juan Pérez de Pandilla recalled that his house stood on the same street as the famous synagogue that had been run secretly by the Vives family and that in 1501, when the tribunal decided to arrest those suspected of attending services, the familiares who carried out the arrests were hidden in his house.[172]

Sometimes carrying out arrests could prove to be extremely dangerous. This was especially true when the tribunal directed most of its activity against the Moriscos, who were armed and could count on a certain amount of protection from their lords. In 1599, several familiares sent by the tribunal to arrest certain Moriscos in the neighborhood of Albarracín were met with armed resistance that had been encouraged by the lord of the village, the count of Fuentes.[173]

At times, familiares acted quite independently, without even waiting for permission from a commissioner or without receiving direct orders from the tribunal. When Francisco Pisa, a merchant and familiar of Grau, received a report from a local citizen who had seen two men engaged in homosexual activity on a nearby beach, he immediately arrested one of the men and had him placed in the local jail. He then went to Valencia to report to the tribunal, which ordered him to bring in the culprit.[174] Pisa's alacrity in responding to a report of sodomy should not be misconstrued. His response no doubt reinforced the tribunal's authority in the town, but it is legitimate to wonder if he would have been quite so eager if the Inquisition's willingness to punish sodomites had not been so perfectly in accordance with communal rejection of homosexual behavior. In moving quickly to arrest a suspected sodomite, Pisa was acting as an official of the Holy Office but equally as a leading member of the community engaged in upholding and enforcing its sexual norms.

Since the role played by familiares in maintaining the Inquisition's network of control was ambiguous at best, we may well ask ourselves why it was necessary for the tribunal to maintain such a large number of familiares even when its activity had substantially declined after the expulsion of the Moriscos. One obvious answer to this question has been alluded to in our earlier discussion of the inquisitorial fuero: familiares were a lucrative source of fines and legal fees.[175] Moreover, the genealogical investigation itself generated considerable fee income that helped support the entire infrastructure of the tribunal, from the secretaries who would usually carry out at least part of it to local commissioners and notaries who would be used in more remote areas. The Suprema also saw that it had some claim to the financial support of the familiares since they were, at least nominally, officials of the Holy Office. Just as the crown levied special taxes on officeholders (media anata), the Suprema required each familiar to contribute to the fabricá de Sevilla (funds earmarked for the Seville tribunal) as part of the costs of his genealogical investigation.[176] In good years, when there were a fair number of applicants, revenues from this source could be substantial. On December 9, 1631, the tribunal reported to the Suprema that between November 18, 1627, and September 16, 1632, the depositario de pretendientes had collected 8,492 reales for this account.[177]

Even more important than their financial contribution, however, was the political support that familiares could provide. The increasingly aristocratic composition of the corps from the early years of the seventeenth century and the insaculación of many of its members meant that the familiares were a far more socially prominent and politically influential group than they had been in the mid-sixteenth century. Faced with the increasing hostility of the Audiencia and the suspicious attitudes of several seventeenth-century viceroys, not to mention strained relations with the canons of the kingdom's collegiate churches and cathedrals, it became vitally necessary for the tribunal to mobilize this support. As the Suprema itself declared in a letter advising the tribunal to turn out all the caballeros who were familiares to escort the officials of the court when they were called on to march in public processions, "such measures are all the more valuable now when the other tribunals are attempting to reduce your authority in every possible way."[178]

Within Valencia city, the most visible way of capitalizing on this political support was through the organization of a chapter of the San Pedro Mártir confraternity. Named for Saint Peter, Martyr, a Dominican inquisitor who was murdered by Cathars in 1252, chapters of the confraternity eventually spread throughout the Spanish tribunals.[179] The ordinances of the Valencian chapter, which were drawn up in 1610, reveal an organization that combined ceremonial, religious, and charitable functions. Theoretically open to all familiares in the district, as each of them paid a fee to the confraternity on receipt of their titles, meetings were comprised almost entirely of familiares from Valencia city and its immediate environs. For the purpose of electing officers, the confraternity was divided into two groups, cavallers and ciutadans, with the prior always belonging to the cavallers and the other posts being equally divided between the two. The organization also had a receiver whose responsibility it was to collect and disburse the fee that the confraternity received from each applicant to the corps for the expenses of the confraternity.[180] Aside from the Procession of the Faith, the most important event that the members of the confraternity participated in was the annual ceremony commemorating the death of their patron saint. Marching in procession behind the inquisitors and officials, the familiares must have been an impressive sight in their special habits and the crosses they wore as insignia of Saint Dominic.[181]

The remaining ordinances reveal that the members of the familiares' confraternity had many of the same concerns as other devout individuals who founded such organizations in the sixteenth and seventeenth centuries. The confraternity had a chapter house with a chapel where the special feast of the Cruz Nueva was to be held and where masses were to be said for the souls of the deceased. Members were to accompany the body of a deceased familiar to its final resting place, and the confraternity was expected to provide a payment of 10 lliures out of its treasury to aid members who found themselves in financial difficulties. By the middle of the eighteenth century, these ordinances had fallen into desuetude, but in 1749, new ones were drawn up by an energetic military officer, José Manrique de la Romana, familiar and colonel of Dragoons, in collaboration with the inquisitors.[182]

By marching with the inquisitors and officials in public processions, the confraternity demonstrated that the tribunal enjoyed the open and explicit support of numerous influential members of Valencia's political elite. But the confraternity had even more direct ways of making its presence felt on the side of the tribunal when it was engaged in a struggle with the Audiencia or another competing agency of government. Since the prestige of the tribunal was closely linked to its ability to defend the fuero and the other privileges of the familiares, the confraternity would occasionally send one of its more distinguished members to court at its own expense to lobby in favor of the tribunal. In 1630, for example, Alexandre Vidal de Blanes, the prior of the confraternity, received permission from the inquisitors to send an ambassador to court to protest certain recent actions by the Audiencia constables. Luis Sorell, a knight of Calatrava, was eventually sent, and the Suprema ordered the tribunal to furnish him with the information that he needed to make his embassy more successful.[183] An analysis of the accounts of the confraternity reveals that it, too, provided a steady source of extra funds for the inquisitors and certain officials. The inquisitors, for example, received 300 reales for attending the feasts of San Pedro Mártir and Cruz Nueva, while the tribunal's nuncio received 200 reales for convening the familiares when the confraternity held a meeting.[184]

Outside of Valencia city, where the tribunal encountered serious difficulties with the canons' council, which continued to resent the fact that the Inquisition enjoyed the fruits of one of their benefices, with city councils eager to seize any opportunity to enhance their prestige, and with bishops for whom the coming of the Inquisition represented a loss of authority, it used the visitation as a way of mobilizing the political support of its familiares. These "political visitations," which really came into their own in the first half of the seventeenth century, had as their ostensible purpose the repression of religious and moral deviance, but their extremely limited geographic range and the small number of cases that they actually turned up versus the time and energy that the visiting inquisitor spent in ceremonial and political activities clearly indicates their real purpose. At the same time, the political visitation was anything but a one-way street. Touring the district's larger towns and organizing bodies of familiares to march in the processions that were such a conspicuous part of every visitation were an excellent way of demonstrating the continued political importance of the Holy Office. But the local familiares also benefited from the presence of the inquisitor. His visitation, with its religious processions and special church services, was an opportunity for them to demonstrate their link with an important national institution, while the special role they played in ceremonies that involved the entire local power elite could hardly fail to enhance their social prestige and political importance.

Perhaps the best example of this reciprocity is provided by the visitation of Inquisitor Ambrosio Roche carried out in 1632. Gandía, Denia, Játiva, and Alcira were the principal stopping places along his route, which was the most frequently visited part of the district during the seventeenth century. These towns, along with Oliva and Carcagente where the inquisitor stopped briefly to rest and obtain a fresh team, were in the heart of the heaviest concentration of familiares outside the immediate area of Valencia city itself. In this region, it was not likely that Inquisitor Roche would find, as he did on his visit to the northern part of the district in 1645, towns refusing to pay the costs of his lodging and transportation.[185] However, even here, where familiares were numerous and politically influential, towns were jealous of their authority, and city councils would seize every opportunity to gain advantage by suddenly refusing to participate fully in certain ceremonies or by insisting on styles of address or marks of courtesy that had not been customary

in the past. During the 1632 visitation, Roche experienced difficulties in Alcira, where the city council at first refused to march in the
procession that preceded the reading of the Edict of Faith.[186] Such
problems made it all the more important for the visiting inquisitor
to surround himself with a large following of familiares, since this
would indicate that the Holy Office still enjoyed significant local
support. To ensure the presence of as large a number of familiares
as possible for the twin processions of the Edict and Anathema,
Roche sent letters ordering all the familiares of the area to assemble
in front of his lodgings before the procession of the Edict.[187] But
the visitation was so popular among the region's familiares that
orders were unnecessary.

On the outskirts of Denia, for example, Roche was met by the
local commissioner, Francisco Rico, the notary, Antonio Mulet, and
a large number of familiares drawn from the entire area around the
city. After effusive greetings, commissioner and notary entered
Roche's coach, while the familiares, their servants, and relations
ranged themselves behind it and followed it into the city, firing their
muskets all the way. This boisterous welcome was atypical, but the
inquisitor was usually met outside town by a delegation that would
include the commissioner and one or more priests as well as a delegation of familiares.[188] In Denia, where six out of the eight city officials
were either familiares themselves or related to a familiar, Roche had
no difficulty in obtaining the eager participation of the city council in
the processions of the Edict and the Anathema.[189]

A large and impressive retinue of familiares was a signal to jealous city councils and to the public at large that the Holy Office had
the political support and the manpower to maintain a strong presence in a given area, while the familiares themselves were prepared to provide lodgings and even transportation to a visiting
inquisitor. In Játiva, Roche stayed in the home of Jerónimo Sanz de
la Llosa, a familiar and knight of Calatrava. On his visit to the
northern part of the district in 1645, the familiares of San Mateo
offered to pay the costs of transporting him to his next destination
after the city had reneged on its promise to pay.[190]

At the same time, local familiares derived considerable benefits
from the visitation. Obviously, their social prestige would be en-
hanced by close association with a high royal official whose visit was
a rare event. Not only did they play a leading role in the proces-

sions of the Edict and Anathema but they were given a special place in church during the ceremonies that marked the reading of these two documents. Local clergy would sometimes protest these arrangements, and, when he was visiting Segorbe in 1649, Roche intervened to prevent the cabildo of the cathedral from removing the bench that had been set up for familiares in the principal chapel.[191] Furthermore, group participation by all the familiares in ceremonies where they rubbed shoulders with the social and political elite of the town tended to obliterate the social distinctions within the group, elevating the labrador and merchant to the level of the cavaller and ciutadà.

The exchange of political and material support for group recognition and social prestige that characterized the relationship between the inquisitor on visitation and local familiares was never more evident than during Roche's sojourn in Játiva from April 22 to May 12, 1632. Met outside the city by a delegation led by Francisco Milán de Aragón, familiar and royal governor of the town, and including the commissioner and several leading familiares, Roche was brought back into the city to lodgings at the home of Jerónimo Sanz de la Llosa.[192] Two familiares also accompanied secretary Julián de Palomares when he went to the city council to ask that it march in the procession of the Edict. (The city council ultimately refused this request, but since three out of the five principal officials were familiares, the city was quite well represented.)

In return for this hospitality and support, Inquisitor Roche was only too pleased to accept an invitation from Milán de Aragón to attend the ceremonies marking the festival of San Pedro Mártir. It is in the phrase that he used to accept this invitation that Roche unconsciously reveals the radical change that had taken place in the underlying purpose of the visitation to the district. He declared that he would attend the festival "with the greatest pleasure, since apart from carrying out a visitation I have come to this city to make myself useful to all those who wish to employ me."[193] As very few actual prosecutions resulted from this or from any other seventeenth-century visitation, it may be inferred that the search for heresy had become little more than window dressing for the real (political) purpose of the visitation.[194]

Apart from its familiares, the Valencia tribunal enjoyed the services of a network of notaries and commissioners (fig. 3). In the

Figure 3. Distribution of Commissioners and Notaries Sixteenth to
              Nineteenth Centuries

Valencia district, the commissioner replaced the obnoxious lieutenant inquisitors whose activities had given rise to so many excesses.[195] During much of the first half of the sixteenth century, these subtribunals were established in every major town beginning about thirty miles from Valencia, but the Concordia of 1568 substituted commissioners and allowed them to be appointed only in the principal towns of Tortosa, Segorbe, Teruel, Gandía, Castellón de la Plana, Denia, Játiva, and Valencia city itself. In fact, this regulation was bent to accommodate certain individuals, and the record reveals commissioners from Onteniente, Mora, Morella, and Jijona, none of which had been included in the original group.[196] Unlike the lieutenant inquisitors, commissioners were not permitted to try cases themselves but merely to collect information and send it back to the tribunal. They could not even arrest a suspect unless they felt that he was likely to flee.[197] Commissioners also carried out genealogical investigations, made arrangements to lodge inquisitors making a visitation in their locality, and were used to interview suspects and administer reprimands in cases of lesser importance. Given the fact that commissioners were primarily from towns with cathedrals or collegiate churches, it is not surprising to find that more than 63 percent of my sample were provosts, canons, or benefice holders in these institutions.[198] In spite of their relatively exalted rank in the ecclesiastical hierarchy, however, the curriculum vitae of applicants reveal them to be the products of an educational system for priests that had long since lapsed into a dull and plodding conformity. José Monterde de Azpeytia, for example, who was a canon in the collegiate church of Mora just outside Teruel, had spent his entire educational career, from grammar school to monastic college in Teruel, only leaving that city to take up residence in Mora where he served for seventeen years before applying for the post of commissioner in the Teruel district.[199]

Since commissioners were confined to relatively few towns outside of Valencia city, it became necessary for the tribunal to recruit ecclesiastical notaries to supplement their activities. Reflecting, perhaps, the new importance of the parish priests in the post-Tridentine era and the Inquisition's desire to align itself more closely with that group even while it attempted its moral regeneration, almost 67 percent of the district's notaries were either parish priests or benefice holders in parish churches or rectories. The parish clergy of Valencia city were particularly well represented, especially those from the wealthier parishes in the center.[200]

Although they were not empowered to carry out arrests, in many other respects the powers and responsibilities of notaries and commissioners overlapped. Where a commissioner was unavailable, notaries would step in to make the arrangements for lodging a visiting inquisitor. Furthermore, notaries, like commissioners, were used to take testimony from witnesses and suspects. Some of these men proved to be as effective and zealous as any inquisitor. During the 1672 visitation, for example, Inquisitor Hermenigildo Jiménez Navarro ordered the inquisitorial notary in Gandía, Francisco Tosca, to follow up on information that had come to him regarding an attempt to find treasure using magic spells and other superstitious means. Tosca not only followed the instructions that he had received but exceeded them as skillful examination of the original two suspects turned up more accomplices, whom he proceeded to interview on his own initiative.[201]

Apart from carrying out these important functions, notaries and commissioners occupied a special place in the network of control. Like the familiares, commissioners and notaries were prominent and visible representatives of the Holy Office so they were likely to be the recipients of information that would lead to cases being formulated by the tribunal. In one example, the commissioner of Teruel received information from several weavers about certain statements of a Protestant character that were made by a certain Anton Gache. The commissioner acted quickly to carry out the arrest and did the initial interrogations of witnesses.[202] But it was precisely in their capacity as clergy that they were uniquely valuable to the tribunal, not only because of the information that they received from their flock but because of their ties to the ecclesiastical network itself. As in any other closed professional group, priests gossip with other priests and tend to have an intense interest in the behavior of their colleagues. It was this interest that led licentiate Pedro Mártir Mateo, one of the tribunal's Valencian notaries, to denounce the activities of Fray Vicente Oriente, a Franciscan whose public ecstasies and relationship with beata Juana Asensio were arousing considerable comment in the city.[203] In another instance, the commissioner of Tortosa, Jerónimo Terca, heard about the flagrant homosexual activities of Melchor Armengol, rector of the tiny village of Bot, from the rector of the neighboring village of Gandesa. After writing the tribunal for instructions, Terca was authorized to examine witnesses and accomplices and accumulate evidence to be used by the tribunal when it formulated its case.[204]

In the light of the preceding discussion of family ties among the familiares of the district and the strong tendency toward endogamy throughout the Spanish bureaucracy, it is not surprising to find that, very frequently, notaries, commissioners, and familiares came from the same or related families. Among the commissioners, six out of the ten in my sample had at least one member of his immediate family in the corps. This group included such men as Dr. Juan Fababuix, a canon in the cathedral of Segorbe who applied to become a commissioner in 1616. At the time of his application, his father, Francisco, was serving as familiar in Vivel where both his paternal and maternal grandfathers and his uncle on his mother's side had served before him.[205]

The relationship is even clearer and more direct in the case of the notaries. Here, a comparison of the overall figures for the social origins of parents suggests the possibility of close family relationships as over 60 percent of both the familiares and notaries were drawn from among artisans and labradores. This indication of broadly similar social origins is strengthened by the fact that notaries and familiares tended to be concentrated in the same geographic areas, with some 57.6 percent of the notaries drawn from the rich silk-producing towns stretching from Alcoy to Almusafes. Not surprisingly, therefore, 29 out of my sample of 55 notaries had one or more familiares in their immediate family, while 40, or 71.7 percent, had one or more among their relatives. An outstanding example of a notary related to a number of families closely tied to the corps of familiares was Mosén Bernardo Calduch, a benefice holder in the tiny village of Chert located deep in the Maestrazgo. Calduch's father and paternal grandfather both served as familiares in Chert, and he was related to no fewer than eight other individuals whose families dominated the corps in Chert and in the nearby villages of Salsadella, Mas des Estellers, and Traiguera.[206] In certain cases, like that of Dr. Francisco Alexandre who applied from Rusafa in 1752, family traditions of service in the corps of familiares provided the inspiration for service as a notary. In his letter of application, Alexandre made a point of declaring that he was applying in order to "emulate" his father and several relatives who had served the Holy Office as familiares from Rusafa.[207]

If, as Kamen has insisted, those who opposed the Spanish Inquisition were a tiny minority of intellectuals and conversos while the Holy Office was overwhelmingly popular with Spaniards of all classes, it was not only because "it helped to institutionalize the prejudices and attitudes that had previously been commonplace in society."[208] By recruiting a large corps of unpaid officials, the Inquisition was able to associate itself with representatives of a broad cross section of Valencian society. The corps of familiares, in particular, was unique among Spain's honorable corporations in containing a majority drawn from the nonprivileged. As a result, an important segment of the population were not merely passive observers of an institution whose aim was to protect and enhance Spanish Catholicism but were participants in its operations and beneficiaries of the social prestige it could bestow.

At the same time as the Valencia tribunal began to lose ground in its struggle with other powerful local institutions, the large and influential corps of familiares, notaries, and commissioners bolstered its political power by providing it with a network of supporters in the most important towns and villages of the district. In this way, a body of men originally formed to combat a perceived threat from religious heresy began to resemble more and more the gangs, clientage networks, or mafiosi that flourished so remarkably in seventeenth-century Valencia.

V

The Converted Jews: From Persecution to Assimilation

The origins of the converted Jews, or conversos, who provided the Valencian Inquisition with 91.6 percent of its victims during the period 1484–1530 may be traced to the great series of pogroms that swept over Spain during the summer of 1391. Everywhere, Jewish communities were attacked and the Jews massacred or forced to convert. In Valencia city, the pogrom began on July 9 when a group of young men forced their way into the Jewish quarter. When the Jews, now thoroughly alarmed, shut the gates to prevent others from entering, the Christians trapped inside cried for help and a mob composed primarily of artisans, vagabonds, and soldiers stormed the ghetto. Amid scenes of religious exaltation, a number of Jews were killed, and many others took refuge in the churches and accepted conversion.[1] The same scenes were repeated, on a smaller scale, when the pogroms spread to Alcira, Játiva, Sagunto, and other places.[2] Deteriorating economic and political conditions in both Castile and Aragon, popular hatred of the Jews for their role as tax farmers and moneylenders, and the vicious attacks launched against them by fanatical anti-Semites like Ferrant Martínez, the archdeacon of Ecija, had combined to severely disrupt the centuries-old pattern of Jewish life in Spain. In spite of official statements deploring the rioting and forced conversions and the protection extended to the remaining Jews by the kings of Aragon and Castile, restoration of the Jewish communities to their former size and prosperity had become impossible.[3]

Faced with growing discrimination and legally barred from holding offices in the towns or in the royal administration, most Jews
found their economic opportunities limited and worked as artisans,
peddlers, and shopkeepers. As a result, the Jewish community
continued to decline, and there was a slow but steady stream of
conversions to Christianity.

The legal and social disabilities that led to the decline of Spanish
Jewry in the fifteenth century did not affect the conversos. During
the first decades of the fifteenth century, there appear to have been
few obstacles to the assimilation of converted Jews into Spanish
society, and even such religious leaders as San Vicente Ferrer, who
dedicated himself to converting the Jews of Aragon, harshly criticized those Christians who refused to accept the converts because
of their Jewish origins.[4] Hard work, financial acumen, and the
traditional role of persons of Jewish origin in finance and revenue
collection made it possible for many conversos to obtain official
positions in the royal administration, enter the church, and join
city councils.[5]

It was in Castile, where the conversos' rapid rise to power on
municipal councils coincided with the intensification of the struggle between the disenfranchised popular classes and the municipal oligarchy, that a virulent form of popular anti-Semitism
emerged. Spurred by the economic distress of the years 1447–
1449 and 1465–1473, this popular hatred culminated in a violent
series of riots reminiscent of the pogroms of 1391, directed not
against the Jews but against the conversos.[6] At the same time, the
entire basis for the conversos' integration into Spanish life was
being called into question. For confirmed anti-Semites like Pero
Sarmiento, the leader of Toledo's violent anticonverso rebellion of
1449, the conversos had continued practicing Judaism in spite of
their nominal conversion. Since they were really Jews masquerad-
ing as Christians, they had no right to occupy municipal offices in
the city of Toledo, offices from which it was alleged they had
already done incalculable damage to the city and its Old Christian
inhabitants.[7] For the chronicler and parish priest of Los Palacios,
Andrés Bernáldez, there was no such thing as a sincere convert.
The conversos consisted of two groups only: those who had left
Spain to practice Judaism openly and those who had remained to
become crypto-Jews.[8]

The conversos' response to this polemic was to lay stress on the traditional church position, which was reiterated by Pope Nicolas V in a Bull of September 24, 1449, that baptism makes all men Christian regardless of their origins "siue Judaei, siue Gentiles."[9] For the converso general of the order of Saint Jerome, Alonso de Oropesa, the conversos' sincerity could not be doubted, and attempts by Old Christians to place the conversos in a separate category were tantamount to "dividing the body of Christ."[10]

It was this controversy over the sincerity of the converted that spawned the first proposals for the establishment of a Spanish national Inquisition, and that very same controversy continues to affect the way in which historians view the operations of the Holy Office during the first phase of its activity. But how Jewish were the conversos? It is on this issue that any moral and religious justification for inquisitorial action against them must rest. If the vast majority of the conversos were secret Jews, then, even though we might criticize the Inquisition's procedures, it would be difficult to deny some moral basis for its actions given the prevailing attitudes toward religious heresy. However, if the conversos can be considered largely Catholic in terms of their religious beliefs and practices, then the Inquisition could be justly condemned for persecuting them for reasons of racial hatred, greed, or political expediency. Historians have been deeply divided over this issue. Some, like I. F. Baer or, more recently, Haim Beinart, have insisted on the essential Jewishness of the conversos. For Beinart, "the conversos were, and remained, Jews at heart, and their Judaism was expressed in their way of life and their outlook."[11] Virtually the opposite position is held by Benzion Netanyahu, who insists that "the overwhelming majority of the Marranos at the time of the establishment of the Inquisition were not Jews but "detached from Judaism, or rather, to put it more clearly, Christians."[12] Yet a third position is represented by Caro Baroja, who holds that some of the conversos formed a distinct religious tendency neither Jewish nor Christian.[13]

Analysis of the cases of Judaizers brought before the Valencia tribunal, however, reveals a complicated picture that does not seem to entirely fit any of these views. When the Inquisition began its operations in the district during the mid-1480s, the conversos appear to have been divided into three broad groups: those who did everything possible to maintain a Judaic style of life and were

Jewish in all but name, those who believed in and practiced both Judaism and Catholicism simultaneously, and those who believed themselves to be fervent Catholics. Representatives of all three tendencies fell into the Inquisition's clutches because even in the case of persons in the latter category, the slightest lapse of memory regarding the performance of a Judaic ceremony or mitzvah or the failure to mention even one person who was present during the performance of such a ceremony in a confession made during a period of grace could, and often did, result in serious trouble with the Holy Office.

The rich and devout Jewish life-style led by Valencian notary Pedro Alfonso and his family attests to the continued strength of Judaism among the conversos long after they had been all but written off by rabbinical observers in both Spain and North Africa. Alfonso and his family observed the Sabbath rigorously and regularly. On Friday evening, candles were lit and food was prepared to be consumed cold on the Sabbath when no work of any kind could be performed. Alfonso practiced Jewish ritual slaughter, and the family observed the kosher dietary rules by rigorously refraining from eating pork or other forbidden items. All the major Jewish Holy Days were celebrated, including Yom Kippur (when the family would be joined by other devout conversos), Passover, and Succoth, when Alfonso would build the ritual Succoth hut with his own hands. Apart from the performance of Jewish mitzvah, Alfonso's immersion in Jewish culture is demonstrated by his ability to speak and read Hebrew. This was so widely known that when a Jew who was carrying a Hebrew book was asked who in Valencia could read it, he answered, Pedro Alfonso. Witnesses also testified that Alfonso and his wife spoke Hebrew in the home.

Alfonso's devotion to Judaism was only equaled by his disdain for Catholicism. According to former servants and other witnesses, he did not maintain any images of Christ or the saints before which prayers could be said. He regularly ate meat during Catholic fast days and took great pains to avoid going to mass. He had also been heard to denounce Christians as idolators because belief in the Trinity implied belief in three separate gods. Finally, Alfonso made no secret of his belief that Judaism was superior to Christianity and frequently declared publicly that he "would rather be a Jew than a Christian."[14]

Frequently, the flame of Jewish belief among the conversos was kept alive by women. In fact, Judaizing was one of the few offenses tried by the Valencia tribunal in which there was a rough equality between the sexes. One of these devout women was Brianda Besant of Teruel. Like Alfonso, Besant was assiduous in observing the Sabbath and the Jewish High Holy Days. In addition, she would pray in Hebrew several times each day and attend services in Teruel's synagogue each Friday evening and twice on Saturday. Besant was also recognized as a leader of Teruel's converso community and would frequently hold services in her own home. On High Holy Days when it was too dangerous to go to the synagogue, she and several other devout conversos would go to a house near the Jewish quarter from where they could hear the Jews pray and sing.

Her rejection of Christianity was complete. She had frequently declared that Christians were her enemies and denounced them as idol worshipers and "believers in many gods instead of one only." She specifically denied the Trinity and was accused of refusing to learn any Christian prayers until after the Inquisition had commenced operations in the city.[15]

Devoutly Jewish conversos maintained a close relationship with the local Jewish community, and their financial support for Jewish worship, charitable contributions, and purchases helped to sustain those communities economically in the face of the growing pressure against them. Both Besant and Alfonso contributed money and oil to the synagogue, while Besant even paid for a reserved seat there so that she could attend prayers on the High Holy Days. Alfonso also gave charity to poor Jews and gave Jews gifts of oil so that they would pray for him when he fell ill. A desire to maintain ritual purity in their lives and religious observances also led these conversos to make certain purchases from Jewish merchants. Jewish butchers were popular as a source of meat that had been ritually slaughtered, and if the converso wanted to slaughter in his own yard, he would frequently hire a Jew to do it.[16] Sometimes Sabbath food was obtained ready cooked from the ghetto, and Besant, Alfonso, and other devout conversos would send flour to the ghetto so that Jewish bakers could bake matzohs for Passover. Alfonso even went so far as to purchase most of his wine from a Jewish-owned tavern. For such devout converted Jews, the existence of a viable and functioning Jewish community close at hand was more than just a source of ritually purified products. They felt themselves to be a part of that community and were considerably less "detached" from it than those Jewish intellectuals of the thirteenth and fourteenth centuries whose rationalism and epicureanism had been condemned by orthodox rabbis long before any large number of Jews had converted. On occasion, the rigid orthodoxy of these conversos exceeded that of the Jews themselves. José Alfara, a Jew from Valladolid who was a witness in the trial of Enrique Fuster, testified that one day when he was visiting Fuster in Valencia, he expressed a desire to witness a Christian procession in honor of the Virgin Mary which was about to take place. Both Enrique and his son Adrian were horrified at the suggestion and refused, declaring that it would be a sin and that the Bible prohibited idol worship.[17]

Enrique and Adrian Fuster, Pedro Alfonso, Brianda Besant, and her husband, Luis de Santangel, were all executed during the period when the Valencia tribunal devoted most of its attention to the converted Jews. There can be little doubt that they, along with hundreds of others like them, "perished at the stake as martyrs to their faith" and were the victims of a religion that they neither liked nor understood.[18]

The term *martyr* cannot, however, be applied to all conversos tried by the Spanish Inquisition. Those within the ranks of the conversos who saw nothing incompatible in believing in both Judaism and Catholicism at the same time also suffered. Sincere believers in the promise of salvation made by both religions, their tragedy was the tragedy of people who assume a degree of religious toleration in an age of religious totalitarianism.

Pedro Besant, Brianda's brother, had been brought up in a profoundly Jewish environment, but he, unlike his sister, had taken pains to learn Christian prayers and observances. At the same time, he was intensely curious about Judaism and had numerous conversations about it with local Jews. One of these, a certain Zacarias, had written down some of the psalms of David for him. The result, as he declared in his 1486 confession, was that during the period in which he confessed engaging in Judaic observances, he derived great pleasure from reciting Christian prayers so that when he awoke in the morning he would first recite the articles of the faith and Our Father and then, after washing his hands, he would say several of the psalms of David that he had been taught. Moreover, he insisted that during this entire period, he "believed firmly and completely in both faiths."[19]

The case of Pedro de Ripoll, a merchant and tax farmer in the town of Albarracín, illustrates how a converso could practice both Judaism and Catholicism while experiencing strong ambivalent feelings that came from an inability to feel entirely at home in either religion. In the course of his trial, witnesses described Ripoll as celebrating the Sabbath and other Jewish festivals, frequenting the company of Jews, and eating matzohs and ritually slaughtered meat in his home. During the same period, other witnesses observed him violating the Jewish Sabbath by working on Saturday, attending mass regularly, and going to confession. During the time when he was most eager to welcome Jews into his home, he was also reported to have denounced his first wife in public as a "mala cristiana" who "had dealings with Jews." In 1473, Juan Montarde, the bailiff of the town, caught him beating his first wife with a stick, but when he ordered him to stop, Ripoll said, "Let me alone . . . leave me with this bad Christian." This tense and conflict-ridden equilibrium could not last forever, and when the Inquisition arrived in the mid-1480s, an abyss opened before Ripoll. His initial reaction was to denounce the Inquisition. "Inquisition, what Inquisition . . . they are robbers, not inquisitors." But soon after, he began instructing the servants not to let any more Jews in the house, had several pigs slaughtered, ate pork for the first time, and began fighting with his second wife over her continued desire to observe Jewish dietary precepts. They began eating separately, and he refused to eat the unleavened bread she bought from the Jewish baker.[20] With the arrival of the Inquisition, Ripoll hastily abandoned his effort to be both a Jew and a Christian, but his previous Jewish observances had made him vulnerable to denunciation. In 1522, after several separate trials, Pedro de Ripoll finally ended at the stake.

The third tendency among the conversos, and the one that church, crown, and Inquisition were ostensibly trying to promote, was to assimilate freely into the wider Christian community. Unfortunately, they could not escape their past, and rigid inquisitorial procedures, which seemed to take little cognizance of shades of guilt, frequently resulted in heavy punishment.

In some cases, the converso had practiced Jewish mitzvah as a

teenager in his parents' home but abandoned Judaic practices soon
after he set up an independent establishment. Jaime Almenara, a
Valencian draper, clearly fell into this category since all the testimony in his case related to the period some 35 to 40 years earlier
when Almenara was between twelve and fifteen years old and still
living in the home of his parents. In fact, he seems to have had only
the vaguest notion of the real significance of the Jewish ceremonies
that he had celebrated so long ago. This was shown when he responded to an inquisitor's question about whether he had ever
observed a fast in honor of Queen Esther. In reply, Almenara declared that "he had fasted not eating all day until evening and knew
that they were Jewish fasts but did not know what they were called
except that he thought that they were in honor of the devil."

In spite of the complete absence of any evidence for Judaic observances as an adult, Almenara's problem was that he had failed to
confess two instances of celebrating Yom Kippur as a teenager in the
confession that he had made during the 1491 period of grace. Evidence of these instances having surfaced, Almenara was promptly
arrested and tortured. These omissions, combined with his failure to
mention the names of his parents and other family members who
celebrated with him, were sufficient to open him up to the charge of
having confessed "falsely and incompletely." After a long trial,
Almenara was condemned to the stake on May 29, 1518.[21]

In the case of Pedro Mateo, a master velvet worker brought to
trial in June 1519, Judaism seems to have been little more than a
flag of convenience required to get through his apprenticeship. All
of the evidence of Judaic observance (Yom Kippur and the Sabbath)
dealt with a period some 40 to 45 years earlier when Mateo was
learning his trade from a succession of converso masters. Since, like
all other apprentices, he lived with the family of his master, he was
in no position to refuse when Antonio Palau's wife insisted that
everyone in the house take part in Yom Kippur observances. Apparently, after he had become established as a master in his own right,
these Judaic observances were forgotten. He married a woman who
was half Old Christian and was regarded by both conversos and Old
Christians as a practicing Catholic who went regularly to mass and
confession. Mateo had become so assimilated that even when he
swore his oaths, they were exactly like Old Christian blasphemies,
and his occasional expressions of doubt about the Immaculate Con-

ception were no different from those expressed by hundreds of Old Christians.[22] Mateo was fortunate; after a long trial lasting almost two years, inquisitors Juan Calvo and Andreas Palacio rejected the prosecuting attorney's call for the death penalty and sentenced him to confiscation of property and perpetual imprisonment.[23]

In certain cases, there can be little doubt that an inquisitorial trial interrupted the process of assimilation, sometimes with tragic consequences. Rafael Baro was another artisan who performed most of his Judaic ceremonies either as a child or when he served converso master artisans during his apprenticeship. In fact, he gave every evidence of being a devout Catholic. He attended mass regularly, went to confession, celebrated Christian holidays and fast days including Lent and Good Friday, and claimed special devotion to the Virgin. Baro was a converso already well on his way to becoming a devout Catholic, but arrest by the Holy Office was a shattering blow to his precarious new identity. On November 16, 1520, a little more than two months after his arrest, Baro committed suicide by hanging himself in his cell.[24]

When the Inquisition began operations in the district during the mid-1480s, it found a close-knit converso community whose relative affluence and local political influence could have made it almost impossible to successfully prosecute any large number of Judaizers. Its success in meeting this challenge was due, at least in part, to the conversos' own social relations. Jews, Old Christians, and conversos had much to tell the Inquisition about the activities and beliefs of conversos who practiced Judaic ceremonies. The fact that the Inquisition was able to make use of witnesses from all of these groups is less a tribute to the perspicacity of judges and prosecuting attorneys than to the ambivalent nature of the conversos' position in Valencian society.

In the famous decree of March 31, 1492, by which Ferdinand and Isabella ordered the Jews expelled from Spain, they stress that the major reason for their decision was the aggressive efforts made by Jews to "subvert" Christians and draw them to Judaism. The decree asserts that the Jews did everything possible to achieve their goal: instructing Christians in the Judaic ceremonies and fasts they had to observe, organizing meetings where neophytes would be instructed in Jewish law, and giving them Hebrew prayer books.[25]

Coolness and reserve rather than the zealous wooing implied by the decree of expulsion seem to have characterized the attitude of Valencia's remaining Jews toward the conversos of the district. Of course, there were rare instances of a Jew whose behavior toward the conversos matched exactly the description of converso/Jewish relations given in the decree of expulsion. In 1488, Saloman Çaporta, a Jew from Sagunto, was fined and exiled for having invited conversos to his home for kosher meals, reading the Old Testament to them in Hebrew, and teaching Hebrew to converso children.[26] Almost equally rare were Jews who openly expressed hostility or disdain for conversos. When Juan Aguilaret went to a Jewish acquaintance in Valencia city and confessed with tears in his eyes that he was sick of Catholicism and wanted to turn Jewish, the Jew replied, "Go along with you, you have worn out one faith and now you want to use up another."[27] Most Jews were willing to provide wealthy converso homes with services like slaughtering or ritual products like matzohs, and they certainly were not unwilling to accept contributions of oil or money for the synagogue or charity for themselves. The danger to the converso and the thing that exposed him to inquisitorial persecution was that the Jews then became a source of information about his activities.

In three separate trials held in 1485, for example, the tribunal found that David and Pastor Enforna were quite willing to give evidence about contributions of oil and money given to the synagogue by three of Teruel's most devout conversos, Francisco de Puigmija, Pedro Besant, and Ursula Navarro. Their testimony was all the more damaging because the Enforna brothers had an official connection with the synagogue.[28] In two of these trials, the Inquisition even received testimony from a Rabbi Samual who had been hired to slaughter animals by both Pedro Besant and Francisco de Puigmija. In Besant's case, the rabbi was able to add that he had observed him performing Jewish prayers some fifteen years earlier. With the exception of fanatics like Çaporta, the relationship between Jews and conversos in the Valencia district seems to have been one-sided. Far from seeking to attract conversos back to their old religion by active proselytizing as implied in the decree of expulsion, the Jews were content to let the conversos come to them for services, products, and occasional instruction while maintaining an attitude of coolness and reserve toward even those who seemed most devout. At Ursula Navarro's trial, for example, Pastor Enforna testified that he considered her "neither Jewish nor Christian."[29] As far as the Inquisition was concerned, many of Valencia's orthodox Jews may well have agreed with such Jewish leaders as Don Isaac Abravanel that it was part of God's plan to punish those who had willingly rejected the faith of Israel. There could be nothing wrong with a Jew testifying against conversos and thereby causing their downfall, for as José Jabez, another contemporary Jewish writer, observed in referring to the conversos, "When the wicked are lost, it is a cause for rejoicing."[30]

During the trial of Manuel Manrana, one of the defense witnesses declared that he believed him to be a "good Christian" because he "got along well with Old Christians, went to mass, ate pork and gave alms to poor Christians."[31] In an age when popular religion consisted of little more than a collection of rituals and social customs, there was no other way to judge, and it was the conversos' failure to conform to the behavioral patterns expected of a Catholic rather than any deeply held religious views that made him an object of suspicion and denunciation for his Old Christian neighbors, servants, and associates.

Occasionally, the converso would be unfortunate enough to run across a hardened anti-Semite who would watch every movement for signs of religious nonconformity. Aldonza Miro had been left impoverished and embittered after she had been reconciled with confiscation of property in March 1491. She made the mistake of criticizing the Holy Office to her neighbor, Diameta Culla, a beata (a laywoman living in pious retirement) who had already denounced three other conversos, one of whom, Frances Vicent, had died at the stake. Her suspicions thoroughly aroused, Culla and her sister Margarita, another beata who lived with her, began watching Miro's every move. Observing Miro and her daughter from a little window from which they could see directly into the main room of her house, the Culla sisters saw her light Sabbath candles and celebrate the Sabbath and eat meat on days prohibited by the church. At Miro's trial in 1501, the only witnesses against her were the Culla sisters and their servant, but that was sufficient, in spite of the fact that Miro had identified the Cullas as her enemies, to have her condemned to death as a relapsed heretic.[32]

Old Christian domestic servants were an especially rich source of testimony for the tribunals. As a servant and dependent of a converso household, an Old Christian could find herself directly or indirectly helping the family to perform Jewish ceremonies. In Pedro Besant's home, for example, even the servants were prohibited from working on Saturdays and were expected to help with ritual slaughtering.[33] At the same time, given the social distance that separated masters and servants in Valencian society, a servant's assertion of her religious attitudes could lead to abuse. In Manuel de Puigmija's devoutly Jewish home, his wife, Violante, beat a servant who refused to eat meat at Lent, and the family prevented another servant from attending mass during the entire two-year period that she worked for them.[34] Both servants had the satisfaction of taking revenge for these and other abuses by denouncing their converso masters to the Holy Office.

But it was not only domestic servants (mainly female) who could be a source of danger to conversos. They were in constant danger from others whom they employed in a variety of capacities. In 1483, for example, Fernando Ligador was denounced for Judaizing by his former apprentice, Rodrigo de Morales.[35] The person who first came forward to denounce Pedro Alfonso, a wealthy Valencian notary and tax farmer who was executed in 1487, was a scribe who had worked in his home, while one of the most important witnesses in Pedro Besant's trial was a man whom he had hired to assist him while he traveled through the district on business. In each instance, the Old Christian had noticed something unusual about the converso's behavior and came forward later to denounce him to the Holy Office.[36] The domestic servant beaten by her mistress, the poor scribe envious of the wealth and influence of the notary for whom he worked on an occasional basis, the manservant paid starvation wages—to all these the Inquisition offered an opportunity for revenge that they would not have had if their masters or employers had been Old Christians.

In constant danger of denunciation by Old Christians, and exposed to grave risks because of their relations with Jews, Valencia's conversos were also vulnerable because of the divisions within their own community. Within families, the appeal of the wider Christian society varied with the individual and generated strong tensions between the more assimilated and those who endeavored to remain faithful to the old ways. Even Manuel de Puigmija, who was rigorous in carrying out a large number of Jewish mitzvah, had been expelled from his parents' home because his father felt that he was lax in his Sabbath obligations.[37] Frequently, tensions such as these produced denunciations. Gracia Garbellent, who had been reconciled during the 1485 period of grace and then continued to carry out Judaic observances, made the mistake of remonstrating with her son's fiancée Beatriz about her habit of saying Ave Maria. She also forced the girl to celebrate the Sabbath, then quarreled with her and ordered her out of the house. In 1491, a conscience-stricken (or perhaps merely fearful) Beatriz came to the tribunal to confess having celebrated the Sabbath in her prospective mother-in-law's home and testified to the large number of other Judaic ceremonies that were regularly practiced there. Gracia's son Juan also provided the tribunal with evidence that led to his mother's condemnation as a Judaizer and execution as a relapsed heretic in January 1492.[38]

Conversos who performed mitzvah were also vulnerable to black-mail from unscrupulous acquaintances whose capacity to extort money from their victims was a direct result of the Inquisition's campaign of persecution against Judaizers. One of these converso blackmailers was Alfonso Fusillo, who made a career out of extort-ing money from his fellow conversos while himself carrying out Judaic observances. Fusillo, who would frequent the homes of many converso families and seek to gain their confidence by recit-ing some of the Jewish prayers that he knew, never lost an opportu-nity to wring money out of conversos who appeared vulnerable to denunciation. In one instance, he insinuated himself into a quarrel between Daniel de Artes and Miguel Ferrer after the former had threatened to expose Ferrer to the Inquisition as a Judaizer and "have all of you burnt." Fusillo calmed Artes and persuaded him not to denounce Ferrer but then proceeded to blackmail Ferrer himself.[39]

Every success that Fusillo had in extorting money from his converso acquaintances and business associates, however, made him more vulnerable to denunciation in his turn. The conversos who paid him and feared him were also in a position to denounce him since he had recited Jewish prayers or celebrated mitzvah in their company. At the same time, by not revealing to the Holy Office the names of conversos whom he knew to be guilty of

Judaizing so that he could blackmail them, he had committed the serious offense of failing to inform the Holy Office concerning evidence of heresy. In the end, Fusillo was arrested when one of his victims denounced him in the course of his trial. Tortured and forced to admit his own Judaizing as well as his activities as a blackmailer, Fusillo was condemned to death not only as a Judaizer but as a "concealer of heretics."[40]

Like any other criminal court under the Old Regime, the Inquisition provided the community with a powerful weapon of social control that could be used to increase the cohesion of already tightly knit communities by permitting them to settle disputes at the expense of unwanted or marginal elements. Under these circumstances, the Inquisition became a powerful new weapon in the social struggle.

In the late 1490s, one of the vendettas typical of all Mediterranean societies of the period broke out in Gandía between neighboring converso and Old Christian families. It started, as many of them did, with a quarrel among women, in this case, Onafranca Guitart, the wife of Pedro Guitart, and Blanca Manrana, Manuel Manrana's mother. The two women fought, and when Blanca retreated to her own home, she was followed by several angry members of the Guitart family carrying weapons and bent on revenge. But when Julio Guitart and several other men invaded the Manrana home and attacked young Manuel Manrana, he fought back and killed Julio with a lance thrust to the face. In revenge, Pedro Guitart killed Francisco Tristany and Francisco Francoli, two close relatives of the Manrana family. Both extended families now became involved in the vendetta, which went on with more killings until even Martín Giner, an important judicial official of the city, who happened to be Pedro Guitart's son-in-law, was assassinated by a member of the Tristany family who was linked with the Manrana. The Old Christian Guitart and their allies, the Fortuny, appeared to be losing the struggle against the combined weight of the Manrana, Tristany, and Francolin families when they decided to denounce Manuel Manrana to the Inquisition. The strategy proved brutally effective. Manuel Manrana was arrested, and after a two-year trial in which he was tortured three times, he admitted to performing some Judaic ceremonies. He was sentenced to die at the stake on September 19, 1505. Not content with this, and with its suspicions thoroughly aroused, the Inquisition moved against the entire clan, and in the years after 1503, eight other members of the Manrana family and six members of the Tristany were tried, and seven were executed.[41]

The Valencia tribunal's activity against the converted Jews may be divided into two major periods. The first of these, a span of only forty-six years lasting from the commencement of its operations in the kingdom in 1484 to about 1530, was a period of intense persecution in which highly motivated inquisitors and officials decimated a weak and divided converso community. During this time, the Valencia tribunal tried 2,160 Judaizers and handed down 909 death sentences. The second period, from 1540 to 1820, witnessed a sharp decline in the number of Judaizers, with only 100 trials taking place. The most intense persecution occurred during 1701–1730 when 55 trials are recorded. Thus, in the period before 1530, the Valencia tribunal had already tried 95.4 percent of the Judaizers it was to bring to trial during the entire 336 years of its history. This second phase was also one of decreased severity, with the tribunal only handing down seven death sentences and suspending thirty-one cases, or 29.2 percent. The precipitate decline in this aspect of the tribunal's activity stands in marked contrast to certain other tribunals where conversos continued to make up a surprisingly large percentage of the accused. Of course, in most of these cases, the tribunals involved were either close to the Portuguese border (Llerena, Galicia) or received a large influx of Portuguese New Christians because of the economic opportunities offered in these areas, or because they were close to Madrid (Toledo). As far as the Valencia tribunal was concerned, the ferocity and intensity of the first phase meant that the majority of devout Judaizers among the Valencian conversos had been either physically eliminated or forced to assimilate, while the relatively small number of Portuguese who made their way to the kingdom provided the tribunal with very few victims.

Apart from a sprinkling of nobles and priests during the first phase of persecution, the social composition of the Judaizers remained substantially uniform. The group was dominated by a middle class of merchants, money changers, and shopkeepers (44.6%) and a popular class of artisans (43%) in the period 1478–1530. After 1540, the tribunal dealt almost entirely with Portuguese, some of whom, especially during the early eighteenth century, occupied important positions in tax farming and the administration of royal monopolies. Many of the New Christians may be placed in an upper middle class of tax farmers and fiscal agents comprising some 34.2 percent of the accused; merchants and shopkeepers comprised another 34.2 percent, and the number of artisans fell substantially (8.5%), indicating the transient nature of the New Christian population. This impression is also confirmed by the small number of soldiers (14.5%) in the group.[42]

Apart from the profound divisions within the converso community and the atmosphere of insecurity and suspicion that surrounded the conversos, three other elements were essential to the tribunal's success in mounting the violent wave of persecution that took place between 1485 and 1530: detailed knowledge of Jewish ceremonies and practices, special procedures that would permit the tribunal to gain an intimate knowledge of the converso community, and a group of committed, even fanatical inquisitors and officials.

Official awareness of and sensitivity to Judaic ceremonies increased rapidly in the fifteenth century in response to the growing national preoccupation with the converso problem. By 1460, Catholic lay and ecclesiastical authorities could turn to Alonso de Espina's *Fortalitium Fidei* (Fortress of the Faith), which provided them with a kind of "master catalog" of typical offenses against the Catholic faith committed by conversos. These twenty-five offenses were divided into three broad categories: specific Jewish ceremonies and customs, ways in which the conversos avoided participation in Catholicism, and deviant or superstitious practices that they engaged in.[43] As this last category of offenses reveals, the process of "demonizing" whereby Spain's conversos were coming to be accused of employing magic, worshiping evil spirits, and committing particularly horrible and inhuman crimes in addition to religious heresy was well advanced.[44]

Espina's catalog not only represented a considerable improvement over the rather sketchy description of Judaic customs described in Eymerich's late-fourteenth-century *Directorium inquisitorum* but its system of classification of offenses provided the Inquisition with a model for interrogation of suspects.[45] This is quite evident from the list of questions that the inquisitor-general ordered the Valencia tribunal to ask conversos coming before it during the

1491 period of grace. Here we find an Espina-style classification of offenses including a fairly complete series of mitzvah (Sabbath, Yom Kippur, Passover, Succoth, and Shivah) and the ways in which conversos violated church precepts (eating meat on days prohibited by the church, refusal to go to confession or take communion, and refusal to attend mass) along with a series of questions that reveal the degree to which the demonizing process had taken hold in official circles. Conversos were to be asked if they had participated in whipping or otherwise abusing a crucifix or image of the Virgin, had crucified and lashed an animal as a way of denying and denigrating Christ's passion, and had invoked evil spirits, employed magic spells, or used other "magical arts" prohibited by the church.[46]

Armed with fairly complete knowledge of the Judaic practices likely to be engaged in by conversos, the tribunal then had to confront the problem of identifying the converso population and gaining an intimate knowledge of the networks of interlocking families that comprised it. For this, the tribunal was able to make highly effective use of the period of grace.[47] Expecting to be fully reconciled with the church and let off with a fine, many hundreds of conversos presented themselves before Valencia's inquisitors and endured the humiliation of being forced to march bareheaded through the streets of the city enduring the taunts and hostile glances of their neighbors. Unfortunately, in the majority of cases, the hope of being free from future persecution proved illusory, and 88 percent of those who came forward during the grace period were subsequently brought to trial.[48]

After 1500, as the conversos became more suspicious, the use of the period of grace as a way of recruiting a pool of potential victims became far less effective. But by that time, the tribunal had already gained a great deal of knowledge about dozens of interlocking families who comprised the converso community, while the use of such innovative techniques as the converso "census" of 1506 allowed the tribunal to monitor changes in family structure and relations.[49] The census includes some 275 extended families from five parishes and gave such information as occupation, marital status, number of children, names of parents and siblings, and previous involvement with the Inquisition. Interestingly enough, several of the individuals listed had recently arrived in Valencia from Italy where they had converted to Catholicism.[50]

Given the ferocious anti-Semitism that pervaded fifteenth- and
early sixteenth-century Spain, the identification of conversos with
Jews, and the process of "demonizing" by which they were singled
out as an especially dangerous element capable of the most heinous
crimes against Old Christians and their religion, it is not surprising
that many of the early inquisitors and officials brought strong feelings of hostility and suspicion to their task. For certain inquisitors
and officials, these feelings manifested themselves in expressions of
profound antagonism toward the conversos and their families, an
antagonism not unmixed with a desire to exploit them for financial
gain. These attitudes were quite persistent and continued long
after the tribunal had ceased to deal with any large number of
converted Jews.

A broad range of anti-Semitic attitudes, from mild hostility to
outright belligerence, were revealed by testimony taken from the
tribunal's staff during the visitations of 1528. The families of
conversos whose property had been confiscated by the tribunal were
particularly vulnerable to the petty tyranny that was exercised by
the officials of the court. According to testimony received from Dr.
Martínez, the judge of confiscated property, both the receiver and
the fiscal frequently insulted those who appeared before the court,
while the receiver was notorious for failing to pay out claims made by
successful litigants "except to those he wishes."[51]

Juan de Velásquez, the chief jailer, appeared to have a particularly exploitative relationship to conversos. Accused by several officials of abusing prisoners verbally and physically, he also used
prisoners as a source of cheap labor in his silk business, forcing
them to work up cloth and then paying them less than the going
rate.[52] Velásquez also exploited the anxiety felt by the wives and
families of the accused. In return for bribes and presents, he allowed members of the family to communicate with their loved ones
from the roof of his house, which adjoined the jail.[53]

Inquisitors themselves were far from immune from anti-Semitic
feelings that affected the way they conducted themselves with prisoners. Juan González de Munibrega, undoubtedly the most overtly
and violently anti-Semitic inquisitor ever to sit on the Valencia
tribunal, was appointed in 1535 after having served as prosecuting
attorney in the mid-1520s. During the six years that he spent on
the tribunal, he carried out a virtual reign of terror during which

the most basic legal procedures were violated, prisoners were left to rot in the Inquisition's jails without being brought to trial, and the inquisitor heaped abuse on the prisoners during interrogation.

In 1538–39, Munibrega thought he had discovered an entire network of Judaizers among certain converso families of Gandía who were suspected of performing Jewish ceremonies and abusing the crucifix with whips when they all took refuge together in the Valldigna Valley during the plague year of 1519. Insight into the way in which Munibrega ran the court may be gained from the case of Miguel Oriola, one of a number of hapless conversos who were swept into the tribunal's net by Munibrega's zealous pursuit of all those involved in the Valldigna conventicle. Oriola, a silversmith of modest means, protested his innocence of any wrongdoing and begged Munibrega to begin his trial so that he could secure his release and support the nine children he had left at home "in much peril and with little to sustain them." Munibrega's only reply to these entreaties was to insist that "no accusation is necessary for you to unburden your conscience."[54] In the end, Oriola spent a total of three years and eight months in captivity without even hearing a formal presentation of the charges against him.

Apart from habitually keeping prisoners in jail without trial for long periods, Munibrega used verbal abuse, threats, lies, and torture to get confessions even to charges that had little foundation. It was one such confession, extorted from a member of the Almenara family, that led to the intervention of the Suprema and cut short Munibrega's career on the court. Pedro Luis Almenara, a wealthy merchant and member of a family that had suffered heavily from inquisitorial persecution, was apparently a devout Catholic who went regularly to mass and confession, visited famous shrines like the Catalan monastery of Montserrat, and served faithfully as a lay official of his parish church.[55] Arrested and accused of having celebrated Yom Kippur along with his parents in Valldigna (when he was six years old), Almenara at first stoutly maintained his innocence, but Munibrega's response was a stream of hysterical abuse: "Ha, you son of a whore, what a cunning one you are. I hope to God that you confess one-third of the heresies that you have committed." Undaunted, Almenara declared that he wished to defend himself and asked for a defense attorney, but Munibrega said, "Take care, if you defend yourself well you will be here more than two years." He then refused to allow the appointment of a defense attorney, remarking, "Now I want to prepare an auto; I have no time to judge defenses." Almenara was then turned over to jailer Fernando de Cabrera, who assured him that there were already ten witnesses against him (there were actually only three) and warned him to "confess if you don't want to die." In the next few days, while Almenara languished in his cell, Cabrera, who had frequently demonstrated his zeal by spying on prisoners late at night, kept his anxiety at a fever pitch by telling him that the confessions made in other trials had implicated his entire family and that what he did not confess now, "he would end by confessing two or three years from now."

In spite of this campaign of psychological warfare, Almenara continued to maintain his innocence. As a result, he was brought to the torture chamber, where to increase his terror, Inquisitor Munibrega told him, "Today's work will be very tedious; do you see those beams, you will have to reach them with your head." After the torture was over, and Almenara was lying on the floor doubled up with pain, Munibrega informed him that he would decide later when to resume the torture "in hours or days, whenever I think its best."[56] It was this threat to renew the torture almost indefinitely that finally broke Almenara's nerve and, aided by leading questions from Inquisitor Munibrega, brought him to confess his participation in the Yom Kippur ceremony. He appeared at the auto de fé of June 22, 1539, and was sentenced to imprisonment and confiscation of property.

In the days and weeks that followed, Almenara became more and more convinced that he had sinned grievously by confessing to something that he had not done. Good Catholic that he was, he was haunted by the thought that his soul would burn in hell for having confessed falsely, and he spurned an offer by Melchor de Perelles to use his influence with Inquisitor Munibrega to lighten his sentence, declaring that "he wanted nothing more than to save his soul." At length, after being confronted by his confessor's refusal to give him absolution because he had perjured himself, he appeared before the tribunal to retract his confession. By this time, however, several of Munibrega's other victims had revoked their confessions, and their cause had received the support of one of Valencia's most powerful nobles, Sancho de Cardona, admiral of Aragon. Cardona, who wanted to weaken the Holy Office in the hope of blunting its campaign against his Morisco vassals, would later pay dearly for his temerity in supporting conversos, but for the moment, the Suprema was forced to send several of its own members to take over the tribunal and hear the cases of those who had retracted their testimony before Munibrega's court.

As a result, the next few years saw the gradual rehabilitation of his victims. Pedro Luis Almenara was at first sentenced to imprisonment at the discretion of the inquisitor-general and to a fine and penitential garment. This was later modified to allow him to return home, but he was restricted to travel only within Valencia city. Finally, by special order of the Suprema, all restrictions on him were lifted, and he was permitted to travel anywhere in Spain.[57]

Miguel Oriola also benefited from the change of regime. After looking into his case, Navarra and Lagasca evidently decided that there was no substance to the charges against him and ordered him released from prison and placed under house arrest within Valencia city. Less than a year later, the two inquisitors terminated the case by allowing him to return to his home in Gandía.[58] As for Munibrega, he was permitted to follow the typical cursus honorabilis of the provincial inquisitor and retire to a lesser diocese, in this case, that of Tarazona in upper Aragon. But when Catholic Spain's ruling circles were thrown into a panic by the discovery of Protestant conventicles in Seville and Valladolid, the old war horse was brought back to service and sent to Seville to help with the large number of cases the tribunal had to prepare. Once there, he behaved in his accustomed manner, quarreling with his colleagues, forcing appeals to the Suprema, and "desiring to burn everyone."[59]

The strongly anti-Semitic attitudes expressed by inquisitors and officials during the first wave of persecution eventually became so ingrained in the minds of Inquisition staff that they formed a permanent part of the bureaucratic tradition and persisted long after the tribunal had ceased trying significant numbers of Judaizers. In 1551, long after the first phase of inquisitorial persecution was over, Baltasar Vidanya, a wealthy converso attorney, came to the tribunal to present a papal brief absolving him of any disabilities incurred through the condemnation of his mother's memory by the Holy Office. Presentation of this brief sparked an immediate protest from prosecuting attorney Luis Ferrer, and the tribunal asked the

Suprema to appeal the brief to Rome in terms that would have done credit to an Alonso de Espina or a Pedro Sarmiento. Allowing conversos like Vidanya to benefit from papal concessions, the inquisitors declared, would only encourage them in their diabolical intention to destroy Old Christians. Already, the tribunal's letter alleged, they had condemned many innocent persons to death acting as judges and royal officers. As lawyers, they cynically helped both sides in judicial disputes in order to lengthen trials and gain more fees, and as doctors, they have murdered their patients by prescribing poisons instead of drugs.[60] Violent persecution of native converso Judaizers was over by the 1550s, but anti-Semitism among inquisitors and officials remained as an enduring legacy of the first wave of persecution.

During the last half of the sixteenth century, merchant-bankers from the Republic of Genoa dominated Spanish imperial finance by handling the transfer of funds from Spain to Flanders. The Spanish treasury paid dearly for its dependence on the Genoese, but Spanish efforts to break free of them in the last quarter of the sixteenth century proved unavailing since no rival network of bankers existed which could provide the same services. After an abortive attempt to substitute a group of Spanish and Portuguese financiers in 1575, Philip II reluctantly turned back to the Genoese, signing an agreement with them in December 1577 which ushered in the golden age of Genoese finance during the last quarter of the sixteenth century.[61]

The failure of their earlier efforts to replace the Genoese did not prevent the crown and its treasury officials from renewing the search for an alternative set of bankers in the seventeenth century. This time their search was rewarded. The union of Spain and Portugal after 1580 and the general expansion of Atlantic trade in the late sixteenth century opened up commercial opportunities that Portuguese New Christian merchants were quick to exploit. Many of these men made vast fortunes by trading in Asian products, investing in the Brazilian sugar industry, and supplying slaves to both Brazil and the Spanish Americas.[62] As a result, when a reformist regime led by Philip IV's chief minister, the Conde Duque de Olivares, came to power in 1621, the Portuguese New Christians were ready and willing to take up the challenge of replacing the Genoese as the crown's principal bankers.

In spite of their key role in Spain's remarkable military and strategic recovery in the first decades of the seventeenth century, however, the Portuguese New Christians found that they had many enemies. The strength of anti-Semitic feeling is demonstrated by the rapid translation into Spanish of a violently anti-Semitic work by Vicente de Costa Mattos, a Portuguese who denounced New Christians as idolators and sodomites and claimed that all heretics were either Jews or descendants of Judaizers.[63] The New Christians were also victims of street violence and the subject of attacks by poets and writers like Francisco de Quevedo. It was the Inquisition, however, that was in the best position to undertake a campaign of persecution. Royal support notwithstanding, anti-Semitic feeling among inquisitors remained strong, and both the Suprema and the regional tribunals remained highly suspicious of the New Christians. In 1586, for example, just at the time when the New Christians were first becoming active in tax farming and military and naval contracting, the Valencia tribunal wrote the Suprema to ask for instructions regarding the Portuguese "confessos" who passed through the kingdom on their way to foreign countries because it was suspected that they were emigrating so as to practice Judaism freely.[64]

Since the New Christians had been able to prevent the Portuguese Inquisition from operating effectively until well into the sixteenth century, Judaic traditions remained strong among them, and evidence of Judaizing was not difficult to find. Moreover, the fact that their business success depended, at least in part, on maintaining relations with the Jewish communities in Amsterdam and Italy meant that they could renew their Jewish traditions by contact with practicing Jews. But the New Christians, like the conversos before them, were vulnerable to attack. The issue of assimilation had divided the community deeply, and the hostility between those who wished to become Roman Catholic and those more closely tied to Judaism was productive of denunciations. María Rodríguez, who testified against Fernán Vázquez during his trial in 1586, was the daughter of Portuguese New Christians who had been imprisoned by the Inquisition in Seville while attempting to leave the Iberian peninsula so that they could practice Judaism. Apparently while still in Seville, she secretly married an Old Christian, but when her father found out, he beat her so severely that she still carried the scars twenty years later. Her second husband was a New Christian, but the women in Valencia's small New Christian community were very suspicious of her, refusing to invite her to meals and showing hostility when she manifested any outward sign of Christian belief. Rebellion against a tyrannical parent combined with anger at Valencia's New Christians were enough to turn her into a more than willing witness and spy who even brought a beata to the homes of her New Christian acquaintances on Saturdays so that she could attest to the fact that no work was being performed there.[65]

A century of inquisitorial edicts, sermons of the faith, and autos de fé had also served to indoctrinate the Old Christian population against any signs of Judaic observance; even a lack of zeal in fulfilling Christian duties aroused suspicion. When Fernán Vázquez was selected as a lay official of the parish church of San Nicolás, the neglectful way in which he performed his duties was enough to arouse the suspicion of the parish priest who considered all his Portuguese parishioners "judíos," a benefice holder in the church who later took it on himself to gather more information about the New Christians of the parish, and a familiar of the Holy Office who happened to belong to the same church. All of these men later testified against Vázquez at his trial.[66]

Old Christian servants were also dangerous. Juana Ana Farragut worked for Cristóbal Gómez during the time he played host to Pedro Méndez Rosete and his wife. Rosete, who had been an important tax farmer and tobacco wholesaler, refused to eat pork while in the Gómez home and pretended to be ill when it was time to go to mass. Ferragut eventually proved an excellent witness and was even able to report on the couple's whereabouts after they left her master's house.[67]

In spite of the fact that certain New Christians were using Valencia as a transit point on their journeys to southern France and Italy and the undoubted presence of a small group of Portuguese merchants like Fernán Vázquez or Francisco Brandon, the depressed economy of seventeenth-century Valencia offered few opportunities, and the majority of the New Christians preferred to settle in Andalucia where they could participate in the Seville trade or in New Castile where there were opportunities in royal finance, contracting, and tax farming. As a result, the Valencia tribunal tried only fifteen New

Christians during the period 1615–1700, when other tribunals like Toledo, Córdoba, and Galicia tried large numbers.

During the eighteenth century, the imposition of a whole series of new taxes after 1707 and the enforcement of the royal salt and tobacco monopolies made the kingdom considerably more attractive to New Christians who were already involved in administering royal taxes elsewhere in Spain.[68] The first decades of the eighteenth century also saw a sharp increase in the persecution of Judaizers by the peninsular tribunals, with 820 appearing in the sixty-four autos held between 1721 and 1727. Valencia contributed only fifty-one cases but, following the national trend, was clearly becoming somewhat more active. In all, the tribunal tried sixty-seven Judaizers in the period 1701–1799, but the majority (55) were tried between 1712 and 1733.[69]

A revealing glimpse into the lives of these early eighteenth-century New Christians is afforded by the case of Simón de Alarcón, who was arrested by the Valencia tribunal in March 1721. Simón came from a family of tax farmers impoverished by inquisitorial persecution. His father, Tomás de Valenzuela y Alarcón, who had been reconciled with confiscation of property by the Toledo tribunal, died when Simón was only six, leaving him with his mother, Isabel de los Ríos, who had been reconciled by the Logroño tribunal. Bloodied but unbowed, Isabel continued to practice Judaism after her release and exhorted Simón to "live like the son of his father."[70]

Fortunately for Simón, his family was well known among the tight-knit group of Madrid New Christian merchants, financiers, and tax farmers whose role in royal finance appeared to be as important under the early Bourbons as it had been under the later Hapsburgs. As a result, Simón was able to enter the service of several of these men, including Manuel de Olivares, an important sugar merchant whose family had been recruited into the ranks of the royal asentistas in the early 1640s, and Francisco de Lara, treasurer of the royal tobacco monopoly. Through these connections, Simón was able to marry María de Molina, the daughter of the administrator of the millones of Antequera. He also met Manuel de Andrade, another official of the tobacco administration, and through him entered the tobacco administration himself, working first in Ciudad Real and then in Zaragoza. He then went to Valencia where he made contact with Felipe de Paz, who, along with his father, Diego, controlled the tobacco monopoly of the entire Kingdom of Valencia. From Felipe he obtained the administration of tobacco in Segorbe and Castellón. This evidently proved quite lucrative; when he was arrested, he had in his possession a substantial amount of cash as well as jewels and silver.

Simón de Alarcón's contacts in Madrid formed a tight-knit group of New Christian families who married among themselves or with other families of known Judaic sympathies. Jewish ceremonies including the Sabbath, Yom Kippur, and Shivah were routinely practiced, and members of the group spoke to one another without the slightest reserve about their firm belief in the Jewish faith. In spite of their efforts to present themselves as devout Catholics, the members of the network and their families suffered grievous persecution at the hands of the Inquisition. In a series of trials sparked by the incautious revelations made by María de Tudela to another prisoner of the Toledo tribunal in 1718, the Madrid, Murcia, Toledo, Córdoba, Granada, and Valencia tribunals virtually destroyed the entire network of New Christian families between 1718 and 1727. Among the victims the Valencia tribunal claimed from among these families were Diego and Felipe de Paz, general administrators of the royal tobacco monopoly for the Kingdom of Valencia, Sebastián de León, Manuel Rodríquez de León, who sold tobacco for the crown in Viñaroz and Torrente, and the members of their families.

Unfortunately for the tribunal, which had expected windfall profits from its prosecution of the New Christians, the evidence suggests that the Paz and their associates were able to remove most of their funds from Spain before they could be seized. By 1724, Felipe and several of his leading associates had been released and were once again offering to take over the tobacco monopoly.[71]

The discrimination and persecution suffered by the Portuguese New Christians during the late sixteenth, seventeenth, and eighteenth centuries stands in marked contrast to the substantial assimilation of the Spanish conversos in the same period. During the sixteenth century, the obstacles the conversos had to face appeared to loom ever larger. Purity of blood statutes spread from the religious orders to Colegios Mayores and cathedral chapters, and by the end of the century, even the Jesuits were forced to exclude conversos in spite of their earlier tolerance.[72] Moreover, the descendants of those punished by the Inquisition were barred from holding public office, carrying arms, exercising certain professions, and wearing certain types of clothing. In a still largely oral society, memories were long, and the officials responsible for carrying out the genealogical investigations designed to trap conversos who tried to enter honorable corporations in spite of the statutes could rely on this collective memory to trace the Jewish origins of conversos claiming to be "pure." Investigators could also rely on the Inquisition, whose records were an invaluable repository of information about converso families. In 1569, for example, the Valencia tribunal furnished the cabildo of the cathedral of Toledo, which had recently (1547) adopted a purity of blood statute, with copies of trials involving the Santangel family.[73] The council of canons intended to use this material as ammunition in its effort to prevent Diego López de Ayala, Hernando de Santangel's grandson, from obtaining a place on the cabildo.[74]

In spite of the ingrained hostility of many inquisitors and officials, however, the Inquisition proved to be a major channel through which the conversos became accepted into the mainstream of Spanish life. This was the result not of altruism on the part of the Holy Office (although there were inquisitors and officials who favored integration) but of necessity. Of all the honorable corporations with purity of blood statutes, the Inquisition was the most penurious and the most politically vulnerable and was therefore not in a position to overlook any opportunity to generate income from relieving the disabilities that it had imposed on converso families or of winning influential friends and allies by allowing certain conversos to become officials, familiares, notaries, and the like.

One of the most common revenue-raising devices used by the Holy Office, especially during periods of acute financial distress, was the commutation of all or part of a sentence or even the complete rehabilitation of an individual from the social disabilities that he might have incurred as a result of the condemnation of an ancestor. In 1520, for example, the Suprema asked the tribunal of Barcelona to estimate how much it could earn by commuting the penitential garments of all persons presently wearing them in view of "la mucha necesidad" in which the tribunal found itself.[75] In that same year, the Suprema ordered a special payment of 150 gold ducats to be made to the inquisitors and officials of the Valencia tribunal to come in part from fees for commutations of habits and prison sentences. In 1531, the Suprema ordered the complete rehabilitation of Onofre Dura and his family. Dura, a wealthy silversmith from Gandía, paid well for the right to hold honorable offices, carry arms, and wear cloth of gold and silver in spite of the condemnation of his father, mother, and grandparents.[76] By the early seventeenth century, the Holy Office had largely abandoned any pretense at enforcement of personal disabilities except as a revenue-raising device. In the instructions issued to Inquisitor Ambrosio Roche for his visitations to Gandía, Denia, and Alcira in 1632, he was specifically told to confine himself to levying fines on the descendants of reconciled or relaxed persons who were holding honorable offices or wearing prohibited clothing, since it was no longer the custom to impose public penance or exile.[77]

One of the principal ways in which the Inquisition was supposed to perpetuate the disgrace of those it had punished was by preserving sanbenitos along with suitable inscriptions in the churches. When these had deteriorated, they were replaced by sheets of linen inscribed with the name, crime, and punishment of the individual. In the Instructions of 1561 and again in 1569, the Suprema charged inquisitors on visitation with the duty of making sure that all the appropriate sanbenitos were in place and hanging new ones when necessary.[78]

In spite of the hard line taken in these instructions and royal support for exhibiting the sanbenitos, there is considerable evidence to suggest that, in practice, the policy was difficult to carry out. Fully realizing the grief and distress that public exhibition of the penitential garments would cause to the families of the victim, some inquisitors were opposed to displaying them. Hernando de Loazes, who was inquisitor in Valencia in 1541, was so affected by the pleas of victims' relatives that he had not replaced a single sanbenito during his term of office and then refused to cooperate with the tribunal when it wanted to renew those in the cathedral after he became archbishop of Valencia.[79]

In other cases, it was opposition from some powerful individual that prevented the sanbenitos from being displayed. In 1644, for example, the Suprema asked the tribunal to account for the fact that not a single sanbenito was hung in the collegiate church of Gandía even though records indicated that thirty-four individuals from that town had been reconciled or relaxed. In reply, the tribunal related that the inquisitor who visited Gandía in 1606 was told that the Duke of Gandía had vetoed placing the sanbenitos in the church. A diligent search of the tribunal's premises then led to the discovery of Gandía's sanbenitos, which had evidently been in storage since the auto de fé when they were first used. By curious oversight, however, Inquisitor Pedro de Herrera y Guzmán failed to take them when he left on visitations to Gandía later that year. The record ends with the information that the duke went out of his way to welcome Herrera y Guzmán when he arrived, but it is legitimate to wonder whether his welcome would have been so warm if the inquisitor had not been quite so forgetful.[80]

Influential conversos were also in a position to do something about the sanbenitos they detested. In 1613, Valencia's inquisitors wrote the Suprema to report that Dr. Guardiola, a judge on the Audiencia, had removed several of the linen sheets that were used to record the names of victims from the front of his chapel in the cathedral. He did this without even notifying the tribunal, but he was so influential that the inquisitors confined themselves to asking one of the secretaries to go to the church and "nonchalantly" explore it to find out where the sheets had been placed. Doubtless, the Guardiola family had long felt the affront of having these obnoxious yellow sheets directly in front of their chapel, especially since they recorded the names of several of their ancestors. By the early seventeenth century, they felt strong enough to act, and the tribunal was so politically weak that it could not stop them.[81]

The image of an inquisitorial secretary skulking through the cathedral to locate sanbenitos removed by order of a converso is an indication of just how far the prestige of the Holy Office had declined since the palmy days of the early sixteenth century. Clearly, the tribunal faced strong and growing opposition to its efforts to perpetuate the infamy of its victims through maintaining sanbenitos. In the face of this opposition, some inquisitors, like Pedro de Herrera y Guzmán, abandoned them entirely, while others, like Hernando de Loazes, had never supported the use of the sanbenitos in the first place. In spite of the Suprema's insistent demands for enforcement of the regulations regarding the sanbenitos, therefore, the tribunal's zeal for them flagged noticeably, and by the mid-seventeenth century, a device that had proved so effective in maintaining the conversos as a class apart was falling into desuetude.[82]

But it was through successfully overcoming the barriers posed by the Inquisition's own purity of blood statute and genealogical investigations that certain wealthy and influential converso families were able to obscure their origins, gain respectability, and integrate themselves more fully into Spanish society. The process by which members of these families were admitted, albeit grudgingly, to the corps of unpaid officials really began in earnest during the early years of the seventeenth century when the Holy Office encountered growing opposition from Audiencias and royal councils and the Suprema was struggling to find ways of rebuilding its political influence at court.

An excellent example of how persistence, influence, and the gradual accumulation of positions in honorable corporations could eventually carry an individual from a "tainted" family into the ranks of the familiares is provided by the case of Vicente Valterra, eldest son and heir to the Count of Villanueva. Vicente's saga began in spring 1627 when he applied to the Suprema for admittance as a familiar of the Valencia tribunal in spite of being single and therefore formally ineligible to serve. The Suprema granted his request and ordered him to be admitted provided that he met the criteria for purity of blood demanded for entrance to the corps.[83] The Suprema's letter drew an immediate protest from the secretaries who were chiefly responsible for verifying the lineage of applicants by checking the tribunal's secret archive. On his mother's side, Vicente was descended from the Santangels, one of the most famous converso families in the Crown of Aragon. The public outcry that the recent admission of his two cousins, Juan Çanoguera and Vicente Sorell, as familiares had caused made the secretaries still more determined to resist opening the door even wider.[84] The Suprema then requested copies of all cases involving the Santangels and documents establishing Valterra's connection with that family. After reviewing this material carefully, the Suprema instructed the tribunal not to admit Vicente and to suspend any genealogical investigation.[85]

The Suprema's letter of August 23 would seem to have ended the case, but just a few days later, it returned to the charge, asking for new copies of all relevant documents and inquiring disingenuously if the tribunal had already admitted Valterra by virtue of its original letter of May 11 dispensing of the requirement that he be married.[86] The cause of the Suprema's strange about-face on the issue was the growing respectability and political influence of the family of the counts of Villanueva. Notwithstanding the failure of Valterra's application to enter the corps of familiares, other members of the family with the same relationship to the Santangels were making progress in their efforts to enter other honorable corporations. The event that appears to have triggered the Suprema's decision to reopen Valterra's case was the admittance of his first cousin, Jaime Millán, to the Order of Santiago, Spain's most prestigious corporate body.[87] As Valterra pointedly reminded the Suprema, he came of a family both numerous and influential whose members occupied important positions and were related by marriage to many of the greatest aristocratic houses in Spain.[88] By May 11, 1629, his demand for a familiatura had acquired enormous momentum. Not only had two other cousins, Luis and Remigio Sorell, been admitted to the Order of Calatrava but the family could now boast ten actos positivos (eight from the Military Orders), so that by the royal pragmática of 1623, Valterra could be admitted without even going through a genealogical investigation.[89]

A family with so many of its members in the prestigious Military Orders and an individual with such great, and growing, landed possessions (Valterra had recently added Canet to his list of villages) could no longer be ignored lest he become a powerful enemy. The feelings of Valencia's secretaries now meant nothing to the Suprema, which summarily ordered them to commence Valterra's genealogical investigation in its letter of October 17, 1629.[90]

Finally, more than three years after he had first applied, Valterra became a member of the corps. The following year, in a now-familiar pattern of using acceptance into one honorable corporation as a springboard to another, he applied to enter the Order of Calatrava. By this time, the Council of the Military Orders was no longer following the pragmática of 1623, and he was aware that representatives of that council would be sent to Valencia to interview the tribunal's secretaries about his lineage. The danger was that Valencia's disgruntled secretaries would balk at testifying and thus delay the entire investigation. But now Valterra had gained the upper hand, and in a letter conspicuous for its aggressive tone, he demanded that the Suprema secretly issue them a formal authorization to testify in his favor and even "compel" them to do so if that became necessary. Needless to say, the Suprema, which had clearly supported Valterra's application in the first place, went along with his demand and issued its authorization on September 26, 1630.[91]

Much the same strategy was used by the next generation of this ambitious family. In 1647, the Suprema approved the application of Francisco Pérez de los Cobos to be a familiar of the Murcia tribunal. By this time, Luis Sorell had become count of Albalat, Valterra's two sons were familiares, and Francisco Pérez de los Cobos was himself a knight of the Military Order of Santiago. Sheer persistence had opened Spain's honorable corporations to this converso family, and the Suprema's order that no one from it was to be admitted in the future without specific permission must be viewed as little more than a pretense of upholding standards that had long ceased to be observed.[92]

An even more significant case, and one that illustrates a growing division within the Holy Office itself about the value of the purity of blood statutes, was that of Tomás Ginart y March, who applied to be an official in August 1699.[93] Ginart y March was descended from the March, Palau, Malet, and Almenara, four of the most notorious families of Judaizers in late-fifteenth- and early sixteenth-century Valencia. Between them, these families had a total of 65 members punished by the Holy Office, including 34 relaxed in effigy or in person.[94] The converso origins of the Almenara family, in particular, were so well known in Valencia that as recently as July 27, 1697, the Suprema had stated categorically that no descendant of that family could even be considered by the tribunal.[95]

In spite of this prohibition, the Suprema was evidently prepared to allow the application to proceed and ordered the tribunal's secretaries to carry out the customary search through the secret archive. Predictably, the secretaries turned up a considerable amount of evidence against Ginart y March's family and were especially concerned to point out that his great grandfather, Francisco March, had married into the Almenara family, "one of those most frequently mentioned in the secret archive."[96]

During the next three years, a series of hearings were held which appeared to further damage Ginart y March's case. Further investigation by fiscal Vicente del Olmo turned up evidence that the genealogy that he had originally presented was fraudulent and that the March family had attempted to obfuscate its connection with the Almenaras by inserting counterfeit documents in the notarial records of the corte de gobernación.[97]

By the end of May 1704, when Valencia's two inquisitors sat down to render judgment, the case against Ginart y March appeared overwhelming, and, after restating all the negative evidence, Inquisitor Diego Muñoz Baquerizo concluded by saying that considering Ginart y March would "greatly dishonor this tribunal." But all along, the inquisitors had been divided on the case. Muñoz Baquerizo's colleague, Juan de la Torre y Guerau, had previously sought to aid Ginart y March by refusing to close the case in spite of the accumulation of negative evidence, and he now emerged as an open supporter. In his written opinion, he dismissed the witnesses against Ginart y March as "few and inconstant" and argued rather implausibly that the older notarial records should be accepted in spite of their glaring deficiencies. Since the inquisitors were now split, the tribunal had no option but to follow Torre y Guerau's recommendation and send the case on to the Suprema for its consideration.[98] Evidently, this was exactly what the Suprema had been waiting for. On June 25, it bent toward Ginart y March, favoring him by authorizing Inquisitor Torre y Guerau to act alone in rendering a final verdict.[99] Since Torre y Guerau's views were already known to the Suprema, it could have surprised no one when he rendered a favorable opinion, and on July 9, 1704, the Suprema authorized Ginart y March's admission as an official of the Valencia tribunal.[100]

The counts of Villanueva were too important for either the Suprema or the tribunal to ignore. The large number of actos positivos that the family had accumulated, especially from the prestigious Military Orders, and its growing wealth and influence made it politically unwise to exclude Vicente Valterra from the corps of familiares. The same cannot be said of the March family. Even though Tomás Ginart y March's grandfather, Jacinto March de Velasco, had been a jurat and represented Valencia city at the Cortes, the family could not lay claim to such distinction at the time of Tomás's application. His father had been a mere ciutadà, and he himself spoke frequently of his own modest circumstances. Judging by this case, the official barriers to the assimilation of the conversos had diminished appreciably. It is not difficult to see in the attitude of Juan de la Torre y Guerau or in that of the Suprema itself a growing acceptance of assimilation within the Inquisition itself.[101] After all, it was an inquisitor, probably Juan Roco Campofrio, who joined in the debate over the purity of blood statutes during the reign of Philip IV and condemned them as a major cause of social division, corruption, and litigation.[102] By the end of the century, even the once taboo Almenara family had become acceptable, and Tomás Almenara, a prominent city councillor in Enguera, was permitted to enter the corps of familiares in spite of the prosecuting attorney's objection that the family was "seriously tainted" with Jewish blood.[103]

By the middle of the eighteenth century, the last wave of persecution was over, and the inquisitorial tribunals saw few Judaizers. Between 1792 and 1820, the last years of its activity, the Valencia tribunal only dealt with six cases, and some of these were of Jews from Gibraltar who came requesting baptism and religious instruction.[104]

Nevertheless, in spite of the virtual disappearance of Judaizing and the complete absence of actual Jewish communities, anti-Semitism remained strong in Spanish society, and for this the Inquisition must bear much of the blame. Within the Inquisition itself, the tendency to accept the conversos did little to allay the suspicion and fear of Jews that underlay the first wave of persecution. At the time of the allied invasion of Valencia in 1705–1707, for example, the tribunal was extremely concerned about the presence of Jewish contractors among the allied forces because it feared that they would try to bring Hebrew books into the city.[105]

For some officials, the Jew remained the incarnation of evil. In a letter to the Suprema dated November 19, 1643, Fray Juan Ponce, a calificador and former Holy Office commissioner in Oran, warned of the imminent arrival of several Jews from that city. The group included Jacob Cansino who was known to Fray Ponce from his days in Oran as a "powerful magician" who could mix up powders and herbal concoctions that bent others to his will even if they had only the slightest contact with them. Fray Ponce assured the Suprema that Cansino intended to bring these magic potions with him to Spain along with some anti-Catholic propaganda of his own manufacture. Saloman Zaporta, another of these Jews, was coming to Madrid to sell slaves. Fray Ponce had no real objection to this so long as Zaporta could be counted on to leave Spain promptly after his business had been concluded. There could be no guarantee of this, however, and the spectacle of Zaporta living at court in a Judaic manner, eating unleavened bread, slaughtering in a kosher style, "mocking our religion and offering prayers for our destruction," was too horrible to contemplate. A worried Suprema responded by ordering the Valencia tribunal to send back any of these Jews who landed without specific royal license.[106]

For such men as Fray Ponce, the Jew was necessarily evil, necessarily an enemy of the Catholic faith. For the popular masses, generations of autos de fé and inquisitorial edicts had associated the Jew with everything dangerous, foreign, and unorthodox. This thinking, which was kept alive by the tattered remnants of sanbenitos that could still be seen in many churches, remained an important element in the Inquisition's continued popularity in spite of the fact that it had itself provided many converso families with the passport to full integration into Old Christian society.

VI

The Moriscos

Until the period just after the conquest of Granada, Valencia's mudéjares continued to practice Islam under the protection of the treaties that had been signed when the kingdom was incorporated into the Aragonese monarchy. These treaties guaranteed full religious and cultural freedom to the conquered population, but, from a legal standpoint, this was mere privilege conceded by the crown and revocable with cause at any time.[1]

For a considerable period after the forced conversion of Castile's mudéjares in 1502, the political autonomy and legal privileges enjoyed by the Crown of Aragon prevented the Aragonese mudéjares from sharing their fate. At the Cortes of Monzón in 1510, Ferdinand swore that he would make no effort to force their conversion, and Charles V felt obliged to take a similar oath on his accession as king of Aragon in 1518.[2] Royal legislation to the contrary, however, the mudéjares of the Kingdom of Valencia had always lived in a changing and insecure environment marked by constant pressure from the growing Christian population. This pressure from below had been primarily responsible for driving the mudéjares from the fertile huerta to the dry farming and mountainous regions in the interior of the kingdom where they remained until the expulsion.[3] The "expulsions" of the fourteenth century also had the effect of removing or greatly reducing the number of mudéjares in the vicinity of the larger towns, which were now controlled by the Old Christians, but this partial segregation of the population of the kingdom did little to reduce the antagonism between the two communities. To the evident differences in religion, dress, and customs was added the new economic role of the mudéjares as the servile tenant farmers of the hated Valencian noblity.[4] As a result, the fifteenth and early sixteenth centuries were punctuated by ugly incidents such as the massacre of Valencia's Islamic community in 1455.[5]

The outbreak of the Germanía revolution in spring 1521 sounded the death knell for the existence of Valencia's mudéjares. The defeat of a viceregal army, partially composed of mudéjares, at the battle of Gandía on July 25, 1521, led to the sack and forced conversion of the mudéjar communities of Gandía, Oliva, Játiva, Villalonga, Guadalest, Penáguila, and Polop. Finally, in March 1522, Germanía forces under el Encubierto, the last and most radical of the Germanía leaders, sacked the mudéjar communities of Alberique and Alcocer.[6]

With the death of Vicent Peris on March 4, 1522, and the surrender of Játiva and Alcira at the beginning of December, the Germanías were defeated, but the partial forced conversion of Valencia's mudéjares during the revolt left the crown and the church in a difficult and ambiguous situation. In Granada and Castile, conversion had been universal, as all Moors who did not wish to convert had been allowed to leave. In Valencia, however, conversion had been partial and hasty so that it was impossible to know for sure which mudéjares had been converted and whether the sacrament itself had been administered properly.[7] At the same time, the question was raised as to the validity of the conversion itself. It was not so much the forced nature of the conversion that concerned theologians and other contemporary observers but the fact that it had been administered by rebels to a loyal population protected by Charles's oath to permit them to practice Islam without interference.[8] It should be noted, however, that even though the church had long accepted the indelible nature of baptism, almost regardless of the circumstances under which it was administered, some influential individuals in Spain continued to express their doubts or at least saw the forced conversion of the Valencian mudéjares as a reason for lenient treatment.[9] For their part, the Moriscos, who had no particular reason to love the faith into which they had been inducted, had returned to their former practices, while the Valencia tribunal, under the leadership of Inquisitor Juan de Churruca, had accepted their conversion as valid and had begun to prosecute backsliders.[10]

Even though Charles had already asked Pope Clement VII to release him from his oath to allow the mudéjares to freely practice their religion, he accepted Inquisitor-General Manrique's suggestion that the entire situation be considered by a special junta made up of members of the leading royal councils with the addition of some jurists and theologians. To provide the junta with information, Manrique created a commission led by Inquisitor Churruca, and then his successor, Andrés Palacio, to investigate the circumstances under which the Moors were baptized and how they had lived since their baptism took place.[11]

Given the attitude of Valencia's inquisitors to the conversions, there could be little hope of an impartial investigation, so it is not surprising that the commission's report laid stress on the care with which the officiating priests questioned the converts about their real desires and performed the rites of baptism.[12] With the report placed before it, the junta deliberated from February 19 to June 1525 and concluded by saying that the Moriscos must remain Christian regardless of their real feelings in the matter.[13] This verdict simply confirmed the policy that Charles had already decided to follow, and on April 4, he decreed that all the baptized mudéjares should be considered Christians. Immediately thereafter, a commission was established to tour the kingdom to notify the Moriscos of the royal decree and of a thirty-day period of grace during which apostates could return to Christianity without prejudice.[14]

Having thrown the prestige of royal government behind the forced conversions, it no longer seemed possible to tolerate the continued worship of Islam among the not inconsiderable number of Valencian mudéjares who had escaped the baptismal water of the Germanía. After obtaining a papal brief from Clement VII which relieved him of his oath to respect the Islamic beliefs of his mudéjar subjects, Charles issued an edict on September 13, 1525, which informed the remaining Moors that no one of a different religion could remain in the kingdom except as a slave. This was followed on October 20, 1525, by an edict ordering all the remaining Moors of Valencia to accept baptism or leave Spain before December 8, 1525.[15] This decision did not receive universal approbation either then or later. On April 3, 1530, Fray Rafael Moner, a Dominican friar and a popular preacher in Valencia, was forced to publicly retract statements critical of the forced conversion.[16]

Of course, Charles V and his advisers were well aware of the fact that the 70,000 to 80,000 Moriscos created by their policy of forced conversion were Christian in name only and that they could not be expected to meet the demands of their new religion without a period of transition. Even before the decree of expulsion was issued, Charles had written to Germaine de Foix, governor of Valencia, asking her to see to it that the converts were instructed properly in Christianity since he knew that there were few priests where they lived.[17] This awareness also explains the outcome of a series of negotiations involving representatives of the Valencian Moriscos. In return for the substantial servicio of 40,000 ducats, Charles agreed that the Inquisition was not to exercise jurisdiction over them for a period of forty years and allowed them to conserve their traditional dress and use Arabic for a period of ten years.[18]

Concern by the royal government and the church over the religious condition of the Moriscos also led to a number of measures designed to make them into genuine converts. For one thing, a network of local rectories was established. To supplement the activity of the rectors who were responsible for the religious instruction and religious practices of their flock, several great missionary campaigns were undertaken before 1609. The earliest of these began in March 1526 just months after the edict of conversion and involved several missionaries including the bishop of Gaudix, Gaspar Davalos. Later campaigns involved the controversial Arabic-speaking Franciscan Bartolomé de los Angeles (1543), the bishop of Tortosa (1567), and groups of Franciscan and Jesuit preachers (1587).[19] The last missionary effort, begun at the instigation of the pope in 1606, was only abandoned with the expulsion itself.[20]

Certain members of Valencia's ecclesiastical hierarchy also interested themselves in the religious education of the Moriscos. In 1566, Archbishop Martín de Ayala published a catechism designed especially for a literate Morisco audience with its Spanish text and Arabic translation on alternate lines.[21] Archbishop Juan de Ribera, who succeeded Ayala later in the century, had a very ambivalent attitude toward the Moriscos but nevertheless threw himself into frantic missionary activity and republished Ayala's text in 1599.[22]

Until the late 1560s, moreover, the crown and even the Inquisition sought to enlist the aid, or at least ensure the neutrality, of the Morisco elite. In the late 1520s, for example, such men as Hazentala, alcadi of Vall de Chelva, and Abdala Abenamir, an influential citizen of Benaguacil, received substantial sums from the crown for not opposing the conversion effort. The Valencia tribunal also enlisted a certain number of leading Moriscos as familiares, in order, as fiscal Luis Ferrer explained in a letter to the Suprema, "to have them ready to assist us in dangerous parts of the district."[23] The tribunal had these Morisco familiares until at least 1568, although they were coming under increasing suspicion as relations between the tribunal and the Moriscos worsened.[24] This group of familiares included members of the Abenamir family of Benaguacil.[25]

As we shall see, these efforts at genuine conversion and assimilation were tenuous and inadequate, but there is evidence to suggest that they achieved some success and that the prospects of assimilation were not as bleak and hopeless as certain contemporary observers and certain modern historians would have us believe.[26] The fact is that the Moriscos of Valencia, like their counterparts in Castile, lived in a society dominated by Hispano-Christian culture, language, and religion, and in spite of the doctrine of taqiyya embraced by Islamic theologians, ordinary Moriscos inevitably came to accept a Hispano-Christian frame of reference even if they continued to resist or reject most aspects of Christianity itself. If assimilation ultimately failed, it was as much due to official paranoia about the military threat represented by the Morisco "fifth column" and the massive rejection of the Moriscos by virtually every segment of Christian society as it was to the obduracy of the Moriscos themselves.[27] As far as the Valencia tribunal was concerned, its basic attitude toward the Moriscos was one of hostility tempered by greed and self-interest. Even though the tribunal had been an early proponent of expulsion, by the end of the sixteenth century, the income it received from Morisco censos, fines, and subsidies and the docility of most of the Moriscos it brought to trial caused it to accept them as a useful "client" group. Unlike Juan de Ribera, the archbishop of Valencia who wrote that he would rather subsist on "bread alone" than tolerate the presence of Morisco heretics among his flock, the Inquisition had become aware that large numbers of Valencia's Moriscos could no longer be considered Moslem in the strict sense.

In spite of the insistence of certain modern historians that the Moriscos preserved the use of some form of Arabic right down to the expulsion, the evidence suggests that large numbers of Moriscos could understand and speak Castilian or Valencian even if they continued to use Arabic among themselves.[28] This, at least, was the conclusion of the junta of Madrid, which had been called into session by Philip II to consider the Morisco problem. Addressing itself specifically to the question of the language that should be used in giving religious instruction to the Moriscos of Valencia, the members of the junta agreed unanimously that this could be done in Castilian or Valencian and need not be done in Arabic as some had proposed, since "generally all the new converts know, or at least understand them." The same panel commented that Moorish-style dress was no longer being used extensively and that the Morisco men were dressing "in the same style as the natives of the Kingdom of Valencia."[29] Unlike some other committees that were formed to consider the Morisco situation, this 1587 junta was unusually well informed and included at least two members with long personal experience of Valencian affairs, Juan de Çúñiga, who had served as inquisitor of Valencia from 1574 to 1579, and Dr. Sapena, the regent of the Council of Aragon and a Valencian judge from a respected old Valencian family.[30]

Even those Moriscos who came from regions where Arabic was still spoken and understood had lost the ability to understand the literary Arabic in which religious texts were written. An example of this would be the Valencian Morisco who stated that he could read and speak Arabic "but understood very little or nothing of the Koran."[31] The direct result of the decline of literary Arabic was the emergence of aljamía literature with texts written in Castilian but using Arabic characters. The use of aljamía certainly cannot be considered positive for the preservation of traditional Arabic culture, as many of the aljamía texts presented bastardized or highly abbreviated versions of the Arabic originals.[32]

The decline of Arabic among the Moriscos did not stop with the emergence of aljamía, however, since many of the religious and polemical works written by Morisco intellectuals for their fellow exiles in North Africa were in Castilian.[33] The de facto Arabic illiteracy among the refugees was given its clearest recognition by Mohammed Rubio, a cultivated and altruistic refugee from Aragon who financed the translation of a series of religious and polemical works from the original Arabic into Castilian.[34] These works were designed for the Morisco refugees of Tunis, where there was a large contingent of Moriscos from Valencia.[35]

Along with the decline in the use of Arabic among the Moriscos went an inevitable deterioration in the practice of Islam itself. This decay was recognized as early as 1568 by a memorialist who wrote that the Moriscos had long since given up "being Moors openly" and described them as a "peaceable and hapless people."[36] Under intense pressure from the church and the Inquisition, the Moriscos were forced to abandon certain external signs of Islamic belief such as the obligation to say five daily prayers.[37] Even more disturbing for the long-term survival of formal Islamic worship among the Valencian Moriscos was the impoverishment and alteration of traditional forms of critically important ceremonies such as those connected with birth, marriage, and burials. In 1583, at the Suprema's request, the tribunal presented a detailed description of the burial rites practiced by local Moriscos and concluded by noting that many of these were not of a traditional Islamic kind but "ceremonies that they have introduced among themselves."[38]

Analysis of the religious practices of Moriscos brought to trial by the Valencia tribunal further reinforces this impression of a decayed and watered-down version of Islam that was embraced more out of custom or a desire to differentiate oneself from a hostile Old Christian community than because it was a live and vital faith. Fully 81.5 percent of the Moriscos tried were accused of practicing just a few of the most elementary Islamic observances, primarily Ramadan, Guadoc, and the Cala. A late description of their practices drawn up by the Inquisition in 1602 lists only two of these (Ramadan and Cala) among the five "commandments" that supposedly distinguished them from Old Christians. These five items are in marked contrast to the much larger list of main offenses drawn up by the tribunal at an earlier period.[39] In evidence drawn from the trial records, circumcision appears to have been quite frequent, but ceremonies like ritual baths, common at an earlier period, were entirely forgotten, and only 1.7 percent participated in the ritual washing of the dead. Overt expression of pride in being Moslem was rare: only 1.2 percent declared their desire to "live and die as Moors," and only 1.1 percent were accused of openly praising Mohammed. Of course, it would be foolish to assert that all of the Moriscos of Valencia were ripe for conversion around the time of the expulsion, but the evidence suggests that large numbers of them were in a phase of religious transition.

Furthermore, in many instances, a Morisco's ignorance of the basic prayers and rituals of Christianity was equaled or exceeded by his ignorance of Islam. Many of the Moriscos who carried Islamic religious writings on their persons or had Islamic religious books in their possession were not only entirely illiterate but had an extremely low level of religious participation and knowledge. Pedro Alamin, who was arrested for carrying a paper containing extracts from the Koran, declared that he had picked up the paper in the road and did not know what it contained since "he cannot read." He had occasionally gone to mass but had never confessed and did not know any of the basic Christian prayers. Apart from having been circumcised, there is no evidence that he had actively participated in any Islamic rite. He was sentenced along with three other men accused of carrying Islamic religious writings as amulets and charms.[40]

Some Moriscos did experiment with Catholicism and Catholic practices, although such experiments did not always have happy consequences. Marco Lardillo, a young Morisco peasant from Carlet, for example, joined one of the confraternities and flagellated himself one Holy Friday. He was arrested after being heard to curse the "evil sect" that harbored such practices.[41] It is also significant that 2.8 percent of the Moriscos tried by the tribunal from 1554 professed a strong attachment to Roman Catholicism.

Scattered evidence of a certain amount of sincere Catholicism among the Moriscos even comes from around the time of the expulsion. The Valencia tribunal itself was forced to write the Suprema for instructions regarding a certain number of Morisco women who had come to the Holy Office voluntarily before the expulsion was announced and who wished to live in a special house established by Archbishop Ribera where they could "carry out their desire to live as Christians."[42]

In this same document, the tribunal referred to the cases of those Moriscos who might now come forward to declare a sincere desire to convert. Alonso de Medallan, a Morisco from Quesa, was one such individual. After having fought in the brief rebellion that followed the promulgation of the edict, he came to the tribunal of his own accord "to confess his sins and ask for penance and mercy."[43]

Even more significant, perhaps, for the potential success of the conversion effort over the long term was the way in which Valencia's Moriscos were beginning to learn basic Christian prayers and rituals under the pressure of indoctrination by village priests. By the early seventeenth century, even among the Moriscos tried by the Holy Office, it was becoming difficult to find those who did not perform basic Christian observances (mass, confession) or recite basic Christian prayers (Our Father) and the articles of faith.[44]

Paradoxically, even some of the religious doubts raised by Moriscos about Catholicism were more reflective of an Old Christian popular perspective than an Islamic one. In the Koran, the Virgin Mary is spoken of with great respect as the "excellent and devout lady" and the Virgin Birth is fully accepted. As a consequence, whatever their differences with Christians on other points of dogma, Morisco intellectuals fully supported this concept. It was exactly the opposite with the Morisco popular masses who consistently expressed the same doubts about Virgin Birth as their Old Christian counterparts.[45]

Moriscos and Old Christians also frequently expressed similar attitudes toward indulgences, even using the same scatological language when referring to them. Marco Antonio Font, an Old Christian alguacil, was deprived of his office and exiled after he offered to "wipe his ass" with the indulgences that a Crusade commissioner was selling in his village. At the same auto, Angela Adori, a Morisco living near Cocentaina, was punished for responding "bulls of my asshole" when she was urged to purchase them along with other Moriscos of the village, and Francisco Tartalico termed indulgences "not glory but shit."[46]

The efforts of an occasional well-meaning missionary or conscientious bishop notwithstanding, the conversion and social integration of the Moriscos depended on a long-term commitment to integration by church and society. Sadly, such a commitment was never made, and by the time Spain's political and religious leaders became aware of the seriousness of the problem in the 1570s and 1580s, prejudice against the Moriscos had become so ingrained that the task had become impossible.

Of all the missed opportunities that punctuated relations between Moriscos and Old Christians in the sixteenth century, perhaps the most significant was the failure to establish an adequate network of parish clergy who could provide religious services and instruction on a day-to-day basis. The need to establish such a network was not even recognized until 1535 when the bishop of Ciudad Rodrigo, Antonio Ramírez de Haro, toured the kingdom and set up 120 rectories in the villages with the largest population of Moriscos.[47]

Almost from the moment of its inception, this system was widely regarded as grossly inadequate and corrupt. For one thing, even though the system had grown somewhat by the 1580s, it was still too small to adequately serve the Morisco population. In the Archdiocese of Valencia alone, only slightly more than one-half of the Morisco villages had rectories.[48] The worst problem with the rectories, however, was not the size of the network but the virtual impossibility of recruiting clergy of sufficient quality and commitment to staff those that had been established. Each rector received only 30 lliures annually, and this amount, which was inadequate to begin with, suffered a serious reduction in purchasing power in the face of rapidly rising prices.

Apart from the enormous difficulty of finding individuals to staff the rectories, the inadequate endowment meant that rectors were compelled to supplement their income by forcing their Morisco parishioners to pay exorbitant fees for religious ceremonies or making them work without wages in their fields.[49] For other rectors, the only solution to their financial woes was to seek other employment even though this meant a high level of absenteeism. Of course, the Moriscos were constantly complaining about their rectors, denouncing them for their eagerness to levy fines for the slightest transgression while caring little for the salvation of their Morisco flock.[50]

But some rectors were so corrupt that they were unwilling to enforce even external religious conformity. While making a visitation to the Sagunto district north of the capital, Inquisitor Alonso Jiménez de Reynoso received testimony from an Old Christian living in the predominantly Morisco village of Gilet indicating that the rector sold local Moriscos licenses permitting them to slaughter animals in accordance with Islamic ritual, permitted Islamic-style marriage ceremonies, and allowed the Moriscos to work on Corpus Christi and other Catholic holidays.[51] And some rectors, while not personally corrupt, were so hostile toward their Morisco flock that they did little more than alienate them.[52]

Recognition of the critical need to reform the Valencian rectories began in the mid-1560s when the junta of Madrid, which met under the leadership of Inquisitor-General Fernando de Valdés, proposed sending commissioners through the kingdom with powers to compel absentee rectors to serve in their posts.[53] The heart of any genuine reform effort, however, would depend on increasing the income attached to rectories while sparing the Moriscos additional financial burdens. Since the ecclesiastical tithes (diezmos) of most Morisco villages were owned by great ecclesiastical institutions or were in private hands, Philip II's first thought was to tax these revenues since they were originally intended to support local churches. Pius V declined Philip's request to tax Valencia's tithe holders, however, and accurately forecast the years of difficulty that the king and other reformers would have in finding money for the rectories when he commented that the tithe holders' cooperation would be extremely difficult to enlist "even for such pious work."[54]

Finally, at a junta held in 1573–74 under the leadership of Archbishop Juan de Ribera, he and the other religious leaders of the kingdom agreed to provide funds from the revenues of the church to found new rectories and raise their stipends to 100 lliures.[55] The drastic failure of this program demonstrated conclusively that below the level of a few enlightened or conscientious prelates and political leaders, the Valencian church as a whole was not prepared to commit itself to the conversion effort, especially if that commitment entailed reduced income for canons, benefice holders, or monastic institutions.

In spite of his ambivalence about the Moriscos, Archbishop Ribera attempted to promote the conversion effort by starting a special fund. This money was then invested and the income used to support rectors in the archdiocese, endow a special school for Morisco children, and provide religious instruction. Unfortunately, none of the other institutions or individuals (who were assessed for the new program) was willing to contribute. Instead of following Ribera's example, ecclesiastical institutions and private individuals petitioned for relief from the king, and cathedral chapters and monastic institutions sent representatives to Rome to protest against any effort to tax their income.[56]

In spite of Ribera's conscientious support, therefore, it appears that little was accomplished in the way of reforming and restructuring the system of rectories. This was admitted by the count of Chinchón in a debate on the Morisco situation held in the Council of State shortly before the expulsion.[57] The drastic failure to establish an effective network of rural rectories and the sporadic and perfunctory nature of the religious instruction offered to the Moriscos on a day-to-day basis could not be overcome by the missionary campaigns of a few well-meaning individuals. As a consequence, the process of conversion remained painfully slow, and the majority of Valencia's Moriscos remained outside the Christian camp until the time of the expulsion.

Quite apart from the inadequacy of the conversion effort, the ability of Islam to survive in the undoubtedly hostile climate of Christian Valencia suggests that its structure had hidden strengths that enabled it to resist the pressures placed on it. One vital element in this structure was the continued existence of dedicated Islamic teachers (alfaquis) who not only offered religious instruction but even acted as judges in private disputes.[58] Some of these men traveled around the kingdom giving lessons in Islamic rituals in private homes. At the auto de fé that was held on September 5, 1604, Gonzalo Plaçuela was punished for opening his home to two Islamic teachers who taught religious ceremonies to a large number of local Moriscos. The teachers were equipped with several Islamic religious works and required their students to demonstrate the ceremonies that they had been taught so they could be sure that they could perform them properly.

Another factor that made the task of conversion difficult was the nature of the Morisco community itself. In spite of the fact that there were many villages with a mixed Old Christian-Morisco population, the Moriscos remained very close knit, with marriage among first cousins very common. As a result, everyone in the community knew instantly when one individual had cooperated with Christian authority in some obvious way like testifying before the Holy Office. Retribution could be swift and deadly in such cases. In 1605, Antonio Roche, a familiar in Carlet, came before the tribunal to testify concerning the sudden disappearance of Luis

Pastoret, a Morisco of the village who was hated by his Morisco neighbors for having celebrated several Catholic religious festivals with the Old Christians of the village and testifying against them before the Inquisition.[59]

Until very late in the century, moreover, those Moriscos who wished to maintain an Islamic life-style could count on a very powerful ally—their lords. The most famous case of complicity between a powerful noble and his Morisco vassals was that of Sancho de Cardona, admiral of Aragon, who was punished by the Valencia tribunal in 1570 for a variety of offenses, including giving the Moriscos of Adzaneta permission to operate a mosque, allowing Moriscos to pass through his territory on their way to North Africa, and encouraging his vassals to resist efforts to convert them.[60] The duke of Segorbe appears to have followed a very similar policy on his estates in the Vall de Uxó, where he allowed an Islamic school to operate freely. Fray José Cebrian, who testified about his experiences in the Vall de Uxó in 1563, recalled that the duke's Morisco vassals were very happy with their lord and that one of them commented, "Here we have such a wonderful señor; we live as Moors and no one dares to say anything to us."[61] So confident were the Moriscos in the protection afforded to them by the nobility that Pedro Aman, who escaped from the Inquisition in 1573, wrote to his friends in Onda encouraging them to resist conversion on the grounds that the nobles would soon intervene to stop the Inquisition from persecuting them.[62]

Of course, with a few exceptions like the admiral, who was also accused of not confessing or taking communion, the nobles were as devout as anyone else in sixteenth-century Valencia.[63] Their support for the religious practices of their Morisco vassals, therefore, was not based on any enlightened respect for religious freedom but on the pecuniary advantages they derived from it. The Duke of Segorbe, for example, regularly received a portion of the estate of his deceased Morisco vassals since it was the Islamic custom to set aside part of the estate for the lord.[64] The Moriscos of Cortes paid their señor a special tax in return for which he allowed them to practice Islamic customs freely and even personally attended their ceremonies and weddings.[65]

While Morisco obduracy and the support they received from the nobility presented formidable obstacles to the integration of the

Moriscos into Valencian society, it was the political and religious atmosphere of the last half of the sixteenth century that really determined their fate. Such events as the rise of the Huguenot movement in France in the late 1550s and the discovery in 1557–58 of groups of Protestant sympathizers in Seville and Valladolid, the Dutch Revolt of 1566, and the second revolt of the Alpujarras in Granada (1568–1570) dramatically increased the level of mistrust and suspicion directed against any group of apparent nonconformists.[66] Furthermore, in the perfervid imaginations of the staunchly orthodox and narrow-minded group that came to power during those years, it appeared likely that Spain's growing list of internal and external enemies would not act in isolation but would join forces to oppose her. Since Valencia's Moriscos were a readily identifiable dissident group, it became all too easy for official circles to see the hand of the French Huguenots or the Ottoman Turks behind every rumor of Morisco resistance. Thus, in 1587, the Suprema solemnly warned the tribunal to be on its guard against a rising by Valencia's Moriscos in concert with the Moriscos of Aragon and the Huguenot prince of Béarn merely because a rumor had reached Madrid that the Aragonese Moriscos were purchasing arms and had dealings with the Huguenots. Lacking any direct evidence, the Suprema simply assumed that the Valencian Moriscos were involved in the supposed plot because of their close proximity to and frequent communication with their Aragonese cousins.[67]

Ordinary Valencians probably thought seldom, if at all, about collusion between the French Huguenots and local Moriscos. They were far more concerned with the corsair attacks that had ravaged and partially depopulated the coast and killed and kidnapped even Christians living far from the sea.[68] By the last quarter of the sixteenth century, estimates of the number of Christian captives in Algiers alone were as high as 25,000, and the authorities seemed powerless to prevent the raids.[69]

It was commonly believed that local Moriscos aided and abetted the corsairs. While the fears of Morisco complicity with the corsairs may have been exaggerated, especially as most of them lived far from the coast, they were not entirely unfounded. In October 1583, fifteen Moriscos of Almería were executed for having assisted Algerian corsairs in an attack on Chilches.[70]

Unquestionably, some Moriscos helped the pirates directly by furnishing guides or military assistance, but a more important part of this collaboration was that many Valencian Moriscos emigrated to North Africa and later returned as corsairs themselves. Abdella Alcaxet, a native of the village of Bellreguard near Gandía, was captured by a squadron of Spanish galleys patrolling the Valencian coast and brought to the tribunal in September 1576. Under questioning, Alcaxet testified that he had left Spain some twenty years earlier with a group of Moriscos from Oliva and served the king of Algiers in two military campaigns. Later, he turned to piracy and made seven corsair expeditions of his own, seizing several Spanish vessels and either forcing the crews to become galley slaves or selling them in Algiers.[71] Some renegade Moriscos even returned to attack the villages from which they had fled. In 1595, during an attack on Teulada, the corsairs killed Antonio Vallés and captured his wife and children. In commenting on this raid, the viceroy of Valencia remarked that the raiders could not have gotten so far inland had it not been for the help of two Moriscos of the village, enemies of Vallés who had fled to Algiers some years earlier.[72]

Official paranoia combined with popular hatred ended by poisoning the atmosphere and shattering the hopes of those few clerics and statesmen who still believed in the possibility of conversion.[73] In official circles, even at the level of the prestigious Council of State itself, extreme solutions to the Morisco problem were being proposed, including such things as mass enslavement of all males ages 15 to 60 or the castration of young men over a certain age.[74] Rejection of the Moriscos on a popular level can be seen in the proliferation of guild ordinances prohibiting Moriscos from becoming apprentices.[75] Morisco physicians, like the Jewish or converso physicians of a century earlier, were being charged with poisoning and maiming their Old Christian patients, and there was a growing demand that Moriscos be excluded from medical schools.[76] This popular hostility resulted in violent attacks on the Moriscos as they streamed toward the ports of embarkation during fall 1609.[77]

During the years immediately following the forced conversion of Valencia's Moriscos, and especially during the tenure of Inquisitor-General Alonso de Manrique, the Inquisition's official policy appeared to reflect the attitudes of moderation and limited toleration that were shared by the emperor and leading members of his administration. The inquisitor-general played a leading role in the series of negotiations carried on from 1525 with twelve representatives of the Valencian Moriscos which resulted in an agreement containing a rather ambiguous clause granting them for the next forty years the same protection from inquisitorial jurisdiction that had been granted to the Moriscos of Granada at the time of their conversion. The document also promised toleration, for a limited period, of Moorish dress, the use of Arabic, the maintenance of separate cemeteries, and even a subsidy for the now-displaced Islamic priesthood.[78]

This moderate approach appeared to be shared by at least a few of Valencia's inquisitors even into the late 1560s. In his remarkable report to the Suprema on the results of his visitation to the Segorbe region in 1568, Inquisitor Juan de Rojas freely criticized the absenteeism of so many local rectors and the greed of the nobility who collected the ecclesiastical rents that should have gone to maintain the churches and levied exorbitant dues and tribute on their Morisco vassals. He was particularly incensed at a recently concluded agreement between the bishops of Segorbe and Tortosa to exclude all the Moriscos of their diocese from attending mass on the grounds that they all lived as heretics and were therefore excommunicated. This, of course, was exactly contrary to the policy of conversion and attraction then favored in official circles, and Rojas demanded that the bishop's order be rescinded immediately.[79]

During the middle years of the sixteenth century, Gregorio de Miranda, who had served on the Valencia tribunal from 1548, played an influential role in the evolution of policy toward the Moriscos. After replacing Antonio Ramírez de Haro, bishop of Segovia, as special commissioner to the Moriscos in 1551, Miranda carried out an extensive visitation to the heavily Morisco areas of the district and became quite popular with Morisco leaders such as the Abenamir family of Benaguacil.[80] In the late 1550s and early 1560s, Miranda served on several special commissions on the Morisco problem that were established by order of Philip II and was reappointed as special commissioner in 1566.[81]

Miranda's policy toward the Moriscos is perhaps best outlined in his summary of the deliberations of the 1561 junta, whose conclusions strongly reflected his views as outlined in several other memoranda. He favored a broad attack on Islamic religious ceremonies and the religious leaders who sustained them as well as a campaign to disarm the Moriscos so as to weaken their resistance. He also favored attracting the Morisco elite by appointing some men of influence as familiares. To carry out a thorough reform of the entire conversion effort, he proposed that a number of special commissioners should be selected to travel through the kingdom. These commissioners would also be empowered to look into abuses ranging from the rampant absenteeism by local rectors to the unauthorized diversion of the revenues of the former mosques into the hands of the nobility which were hampering the conversion effort.[82]

These ideas, as embodied in the resolutions of the junta of Madrid which met at the end of 1564, might have opened a new and more promising phase in the relations between the Morisco community and the state.[83] They did lead to the reappointment of Miranda as commissioner and to his selection of a number of Morisco leaders as familiares, including several members of the influential Abenamir family. What is questionable, however, is the degree to which someone like Miranda represented mainstream views within the Inquisition, much less in society as a whole. Of course, the evidence suggests that Miranda himself hoped to profit from his commission by collecting fines and had appointed a special treasurer for them. When he learned of this, Philip II ordered him to desist on the grounds that this would alienate the Moriscos and undermine the entire purpose of the commission.[84]

Another point of view, which was diametrically opposed to that of Miranda and other moderates, was expressed by Inquisitors Pedro de Çarate, Francisco de Arganda, and Juan de Llano de Valdés in their reply to a memorial that had been submitted to Philip II by Jerónimo Corella of the Council of Aragon. Corella, who was a moderate on the Morisco issue, called for another, more intensive conversion campaign and contended that the relative failure of the conversion effort thus far was the result of a lack of resources rather than the impossibility of the task. Taking a rather broad hint from the Suprema, which had sent them the memorial for their comments on the result of so many years of "using the Moriscos with softness and moderation," the three inquisitors rejected the entire notion of conversion and called for more intense persecution including capital punishment for first offenders.[85] Even though the moderation with which the Valencia tribunal carried out its judicial responsibilities during the period belied the violent tone of the memorial, the official position taken by the tribunal on this occasion could only add strength to those demanding a drastic solution to the Morisco problem.

Certainly the tribunals' actions with regard to the Moriscos were more reflective of ambiguity and greed than either the positive attitude and optimism so often expressed by Gregorio de Miranda or the outright hostility of Llano de Valdés. In 1528, Inquisitor-General Manrique modified the (already somewhat ambiguous) provisions of the 1526 agreement to allow the Inquisition a virtually free hand in the persecution of Moriscos on the grounds that they were continuing to practice Islam.[86] For its part, the Valencia tribunal had largely ignored the 1526 agreement and brought small numbers of Moriscos to trial almost every year from 1526 to 1540.[87]

Complaints by the Valencian nobility led to a virtual cessation of inquisitorial persecution between 1541 and 1543.[88] The period 1544–1546 saw the resumption of activity, with 165 cases tried in those years. Pope Paul III's brief of August 2, 1546, however, had the effect of virtually nullifying inquisitorial authority since it allowed confessors to be appointed who would be empowered to absolve Moriscos for crimes against the faith and relieve them and their descendants from all disabilities.[89] This brief, combined with a provision of the Valencian Cortes of Monzón of 1547 calling for "postponement" of proceedings against the Moriscos, led to a sharp decline in the tribunal's activity.[90] From 1554 to 1557, for example, only six Moriscos were tried, while at the auto de fé held on March 14, 1557, the forty-nine Moriscos who appeared were natives of Aragon and Catalonia who had moved to the district and were therefore not covered in the Cortes resolution of 1547.[91]

Behind the scenes, however, the tribunal was preparing to recover its lost authority by gathering evidence against nobles who encouraged their Morisco vassals to practice Islam and by sending letters to the Suprema describing the Moriscos' Islamic life-style.[92] In the 1560s, the tribunal unleashed a new wave of persecution. This time, however, its activity was rather more selective: it concentrated its attention on destroying the Morisco community's religious and political leaders. This approach was very much in line with the program of conversion/repression as set forth at the Cortes of 1563–64 and was specifically endorsed by the Suprema in 1565.[93]

In pursuit of this objective, inquisitors on visitation, like Juan de

Rojas in 1568, carefully drew up lists of leading Moriscos who were to be prosecuted as soon as possible after the conclusion of the most recent period of grace.[94] Morisco political leaders such as Vicente Cortes, who had come to Valencia as a special representative of the Morisco community, or Alfonso Bastante and Jaime Bolaix, who led the Moriscos of Vall de Uxó in an angry confrontation with the Bishop of Tortosa in May 1568, were also prosecuted.[95]

On July 1, 1567, after a consultation with the Suprema, the Valencia tribunal issued an order to arrest Cosme, Juan, and Hernando Abenamir, probably the most important and widely respected members of the Morisco political elite. In spite of Gregorio de Miranda's campaign to win over the Abenamirs, a campaign that resulted in making Cosme Abenamir a familiar, his colleagues on the tribunal had been gathering evidence against the family since March 1556. Testimony in the case reveals Cosme's religious position as somewhat ambiguous. In spite of being a strong and vocal defender of Islam, even asserting that it was superior to Catholicism in a conversation with Gaspar Coscolla, an Old Christian merchant living in Benaguacil, Cosme testified that he had been married according to the rites of the church and recited the Our Father and Ave Maria during his first interrogation. On this occasion, Cosme was able to purchase a pardon from Inquisitor-General Diego de Espinosa for the substantial sum of 7,000 ducats, and he and his brothers were allowed to return to their homes. But their cases were only suspended, and even the Inquisitor-General's pardon could not save Cosme from being rearrested in December 1577.[96]

At the auto de fé of 1568, it was the turn of Islamic religious teachers. After Valencia's inquisitors angrily rejected a suggestion from the Suprema that it might be wiser to read out the alfaquis' sentences at a private ceremony to avoid offending the Moriscos, ten leading alfaquis appeared among the forty-nine Moriscos sentenced at the auto.[97]

The inability of the Inquisition to support its campaign against the Moriscos by confiscating their property would sooner or later have forced a halt in this intense activity given the tribunal's extreme financial penury during the middle years of the century. Confiscation of Morisco property, however, had been prohibited by a royal order issued at the Cortes of Monzón of 1533 which provided that the property of a Morisco condemned for heresy should pass to his Catholic heirs and protected any rights that his señor had in the property. At the auto de fé of July 7, 1566, the tribunal simply ignored this law and proceeded to confiscate and sell the property of the Moriscos who were reconciled. This brought an instant protest from the estates of the kingdom, which sent two ambassadors to court.[98] Assured of the Suprema's full support for its actions, the tribunal did the same thing with the property of those reconciled at the auto of 1568. Realizing that new protests would be entirely unavailing unless the tribunal was granted some form of financial compensation, the Cortes this time offered to provide a subsidy of 1,000 Valencian lliures.[99] Even though this offer was rejected, it did lead to a complex series of negotiations among the viceroy, representatives of the Morisco community, and the tribunal, which resulted in the agreement of October 12, 1571. This agreement, which was accepted with a great show of reluctance by the tribunal, meant that the Moriscos agreed to tax themselves to support the Inquisition. In return for this subsidy, which amounted to 2,500 lliures annually, the tribunal agreed not to confiscate Morisco property in the villages included under the agreement and to limit its fines to a maximum of 10 ducats. These fines were to be expended only on supporting or embellishing the rectory in the Morisco victim's home village or to pay the costs of feeding poor prisoners. During the negotiations for this agreement, the tribunal had also committed itself to restoring the property that it had seized illegally. Once the agreement was concluded, however, the tribunal ignored its ameliorating clauses. The property that had been confiscated and sold was never returned to its owners, and the 10 ducat fines that were routinely levied after 1571 were simply incorporated into the tribunal's regular income instead of being used for pious works or the relief of poor prisoners.[100]

During the 1570s and early 1580s, the paranoia that was beginning to grip government circles spread to the Valencia tribunal, making it supersensitive to any rumors of collusion between local Moriscos and Spain's internal or external enemies. The second revolt of the Alpujarras (1568–1570) stirred fears of a simultaneous rising by the Moriscos of Aragon and Valencia, while the arrival of Moriscos from Granada after their defeat was regarded as highly dangerous by all of the crown's representatives in the kingdom.[101]

In 1578, several Moriscos were accused of having received in their homes two emissaries of the king of Algiers, who had arrived with letters for the Moriscos of Aragon and Valencia.[102] The obsession with Morisco conspiracies, however, left the tribunal vulnerable to manipulation by unscrupulous individuals who were well aware that to denounce someone for being in contact with Turks or North Africans or French Huguenots virtually guaranteed his arrest regardless of how flimsy the evidence really was. In 1581, the tribunal's watchfulness appeared to have paid off in a big way with the discovery of a plot involving leading Moriscos from Valencia and Aragon. This seemed to be nothing less than the long-awaited grand conspiracy involving a rising by the Aragonese and Valencia Moriscos in concert with all of Spain's enemies, and for several years thereafter, the tribunal was busily engaged in arresting and trying the plotters. In this instance, zeal seems to have been stronger than discretion, and it was not until 1584, when the tribunal received testimony from Lorenzo Polo, then at the peak of his career as an informer (see below) to the effect that the so-called plot was a complete fabrication that prosecution was halted. Since Polo's testimony had proven to be so reliable in the past and since it was supported by no less than twenty-four other witnesses, Gil Pérez and Alonso Conejo, the chief "discoverers" of the alleged plot, were arrested and convicted of perjury.[103]

During the first half of the 1570s, the Valencia tribunal increased only slightly the level of anti-Morisco activity that had been attained during the 1560s. But by the last half of the decade, the figures reveal a rising trend of activity that was to continue right through the mid-1590s.[104] In part, of course, this increased activity reflects national political trends and the tendency to regard any Moriscos, no matter how assimilated, as a potential danger to Spanish security.

As far as the Valencia tribunal was concerned, this national trend was greatly reinforced by the spectacular revelations of Lorenzo Polo. Polo was the scion of one of the wealthiest and most distinguished Morisco families in Teruel. His family, along with several interrelated Morisco families living on the same two streets of the city, had converted to Roman Catholicism voluntarily in 1501 and were well known for an ostentatious display of Catholic orthodoxy. They were so well accepted as Christians that they had been able to intermarry freely with Old Christians, enter the priesthood, join confraternities, and carry arms—even in coastal districts, at a time when Moriscos who carried arms openly were regarded with great suspicion and subject to arrest. In 1575, when the Moriscos of Aragon were disarmed, Polo's father and other leading members of these families successfully petitioned the crown for the restoration of their weapons on the grounds that they should be considered Old Christians.[105] This secure and comfortable world came to a sudden and shattering end on May 2, 1578, the day that Polo walked into the headquarters of the Inquisition and laid a series of amazing allegations before the startled inquisitors. According to him, he and his entire family as well as all the other families living in that part of the city were secret Mohammedans and had been so ever since their voluntary conversion many years before. During the next several years, up to the mid-1580s, Polo and certain other members of Teruel's Morisco community testified against their erstwhile friends, and the tribunal was able to shatter what was arguably the most tight-knit group of Islamicizing Moriscos in the kingdom.[106]

For the inquisitors of the Valencia tribunal, the revelation that the same Morisco families that Inquisitor Juan de Rojas had once lauded for their "good and Christian lives" were secretly practicing Islam must have been profoundly shocking. During the early 1580s, the tone of inquisitors' letters about the Morisco situation becomes harsher, less compromising, and less hopeful about the possibility of conversion. It was in 1581, as dozens of Teruel's Moriscos were being brought to trial, that Valencia's Inquisitor Alonso de Reinoso first suggested the idea of expulsion in a letter to the Suprema.[107] The external conformity and inner apostasy of the Moriscos of Teruel also figured in the violently anti-Morisco tract written by Martín de Salvatierra in 1587. Salvatierra, who had been inquisitor of Valencia in the early 1570s, singled out the "wickedness and ill-will" demonstrated by the Teruel Moriscos as a way of showing the futility of any further conversion efforts and justifying such extreme measures as castration of young males and expulsion.[108]

In what seems almost to have been a reaction to the sharp increase in corsair activity against the Valencia coast after the Hispano-Turkish truce of 1580 (raids on Calpe and Chilches in 1583 and Altea, Polop, Moraira, and Callosa in 1584) and the Teruel affair, the Valencia tribunal greatly intensified its persecution of Moriscos.[109] Between 1585 and 1595, the tribunal punished a total of 1,063—more than in any comparable period either before or since. There was a drop almost to the level of the late 1570s in the period 1595–1599 (162 cases) and then a resumption of a level of activity similar to that of the mid-1580s through the period of the expulsion and beyond.[110]

On a national level, the controversy over the ultimate fate of the Moriscos continued, but by the first years of the seventeenth century, the idea of expulsion was gaining more and more adherents. At a meeting of the Council of State on January 30, 1608, a majority of the members spoke as though the decision to expel the Moriscos of Valencia had already been taken, and even those members who seemed to oppose it could offer but feeble resistance.[111]

At the Council of State session of April 4, 1609, the expulsion of Valencia's Moriscos was finally approved in light of the fact that the success of truce negotiations between Spain and the United Provinces had removed concern about foreign military interference and freed Spanish resources for the operation.[112] The decree of expulsion itself faithfully reflects the views of hardliners like Juan de Ribera or the mayordomo, Gómez Davila, with its acceptance of the collective responsibility of the Moriscos for plotting with Spain's enemies and the complete failure of conversion.[113] In making a special point of the need to "placate" God who had been so grievously offended by the Moriscos, moreover, the royal decree seems to reflect the fears of divine punishment of Spain for tolerating known heretics which was so often expressed in letters and memorials around the turn of the century.[114]

As far as the Valencia tribunal itself was concerned, the decree of expulsion seemed to come as something of a shock. Even though three of its inquisitors had been among the earliest proponents of expulsion, later memorials from the tribunal or those closely associated with it had emphasized the need to force genuine conversion. In a letter written to the king in 1583, Valencia's inquisitors boasted that they had eliminated at least one major obstacle to the conversion effort by executing or imprisoning all the leading Islamic religious teachers.[115] In spite of its outward show of dissatisfaction with the Moriscos, the tribunal was profiting from the Morisco presence both through the subsidy provided in the Concordia of 1571 and from the 10 ducat fines that it routinely levied and pocketed. The tribunal's willingness to accept and profit from the Moriscos is clearly demonstrated by the fact that, like many Valencian nobles and ecclesiastical institutions, it made loans to Morisco villages, one as late as June 20, 1609, two and one-half months after the Council of State had decided on the expulsion.[116] Such loans actually helped Moriscos to expand into primarily Old Christian districts.[117]

The tribunal's attitude was further demonstrated by Inquisitor licentiate Bartolomé Sánchez during the deliberations of the ecclesiastical junta that was organized to consider the Morisco problem in November 1608. As reported by Fray Antonio Sobrino, a calificador who strongly supported renewed conversion efforts, Sánchez voted with the majority in rejecting the idea that the Moriscos were all incurable heretics and in favoring their inclusion—whether forced or voluntary—in the rites of the church.[118] But what probably shows the tribunal's acceptance of the Morisco presence more than anything else was the June 1606 memorial that was sent to the Suprema by Nicolás del Río, one of the tribunal's secretaries. This memorial, which could not have been sent without the explicit approval of the inquisitors, called for a dramatic increase in the arrest and trial of Moriscos, including those six hundred individuals already noted in the Inquisition's files with only one witness against them who were therefore not normally subject to persecution. These additional prisoners, and others brought in through the modification or suspension of other procedural safeguards, would then be heavily fined to provide funds for a new prison specially designed for Moriscos. Not only would this prison be more commodious than the old one but it would be equipped with a large chapel presided over by a well-trained chaplain who would provide them with religious instruction. Del Río's conception of this prison was that it should lead to the rehabilitation and not merely the punishment of its inmates. Instructed by the chaplain, watched over by a staff of warders, those prisoners who demonstrated proficiency in their religious observances could hope for a reduction in their sentences and eventual freedom.[119]

For its part, the Suprema received this suggestion favorably. In response to proposals made by the tribunal, it began commuting the sentences of a number of wealthy Moriscos then serving in the galleys in return for a substantial money payment. By January 30, 1609, three months before the Council of State resolution, construction of the new model prison was well under way, and the Suprema was in the process of selling more commutations so that it could be completed.[120] Del Río's proposal and the fact that the Valencia tribunal had dropped its earlier insistence on expulsion indicate a significant and growing division among the Moriscos of the district during the late sixteenth and early seventeenth centuries. Insight into this split may be gleaned from comparing data about the particulars of trials with information about sentencing. Broadly speaking, this evidence reveals that the Moriscos brought to trial by the tribunal fell into two main groups. The first, and largest, comprising 52.2 percent of the accused in the sample, were those who demonstrated a willingness to cooperate with the Holy Office either by coming in to denounce themselves voluntarily or by confessing at one of the early hearings during the trial. Their cooperation was rewarded with relatively light punishment. Fully 72.9 percent of this group received sentences of reconciliation accompanied by fines (11%) or, more frequently, religious instruction (25.9%).[121] By the 1580s, it appears that many Moriscos had come to accept the Holy Office as a relatively benign institution where they could confess their sins and expect to receive lenient treatment. For its part, the tribunal relied on the Moriscos for a good part of its revenues while coming to accept them as a not entirely irredeemable group whose practice of Islam was gradually fading.

In marked contrast to this cooperative or docile group were the "resisters," persons against whom there was substantial evidence but who refused to admit anything. It was against this group, comprising about 40 percent of the accused, that the tribunal turned the full force of its persecution and laid down its heaviest sentences. Of these negativos, 23 percent were sentenced to galley service, 17 of them to eight years to life, while 7 were relaxed. The existence of this sharp dichotomy among the Moriscos tried by the Valencia tribunal reveals that the Moriscos were no longer a monolithic group, while the tribunal's pedagogy of punishment could not have failed to further isolate the large but vulnerable group of die-hards.

For the first few years after the expulsion, the tribunal maintained the intensity of its anti-Morisco activity, punishing no less than 258 Moriscos between 1610 and 1614.[122] This activity was sustained by the fact that not all the Moriscos had actually left Valencia, while others returned either as pirates or because they found living conditions in North Africa intolerable.

In the first place, there were those Moriscos who resisted the expulsion order. In October 1610, two widely separate rebellions broke out, one in the Muela de Cortes valley region in the hills above the Júcar and the other in the coastal region around Guadalest. In the course of these risings, the Moriscos murdered priests and destroyed or desecrated churches, thus making themselves liable to inquisitorial persecution.[123] In addition to this group of rebels, several thousand Morisco children had remained behind after their parents had left.[124] Since many of these children had been taken into the homes of Valencian Old Christians, the government allowed them to remain in the kingdom, even though it made strenuous efforts to locate and count them. The tribunal, for its part, was kept busy hearing the confessions of these poor creatures who were brought to the Holy Office by their new masters.

Disappointing the hopes of those who felt that the expulsion would deprive the North African corsairs of critical assistance and therefore lessen the effectiveness of attacks on Valencia's ravaged coasts, the period 1610–1619 saw a dramatic increase in corsair activity and a sharp upswing in the number of captives seized.[125] Inevitably, military countermeasures netted a certain number of prisoners, and among these were to be found former Valencian Moriscos who served the corsair captains as soldiers, sailors, and guides.[126] According to a royal order addressed to the viceroy marquis of Caracena in February 1615, the Holy Office was to have jurisdiction over such persons even though they had been arrested by secular authorities for their crimes.[127]

A typical case of this kind was that of Amet Moro. A native of Benillup, Moro had gone to Algiers at the time of the expulsion, where he lived for three years. During that time, he turned corsair and served on several corsair boats engaged in raiding Spanish shipping. He was eventually captured and made a slave in Valencia city. At the outset he pretended, with some success, to be a Moor but was finally brought before the Holy Office after he was captured, along with several other slaves, while trying to escape. In his testimony before the tribunal, he admitted his Valencian birth and baptism but showed clear signs of repentance and a desire to receive instruction in Roman Catholicism. Seemingly unimpressed by this, the tribunal handed down the relatively severe sentence of perpetual imprisonment with the first three years to be spent in

galley service.[128] The harshness of this and other sentences that the
tribunal was handing down in such cases earned it a rebuke from
the Suprema in the following year.[129]

After the mid-1620s, the number of Moriscos tried by the Valencia tribunal begins to decline sharply until, by the 1640s, they came
to represent a tiny percentage of its overall activity.[130] During the
eighteenth century, even this very low level of activity had been
further reduced, and the Moriscos who had provided the tribunal
with 73.2 percent of its victims between 1560 and 1614 only accounted for thirteen cases between 1700 and 1820.[131]

As A. Domínguez Ortíz and Bernard Vincent have already observed, historical circumstances had deprived the Moriscos of the
elaborate social hierarchy so typical of early modern society.[132] Formation of a Morisco aristocracy, complete with large landed estates
and ties of vassalage, was made virtually impossible by the fact that,
with some exceptions, the bulk of the old Islamic leadership had
fled. Even someone like Cosme de Abenamir, the leader of a widely
respected family, was still a vassal of the Duke of Segorbe and was
forced to resign his familiar's commission at the duke's command.[133]

A hierarchy of religious leaders also failed to develop, in part
because in Islam itself the priesthood was not a well-defined group
and in part because such Islamic priests and religious teachers as
there were had to operate in secret.[134] Indeed, there is some evidence to suggest that Islamic religious teachers—the alfaquis and
tagarinos that were the subject of so much inquisitorial
persecution—came from the very lowest segment of the Morisco
population.[135] A combination of Old Christian hostility and discrimination and social pressure from the Morisco community itself made
conditions unfavorable for the development of a new class of Morisco
Catholic priests.

Creation of a class of professionals also proved to be quite difficult.
The ordinances of professional organizations regularly discriminated
against Morisco notaries, while Morisco physicians were viewed
with envy and distrust by their Old Christian colleagues and perse-
cuted by the Inquisition.[136] The biased attitude of Old Christian
professional groups rather than any inherent lack of ability, therefore, explains the tiny percentage of professionals (0.4%) among the
Moriscos tried by the Holy Office.[137] This is one of the lowest percentages of professionals of any group tried by the Inquisition.[138]

Strong Old Christian hostility could not prevent the Moriscos from becoming merchants; Vicente and Juan Baya Mallux, for example, formed a mercantile company in 1571 and prospered trading in silk, wool, sugar, and cattle.[139] Morisco muleteers also played a critical role in carrying goods from one region to another. So important were the Moriscos to the trade of the important inland town of Cocentaina that the city fathers complained that with the expulsion, "the greater part" of long-distance trade had come to a halt.[140] But given the paucity of well-established commercial routes in this still rudimentary society, muleteers were often merchants themselves.[141] Among the Morisco victims of the Holy Office in Valencia, 8.8 percent were merchants, and of these, more than half belonged to that class of petty shopkeepers and itinerant traders who played such an essential role in the Valencian economy.[142]

Drawing on their tradition of fine woodworking and metalworking, and sustained by the need for self-sufficiency in the isolated villages where most of them lived, the Moriscos frequently engaged in crafts.[143] This is reflected in the occupational structure of those tried by the Holy Office: some 19.2 percent were artisans, including shoemakers (in spite of the opposition of Valencia's shoemakers' guild), basketmakers, butchers, metalworkers, and stonemasons.

The overwhelming majority of the Moriscos tried by the Valencia tribunal, some 64.9 percent, gained their livelihood from agriculture. Although most of these peasants were quite poor, in many cases farming tiny plots, others were moderately well off.[144] Recent studies of landholding in several Valencian towns with large Morisco populations have revealed glaring inequalities, with the top 10 percent holding 38 to 50 percent of the land.[145] Among this small elite were to be found moneylenders and peasants with a variety of interests; for example, Gaspar Mois had holdings that included olive oil mills, olive groves, mulberry trees, and wheat fields.[146] It was from among this group that the tribunal could hope to make substantial financial gains either through confiscation of their property when they lived in villages not covered by the Concordia of 1571 or, more commonly, by allowing them to buy their way out of galley service or other heavy sentences for substantial sums of money.

In Islam, as in Judaism, many key religious rituals were performed primarily in the home and closely linked to family life. As a result, in both cases, women formed a relatively high percentage of those tried by the Holy Office.[147]

The figures on marital status reinforce the impression of the Moriscos of Valencia as a settled and relatively stable population of agricultural workers and peasants. More than 66 percent of the Moriscos whose marital status is stated in the records were married at the time of their arrest, while another 20 percent were widows or widowers. In spite of the mass flight of dozens or even hundreds of Moriscos from certain villages, therefore, their strong family orientation would appear to support Nicolás del Río's view of them as fearing nothing more than being forced to "leave their land and homes." Interestingly, del Río used his perception of the Moriscos' attachment to home and land not as a justification for expulsion but to support his proposal, which was designed to rehabilitate a significantly large number of Morisco offenders.[148]

Nevertheless, in spite of the obvious economic value of such a stable and productive population and the lack of any real threat of rebellion, social and political pressure for expulsion had become overwhelming by the first years of the seventeenth century. In this case, the proximate cause was not the actual (frequently moderate) outcome of inquisitorial activity but its inevitable social by-products: racism and discrimination. It was the spectacle of so many Moriscos being paraded before the eyes of the Old Christian population at the frequent autos de fé that did so much to artificially maintain the separateness of a community already moving toward assimilation. Of course, inquisitors like Bartolomé Sánchez knew that most of their victims were accused of trifling offenses, but the tribunal had taken an official position on the expulsion issue in the early 1580s, and the inquisitors of the early seventeenth century were neither strong enough nor independent enough to challenge the harsh and uncompromising mood that had taken hold in Spanish ruling circles and ended by sealing the fate of a community that had lived in Spain for hundreds of years. Carried out with brutal efficiency, the expulsion of the Moriscos represents the greatest achievement of Lerma's undistinguished regime. But, like so many of the other accomplishments of the imperial age, its results were deeply disappointing, weakening instead of strengthening the Spanish monarchy, undermining the Valencian economy, and lending further support to the black legend of Spanish intolerance.

VII

Illuminism, Erasmianism, and Protestantism: The Problem of Religious Dissent

In spite of the attention that Spanish Protestantism has received over the centuries, scholars have been skeptical about its real or potential impact on Spanish society. This view was perhaps best expressed by Lea who declared that it was unlikely that the small number of Spanish Protestants could make a "permanent impression on the profound and unreasoning religious convictions of Spain in the sixteenth century."[1] He and others have also rightly emphasized the benefits that accrued to the Inquisition from its discovery of Protestant "cells" in Valladolid and Seville and the spectacular autos de fé of the late 1550s and early 1560s. Given the small number of actual native Protestants punished at these and other proceedings, it might seem almost as though the Inquisition had grossly exaggerated the importance of the threat so as to reverse its flagging fortunes and render itself indispensable to the monarchy.

Of course, it would be foolish to deny that the Inquisition reaped substantial political and financial benefits from its persecution of Protestants, but, in my view, it would be equally foolish to underestimate the gravity of religious dissent and disaffection among the Old Christian population. In many regions, popular Christianity was neither "profound" nor "unreasoning"; it simply did not exist.[2] In other areas, even in places like the Archdiocese of Toledo with its large number of parish clergy, less than 40 percent of those the

Inquisition interrogated before 1550 could recite the basic prayers.[3] In Valencia, the tribunal found that only 8.7 percent of those tried for common blasphemy from 1554 to 1820 even mentioned the name of Jesus in their curses.[4]

Ignorance of the basic tenets of Christianity could prove to be as much of a barrier to the spread of religious heterodoxy as it was to official efforts to cathechize the population. What really concerned the church and the Inquisition, however, was the widespread doubt about or outright rejection of important Catholic dogmas and a pervasive anticlericalism expressed in everything from the picaresque novel to a statement by Lorenzo Sánchez, himself a notary of the Inquisition, who once declared that "tithes are ours, and the clergy are our servants."[5]

The Inquisition punished such statements under two general and overlapping headings: blasphemy and propositions. In their most serious form, both of these categories were designed to trap individuals who had made statements contrary to Catholic dogma and tending to a denial of faith.[6] In practice, the really serious forms of these offenses were not the blasphemous swearing that often accompanied games of cards or dice or the proposition, which represented the widely held belief that fornication between single people was no sin, but those statements that implied hostility to the church and rejection of its teachings. In Valencia, 50.3 percent of those punished for blasphemy between 1554 and 1820 were convicted for cursing and denying God and the saints. More significant of the widespread rejection of the position that the church claimed for itself was the fact that fully 24.2 percent of those convicted for propositions expressed doubts about the church's authority in matters of faith.

Although blasphemy was theoretically a less serious charge than propositions, there were at least some among the mass of ordinary people (mainly artisans and peasants) charged with this offense whose statements and actions betrayed a profound religious malaise. Cristóbal Ballester was one such person. This cavaller, the nephew of the governor of the estates of the admiral of Aragon, was a restless individual who moved incessantly around the district and lived separated from his wife. Convicted of blasphemy for the usual profanity, his refusal to go to confession, attend mass, or observe fast days reveal him as another one of the many Old Christians whose ambivalent attitudes about Roman Catholicism were a cause of increasing concern to the church in the turbulent 1560s.[7] Even more alarming from the standpoint of the church was that some people's blasphemy took the form of mocking church observances. Almost 13 percent of those convicted of blasphemy were accused of such mockery, which consisted primarily of satirical references to church ceremonies or the sale of indulgences but occasionally became sacrilegious. In 1665, Francisco Dalmau was accused of ridiculing Holy Week and habitually taking over the pulpit just before mass began to deliver an absurd and mocking sermon.[8]

But the ignorance, indifference, or downright hostility that characterized popular attitudes toward Catholicism all over Spain was counteracted, at least in part, by a broad-scale effort at religious reform and renewal that affected both monastic and secular clergy and involved pious laymen as well.[9] Within the monastic orders, this reform movement had a double thrust: institutional and individual. On an institutional level, the reformers wished to return to the simplicity and poverty prescribed in the primitive rule of the order. Closely linked with this, they offered each monk a new form of spirituality with strongly mystical overtones. This recogimiento tendency, as it came to be called, was an interiorized form of Christianity by which each individual sought to achieve union with God by searching within himself and following a course of methodical mental prayer.

By the beginning of the sixteenth century, this tendency was becoming popularized by such authors as García de Cisneros in his *Excercitatorio de la vida espiritual* (1500) and by groups of laymen and clergy who were strongly influenced by the works of the Catholic mystics which were becoming available in Castilian translation.[10] These groups frequently formed around a beata, a woman who had adopted a religious life without necessarily joining an order and who was regarded as having exceptional spiritual gifts.[11] This Illuminist movement, as it came to be called, eschewed the long and complicated spiritual exercises followed by the members of religious orders and promised that everyone who spontaneously accepted the enlightenment of the Holy Spirit could achieve a supreme and immediate union with God.[12] The egalitarianism and religious fervor of the Illuminists was an important source of religious renewal among the laity during the first decades of the sixteenth century, and Illuminist preachers under the leadership of Juan López de Celain (who was executed as a Lutheran in 1530) were even recruited by the admiral of Castile, Fadrique Enríquez, for an abortive campaign to evangelize his estates.[13]

The problem with Illuminism, however, as with all forms of mysticism, was that in upholding mental prayer, meditation, and direct communication with God as the most exalted form of religiosity, the Illuminists tended to downplay the importance of obedience, church observances, and good works.[14] The relationship of sexually frustrated priests and monks with the female beatas also posed the danger of sexual license, especially since Illuminism, in its most extreme form of Dejamiento, held that nothing could be sinful if it came from God. In Dejamiento, the believer combined a complete abandonment to the will of God with a doctrine of the impeccability of those whose souls were closest to God. The belief in impeccability led devotees to engage in daring sexual experimentation, which they not only believed was pleasing in the sight of God but would also aid them in achieving spiritual perfection. Moreover, beatas like Isabel de la Cruz posed special problems of their own. As women leading sexually mixed groups that frequently included male priests, they upset the traditional concept of a male-dominated church.[15] At the same time, the powers that they claimed for themselves frequently extended to setting aside church precepts (such as fast days), on the grounds that they were irrelevant or unnecessary for their devotees. This amounted to a substitution of private judgment for the rule of authority and could almost be construed as setting up a rival to the established church. Finally, apart from these doctrines that could more or less be accommodated within church tradition, there was another element to Illuminism that drew the special ire of theologians. Like all Spanish mysticism, it was hostile to scholastic theology, which, in its late-fifteenth-century form, seemed to provide little more than a field for abstract and involved theological disputes without reference to scripture.[16]

In light of all of this and the fact that many of the early sixteenth-century Illuminists were converted Jews, the Inquisition began taking an interest in the movement.[17] The tribunals where Illuminist activity was most concentrated began making arrests in the mid-1520s, and, in a series of trials lasting until the late 1530s, the leading representatives of the early Illuminist movement were punished.[18] In September 1525, the Inquisition also issued the first of its condemnations of Illuminist doctrine, which resulted in part from a visitation to Illuminist-infected zones of the Archdiocese of Toledo by a special inquisitorial commission appointed by Inquisitor-General Manrique.[19] This did not end the movement, however, and there were several more waves of Illuminist activity that attracted the attention of the Inquisition in Extremadura (1570–1582), upper Andalusia (1575–1590), Seville (1622–1630), and Valencia (1668–1675). Even after the major foci of the Illuminist movement had been destroyed, the tribunals continued dealing with isolated cases down to the end of the eighteenth century.[20]

The Valencia tribunal's experience with Illuminism was minimal in the sixteenth century as Valencia was far from the major centers of Illuminist activity in New and Old Castile. In January 1538, the tribunal punished Esperanza Martorella, called "the beata" for asserting, among other things, that she had frequent conversations with the angels, that God had given her the power to live without eating just like certain saints, and that she would receive the blessing of God, the Son, and the Holy Spirit whatever her sins and transgressions. While it is true that the tribunal classified this case as "Illusiones," Martorella's ideas and attitudes appear to fit comfortably into one or another of the lists of Illuminist propositions condemned by the Holy Office.[21] Certainly, her claim to be able to live without eating indicates that she believed herself to be in possession of a special state of spiritual perfection. She even testified that while she was in the inquisitorial prison awaiting trial, God had informed her that she would emerge from the ordeal "without shame."[22]

My analysis of the relaciónes de causas and cases during the seventeenth, eighteenth, and nineteenth centuries yields thirty-nine cases, with the last one in 1818.[23] These were not very frequent occurrences, however, averaging little more than one every ten years from the mid-1620s to the late 1660s, when the pace of prosecution definitely increases.

It was in spring 1668 that the Valencia tribunal, for the first and last time in its history, stumbled on a group of Illuminists similar to those discovered by the Toledo tribunal in the 1520s or the Llerena and Córdoba tribunals in the late sixteenth century. This group was made up of eight individuals who formed around a young (25) married woman named Gertrudis Tosca, whom they all regarded as their "spiritual mistress."[24] Like other beatas who played an important role in Illuminist groups, Tosca laid claim to great spiritual power. She said that she knew the mind of God and could tell if a deceased soul had mounted to heaven. At one point, she even declared that God had made her into another God on earth.[25] Like the early sixteenth-century practitioners of Dejamiento, she informed her followers that they should surrender themselves completely to the will of God even in matters normally considered sinful.[26]

Her disciples, including three priests, Remigio Choza, José Navarro, and Dr. José Torres, a benefice holder in the parish church of San Juan del Mercado, "worshiped her as a saint" and believed she was "especially illuminated with the Holy Spirit" and was "impeccable and confirmed in Grace."[27] This belief in Tosca's impeccability combined with the extravagant worship that the disciples accorded her, which included frequent kissing on the hands, mouth, and breast, led naturally to carnal excesses. All three priests became her lovers, sometimes performing the sex act openly in front of or even in the same bed as the female disciples. They justified this conduct to themselves and others as a way of advancing to perfection. Once when Luisa Choza, Remigio Choza's sister, was sleeping in the same bed with Tosca, the priest entered the room, undressed, and proceeded to have sexual relations with her. When Luisa reproached him about this, he answered that these carnal acts had been ordained by God and "were perfection, not sin."[28] José Torres, who admitted having intercourse with Tosca on thirty occasions, two of them in the communion chapel of the parish church of San Miguel, even claimed that each time they consummated the sexual act, a soul would be released from purgatory.[29]

Tosca's exalted conception of her own spiritual powers also led her to take on an almost priestly role among her devotees. She was obsessed with the desire to administer communion in her own home and did administer a form of communion to Torres. She also partially supported herself on alms given to her by her followers; she assured them that giving her the alms that they would normally have given at mass was exactly the same as giving them to the priest in church.[30]

The little group finally broke up because Tosca failed to justify her claim to possess extraordinary spiritual powers. The end came when Angela Sinisterra, one of her most recent devotees, decided to test her abilities by bringing her a blind man to cure. At first reluctant, Tosca attempted to bring about a cure and failed. This, in turn, led to a grave spiritual crisis for her, and shortly thereafter, she and some of her followers approached one of the tribunal's calificadores, who presented their confessions to the tribunal.[31]

Spontaneous confession combined with a remarkable reluctance by both the inquisitors and their consultor to use the words "heretic" or "Illuminist" when referring to the accused were responsible for the relative leniency with which they were treated. Except for Josefa Clement, who was admonished and given spiritual penalties, the cases of all the women in the group were suspended.[32]

The priests were treated with greater severity, although the final sentences were more a reflection of the Suprema's harsher attitude than the relative leniency advocated by the tribunal and its consultor. In the case of Torres, for example, the Suprema added exile, confiscation of property, and loss of ecclesiastical benefice to the abjuration and reclusion prescribed by the tribunal.[33]

So ended the Valencia tribunal's most important brush with Illuminism. One can only surmise that its failure to use the term "Alumbrado" in connection with these cases reflects a reluctance to make a martyr out of someone who had a popular reputation for extraordinary spiritual grace and virtue. The disastrous case of Padre Simón had taught the tribunal the virtues of discretion and the limits of its power over popular religious figures.[34] This impression of caution by the tribunal is supported by its reluctance to actually arrest the accused once their initial confession had been received and by its insistence on reading their sentences in private rather than holding a dramatic auto de fé.[35]

The edict of September 23, 1525, which condemned forty-eight propositions stemming from the beliefs of the "alumbrados, dejados o perfectos," and the trials of leading Castilian Illuminists during the mid-1520s and 1530s placed the Spanish reform movement on the horns of a cruel dilemma. The Illuminists and other reformers could throw in their lot with the Lutheran movement and abandon the Roman Catholic church altogether or they could resign themselves to accepting the Spanish Catholic church with all of its imperfections. Like the Italian spirituali, although for different reasons, neither of these alternatives was feasible.[36] For one thing, apart from a few Spaniards who had witnessed the dramatic events at the Diet of Worms and a few hardy German or Flemish merchants who talked about it during their journeys through the Iberian peninsula, Lutheranism was virtually unknown in Spain. Furthermore, an Illuminist-Lutheran alignment was also made more difficult by significant doctrinal differences, notably, over justification and the role of Christ.[37] By the 1520s, however, the Spanish reformers could no longer entirely accept conventional church practices or reconcile themselves with the institutional church.

A middle way, which could allow them to pursue their goals within the Catholic Church while affording them some protection from the Inquisition, was indicated by the favor shown to the works of Erasmus in official circles during the 1520s and 1530s. That this should be the case was more the result of a favorable (if temporary) conjuncture in imperial foreign policy than the fact that certain court officials were pro-Erasmian during this period.

As a consequence, for approximately twenty-two years, there was a tacit agreement between Erasmus's position on the need to reform radically and restructure the Catholic Church and the orientation of imperial policy. In concrete terms, the result was that influential courtiers and high-ranking administrators openly favored Erasmus, supported the translation of his works into Spanish, and extended their protection to intellectuals with a pro-Erasmian point of view. Since one of these high-ranking officials was Inquisitor-General Manrique himself, those who identified themselves with Erasmianism could even hope to enjoy a measure of protection against inquisitorial persecution. It was under Manrique that the Inquisition was given specific responsibility for curbing the already mounting chorus of criticism of Erasmus in Spain.[38] Manrique also presided over the theologians' commission that was convened on June 27, 152⅓, to debate the orthodoxy of Erasmus's work. Six weeks later, Manrique dismissed the commission because of an outbreak of plague in Valladolid, although some have suggested that he wanted to avoid a negative verdict.[39] Regardless of Manrique's intentions, it never reconvened, and the result was to perpetuate the status quo in which Erasmus's works were allowed to circulate freely.[40]

But the official support that Erasmus enjoyed and the protection that such support afforded had unintended and unforeseen effects on the native Spanish reform movement. The fact is that Erasmus's stress on mental prayer and his tendency to downplay the importance of formalized religious observances radicalized the Spanish reformers and moved some of them considerably closer to a Protestant or proto-Protestant position.

The impact of these Erasmian ideas on the intellectual and religious climate of Valencia in the 1530s was reflected in the trial of Miguel de Mezquita whose strong antipapal views found support in Erasmus's *Sileni Alcibiadis*, which had been translated by Valencian Bernardo Pérez de Chinchón and published in 1529.[41] Under interrogation, he admitted to owning copies of the *Enquiridion* and the *Colloquies*. The influence of the latter work on his religious practices can be seen in his manner of confessing every day in private. This "confession to Christ" prescribed by Erasmus in his *Colloquium senile* gave rise to an interesting exchange between Mezquita and his judges who tried to trick him into declaring that private confession alone was sufficient. A few years earlier, the Córdoba tribunal had tortured Diego de Uceda for admitting that he believed that the most important form of confession was private, but Mezquita insisted that oral confession before a priest was necessary at least once a year. This seemed to be enough for the inquisitors, who ordered him released.[42]

Official protection, the support of powerful nobles like the marquis of Villena in Castile or the duke of Calabria in Valencia and, above all, the favorable conjuncture in imperial policy were sufficient to protect the Erasmians of the 1520s and the 1530s from severe punishment even if they were brought to trial by the Inquisition.[43] The shift in imperial policy toward the German Lutherans which took place after the failure of the Regensburg conference and the hardening of papal attitudes under Julius III and especially Paul IV Caraffa (1555–1559) heralded a change in the way that the Spanish Inquisition would deal with religious tendencies that appeared compatible with Lutheranism. Already from the early 1540s, the Inquisition began to intensify its censorship activity.[44] In 1551, the Spanish Inquisition published its first index of prohibited books. This catalog was based on the University of Louvain Index of 1546 but added those works that the Inquisition had prohibited by edict as well as a whole series of general prohibitions on specific categories of books, which greatly increased its impact.[45] The death of Inquisitor-General Francisco García de Loaysa on April 22, 1546, and the selection of Fernando de Valdés to replace him brought to the Inquisition's highest office a man who had an almost visceral hatred of all forms of spirituality.[46] It was Valdés, with the help of his spiritual counselor, Melchor Cano, who presided over the destruction of the "Protestant" cells of Seville and Valladolid in 1558–1560 and unleashed the wave of persecution that included many native "Protestants" during the mid-1560s.[47]

It can scarcely be doubted that in most of these cases, the Inquisition was dealing not with true Protestants but with the evangelical and reformist strain in Spanish Catholicism. It is also undeniably true that Valdés exaggerated the threat and used it to solidify his own position and that of the institution he served. Nevertheless, the evolution of Spanish reformers from the first generation of the 1520s to the second generation of the 1540s and 1550s had moved them toward a doctrine of justification by the will of Christ in which works were seen to flow from and depend on faith.[48] Of course, this was not exactly justification by faith alone, but it was close enough to cause the Inquisition and the authorities serious and legitimate concern.

Related in time and substance to the inquisitorial crackdowns in Seville and Valladolid was the Valencia tribunal's persecution of the little group of Erasmians that formed around the Valencian noble, Gaspar de Centelles y Moncada. Centelles was the scion of a distinguished Valencian family that was linked by marriage to the counts of Gagliano. His grandfather, Pedro Sánchez de Centelles-Calatayud, was the first lord of Pedralba.[49] His humanistic intellectual concerns and evangelical religious orientation were nurtured at the imperial court during the mid-1530s.[50] After returning to Valencia sometime in the late 1540s, Centelles served as one of the four oidors de compte for the noble estate at the Cortes of Monzón of 1542. Ten years later, after quarreling with the fifth duke of Gandía, he became deeply involved in the violent feud that pitted the Pardo de la Casta against the Figuerola and involved such leading noble families as the Borja and the Aragon-Sicilia. As a consequence, Centelles was exiled to his estates by express order of Philip II.[51]

With plenty of time on his hands now that he was no longer involved in Valencian politics, Centelles returned to the intellectual concerns of his youth and became the center of a small group of humanists who carried on a vigorous correspondence and occasionally visited the palace in Pedralba to debate the religious issues of the day. The group included Miguel Pérez, a student who was reconciled in 1567, Pedro Luis Verga, reconciled in 1567 and relaxed in 1572, Dr. Sigismundo Arquer, a former fiscal of the Council of Aragon in Sardinia who was relaxed by order of the Toledo tribunal in 1571, and Jerónimo Conques, who was condemned to abjure de vehementi in 1564.

The tenor of this group's religious views can be best understood from the extensive correspondence between Arquer and Centelles and conversations held in Pedralba itself. In a series of letters written between 1548 and 1557, Arquer stressed the critical importance of Scripture as the basis for any true Christianity and praised those who became the "lambs of Christ without needing anyone to expound the gospel to them." Arquer also stated his belief that the faithful would have to rely utterly on God for their salvation since they were too weak to observe His law. It is little wonder that the theologians who reviewed these letters for the Toledo tribunal agreed that these propositions were strongly reminiscent of Lutheran ideas regarding works, observances, and spirituality.[52] Later, when Arquer stayed in Pedralba as a guest of Centelles, he became involved in a conversation with Jerónimo Conques concerning the Eucharist in which he specifically denied any change in the substance of the bread and wine.[53]

Conques, a benefice holder in Valencia's cathedral, was certainly more moderate than Arquer and claimed at his trial that he had rejected his view of the Eucharist. Instead of sharing Arquer's almost Lutheran position, Conques approached the church from an Erasmian standpoint. In his correspondence with Centelles, he deplored the way in which the ceremonies of the church were neither "meritorious nor useful" when carried out by those whose only desire was to make an outward show of piety. Claiming to be disgusted by the vulgarity and ignorance of certain local preachers, he intended to write a treatise on preaching based on Erasmus's *Ecclesiastes*.[54]

In 1571, after a long trial during which he proved himself a stubborn and resourceful antagonist, Arquer was executed by order of the Toledo tribunal. As for Conques, even though his theological position cannot be characterized as any more than moderate reformism, he, like Seville's Dr. Constantino some years earlier, had the misfortune to be part of a wider struggle involving the Inquisition and the canons of the local cathedral chapter. By his own admission, Conques had been one of those responsible for ejecting Inquisitor Francisco Ramírez from the seat that Valencia's inquisitors had occupied in the choir.[55]

Wounded but still dangerous, the tribunal found a way of avenging itself on the overbearing canons by punishing and humiliating one of their number who had made himself vulnerable because of his correspondence with Centelles. It is not difficult to imagine the inquisitors smiling inwardly as they sentenced Conques to two years of reclusion in the monastery of Nuestra Señora de Socorro outside the walls of the city. There, this detester of mindless devotions who had once helped Centelles wean Francisco Fenollet away from mechanically reciting his rosary was forced to say three parts of the rosary of Our Lady each day, amounting to 15 Our Fathers and 150 Ave Marías, and this avid correspondent could neither write nor receive letters without the express permission of the inquisitors.[56]

In December 1562, Centelles himself was arrested by the Valencia tribunal, which had been gathering information about the Pedralba group since the spring and was particularly eager to prosecute him because of the potential windfall it would receive in confiscating his estate.[57] After a prolonged period of depression during which he lived for seven months without opening the blinds that covered the windows of his cell, he recovered and took an aggressive tone with the theologians who came to convert him. Finally, when his defense attorney asked him to sign a statement in which he specifically recognized the Roman Catholic church as the only church of God, he refused and was condemned as a heretic at the auto de fé of September 17, 1564.[58]

According to the account that was sent to the Suprema by Inquisitor Bernardino de Aguilera shortly after the auto de fé, Centelles was at first adamant in his refusal to listen to any of the friars who were trying to get him to repent and publicly embrace Catholicism. But when the sentence was read out, he appeared to have been stricken by remorse and fell on his knees begging forgiveness of God and the assembled multitude and declaring that "burning was nothing to what he really deserved" because of his crimes and the bad example he had given. A few moments later, however, after he had been led back to the city hall, he appeared to have repented of his earlier weakness. Tearing off the cross that the friars had placed around his neck, he threw it to the ground and cursed "those who had made him worship idols." At the end of the ordeal, just before he was to be garroted, Centelles confessed and appeared to have repented of his earlier defiance, but when confronted once again with the demand for a confession of faith in the Catholic church, some observers said that he had refused to swear; others said he had.[59] On that ambiguous note ended the Valencia tribunal's most serious encounter with native Spanish Protestantism.

For the remainder of the century, the tribunal dealt with a few small and insignificant groups of native Valencians whose religious views were extreme enough for the tribunal to class them as "Lutherans." As it had from the mid-1520s, the tribunal confronted real Protestantism in the sense of conscious belief in and practice of Lutheranism and Calvinism largely in the shape of foreigners living, working, fighting, or traveling in the district.

An analysis of the sociological data drawn from the case summaries reveals that the overwhelming majority of those charged with "Lutheranism" were not only of foreign origin but were a typically transient population that put down few roots in Valencian society. One of the most revealing indications of this is a remarkable preponderance of young men and an almost total absence of individuals over 40 years old. More than 74 percent of those whose ages are known were between 20 and 30 years old, while only 10.5 percent were over 50. The impression of a young and rather transient group is reinforced by the data on marital status, which reveals that 82.6 percent were single at the time of their arrest. The offense was also overwhelmingly male, with only 2.1 percent of the cases involving women. Occupational data also serve to confirm this general picture. Only 4.3 percent were peasants, while 22.5 percent were artisans and fully 54.3 percent soldiers either from invading forces like the Allied armies during the War of the Spanish Succession or from the Spanish regiments themselves, which were filled with foreign recruits, especially during the eighteenth century.

Among the very first cases of Lutheranism tried by the tribunal was that of a German merchant named Blay who was associated with one of the companies of German merchants who were active in Valencia during the first half of the sixteenth century. Although Blay made no secret of his sympathy for Martin Luther and his ideas, there is little evidence to suggest that he was a Lutheran in any formal sense or that he had had any direct contact with the incipient Lutheran church in his native land. He seems to have approved of Luther mainly when he opposed clerical celibacy on the grounds that if priests or monks were of such weak character that they could not be without a woman, it would be better for them to marry than live in mortal sin. He also claimed (mistakenly) that Luther had declared that persons should come to confession voluntarily. Apart from this, the fragmentary record of the case reveals nothing about any belief in justification by faith, hostility to the ecclesiastical hierarchy or the pope, or any of the other core doctrines of Lutheranism. After a brief trial, Blay was sentenced to perpetual imprisonment and confiscation of his property.[60]

Germany also gave to the Valencia tribunal one of its most curious cases, involving John Heinrich Horstmann, a well-educated religious charlatan. Baptized a Catholic and given a good Catholic education by the Jesuits, Horstmann decided at around age 25 to leave his native Borgenstreich and wander Europe, supporting himself by teaching languages. Finding that this alone was insufficient, he soon discovered that he could profit from the rivalry between Protestant and Catholic by feigning conversion. In Protestant lands, he pretended to be a recent convert or a Catholic ready for conversion, while in Catholic countries, he became a Lutheran who wished to be baptized into the Holy Catholic Church. His excellent education and dignified bearing won him the support of powerful patrons in many places who were not only willing to sponsor his "conversion" but gave him small sums of money and even allowed him to tutor their children. In Perusia, for example, he lived in the home of the local inquisitor and received a purse of 30 escudos from the city. By the age of 89, when he was arrested by the Valencia tribunal, he had supported himself this way for more than fifty years and admitted to having been baptized on twenty-one separate occasions. He had even gone so far as to have himself circumcised in Amsterdam and practiced Judaism there for eight months while being supported by the Jewish community. Finally, in 1746, he returned to Spain, which he had visited twenty years earlier, and was baptized at Cádiz, Granada, Córdoba, and Valencia, where he lived for a time in the archbishop's palace. Horstmann's spectacular career finally came to an end when the Valencia tribunal arrested him on June 23, 1752, after receiving a letter from the Seville tribunal describing him and his activities. After his arrest, Horstmann told his story fully and without showing any remorse. He claimed to have always been a devout Catholic and only pretended to be a Protestant in order to get money and tutoring jobs. By February 1752, however, he was seriously ill, and as death approached, this religious chameleon and mountebank showed his true allegiance by refusing confession and the last rites of the church. When one of the priests who had gathered in his cell asked the by now mute prisoner to indicate whether he wanted to die as a Calvinist by squeezing his hand, Horstmann gripped it so hard that the priest had to call for assistance to loosen it. Immediately after his death on February 28, Horstmann was buried in a box of quicklime in the courtyard of the Inquisitor's palace, and at an auto de fé held on August 26, 1753, he was burnt in effigy by express order of the Suprema.[61]

Of much greater concern to the tribunal than the far-off German Lutherans were the French Protestants, especially after the Huguenot movement began to gain strength in southwestern France in the mid-1560s. The opportunities provided by Valencia's expanding economy provided a powerful lure for French immigrants, and modern estimates of the number of Frenchmen in the kingdom range as high as 30,000 for the period around 1600.[62] Certainly, the dangers of Protestant subversion appeared greater wherever the French settled in considerable numbers, especially in the northern part of the inquisitorial district. In 1574, the tribunal favored placing an additional commissioner in Morella because of the large number of French immigrants in that region.[63] In 1566, Sebastian Gutiérrez, who had stumbled across what appeared to be an entire Huguenot conventicle among the French living in Teruel, declared that the "very air" was infested with heresy in many places and that if the French were not watched carefully, the "infection would spread from Catalonia and Aragon to the rest of Spain."[64]

Apart from the fact that there were Huguenots among the French immigrants, there was also the ever-present danger of book smuggling from France. In 1567, for example, Cardinal Granvelle wrote to warn that the Huguenots were hoping to provoke disorder in Spain by sending quantities of subversive books. In June 1568, the Suprema wrote provincial tribunals to take extra precautions because of an alleged plot by the Huguenots to smuggle Protestant books into Spain utilizing compartments ingeniously fitted into wine casks.[65]

Given this degree of apprehension, which was no doubt heightened by fear of Spain's traditional enemy, the actual threat posed by the French immigrants seems to be weak. Certainly, an analysis of the cases of Frenchmen tried for Lutheranism by the Valencia tribunal reveals some who were strongly in the Protestant camp and had a good understanding of Protestant beliefs. The vast majority, however, occupied a kind of religious gray area, neither Catholic nor Protestant, frequently filled with anxiety about their religious position and willing, sometimes even eager, to reconcile themselves with the religion of their adopted country.

One of the very few French immigrants who can be said to have been a firm Protestant was Mateo Alari, who was sentenced to death at the auto de fé of April 19, 1587. Alari, who rejected confession, papal authority, indulgences, and the worship of saints, resisted all of the many efforts to convert him and declared that he intended to live and die as a Lutheran.[66]

In contrast, the case of Jerónimo Martorell, who was executed for the same offense in 1583, appears to be that of a person with a weak religious affiliation who was trapped by an unfortunate family situation. Martorell, who was a linen weaver, had left his native village some thirteen years earlier and served as an apprentice in Catalonia before setting up his own shop in Villafames. According to testimony by a number of defense witnesses, he lived as a Catholic while in Villafames, attending mass regularly, performing pious works, and going to confession. Unfortunately for him, the two young apprentices that he hired were Frenchmen who had been exposed to one degree or another to the Huguenot movement. Goaded by his apprentices who boasted of their disdain for Catholicism, Martorell began opening expressing Protestant or heretical views in conversation with them. The situation was further complicated by the fact that both young men were suitors for his daughter's hand. Since Martorell did not wish either of the men to be his son-in-law, he alienated both of them and lost his daughter anyway: she eloped with Guillén Mateu, who was going to be the chief witness against her father. When Mateu and Juan Philippe, the other apprentice, were arrested by the tribunal, they had no compunction about denouncing their former master as a Protestant. Driven by a fear of torture, Martorell then confessed to the charges, only to partially revoke his confession a few days later. With this revocation, of course, his case became considerably more serious, and the charge of being a "feigned, counterfeit penitent" was added to the rest. In spite of the fact that the testimony of the two apprentices had been at least partially invalidated by defense witnesses who testified that they were the accused's mortal enemies, Martorell's revoked confession had sealed his fate. Like so many others, he was the victim of ignorance about the inner workings of the Holy Office.[67]

Cut off from actively practicing their religion and exposed to the rich and splendid ceremonial of the Spanish Catholic church, French Huguenots settled in Valencia found themselves drifting back to the religion into which many of them had been baptized. In the case of Juan Casanyosas, who had rebelled against his strict Catholic father and claimed to have been a Huguenot from age ten, the reversion to Catholicism took the form of growing doubts about Protestant beliefs such as the futility of prayers to the saints. According to Casanyosas's account, he had begun to waver in his beliefs after he had heard sermons that "touched his soul" while living in Valencia. It is curious to note that Casanyosas made no attempt to conceal his Protestant views while in the secret prison. In fact, he behaved in such a way as to almost invite punishment by arguing points of religion with Jerónimo Biosco, a priest who shared his cell, and by singing Lutheran songs so loudly that they could be heard by the other prisoners. The impression of a person seeking a kind of expiatory punishment is borne out by his rapid and complete confession and his refusal to present any formal defense.[68]

In other instances, conversion to Catholicism was a much more open and conscious process in which the individual's confession at the bar of the Holy Office was an act of final and complete rejection of a Protestant past. David de Cabanès, a French journeyman who came to the Inquisition of his own accord in 1612, had been brought up as a Huguenot by his parents. After coming to Valencia in 1606, Cabanès served several masters, all of whom taught him the rudiments of Catholicism. He attended mass and went to confession but never felt comfortable enough to mention his Huguenot past. For Cabanès, spontaneous confession before the Inquisition was evidently a way of removing the guilt that he felt and more firmly establishing his new religious identity.[69]

From the perspective of the Valencia tribunal, therefore, it appears that the authorities' fear of religious subversion coming from the large group of French immigrants in the kingdom was largely unfounded. Dedicated Protestants with a sophisticated understanding of Protestant theology were rare among them, while the tug of Spanish Catholicism was strong even for someone like Martorell. Doubtless, some Frenchmen were able to communicate their religious ideas to Spaniards and others smuggled in prohibited books, but the impact that they could have on the native population was minimal because of their own internal divisions, isolation, and lack of strong commitment to the Protestant cause.

By the end of the sixteenth century, the decline in Protestant conversion efforts and the relative stability of European religiopolitical frontiers led to the emergence of a new policy with regard to foreign Protestants. This policy, which was to be followed with several interruptions until the final years of the Inquisition, involved tolerating their presence so long as they gave no offense to the Catholic religion. At the same time, Protestantism continued to be one of the Inquisition's principal enemies, so that vigilance remained high to prevent even the possibility of religious subversion. Moreover, at various times during the next two centuries of its history, the Inquisition helped the cause of Roman Catholicism by becoming a kind of conversion bureau for foreign Protestants, especially from places where Catholicism had retained its strength as a religious alternative.

This policy really began in 1597 when the Suprema issued an administrative order to all tribunals instructing them that merchants or sailors arriving from Hamburg or other German ports should not be molested because of their religion unless they had offended Roman Catholicism in Spain itself. Even if this had occurred, only the property of the individual who actually committed the offense was to be seized and not, as hitherto, the entire cargo of a vessel.[70]

When peace was made with England in 1604, one of the provisions of the treaty provided that King James's subjects would enjoy the same toleration as that extended to the Germans some years before.[71] While in Spain, they were not to be prosecuted for an offense against Catholicism committed previously. They were not to be forced to enter churches, but if they did so, they were expected to show the same reverence to the Holy Sacrament as anyone in the congregation. If they encountered a religious procession, they were either expected to kneel out of respect for the Holy Sacrament or avoid seeing it by entering a doorway or going up another street.[72]

Even before it had officially transmitted the relevant articles of the peace treaty to the provincial tribunals, the Suprema laid down the policy that was to be followed toward those English or Scottish Protestants who wished to convert. Those coming forward voluntarily could be heard by commissioners at the ports who would interrogate them as to their religious practices and refer them to the tribunal. After reviewing this testimony, the tribunal had two options: if the individual had had sufficient religious instruction or had once practiced Catholicism, he could be reconciled in the audience chamber and given spiritual penalties; if instruction was considered incomplete, they were to be absolved *ad cautelam* and remanded for religious instruction.[73] In 1609, when the twelve-year truce was signed with the United Provinces, the Dutch received the same privileges previously accorded to the English and Scots.[74]

Of course, such toleration, limited though it was, ran counter to the deepest social values of a society that had long prided itself on its fanatical opposition to any form of religious heterodoxy. Valencia's Archbishop Juan de Ribera expressed this attitude very well when he protested the 1604 peace treaty on the grounds that making peace with infidels is prohibited by divine law, while the evil example of the English Protestants openly practicing their religion might provoke heresy among the faithful.[75]

For its part, the Suprema lost little time in introducing arbitrary and illegal modifications to the treaty provisions. In 1612, it asserted a distinction between transient and resident foreigners. Resident householders were expected to practice Catholicism and were subject to the Inquisition in matters of faith. In May 1620, the Suprema insisted that no foreigner living in the port towns could maintain an inn and cautioned the tribunal that close watch should be kept on such persons so that "the plague of heresy" would not be revived.[76]

With the renewal of hostilities between Spain and Holland (1621) and England (1624), the privileges contained in the earlier treaties became null and void, and the Inquisition once more took up the persecution of English and Dutch Protestants found in Spain. Even after peace was restored with those countries, the Suprema insisted that port commissioners and other officials furnish periodic reports of the activities of resident Protestants, including their religious practices, where they lived, and who they received in their lodgings.[77]

On occasion, the hostility and ill-will fostered by years of conflict would burst forth in ways that made it difficult for Spain to disengage itself from the struggle with the Protestant powers. Given Spain's military weakness in the late 1640s and 1650s, the Treaty of Münster of October 24, 1648, by which Spain made peace with Holland in return for recognizing her as a sovereign state, was vital if she expected to continue the war against France with any degree of success. Serious violations of the treaty, one of whose provisions promised that Dutch subjects should not be molested on account of their religion unless they caused scandal, might have strengthened the anti-Spanish party in Amsterdam and brought the Dutch back into the war. Nevertheless, Philip IV's weak government found it extremely difficult to get the Inquisition to respect the provisions of the treaty. One of the most glaring examples of the Inquisition's disregard for Spain's international obligations during this period is provided by the Valencia tribunal's arrest of Paul Jerome Estagema in 1651. Estagema, a native of Hoorn, was evidently closely connected with the Dutch peace party as two of its leading members, the Dutch ambassador to Spain and the Dutch plenipotentiary at the Münster peace conference, repeatedly petitioned the king for his release. After consulting with the Council of State, Philip meekly wrote to the tribunal to request that the case be resolved as quickly as possible paying due attention to the provisions of the peace treaty. This letter was ignored, and it was only in mid-December, after further petitions by the ambassador, that the Suprema ordered the tribunal to terminate the case and report the sentence, which caused the tribunal no great concern since the trial had already been concluded on September 7.[78] In general, however, the majority of the ninety-one Protestants seen by the tribunal in the seventeenth century were soldiers. These were drawn from among foreigners in Spanish service, such as a German mercenary quartered with his regiment in Gandía who presented himself before the commissioner there in 1664.[79]

In the eighteenth century, 87 of the 148 foreign Protestants seen by the tribunal were soldiers. The situation was a little different from the previous century, however, because the Protestant conversions began with the arrival of Allied forces in late 1705. At first, the tribunal was filled with apprehension and issued several decrees forbidding fraternization with the Allied army. In the end, these fears were exaggerated; Archduke Charles, who resided in Valencia from September 30, 1706, to March 7, 1707, sought to gain popularity through a fervent display of piety and regular church attendance.[80] As a result, Protestant influence on the native population was nil, while the Inquisition reaped a harvest of conversions.

Given the fact that no significant Protestant movement arose on Spanish soil, it is no surprise that modern historians of sixteenth-century Spain have been extremely skeptical of the depth and severity of the Protestant threat to Spanish Catholicism. Nevertheless, the alarm voiced by contemporary observers like Charles V must be placed within a contemporary context and not dismissed simply because we have the benefit of hindsight. The Seville and Valladolid conventicles were not merely "isolated pockets" but emerged from a society that had been well prepared to receive Protestant ideas by the native Illuminist movement and by the Erasmianism that became so widespread in intellectual circles during the 1520s and 1530s. At least potentially linked with these movements, especially with their stress on greater egalitarianism in religion, was popular anticlericalism and the rejection of certain Catholic dogmas by the popular masses. Since Spain, like the rest of Catholic Europe during the late fifteenth and early sixteenth centuries, harbored powerful forces critical of the Catholic church as then constituted, the failure of Protestantism was not because it was essentially alien to the Spanish or Latin mentality. Instead, that failure was the result, above all, of prompt and effective action by the Inquisition.

The Inquisition's efforts to neutralize this threat included the selective repression of native sympathizers and potential sympathizers and the identification of "Lutheranism" with Judaism and Islam, which were already detested by the majority of the Old Christian population. This was done, above all, through the regular readings of the Edict of Faith in the cathedrals and churches of Spain where the Inquisition's version of Protestantism was given its place just after a description of the Judaic and Islamic heresies.[81] All three of these "sects" were presented in opposition to "Christianity," which was made synonymous with "what is believed and upheld by our Holy Mother the Roman Catholic Church."[82] The success of this strategy of "inoculation" may be seen from the testimony of Gaspar Coscolla, an Old Christian merchant, regarding a conversation he had had with a member of the Morisco Abenamir family concerning the relative merits of Catholicism and Islam. When the Morisco expressed astonishment that Coscolla could still maintain the supremacy of Catholicism when he "knew the truth" about Islam, Coscolla replied that for him "Mohammad was just like Martin Luther."[83]

In confronting the challenge of Protestantism, therefore, the Inquisition had to deal with a difficult and complex problem. In the Spain of the 1520s and 1530s, with the Comunero Revolution of Castile and the Germanía of Valencia a very recent memory and with a growing wave of criticism of the Catholic Church an everyday reality among all classes, the chances for religiopolitical subversion were good. The failure of the incipient Spanish Protestant movement was the result of the Inquisition's success in applying its triple strategy of selective repression, inoculation, and absorption. The defeat of Spanish Protestantism, moreover, served to enhance the authority and prestige of the Inquisition both at home and abroad. Within Spain, the Inquisition had proven its worth to a nervous royal government that now moved to place the tribunal's finances on a permanent basis. Abroad, the growing reputation of the Spanish Inquisition as a bulwark of Catholicism made it the first resort of foreign Protestants who wished to join the Catholic church while resident in Spain.

VIII

The Inquisition in the
Post-Tridentine Era

Within the vast reform movement that swept over Europe between 1450 and 1650, the Council of Trent (1545–1563) occupied a very special place. On the one hand, by setting forth a statement of orthodox Catholic belief on such key issues as justification, it represented the final collapse of any hope of reconciling the Catholic and Protestant religious positions.[1] On the other hand, it was responsible for establishing the guidelines for a broad program of church reform that drew its inspiration from Erasmus, Johann Geiler of Kaisersberg, and Savonarola, among others, and was supported at the council by such figures as Cardinals Pole and Morone and Juan Bernal Díaz de Luco, bishop of Galahorra.[2]

As outlined by the council and implemented by the church, the Tridentine reform attempted to change both popular religious culture and the role of the priesthood itself. Within the context of this movement, the Inquisition played an important if ancillary role alongside bishops, provincial councils and synods, parish priests, and even laymen like Philip II who made the council's decrees the law of the land on July 12, 1564.[3] The Inquisition's alignment with the effort to implement the Tridentine decrees determined much of its activity right down to the time of its abolition in the early nineteenth century and shifted its focus away from the ethnic minorities and religious heretics who had taken up most of its attention in the first period of its history and toward the mass of the Old Christian population whose religious orthodoxy was never seriously in doubt.

Blasphemy was certainly one area of inquisitorial activity that greatly increased as a result of the Tridentine concern with reasserting the separation between the sacred and profane.[4] Of course, blasphemy defined as expletives showing disrespect for the sacred had long been punishable under secular law. In 1462, Henry IV prescribed severe penalties for this offense, including scourging and cutting out the tongue, while Ferdinand and Isabella, in their laws of 1492 and 1502, detailed a whole list of commonly used expletives for which penalties were provided, ranging from a brief period of imprisonment for first offenders to piercing the tongue for the third offense.[5] In 1532, Charles V reflected the concern of secular jurisprudence with offenses against public morality by urging his *corregidores* to show special zeal in the punishment of blasphemy, usury, concubinage, and other "public sins."[6] The ecclesiastical courts also claimed jurisdiction over blasphemy, and at the Council of Seville of 1512, the bishops imposed fines and imprisonment on clerics and laymen convicted of this offense before their tribunals.[7]

Given all this legislation and the established role of secular and ecclesiastical courts in the repression of this offense, it is logical that the Inquisition would show some reluctance to become involved in such a well-worked area of judicial activity. The tradition of the medieval Inquisition as expressed by Eymerich limited inquisitorial jurisdiction only to those expressions that smacked of heresy, such as a statement implying doubt about God's omnipotence or an expletive calling the Virgin Mary a "whore," which implied disrespect for the Virgin Birth. These expletives, which were termed "heretical blasphemy," were seen as distinct from those that in no way denied the articles of the faith and should therefore be judged by other tribunals.[8] Internal legislation by the Suprema also reflected this tradition, and as late as 1547, it insisted that a whole series of expressions commonly uttered in the heat of anger or frustration such as "I renounce God" or "May it spite God" fell outside inquisitorial jurisdiction.[9]

Apparently, the cautious approach adopted by the Suprema was not followed by the regional tribunals. Complaints voiced by delegates to both the Aragonese and Castilian Cortes in 1510, 1530, and 1534 indicated that inquisitors were routinely imprisoning orthodox persons for words uttered in the heat of passion or frustration.[10]

Nevertheless, given the amount of competition and the small profit that could be wrung out of such cases, the Inquisition had little interest in them, and they comprised a very small part of its overall activity. The Valencia tribunal only tried six individuals for blasphemy before 1530.[11] It was only after 1560, when the Inquisition was enlisted in the struggle to remodel popular culture and enforce respect for the sacred, that its activity in this area began to increase. Between 1540 and 1614, the tribunal heard 227 cases, with 29 in 1587 alone.[12]

Analysis of the social origins of those accused of blasphemy before the Valencia tribunal leaves no doubt that this offense was committed by individuals from every social group. The nobility was represented by 2.3 percent of the accused, while 65.2 percent came from the popular classes including artisans, peasants, soldiers, and servants. The offense was also overwhelmingly male: men comprised more than 91 percent of the offenders.

In spite of the well-established principle that the Inquisition's jurisdiction over blasphemy extended only to statements of a heretical nature, the vast majority cited in the cases were expletives in common use to which no heretical intention could be imputed. Over 50 percent of the cases involved statements renouncing God or the saints, usually in a moment of rage and frustration. A typical case was that of Jerónimo Merin, an illiterate velvet worker who came to the tribunal in 1612 to denounce himself for having renounced God and his saints after losing his ball during a game of pelota.[13] The Inquisition recognized the comparative mildness of such expletives and their insignificance from a religious standpoint by treating the accused with comparative leniency. Only six individuals were tortured in the course of their trials, and only 3.5 percent were sentenced de vehementi.

Blasphemers also received the mildest punishments of any group of offenders appearing before the bar of the Holy Office. Only 1.3 percent were sentenced to death and 7.9 percent given terms of galley service. Almost half (48%) of the cases ended in suspension, and almost 31 percent were merely admonished in the audience chamber and sent on their way.

Offenders who received the severest sentences were usually found guilty of uttering expletives of a more serious nature. In the case of Miguel Ferrer, who was sentenced to spend ten years in the galleys on May 3, 1647, the more common expressions were combined with violent ones like "Christ the cuckold" and "the Virgin Mary was a whore and Saint Christopher her pimp." In addition, Ferrer was a repeat offender (he had been convicted of a similar offense in 1643) and a prisoner of the crown. Interestingly, the Suprema went along with the harsh sentence handed down by the tribunal but downgraded its recommendation of a de vehementi abjuration to abjuration de levi, clearly recognizing that even such violent expletives as those uttered by Ferrer had little religious significance.[14]

One important indicator of the Inquisition's success in remolding popular attitudes is the number of people who were coming forward by the seventeenth century to denounce themselves or their friends for expletives that they would never have paid the slightest attention to a generation earlier. In the Spain of the seventeenth century, every man (and woman) became his own inquisitor, having been taught through the Inquisition's "pedagogy of fear" to scrutinize his own words and actions and those of his neighbors for any sign of nonconformity. So it was that when María de la Bresa, a tailor's wife from Valencia, heard Catalina Rico, her neighbor, declare bitterly that "God laughs at her misery," she came directly to the tribunal to report her.[15] An entire society had now learned to move in lockstep with the demands of the baroque cultural, religious, and political monolith.[16]

A second major objective of both Catholic and Protestant reformers was to impose an ethic of decency, modesty, and self-control onto the moral life of the laity.[17] The concern for public morality is what prompted the repression of concubinage by the Inquisition as well as the secular courts. Typical of this sort of case was the Valencia tribunal's prosecution of Nicolás Flores, a familiar of the Holy Office and a wealthy labrador of Las Useras, for living openly with a married woman of the village. Evidently, Flores was an incorrigible offender who had been tried for the same offense on three previous occasions and had scandalized the entire village by his conduct. The rather mild punishment handed down by the tribunal in his case—a 30 lliure fine and ten days of spiritual exercises in a local monastery—could hardly have had much impact on such a personality.[18] Interestingly, the Inquisition's sentence in this case appears to have been considerably milder than that handed down by the Council of the Military Orders in a similar case that it tried in 1700. In this instance, a notary of the village of Almonacid was accused of having sexual relations with a series of married women. The council sentenced him to four years of exile from the village.[19]

Closely related to the effort to reform popular morality was the inquisitorial campaign against the proposition that simple fornication was not a mortal sin. Eymerich's *Directorium* is silent on this subject, and it appears that the Inquisition did not even begin to deal with cases of this kind until 1559–60. By the cartas acordadas of November 20, 1573, and November 20, 1574, the Suprema ordered the local tribunals to treat simple fornication as if it were a heresy and include it in the Edict of Faith.[20] On December 14 of that year, the Valencia tribunal, on orders from the Suprema, published a special edict declaring that it was heretical to assert that simple fornication was not a mortal sin.[21] From the mid-1550s, inquisitorial prosecution of these cases began to increase markedly, and from 1554 to 1820, over 25 percent of the Valencia tribunal's cases of propositions involved simple fornication.[22]

Bigamy was another sphere of activity that was closely related to the Inquisition's role as enforcer of post-Tridentine sexual morality. From the twelfth century, the church had declared marriage a sacrament that could be enjoyed only once during the lifetime of both partners while the other partner is still alive.[23] Since neither priest nor witnesses were required to be at the ceremony, however, church authorities could exercise little control over marriage and there were frequent clandestine marriages of a bigamous character. In response to this lamentable state of affairs, the church fathers at the Council of Trent reinforced the sacrament of marriage by stipulating that banns had to be published three separate times before the ceremony and that it would be valid only if performed before a priest and two or three witnesses. The marriage would then have to be recorded in the parish register.[24]

It was against this background that the Inquisition began to increase its activity in this area. As early as 1563, the tribunal wrote the Suprema to demand a crackdown on bigamists because of their disrespect for the sacrament.[25] Doubtless, the Inquisition was called on to play the major role in the repression of bigamy because, as an empirewide institution with a well-developed tradition of exchanging information among the several tribunals, it was best suited to enforce the law, especially since the offense frequently involved movement from one region to another. The jurisdiction of the ecclesiastical courts over all marital cases was given proper recognition by providing that after the conclusion of inquisitorial proceedings, the ordinary would decide which of the women was actually married to the accused.[26]

An example of cooperation among the several inquisitorial tribunals is provided by the case of Miguel Romero, a Valencian who had emigrated to the New World and settled in Havana. The case was instigated by the Cartagena tribunal, which had received information leading it to believe that Romero had been married forty years earlier in the village of El Grao just outside Valencia city. In response to the Cartagena tribunal's request for information, the Valencia tribunal sent a Holy Office notary to El Grao to investigate. The notary was successful in finding Josefa María Días, Romero's first wife, as well as the original marriage record, which had been noted in the parish register. After a copy of this information was forwarded to America, Romero was arrested and sentenced to four years in an African presidio.[27]

Bigamists coming before the Valencia tribunal were overwhelmingly male (85.5%) and largely young (79% were age 40 or less). Analysis of status and occupational categories reveals bigamy to be an offense that involved all classes, from cavallers (7.6%) to beggars (2.1%), but with a heavy concentration among those whose occupations either required them to have a high degree of mobility or permitted them to pick up employment almost anywhere. It should not, therefore, be surprising to learn that almost 11 percent of bigamists were soldiers or that artisans comprised almost 42 percent of the accused.

Penalties handed down by the tribunal were relatively mild. First of all, in spite of the fact that the Inquisition's claim to jurisdiction was based on the idea that the bigamist had impiously abused the sacrament of matrimony, all of those accused before the Valencia tribunal were only judged "lightly suspect" of heresy, which clearly indicates how little concern there really was with the religious implications of the offense.[28] The harshest penalties handed down were periods of galley service (23%), but no one received the ten-year term prescribed in Philip II's ordinance of 1566.[29]

It is undeniable that there were a goodly number of scoundrels and frauds who used multiple marriages as a way of gaining a livelihood or improving their position. One of the bigamists who appeared in the Valladolid auto de fé of October 4, 1579, admitted to having married fifteen times in the space of ten years and then disappearing with whatever property he could obtain.[30] In the case of Pedro Pérez de Novella, who was brought to trial by the Valencia tribunal, the motivation for his second marriage was clearly the hope of social and professional advancement. His first wife was the daughter of a labrador, and he was the son of a notary. After living with his first wife for nine years, Pérez de Novella deserted her and his two children and went to Castellón de la Plana, where he pretended his wife had died, and married Antonia Amiguet, the daughter of the local alguacil mayor. Since the office was venal and Antonia was the alguacil's only child, she brought this office with her in her dowry. At her father's death, which occurred shortly after the marriage, Pérez de Novella took his place as alguacil mayor, thereby fulfilling his long-standing goal of occupying an honorable position, an ambition that his first wife's lowly origins would have made nearly impossible in the status-conscious eighteenth century.[31]

The relative leniency of the Inquisition with regard to cases of bigamy and the way it made every allowance for extenuating circumstances may have amounted to tacit recognition by the Holy Office of the cost in human terms of the church's attitude toward marriage. The indissolubility of the marriage bond simply made it impossible for people to resolve problems of infidelity or incompatibility except through illicit means such as contracting a second marriage. Juan Bastit, a French stonecutter, was forced by the lack of economic opportunity in his home province to journey to Spain to seek employment. On returning from one of these journeys, he found that his wife had had an illegitimate child by a man who had once had an affair with her mother. Disgusted by his wife's behavior, Bastit took the road to Spain once more and eventually settled in Rubielos, where there appears to have been a small colony of French artisans. He was able to persuade two of these men to swear that his first wife had died so that he could marry a local girl.[32]

Parental control over marriages and arranged marriages was another fertile source of dissatisfaction and marital instability. María la Jaqueta, the illegitimate daughter of a high-ranking benefice holder in the town of Tours, was forced by her mother to marry one Pierre Verdier whom she described as a "drunkard and misogynist." He treated her so badly that she fled in the company of a young Frenchman who then forced her to marry him by threatening to place her in a bordello if she refused. Destitute and entirely dependent on her paramour, María had little choice but to agree, even though she was well aware that she was breaking the rules of the church. Unfortunately for María, the village where the pair settled contained a small group of French immigrants, several of whom had known her previously. Denounced to the tribunal, she was convicted of bigamy and sentenced to 100 lashes. It is difficult not to have a certain compassion for this 23-year-old girl who had so little control over her own life and who was the victim, successively, of mother, husband, lover, and Inquisition.[33]

Apart from heresy itself, sodomy and bestiality were the crimes that inspired the greatest repugnance in the hearts of princes, jurists, and legislators during the entire early modern period. These were the crimes "committed against the natural order," the "abominable sin," the crime that was so disgusting that it was "horrid even to pronounce it aloud" according to a public prosecutor who was responsible for a sodomy case in 1740.[34] Harsh penalties were prescribed for both crimes in civil legislation. In the medieval Partidas, both were punishable by death, while in their edicts of August 22 and 27, 1497, the Catholic Kings declared that those found guilty of such crimes were to be burned alive in the place where the crime had been committed. The criminal code of Valencia also contained ferocious penalties mandating death by fire for those over twenty years of age and scourging and galleys for minors.[35]

Evidently, the early Inquisition had demonstrated a certain interest in these offenses, but by its decree of October 18, 1509, the Suprema ordered the Castilian tribunals to leave them in the hands of the secular and ecclesiastical courts. In Aragon, however, popular hostility toward sodomites as expressed in the Valencian rioting of 1519 and the presumed connection between sodomy and the Islamic minority resulted in a request to Pope Clement VII for a brief placing it under inquisitorial jurisdiction.[36]

The papal brief was issued on February 24, 1524, but the Aragonese tribunals seem to have made little use of their new powers until after 1560, when the Inquisition began its campaign in support of post-Tridentine sexual morality and Christian marriage.[37] In Valencia, the tribunal appears to have been virtually inactive against sodomy before 1570.[38] From 1571 to 1700, however, there were 283 cases of sodomy and bestiality and another 226 between 1701 and 1820.[39]

In this as in other areas of its growing jurisdiction, local inquisitors rather than the Suprema took the lead. As early as March 1554, Valencia's inquisitors wrote to request permission to proceed aggressively against sodomites. In 1572, the tribunal wrote that it had eight men in prison awaiting trial on charges of sodomy and that many more could be indicted "if the public could be assured that the Holy Office had jurisdiction over such cases."[40] Just a few months later, on January 28, 1573, the tribunal wrote again, this time to ask that the Suprema allow it to place the offense in the Edict of Faith.[41] In the following year, the Suprema bowed to this pressure and permitted the Aragonese tribunals to include sodomy in the edict.[42]

In spite of its special powers, the tribunal had difficulty asserting its jurisdiction over certain offenders, particularly those whose position allowed them to enjoy the protection of their own "fuero." In 1572, we find the Suprema ordering the tribunal to refuse to surrender the Minim Friar Pedro Picasso to the provincial of his order who was demanding custody, and between 1571 and 1573, the tribunal struggled to assert its jurisdiction over Pedro Luis Galcerán de Borja, the grand-master of the Order of Montesa.[43] In these cases and many others, the Inquisition was successful in defending its jurisdiction, but we must assume that other courts did continue to hear a certain percentage of the sodomy cases.

In spite of its inclusion in the Edict of Faith, inquisitorial procedures in these cases belie any connection between sodomy and heresy. The original papal brief had specified that local law was to be followed, and, in 1572, the Suprema refused to consider a request by the tribunal that would have allowed it to treat such cases as procesos de fé.[44] As a result, in accordance with Valencian criminal procedure, the names of witnesses were not kept secret and there was even open confrontation between witnesses and the accused. During his long trial, Melchor Armengol was permitted to draw up special lists of questions to be put to the two chief witnesses against him and was allowed to confront them in open court where he was able to reveal certain discrepancies in matters of detail through cross-examination.[45] Sometimes the use of ordinary judicial procedures with the right of cross-examination would be of considerable help to an accused. In the case of Fray Manuel Sánchez del Castellar y Arbustan, who was accused of sodomy before the Valencia tribunal in 1681, cross-examination revealed that the accusation was little more than an elaborate plot hatched by other friars jealous of his position in the order.[46]

The Suprema also took a considerable interest in these cases, probably because they frequently involved harsh punishment of Old Christians and insisted that proper judicial procedures be followed. In 1624, for example, the Suprema sharply rebuked the tribunal for the sodomy cases included in the relaciones de causas of the previous year because the accusations were poorly substantiated.[47]

Statistical analysis of the data taken from the relaciones de causas reveals that both sodomy and bestiality were crimes committed largely by unmarried young men. Some 98.7 percent of those accused of sodomy were males, although five women were accused of lesbianism. The figures for bestiality yield remarkably similar results, with 98.9 percent of the accused being males. The age profile of the two groups was also quite similar: 74.9 percent of the sodomites and 77 percent of those accused of bestiality were under 40 years of age. These two crimes also exhibit the highest percentage of unmarried offenders of any dealt with by the tribunal—70.2 and 90 percent, respectively.

Analysis of the information abut occupation and status, however, reveals some sharp differences in the sociology of those accused of these crimes. Sodomites were widely distributed across the occupation/status range, with small groups of cavallers and ciutadans (2.9%), professionals and merchants (5.5%), and clergy (18.9%). In contrast, persons of higher social status are almost entirely absent among those accused of bestiality: there was a complete absence of knights and ciutadans and only one cleric. For both offenses, the largest proportion of offenders were artisans and peasants, but while the percentage of artisans was remarkably similar (27.5% for sodomites and 30.6% for bestiality), the percentage of peasants (34.6%) was much higher for bestiality than it was for sodomy (10%), reflecting the rural nature of that crime. As one would expect, both offenses had a high percentage of accused from marginal groups or occupations where there was a high degree of mobility and consequently little opportunity to develop a settled family life. Thus, both offenses have similar percentages of slaves and vagrants, 7.0 and 10.2 percent and 7.0 and 6.1 percent, respectively.

Without doubt, the most politically powerful individual ever arrested on charges of sodomy by the Valencia tribunal was Pedro Luis Galcerán de Borja. Not only was the grand-master the son of the third duke of Gandía and related to most of the leading nobles of the kingdom but he was also the leader of one of the most powerful and violent of the aristocratic "bandos" that had so disrupted Valencian society during the 1550s.[48] Arrested in 1571 on testimony from several of the order's commanders, he was given exceptional treatment and permitted to run the affairs of the order from comfortable apartments that had been set aside for him.[49] Ignoring Borja's persistent refusal to recognize the Inquisition's jurisdiction and the considerable political pressure that was brought to bear by members of his family, the tribunal and the Suprema pressed the case.[50] Direct evidence was provided by three of his servants, one of whom, Gaspar Granulles, had fled to Rome where a warrant was issued for his arrest in November 1572.[51] Given the strong political influence being exerted on the accused's behalf, especially by Archbishop Ribera, and the fact that Martín de Castro, the principal witness against him, revoked his testimony, a split verdict on the tribunal is not surprising.[52] The Suprema chose to accept the view of hard-liner Juan de Rojas who had voted for a heavy fine and four years of exile, although it modified exile to ten years of reclusion in the castle of Montesa and a fine of 6,000 ducats.[53] Even this sentence could hardly have been expected in such a case but for the fact that the Valencian nobility, in general, had become somewhat discredited in the eyes of the king because of their support of the religion and customs of their Morisco vassals and that many of them had been, or were about to be, punished by the Inquisition.[54] In the end, of course, the crown's need for the political support of the Borja family outweighed its desire to punish sodomites, and, in 1591, Borja was absolved and rehabilitated politically by being granted the post of viceroy of Catalonia.[55]

If political influence and social prominence saved Borja from the harsh punishment that many a lesser man had to suffer for similar offenses, the lack of such influence may well have condemned Melchor Armengol to harsher punishment than he might have otherwise received. Armengol was rector of Bot, located in the Sierra de Montenegrelo in the extreme northern part of the district. Unlike many other parish priests, he was scrupulous in carrying out his duties; but, since the income from his benefice was barely sufficient to meet expenses, Armengol was eager to take advantage of any opportunity to increase it by asserting control over church property and acting to farm the ecclesiastical tithe. His efforts to do this, however, made him a number of enemies among the village elite, including his former sacristan and the leader of the village council, Juan Altadill. Armengol also alienated his parishioners by evicting mothers with young children from church if their infants cried during services. Furthermore, this remote region, like other parts of the sprawling inquisitorial district, was afflicted with serious clan rivalries and banditry. Armengol had close ties with one of the bandit leaders, while his enemies were linked to the leader of the opposing group. In spite of his general unpopularity, however, he employed the son and nephew of two of his principal enemies as servants and sodomized them and another boy in his bedroom in the rectory, in a hut outside of the village, and in a lodging house in the city of Tortosa.

These activities, which apparently went on for some time, eventually became known to one of Armengol's bitterest enemies, Juan Çabater, the rector of neighboring Gandesa, with whom Armengol had significant disagreements and a pending lawsuit. Seeking to destroy his enemy, Çabater denounced Armengol before Jerónimo Terca, canon of Tortosa cathedral and the Holy Office commissioner for the region. After receiving this initial testimony, Terca was told to follow up his investigations by calling in other witnesses, and within a few weeks an impressive body of evidence had emerged concerning Armengol's sexual relations with the boys, including Agustín Villavert's assertion that he had been repeatedly raped on the rector's bed and that the sexual act had always been consummated.

In his long and brilliant defense, which included face-to-face confrontations with the boys, Armengol was able to establish what to a modern mind would appear to be reasonable doubt, especially with regard to the incidents in Tortosa, chiefly by pointing out inconsistencies in prosecution testimony. However, he was unable to shake the testimony of the third boy, José Prat, who declared that Armengol had kissed him and touched his genitals, and in this instance he was reduced to lamely asserting that Prat must have been induced to testify by one of his enemies. In the end, the tribunal, which was chary of offending local elites and wanted to extend its system of familiares into the Bot region, sentenced Armengol to be degraded from clerical orders, deprived of his office and benefice, and given three years of galley service.[56] The case of Melchor Armengol, like many cases of superstition and others that we have referred to, is a good illustration of the role that reputation and the whole context of personal relationships can play in inspiring judicial denunciations. Although the allegations against him were probably largely true, Armengol was himself a victim not only of his own bad temper but of the tragic condition of many of Valencia's country parishes where the priest was forced into poverty, absenteeism, or worse because powerful village elites controlled parish business and finances.

As stated above, both sodomy and bestiality were committed primarily by unmarried men whose occupation or circumstances made it difficult or impossible for them to live a normal family life even if they had been disposed to do so. Typical of this group were individuals like Ali, the black slave of the viceroy's mayordomo, who was accused of having sexual relations with two young men, one of whom was a part-time agricultural worker and the other a vagrant some 15 or 16 years of age.[57]

Another marginal individual who paid with his life for the social prejudice against bestiality was Pedro Juan, a watchman in the village of Montesa. There was only one witness to this act, which occurred in broad daylight just outside the town walls in March 1621. The witness, Gracia Navarro, was out gathering herbs when she saw Juan having sexual relations with a mule whose legs were tied apart. She ran immediately to tell several labradores whose farms were close, and these men apprehended Juan and held him while they summoned the local familiar. Juan escaped but was recaptured the following day by the familiar and one of the labradores and eventually brought before the tribunal. In his defense, Juan alleged that he drank heavily and was habitually drunk and that he had only entered the mule's privates "a little way." His habitual drunkenness was partially contradicted by the testimony of several witnesses who also declared that semen had been streaming out of the mule's backside shortly after the alarm had first been given. Even though the tribunal was able to verify Juan's claim to be a devout Catholic, this did him little good. He was given a sentence of death, which was carried out along with the senseless execution of the perfectly innocent animal after the auto of July 4, 1621.[58] It is interesting to note that the verdict in this case was unanimous and that one of the members of the tribunal at this time was Inquisitor Alonso de Salazar y Frías, the savior of the witches of Navarre and Guipúzcoa a decade earlier. It would be many generations before the enlightened attitude that Inquisitor Salazar y Frías showed in the case of the witches would be extended to those convicted of bestiality.

Curiously, the working legal definition of the sin/crime of sodomy that was used by both the secular courts and the Inquisition included certain forms of "unnatural" sexual relations between men and women. As late as 1780, Antonio Gómez included any form of sexual relations that made use of any artificial methods in his definition of sodomy, and on November 29, 1644, a man was burnt to death in Madrid after having been accused by his wife of having anal intercourse.[59]

The Valencia tribunal also tried a certain number of persons (5.6% of sodomy cases) for this offense, which was termed "imperfect sodomy" by the canonists.[60] Use of confessors to force their penitents to bring cases of solicitation before the Holy Office was evidently extended to instances of anal sex as well, and the late sixteenth and early seventeenth centuries saw an increasing number of women coming to the tribunal to denounce their husbands and lovers. Evidently, some of these relationships were extremely unhappy, so the Holy Office in this instance provided an outlet for the frustrations and anger of women who had been battered emotionally, physically, and sexually by their partners. Isabel Juan Ramírez, for example, who came to the Holy Office on February 6, 1609, on the advice of her confessor, testified that her husband, a baker, had attempted anal sex with her on numerous occasions and beat her when she refused.[61] Some women were unable to avoid engaging in this form of sex in spite of being aware of its illicit nature. Esperanza Agut, the wife of a labrador from the village of

Artana, came to testify that her husband had forced her to have anal sex with him even though she begged him not to because she knew it was a grave sin.[62]

The majority of the sodomy cases tried by the Valencia tribunal involved a relatively small number of sexual acts with few partners.[63] In fact, the tragic case of Juan Ximénez, who became despondent after his arrest on sodomy charges and committed suicide in his cell, involved repeated homosexual acts committed over a ten-year period with just one partner.[64] About 20 percent of the cases involved multiple sexual acts committed with numerous partners. One of the most remarkable cases of this kind involved Jesualdo Felizes, the brother-in-law of the count of Albalat. Felizes not only forced a succession of servant boys to have sexual relations with him but also paid for sex with the boy musicians of the chapel of San Andrés and sodomized his two nephews on twenty-two separate occasions. Felizes would usually act as the aggressor in these trysts, but sometimes, as with Domingo Meris, the lovers "sodomized each other mutually." Evidently, Felizes's family, consisting of his mother, Jerónima Arazil, and brother, Fray Vicente Felizes, were quite complaisant about his sexual preferences. On one occasion, Fray Vicente even persuaded the mother of one of Felizes's boy servants to coax her son to return to the house after he had fled these sexual advances. Felizes habitually slept in the same room as his mother, along with one of his boy lovers. He even went so far as to perform his sexual acts in her bed and in one instance scourged one of his lovers there after sodomizing him. Felizes was eventually denounced to the Holy Office by Dr. Juan Val, rector of the Colegio de San Jorge in Valencia, who had heard rumors about his activities while on a visit to Meliana where the family resided after it left Valencia.

The fact that Jesualdo Felizes could carry on his extraordinary sexual career for more than a decade without ever being denounced to the Holy Office is only partially attributable to his high social standing. Of course, his rank made his servant lovers unwilling to denounce him as they probably felt it would be futile. As José Bermudez, who had been sodomized by Felizes twice a day for seven years, put it when asked why he had not denounced his master, "What good would that have done, he would only have beaten me." But Felizes was also able to exploit the existence in

Valencia of networks of young homosexuals and the apparent acceptance among young men, even in this land with a tradition of
lynching sodomites, of a certain amount of homosexual behavior
among friends. Certainly his sexual relations with the boy musicians of San Andrés, several of whom admitted during his trial that
they had sexual relations with one another, attest to the existence of
such groups.[65] In 1796, just eleven years after Felizes was sentenced, we learn of another such group from the spontaneous confession of Benito Campany. The previous year, Campany, who was
an art student, went with several of his friends to the harvest at
Játiva. After buying a watermelon for refreshment, they all climbed
up on a pile of hay and proceeded to pull off their pants and
sodomize each other in turn. The casual and spontaneous nature of
this episode and the youth of those involved, ranging from 8 to 16
years of age, indicates that we are not dealing with a group with
definite sexual preferences but rather with boys who accepted homosexual activity as part of their relationship with one another
regardless of their ultimate sexual choices.[66]

The attitude of many inquisitorial officials toward sodomy and
bestiality was best summed up by Dr. Pérez, the tribunal's prosecuting attorney in the case of the master of Montesa, who demanded the death sentence on the grounds that failure to punish
such a "heinous" crime would bring divine retribution in the form
of "famine, plague and earthquakes."[67] In reality, as the sentence of
the master himself was to indicate, the punishments handed down
by the Inquisition for sodomy and bestiality were considerably
milder than the violent antagonism expressed by its prosecuting
attorney would seem to imply. According to a memorial analyzing
the tribunal's policy toward these offenders presented to the
Suprema in 1687, the harsh laws of the Valencian criminal code had
been followed in many cases until 1628, when the tribunal executed its last sodomite. Since the memorial speaks of "the lack of
conclusive proof" in certain of these cases, it is safe to assume that
one reason for this apparent leniency was the Suprema's strictures
on the inadequacy of proof in certain cases that had been presented
to it some years earlier.[68] The suspicion that the Suprema was
behind this change of heart by the tribunal is confirmed later in the
memorial when the inquisitors comment on the case of Carlos
Charmarino, a sailor whose sentence of death by burning and confis-

cation of property by the tribunal was reduced by the Suprema to
200 lashes and ten years of galley service. By 1656, the Suprema's
more lenient policy was beginning to make itself felt on the tribunal. In the case of Juan Antonio Jirado, the consulta de fé divided
with several votes for the death penalty, but Inquisitor Antonio de
Ayala Verganza and the ordinary of the Archbishop opted for 200
lashes and ten years of galley service "because in similar cases
sentences had been reduced by the Council." As it turned out,
Inquisitor Ayala Verganza had interpreted the Suprema's mood
correctly, as it sentenced Jirado to only five years of galley service
followed by eight years of exile. Finally, the authors of the memorial, Inquisitors Jiménez Navarro and Francisco Espadaña, commented on their own policy in sentencing certain slaves whose
cases had presented themselves that year. Following the "lenient
policy ordered by your Eminences for these many years," they
said, it had been decided to punish them with scourging and order
their master to sell them outside the kingdom rather than sentence
them to death or a term of galley service.[69]

Analysis of sentences handed down for sodomy and bestiality
appears to substantiate the impression of leniency conveyed in the
1687 memorial. Contrary to Valencian criminal law, only 6.7 percent of sodomites and 5.8 percent of those convicted of bestiality
were given death sentences, and confiscation was mandated in only
1.7 percent and 1.1 percent of these cases, respectively. Instead, as
indicated in the memorial, a high percentage of sentences for these
offenses involved galley service (13.8% and 19.7%), scourging
(14.1% and 24.4%), and exile (18.8% and 32.5%). But there were
many even milder punishments like reclusion in monasteries for
clerical sodomites or fines. Interestingly, especially given the seriousness with which these offenses were treated in the criminal
code, the percentage of suspensions was extremely high: some 63.2
percent of sodomizers and 44 percent of cases of bestiality. This was
especially true in the eighteenth century when the high percentage
of suspensions merely confirms the long-term trend toward leniency in these cases that was the subject of the 1687 memorial.[70]

The moderation with which the Inquisition treated those accused of sodomy and bestiality seems all the more remarkable
considering the profound social prejudice against such offenders.
But the law, as E. P. Thompson has pointed out, must be seen both

as "particular rules and sanctions which stand in a definite and active relationship (often a field of conflict) to social norms" and "in terms of its own logic, rules and procedures."[71] Like the judges of the Paris Parlement with regard to another class of offenders equally abhorred by popular opinion, witches and sorcerers, the members of the Suprema were concerned to protect the integrity of the procedures and legal traditions that gave expression to inquisitorial law and prevent lesser tribunals from abusing them.[72] Like their counterparts in Paris, the members of the Suprema became more and more concerned about the procedural irregularities and difficulties of proof that characterized such cases as time went on. This concern led them not only to insist on more effective procedural guarantees but to a pattern of reducing the sentences that local inquisitorial tribunals in imitation of local law had handed down in these cases. A new "style" or tradition was in the process of formation, and, within a few years, the local tribunals, whose judges were after all dependent on the Suprema for preferment, adopted it as their own. In its leniency toward sodomites, as in many other respects, the Inquisition was more enlightened than the secular courts, which were still handing down death sentences for sodomy and bestiality in the middle of the seventeenth century. Before 1750, however, the secular courts with jurisdiction over these offenses had adopted the style of the Inquisition, and centuries of violent persecution and brutal punishment for homosexuality were drawing to a close.[73]

An even more striking example of the Spanish Inquisition's progressive approach to an offense that was treated with great severity elsewhere is provided by its treatment of those accused of sorcery. The Spanish Inquisition's cautious and moderate attitude stands in sharp contrast to the witch hysteria that gripped much of northern Europe, and it is all the more remarkable because its jurisdiction over crimes involving sorcery depended on the medieval scholastic definition of all forms of magic as demonic and heretical.[74] In spite of this, most Spanish inquisitors were able to resist popular pressure for harsh and summary punishment of persons popularly reputed as witches and refrain from systematically imposing learned notions of diabolism (with which they were quite familiar from their knowledge of works like the *Malleus Maleficarum*) on the popular magical traditions that provided the raw material for the trials. In the end, what counted for the Spanish Inquisition was not the formal scholastic notion of pacts with the devil and apostasy from the faith but the concept that the church's monopoly on supernatural remedies was being undermined and its rituals and prayers misused by magicians.[75] This approach, which emphasized the post-Tridentine effort to enforce respect for the sacred rather than a desire to extirpate a dangerous new cult of devil-worshiping heretics, provided the basis for inquisitorial activity in this field and prevented Spain from becoming the scene of the massive witch persecutions that caused so much suffering in the rest of Europe.

In a country where the traditions of scholasticism dominated intellectual life throughout the early modern period, the Spanish Inquisition's attitude toward sorcery could hardly have been the result of an "enlightened" rationalist negation of the power of the devil or the ability of witches to harm men and animals with his assistance. In fact, fifteenth-century Spain saw the publication of some of Europe's earliest witchcraft treatises, and as late as 1631, in a work that was warmly approved by Dr. Baltasar de Cisneros, calificador of the Zaragoza tribunal, Gaspar Navarro fully accepts the reality of the Sabbath, diabolical pacts, and maleficia and called for the exemplary punishment of witches.[76] The scholastic link between sorcery, diabolism, and heresy also received support from Inquisitors like Arnaldo Alvertín, who in 1535 proclaimed himself a firm believer in all the horrors that witches were accused of.[77] In fact, Dr. Alonso Becerra and licentiate Juan del Valle, who voted death sentences for the witches condemned at the famous auto de fé of November 7, 1610, in Logroño, represented a respectable minority view in a tribunal that had never explicitly denied the reality of witchcraft.[78]

In matters of judicial procedure, what really counted, however, was the climate of opinion on the Suprema itself. In 1562, Inquisitor-General Manrique convened a junta of judicial experts (including future Inquisitor-General Valdés) and theologians to discuss the issues raised by an outbreak of witch persecution in Navarre.[79] As a result of the discussions held by the members of this assembly, the Suprema issued a series of instructions that set the tone for the Spanish Inquisition's future attitude toward witchcraft. Essentially, these instructions instituted procedural safeguards that made it impossible for Spain to experience the massive witchcraft persecutions soon to become common in much of the rest of Europe.[80]

That the Valencia tribunal followed the majority of Spain's provincial tribunals in adopting a moderate policy toward the kinds of sorcery cases that could easily have resulted in accusations of demonizing and triggered witch panics elsewhere in Europe is illustrated by several sixteenth- and seventeenth-century cases. Vicenta Malpel, a fourteen-year-old servant girl who had become widely known in Valencia for her visions of the Virgin Mary and the infant Jesus as well as her ability to predict the future and find missing or stolen objects, also claimed that the devil visited her in the shape of a "gentleman" dressed in black silk. Arrested by the Holy Office after she had been denounced by five witnesses, she admitted the charges, but the consulta voted for torture because she was "suspected of a pact with the devil." After being brought to the torture chamber (but not actually tortured), she confessed that the devil had appeared to her the first time after she had received a brutal beating from her mistress and told her that if she wanted to secure better treatment, achieve fame, and become known as a saint, she should pretend that she had visions of holy figures and that when people came to question her about them he would tell her what to say. She also testified that she had had sexual relations with the devil on numerous occasions during the last two years even though she had remained a virgin. Although Vicenta denied that she had surrendered her soul to the devil or signed any agreements with him, it would have been quite easy for her interrogators to have gotten her to admit diabolical pacts and virtually any other form of diabolism had they been so inclined, since she was a highly suggestible person who was described as frequently contradicting herself during her testimony. Evidently, there was no disposition to do this, and this adolescent, whose resemblance to the child witches of Germany or Salem must strike anyone familiar with the history of witchcraft, was merely sentenced to appear in the following auto de fé with the insignia of an invoker of the devil, public shame, and a period of reclusion in a monastery to be determined by the tribunal.[81]

Isabel Patris was another individual who would certainly have been given the death penalty if her trial had been held before a tribunal in northern Europe. Patris, who evidently practiced both amatory and curative magic, sometimes in direct competition with local physicians and exorcists, was widely reputed to be a witch and was accused of killing many persons with her evil spells, especially those who refused her alms. In spite of this local reputation and several specific accusations of maleficia, including the death of a woman shortly after Patris had visited her, the tribunal resisted any temptation to turn a case of popular magic into diabolism and instead sentenced Isabel to abjuration in the audience chamber and eight years exile from the district.[82]

In another case in which the tribunal might easily have crossed the line from amatory magic to diabolism, the sentence was harsher but probably because of the sacrilegious activities that emerged from the testimony rather than any fear that it had encountered a member of a real witch cult. Teresa Agustí, who admitted having made a pact with the devil and removed her cross and rosary for fifteen days so as to find out if her lover was coming to see her, had also been heard to threaten her lover with retribution after he left her "even if she had to give her soul to the devil." After his death, which occurred shortly after this threat was uttered, Dr. Morales, the physician who attended him, commented that his symptoms were so irregular that they could not have come from natural causes and must have been the result of some witchcraft. Rather ominously, these charges influenced the tone of the prosecuting attorney's accusation in which Agustí was charged with "passing to the side of God's enemies" for setting aside her rosary and cross, with "diabolical witchcraft" for casting the spell that caused her lover's demise, and with an explicit pact with the devil. In spite of this overheated rhetoric, which might easily have led to a charge of diabolism, the tribunal continued to act with the moderation that had long characterized the Inquisition's response to witchcraft accusations by absolving de levi and making her appear in church wearing the insignia of one convicted of superstition and imposture (*embustería*). She was sentenced to verguenza, exile from Valencia, and four years in the women's prison where she was to have a calificador to govern her spiritual welfare. After generations of moderation, the Valencia tribunal was not going to allow itself to be stampeded into accusations of diabolism or accepting vague and unsubstantiated testimony about murder by magic.[83]

Living before the advent of modern medicine, sanitation, organized fire brigades, and emergency services, early modern Europeans, like their ancient and medieval predecessors, were vulnerable to a variety of diseases and misfortunes whose catastrophic consequences have been prevented or limited in the highly sophisticated European societies of today. Early modern Valencia was no exception to this rule, and a brief glance at Porcar's chronicle of the early seventeenth century reveals a full range of catastrophic events, including outbreaks of plague, numerous fires, severe thunderstorms, and long periods of drought.[84] Like the primitive religions that it replaced, Catholicism sought to help afflicted humanity by propitiating the supernatural forces (the wrath of God) that were believed to have caused these problems.[85] The church was commonly regarded as a vast repository of supernatural power and sometimes directly encouraged this view by accepting and supporting certain miraculous events if they appeared to lend support to the faith and by creating a litany of usages designed to draw down God's blessing on the tiny struggles of everyday life.[86]

Thus, it is hardly surprising that in spite of the careful attempt made by at least some clergy to indicate that the effectiveness of specific prayers or any other observances depended ultimately on the will of God, it became widely accepted that, with the proper formula and devices, man could manipulate the supernatural. It was this belief, encouraged directly or indirectly by the church, that provided the basis for the activity of the early modern magician who frequently incorporated cult objects or Christian prayers in his charms and incantations.

Since the prestige of the church itself was so heavily dependent on its ability to mobilize supernatural forces on man's behalf, its attitude toward popular superstitions was highly ambivalent. If the intercession of the supernatural was sought through observances approved by the church, such as rogations or exorcism, this could only increase devotion, especially if the believer demonstrated a genuine trust in God and did not seek any specific material gain. However, the post-Tridentine church's desire to reassert respect for the sacred made it sensitive to any attempt to invoke the supernatural for illicit or materialistic purposes, especially when officially sanctioned forms of intercession were used in unacceptable ways.[87] This new sensitivity led to Sixtus V's bull of 1585 against magic and brought the Inquisition into the struggle against popular superstition.

The three most important kinds of superstitious error prosecuted by the Valencia tribunal were divination (51.8% of all cases), love magic (25.9%), and curative magic (17.7%). Divination included such practices as attempts to predict the future or affect the outcome of future events. In 1604, for example, the Valencia tribunal sentenced Alonso Verlango to a reprimand and two years of exile for, among other superstitious practices, hiring a woman to bring about the resolution of a lawsuit by performing several conjurations that combined the invocation of saints and demons.[88]

The most common form of divination, however, was the effort to free enchanted treasure. This form of divination provided the tribunal with 34.5 percent of its cases of superstition and had become so common in the kingdom by the early eighteenth century that the Suprema wrote to ask that the archbishop order parish priests to denounce it from the pulpits.[89] The time, trouble, and expense involved in hunting for enchanted treasure frequently meant that such "expeditions" were organized like business partnerships and involved men with a certain amount of wealth.

One group of intrepid treasure hunters, which included such luminaries as Melchor Gamir, a jurat of Valencia city, and Melchor Moscardo, an official of the criminal chamber of the Audiencia, began by purchasing a Moorish slave who enjoyed some reputation as a magician and who promised to find them an enchanted treasure. After making several fruitless attempts, the slave finally admitted that he had only made the claim to avoid work. The partners then sold the slave but without abandoning their belief in the possibility of liberating enchanted treasure, although it did make them a bit more cautious about investing any more money. This time, they simply came to an agreement with the owner of another Moorish slave who claimed to be a master of "natural magic" which would provide him with a share of any treasure that was discovered. After this slave also failed to deliver on his promises, the members of the group, who were well aware of the Inquisition's attitude toward this sort of activity, felt it necessary to denounce themselves to the Holy Office for "any trace of superstition that might have become involved in these things."[90] Confronted with the evidence of such practices in late-seventeenth- and early eighteenth-century Valencia, the historian can only lament that the energy and persistence shown by these groups in the pursuit of imaginary treasure could not have been turned to the creation of real wealth in a region where enterprising businessmen were in short supply.

At a time when the church continued to claim that prayers and even sacraments could have curative power, the Inquisition's attack on those practicing healing magic must be seen as a way of protecting the church monopoly against unwelcome interlopers. In the case of Anna Rodríguez, a curandera who was accused of witchcraft by her neighbors, the tribunal entirely ignored the charge of sorcery and simply ordered her not to engage in any more healing.[91] Less easy to decide was the case of Blas Olaria, the parish priest of El Castillo, who, for a fee of three sueldos, provided sick people with special amulets and said prayers for their recovery. At his second trial in 1651, he argued that the saints themselves had given charms to those who had become ill through enchantment and that "many" other priests did exactly as he was doing. This forceful and effective argument was enough to produce dissension among the calificadores, and the Suprema had to step in to insist that the case be prosecuted.[92]

Evidence that the campaign against magical healing was having some impact on the practitioners themselves comes from the fact that known healers were becoming more reluctant to perform their functions. In 1642, it took the intervention of the governor of Castellón de la Plana himself to persuade Juana Font to cure a woman who claimed that she became ill after quarreling with her.[93]

Love magic, which comprised more than one quarter of the cases of superstition tried by the Valencia tribunal, was largely carried out by women in an effort to cope with a world that had dictated their extreme powerlessness and subjugated them to husbands and lovers. In their pathetic and ineffective attempts to assert some measure of control over the men in their lives or to attract the attention and affection of the men they desired, Valencia's women could draw on a rich popular tradition of incantations, rituals, and magical concoctions and on the support of networks of other women with similar concerns. Knowledge of magical practices and contacts with well-known practitioners of the magical arts were shared among the women comprising these networks, but jealousy, competition for lovers among some of the women, and bitterness over the failure of amatory magic to produce any positive results tended to make these networks highly unstable and productive of multiple denunciations to the Holy Office. Once they were brought before the bar of the Holy Office, their tendency to mix Christian prayers with superstitious incantations and frequent if perfunctory invocation of the devil left these women open to charges of "irreverence" for the sacred, "profane observance," and "sacrilege" even though it was agreed that formal heresy was never an issue.[94]

The case of Esperanza Badía, who was incarcerated by the Valencia tribunal on November 26, 1653, provides an excellent example of the kind of woman most likely to become involved in amatory magic on what might almost be termed a "professional" basis as well as the shifting and unstable personal relations that eventually resulted in denunciations to the Holy Office. Orphaned at nine when both her parents died, she was married at age thirteen to Francisco Mayner, a bookseller who deserted her shortly after the birth of their only daughter. Badía then moved to Valencia city where she became a nursemaid in several homes and attracted the attention of a prosperous labrador. It was on this individual, Andrés Berenger, that she first used amatory magic to "tie" him more closely to her and induce him to keep his promise to marry her. In the end, the marriage never took place, since Badía's husband was known to be still alive and she lacked sufficient funds for the expenses involved in the annulment process. Poverty stricken, deserted by her lover, and with her last hope of marriage now gone, Badía began to supplement her meager income by practicing amatory magic (reciting magical incantations, mixing up potions) as part of a network of women much like herself. Within this group, Badía was among the most active practitioners of love magic, frequently working for women like Celedonia Lazero, with whom she lived for a time and from whom she received money on three separate occasions for mixing a magic potion that would cause her lover to return. Badía also taught other women incantations and was herself taught by others like María la Catalana, who evidently enjoyed considerable prestige as a practitioner of amatory magic, in part because she had once been convicted of superstition by the Inquisition. At the time of Badía's arrest, María was living in Valencia in violation of the four years of exile to which she had been sentenced. This did little damage to her business, however, and she kept busy casting spells, reciting amatory incantations, and mixing potions for a large number of clients including Esperanza Badía herself.

In the end, this group came to grief after Badía was denounced by her erstwhile friend and client, Esperanza Coll, with whom she had quarreled over a man. With Coll's testimony, of course, the relative anonymity that had protected the network was breached, and the tribunal reaped a rich harvest of denunciation and arrests.[95]

The widespread practice of amatory magic in sixteenth- and seventeenth-century Europe and the persecution of its practitioners may well be two sides of the same coin. The "European marriage pattern," which was well in place by the early sixteenth century, entailed later marriage and was characterized by a large percentage of women who never married.[96] The competition for any available men must have been ferocious, and those women without dowries or special physical attractiveness utilized every means, licit or illicit, in the struggle. The persecution of such women by the Inquisition and secular criminal courts of Europe may tell us more about society's inability to assimilate the large number of women who were no longer under masculine rule than about any new and dangerous heresies or diabolism involved in amatory magic.

In his sermon preached at the opening of the second session of the Council of Trent on January 7, 1546, the bishop of San Marco in Calabria laid stress on the theme of the internal reform of the church that was to become one of the principal objectives of conciliar legislation. According to the bishop, the "decay in church morality had provided the dissidents with the weapons with which to attack us," and while few believed that the mere reform of abuses would lead to a reconciliation with the Protestants, there could be little doubt that a reformed church would be in a better position to hold the line against further Protestant advances.[97] The primary thrust of this reform, as Bishop Del Monte declared before the session of February 8, 1547, was "the revival of the pastoral ministry—the cure of souls."[98] The new post-Tridentine church, unlike its medieval predecessor, was to be a parochially grounded institution with priests thoroughly trained in theology, preaching in accordance with Catholic dogma, administering the sacraments in a proper and respectful manner, and setting a high moral standard for the laity.[99]

Unfortunately, as many at the council were aware, the mid-sixteenth-century priesthood fell far short of this clerical ideal. Ease of access to clerical orders and the lack of any uniform theological education led to the creation of a priesthood deficient in theology, incapable of preaching, and prone to doctrinal error.[100] Bishops' frequent absenteeism and their inability to exercise control over the priests and benefice holders in their dioceses resulted in a scandalous laxity of morals and an undisguised disdain for ecclesiastical responsibilities. Of course, the fathers of the council recognized these shortcomings and in Sessions XX and XXII passed decrees reforming the moral lives of the clergy and establishing the principle that clerics should be educated in theology in seminaries. But passing a series of decrees, however well intended, was not the same as actually achieving the reform of clerical life. It would take generations to finally achieve the goal of establishing diocesan seminaries, for example, and meanwhile there were a great many pulpits from which indifferent, bad, or even dangerous ideas were pouring forth each Sunday. Regardless of the decrees at Trent, episcopal authority remained weak and many bishops continued the absenteeism that had frustrated earlier efforts to reform the moral behavior of the diocesan clergy.[101] The attainment of a genuinely reformed priesthood would take time, possibly generations, but time was what the mid-sixteenth-century church did not have. Faced with the Protestant threat and with the Protestant rejection of such critical Catholic institutions as clerical celibacy and confession, the Catholic church had to curb the worst abuses and doctrinal errors of the clergy even though the institutions of genuine reform were not in place. It was this realization of the urgency of finding at least a partial solution to the problem of the clergy that led Pope Paul III to issue a bull specifically prohibiting the preaching of scandalous or erroneous propositions and Pius IV to grant the Spanish Inquisition jurisdiction over the disrespect for the sacrament of penance implied in solicitation in the confessional.[102]

Given the low level of theological instruction among the clergy and the importance of preaching as a form of propaganda, it was to be expected that the Holy Office would find a great many preachers who made foolish or theologically unsound statements from the pulpit.[103] Of course, the excesses that the new post-Tridentine religious sensibility detected in many popular sermons were often little more than the result of a preacher's attempts to entertain or captivate his flock.[104] In other cases, however, popular sermons revealed a depth of ignorance and misinformation that must have been profoundly troubling to the Holy Office. An excellent example of this is provided by the case of Dr. Gaspar Livera, a respected benefice holder in the parish church of San Andrés of Valencia whose degree in theology seems to have been little more than a license to preach doctrinal errors. Among the propositions that the Holy Office was later to qualify as "heretical" and "erroneous" were Livera's assertions that the Virgin Mary had been ordained in both major and minor orders and that she was a true pope with the power of the keys like Saint Peter.[105] On one occasion, Livera, who was evidently something of a Valencian patriot, preached a sermon in honor of Valencia's patron saint, Vicente Ferrer, in which he asserted that since he was the most virtuous and perfect of all the saints, he was the only one who could rightfully be called the "saint of God." Evidently, the tribunal and the Suprema felt that Livera's case was serious enough to merit exceptional punishment, so that in addition to the customary obligation to retract his errors in the same pulpits in which they had been uttered, he was sentenced to be perpetually deprived of the right to preach.[106]

The fact that Livera was able to demonstrate at his trial that many of the propositions that formed part of the accusation were taken from printed sermons written by others is an indication of just how deep seated doctrinal error was in the post-Tridentine Valencian church. In fact, as the Valencia tribunal was to find out for itself, the presence of a doctrinal eccentricity within the tradition of a particular ecclesiastical institution would make the leaders of that institution close ranks around any of their number who was brought before the Holy Office for making statements consistent with that tradition. On December 6, 1628, Fray Jerónimo Navarro, a prominent Jeronimite preacher, was brought before the tribunal after having been denounced by several of his fellow monks for propositions that he had uttered during sermons in the chapel of the Jeronimite monastery in Gandía where he resided. Among these were the statements that when the church beheld Christ beaten and disfigured after the passion, it neither recognized nor wanted him for its savior and that the fathers of the Old Testament had a faith that was "formless, irregular and unpleasing." A search of Navarro's papers revealed another thirty-six propositions, many of which were qualified as heretical, which were drawn from the writings of a number of different monks of the order, including a very well-respected master of theology since deceased. As this meant that "false doctrine" was fairly widespread at the monastery, the Suprema intervened to toughen the provisions of the sentence first handed down by the tribunal, and, in addition to forcing Fray Jerónimo to retract his statements, he was not to be permitted to preach without the permission of the inquisitor-general.[107]

Punishment of a monk for maintaining theological ideas that were widespread and accepted as orthodox within the Jeronimite Order stirred up a hornet's nest of opposition among the superiors of the order which was quickly felt by the monks who had denounced Navarro before the tribunal. Testifying before the Inquisition was a violation of the rule passed on May 24, 1612, which prevented any monk from going before the Inquisition to denounce a fellow monk without the express permission of his superiors.[108] A visitation to the Gandía monastery by officials of the order resulted in charges being lodged against the monks who had testified against Navarro, and they were all removed in disgrace to other monasteries. As one of the monks commented in a letter to the Suprema some years later, not only had his own once-flourishing career in the order been ruined by his decision to testify before the Holy Office but, in light of the punishment that he and the others had received from his superiors, it was extremely unlikely that any monks would be willing to come forward in the future.[109]

Within the context of the reform of the church that was set in motion at the Council of Trent, the Spanish Inquisition's attempts to repress the worst excesses of erroneous doctrine were appropriate and laudable. The profound dissensions within monasteries and the animosities among the religious orders whose members dominated Spanish education, however, meant that the Inquisition came to be seen as the ideal instrument for destroying personal and intellectual enemies and punishing those whose ideas appeared to conflict with established orthodoxy. This, combined with book censorship, contributed to the decline of Spanish institutions of higher education, which in their heyday during the middle years of the sixteenth century had contributed so much to European intellectual life.[110]

It was the tension between reformers and conservatives in the

Franciscan monastery of San Antonio of Mora, of which he was the superior, which brought Fray Anselmo de Gracia to the tribunal on November 22, 1680, to denounce himself for uttering a potentially heretical proposition. Fray Anselmo admitted that during a moment of intense frustration he had declared in the hearing of several monks who were most strongly opposed to the reform that if some were given crowns in heaven for their travail on earth then he would receive several. Evidently, Fray Anselmo was afraid that his enemies in the monastery would denounce him and distort his words to make them seem worse than they were and had come before the Holy Office to forestall them.[111]

The strong rivalries among the orders that were based in part on differing theological traditions were highly productive of denunciations. In November 1698, for example, Augustinian Fray Ignacio Soso was denounced by the Oratorian, Dr. Tomás Tosca, for certain propositions that he was planning to defend publicly to gain the degree of doctor of theology at the University of Valencia. The case was eventually suspended after Soso testified that the propositions that he intended to defend were considered orthodox within the theological traditions of the Augustinian Order and offered to formally submit himself to the authority of the Holy Office. Even so, the fact that immediately on receiving this complaint the Inquisition imperiously ordered the suspension of proceedings at the university was a chilling example of the power that it had assumed over Spanish academic life.[112]

In the struggle between the "novatores" and the supporters of traditional scholasticism, the traditionalists had a powerful ally in the Inquisition. The latter, except for a brief period during the 1520s and 1530s, had never been a friend of innovation, and by the early seventeenth century with the publication of the restrictive index of 1583–84, it had clearly ranged itself on the side of the traditionalists.[113] The sure knowledge that he could count on the Inquisition's support against his intellectual opponents is what brought Dominican Fray Pedro Juan Imperial to the tribunal to roundly denounce the antischolasticism of certain members of the faculty of the University of Valencia which had been made especially obvious at an oral disputation that he had recently attended.[114] It was pressure from reactionaries like Fray Pedro Juan and the ever-present threat of intervention by the Holy Office that transformed the University of Valencia from the intellectually avant-garde institution that it was during the early and middle years of the sixteenth century to the bastion of intransigent scholasticism that it became by the end of the seventeenth century.[115]

So pervasive was the atmosphere of fear and conformity in intellectual circles that by the end of the seventeenth century, Spain's theologians had become their own inquisitors and denounced themselves whenever they suspected that they had made a statement of doubtful orthodoxy. In June 1691, for example, Fray Silverio Garcerán, reader in philosophy at the monastery of La Merced in Elche, came to denounce himself for certain propositions that he had stated during an oral examination for the post of reader in theology.[116] Some months later, a Carmelite, Fray José Marti, denounced himself for what he felt might have been a heretical proposition that he had uttered during a sermon.[117]

In seminaries and monastic colleges, in universities and from the pulpit, the intellectual leaders of early modern Spain were the secular and regular clergy. The fact that more than 30 percent of those brought before the Valencia tribunal on charges of uttering heretical or dangerous propositions were clerics indicates that the Inquisition was deeply committed to creating and maintaining the impression among this influential body of men that safety and preferment lay in treading the well-worn path of orthodoxy, however imprecise its definitions.

The centerpiece of the Council of Trent's definition of specifically Catholic doctrine was its clear statement of the centrality of the sacraments in the practice of Christianity.[118] At the same time, there was an uncomfortable awareness, fed by the personal experience of many who attended the council, that under present conditions, the sacraments were being administered badly and without proper reverence.[119]

One of the most glaring examples of the irreverence that concerned the fathers at Trent was solicitation, by which clerics appeared to demonstrate their disdain for the sanctity of the sacrament of penance by attempting to seduce their penitents while hearing their confessions.[120] The opportunities for such illicit behavior were considerable given the fact that the confessional, which provided a physical separation between priest and penitent, did not exist before the mid-sixteenth century and was probably not widely used in the Kingdom of Valencia until the late eighteenth or early nineteenth century. An edict issued by the tribunal on November 3, 1781, complains of the disregard of many previous orders to employ confessionals and speaks of confessions being heard in oratories and private chapels in much the same terms as a similar decree issued 156 years earlier by the Suprema.[121]

Alarm over the discovery of proto-Protestant conventicles in Seville and Valladolid in the late 1550s and the critical need to reassert the validity of the sacrament of penance in the face of Protestant rejection led to a growing concern over solicitation in reformist circles. Since the episcopal courts were notorious for taking a lenient view of this offense, Pope Pius IV, in 1561, granted the Inquisition jurisdiction over the heresy implied by such obvious abuse of the sacrament.[122] By 1563, a letter from the Suprema recorded approvingly that several tribunals already had cases pending, although it was decided provisionally not to include the offense in the Edict of Faith.[123] In 1622, Gregory XV widened the definition of the offense to include what was said before and after confession, even if it had only been a sham confession.[124]

In spite of papal fulminations and the repeated denunciation of solicitation by theologians and moralists, however, auricular confession presented many dangers and temptations for both priest and penitent. The role of the confessor as spiritual and moral adviser encouraged a certain intimacy, while the confessor's obligation to ask searching questions about the sexual lives of his penitents provided him with the opportunity to bring his own sexual needs and experiences into the discussion. Since the institution of celibacy inevitably posed a series of grave psychological problems for many priests, such topics could easily lead to the verbalizing or acting out of sexual frustrations.[125]

For some of the women who were victims of sexual solicitation, the experience of a confessor breaking his sacred trust was profoundly shocking. Mariana Llorens, a young woman from just outside Valencia city, was so upset by a series of improper questions put to her by her confessor that she felt suffocated and had to run out of the church without even receiving absolution. This incident disturbed her so much that it caused intermittent bouts of depression that were only relieved after she testified about the incident before a calificador of the Holy Office four years later.[126]

Certain women were more than willing to listen to the indecent language and illicit proposals of their confessors, however. Marital relationships that were inadequate emotionally and physically left many women unfulfilled and eager for the attentions of the priests they saw for confession. Such a relationship promised the fulfillment of sexual and emotional needs while offering a greater degree of safety from a jealous and brutal husband than would a relationship with a male friend or neighbor. María Palomino, who enjoyed a series of relationships with a number of her confessors over about a ten-year period, had a husband who frequently beat her and forced her to have anal sex. Needless to say, María came before the Holy Office only because her new confessor had refused to absolve her until she had done so.[127]

One of the most remarkable aspects of the Inquisition's persecution of this offense was the extreme difficulty of obtaining enough evidence to bring an accused to trial. The gradual acceptance, by the end of the sixteenth century, of the requirement of two independent witnesses to initiate prosecution created a significant obstacle and allowed some individuals to continue their profligate careers with virtual impunity.[128] Of course, there were many reasons women might be reluctant to come forward to present their charges. The parish priest was a powerful individual, especially on a village level, and had many ways of revenging himself on those who had testified against him if the courts did not remove him from the scene. In the case of nuns, who were entirely subordinate to male spiritual directors, sheer ignorance played an important role in limiting the number of denunciations. In 1750, Dr. Domingo Campillo, special commissioner for the investigation of charges that had been brought against Padre Esteban Hespanique, found that even though Hespanique had been pouring filthy words and suggestions into their ears for four years, his penitents in the convent of Santa Teresa of Teruel failed to denounce him because they were unaware of the nature of the offense.[129] Other women, like María Palomino, who was tied to a brutal and unsatisfying marriage, would have little reason to come forward unless forced to do so.

In the last analysis, it was the reputation of the individual in his monastery or among his parishioners that determined his fate. Padre Hespanique's practices had simply become too widely known in the convent to escape notice. In the case of Juan Bautista Catalá,

the rector of Yátova, the eight denunciations that had been received against him before he came to denounce himself to the
tribunal in October 1763 were as much a product of the village's
rejection of him as their priest as with his illicit sexual activity. The
evidence even suggests that his activities during and after confession were regarded with a certain tolerance until he had alienated
enough people in the community by the way he performed his
office to leave himself defenseless. Witnesses described his frequent absences from his church, slipshod celebration of mass, and
misuse of funds earmarked for masses for the dead. At one point,
he was even said to have cut the communion loaf in pieces at the
altar in full view of the congregation. In another instance, he simply went too far with his sexual activity. Catalá's friendship with
Miguel Lisarde remained close in spite of the fact that he had
engaged in sexual foreplay with his 21-year-old daughter during
and after confession, made off-color remarks to her in public, and
"spent many nights" with her in the rectory. Their relationship was
destroyed when Catalá's lust for Antonia Lisarde became so great
that he got her to promise that she would marry the brother of one
of his servants. This agreement, which would have allowed Catalá
to enjoy her sexual favors while her complaisant husband looked
the other way, was contested by Miguel Lisarde, who went to court
and got a judgment freeing his daughter from this unwanted entan-
glement. As a result, Catalá no longer visited the Lisarde household as he had frequently done before the lawsuit, and Antonia
Lisarde no longer came to confession with him and later denounced
him for solicitation.[130]

A sociological analysis of solicitantes coming before the Valencia
tribunal reveals a considerable preponderance of the regular clergy
over the seculars, with the former accounting for 67.5 percent of
the accused. Furthermore, among the regulares, the various orders
of Franciscans accounted for fully 46.8 percent of the cases as opposed to only 6.3 percent for the Dominicans and 3.9 percent for
the Jesuits. The age profile indicates a heavy concentration of solicitantes (76.3%) among ages 31 to 50, when the discipline of
seminary or monastic college was over and priests and monks acquired the greater freedom of movement that came with taking
charge of a rectory or preaching and confessing at several locations.

As far as punishment was concerned, since there was no actual suspicion of heresy involved in any of these cases, all accused were sentenced to abjuration de levi. The graver corporal penalties such as relaxation or galley service or scourging were entirely omitted (although some monks were "disciplined" with a whip when they arrived at the monastery chosen for their reclusion). For the regulars, there was reclusion in a monastery selected by the tribunal, deprivation of the right to confess, and sometimes deprivation of other sacramental functions. For the seculars, there was reclusion, deprivation of benefice, fines, disciplines, spiritual exercises, and suspension from confessing and other spiritual functions.[131]

Although Lea asserts that "the penalties inflicted were singularly disproportionate to the gravity of the offense," it should be borne in mind that these were grave penalties to inflict on a priest or monk as they involved disgrace, loss of benefice or career, and long periods of exile.[132]

During the last and longest phase of its history, roughly from 1560 to 1820, the Spanish Inquisition joined the official church and the baroque state in a gigantic effort to remodel popular culture and the priesthood along the lines demanded by the Tridentine reformers. But if the repression of such offenses as blasphemy and propositions served to enforce respect for the sacred and helped rid pulpits and classrooms of unsound theology, it also had the effect of promoting a stultifying conformity that robbed both popular and elite culture of their creative spontaneity. Punishment of bigamy and solicitation may have helped to promote public respect for the sacraments of holy matrimony and penance but did nothing to resolve their root causes. By the late seventeenth century, even its once-innovative position on witchcraft accusations was beginning to appear less novel as other European judicial institutions ended or significantly reduced witchcraft trials. Like most of the other institutions of Hapsburg Spain, the Inquisition had become profoundly conservative, willingly sacrificing genuine reform to stability and demanding explicit acceptance of a set of obsolete intellectual concepts and moral standards.

IX

Decline and Abolition of the Holy Office in Valencia

On December 16, 1705, the city of Valencia was occupied by a small force of Allied soldiers under the command of Juan Bautista Basset y Ramos. Shortly after the Allies entered the city, most of the nobility and royal officials fled the kingdom for the safety of Bourbon-controlled Castile.[1] The most conspicuous exception to this mass exodus of Valencia's traditional governing classes was her two senior inquisitors, Juan de la Torre y Guerau and Isidro de Balmaseda. Remaining at their posts throughout the Allied occupation, the inquisitors not only succeeded in maintaining order within the city but were also able to keep Bourbon military and political leaders supplied with a steady stream of intelligence.[2]

When the disastrous battle of Almansa on April 25, 1707, led to the withdrawal of Allied forces, the city was once again left defenseless, and the arrival of a messenger from the advancing Bourbon army on May 6 led to an outbreak of rioting during which a mob stormed the city hall and arms were distributed to the people. At this critical moment, the tribunal, led by its indefatigable chief, Isidro de Balmaseda, stepped into the breach. After hiding the terrified jurats in the palace of the Inquisition where they would be safe from the mob, Balmaseda ordered the religious communities to organize processions to pray for the city's deliverance while sending his officials to make contact with the heads of the craft guilds and others with influence over the popular masses to quell the rioting. After a message from the Bourbon commander assuring the city that it would not be put to the sack if it surrendered was received by the auxiliary bishop, Balmaseda felt free to allow the jurats to leave the palace so that they could officially welcome the royalist forces, while sending several officials of the Inquisition to convince the archduke's remaining supporters to lay down their arms. These delicate negotiations successfully concluded, the city surrendered without a struggle to the duc d'Orléans.[3]

In what may have been its finest hour, the tribunal had saved the city from all the horrors and cruelty of war to which a useless resistance would have exposed it.[4] Furthermore, during the long months of occupation, it had emerged as the leading element of the city's political elite, protecting and defending its weaker members against the popular masses. Its prestige had never stood higher, and in a marginal note scrawled on the tribunal's final report, Inquisitor-General Vidal Marín ordered the Suprema to write the tribunal to congratulate it for the exemplary manner in which it "had conducted itself during that critical period."[5]

After the city had surrendered, the inquisitors gave further proof of their unqualified loyalty to the Bourbons by prosecuting those who had collaborated with the Allied government or had shown any sympathy for the Allied cause. This prosecution was carried on in two ways: by virtue of the Suprema's edict of October 9, 1706, which ordered penitents who had been urged to disobey Philip V to denounce their confessors to the Holy Office, and by using the tribunal against any Allied loyalist who could be shown to have committed an offense that fell under inquisitorial jurisdiction.[6]

In summer 1707, Balmaseda pressed charges against the abbot and monks of the Cistercian monastery of Poblet and ordered the arrest of Fray Mario Andreu, the monastery's administrator for the villages of Quart and Aldaya who had been instrumental in keeping them loyal to Archduke Charles.[7] At the same time, the tribunal ordered the arrest of Fray Peregrin Gueralt of the Servite order who had carried intelligence to the archduke's forces.[8] As a member of the special tribunal that was established to punish those who had served the archduke, Inquisitor Balmaseda also came into conflict with the archbishop and his officials who had made no secret of their sympathy for the Allied cause even after the recovery of the city by the Bourbons. After a confrontation with the vicar-general over his treasonous correspondence with Allied generals, Balmaseda was very nearly placed under ban of excommunication.[9]

The Valencia tribunal's outstanding record of loyalty to the Bourbon cause in an otherwise "rebel" province did not go unrewarded. Sometime in early June 1708, the crown granted the tribunal 3,400 lliures in revenues to be drawn from the village of Alaquàs. Evidently, the inquisitors must have enjoyed excellent relations with Melchor de Macanaz, the chief Castilian minister in the conquered province, as he moved quickly to make the revenues available to them and earned their praise for his demonstration of "courtesy and affection" for the Holy Office.[10] Ironically, the same inquisitorial tribunal that Macanaz had so willingly assisted in the days of his glory also benefited from his disgrace. After the publication of a papal decree condemning as heretical the strong memorial of royal perquisites that he had drawn up for the Council of Castile in December 1713, he was banished to France. Tried in absentia by the Holy Office, he was sentenced to perpetual exile and the loss of all of his property.[11] Among the dividends that came to the Inquisition's treasury as a result of this case were more than 9,300 lliures that the Valencia tribunal received between 1716 and 1723 from property that had been awarded to Macanaz by the crown during his sojourn in the kingdom.[12]

Buoyed by the firm support of Philip V (1701–1746), the Spanish Inquisition in general, including the Valencia tribunal, made a significant political and financial recovery during the first decades of the eighteenth century. In Valencia, overall activity increased dramatically to 1,323 cases between 1701 and 1750, as opposed to the 451 recorded between 1651 and 1700. This increase was especially impressive if we compare it to the activity recorded during the slack years of the majority of Charles II (from 1675), when the tribunal only logged 113 cases.

The tribunal's excellent relationship with the crown during this period is demonstrated by the employment of its inquisitors in a variety of special assignments. In 1746, for example, Inquisitor Francisco Antonio Espinosa was given the responsibility for carrying out a visitation to Corpus Christi seminary, of which King Philip V was founder and patron.[13] Several years later, Inquisitor Fernando de Urbino was selected by the crown to carry out a visitation to the troubled Cistercian monastery of Valldigna.[14]

The tribunal's financial condition, which had already deteriorated during the last years of the reign of Charles II, continued to worsen during the War of Succession as a result of the Allied occupation and the devastation caused by the Bourbon reconquest.[15] In February 1706, the tribunal wrote the Suprema to comment that it had been unable to collect most of its revenues for that year because of the "ruinous" condition of the local economy.[16]

As the 1706 letter clearly indicated, the tribunal's financial condition depended absolutely on the general condition of the economy and particularly on the agricultural sector. The restoration of peace and stability under the Bourbons led to a period of significant economic recovery beginning in about 1713. Between 1713 and 1787, the population of the kingdom virtually doubled to about 770,000, and, as a consequence of this increased population pressure, much new land was put under cultivation. Overall agricultural output increased significantly, while productivity was improved through a large number of private irrigation projects. Peasant incomes increased as a result of the spread of rice cultivation (in spite of official opposition) and the increasing use of rural labor by Valencian silk producers, and the production of raw silk more than doubled between 1740 and 1770.[17]

The impact of these trends on the rural rents—on which the fortunes of the Valencia tribunal depended—could not have been more positive, with 300 to 400 percent increases in the tithe in virtually all areas.[18] As a result, the tribunal's financial condition improved dramatically, with overall revenues almost tripling between 1727 and 1797. Increases were particularly dramatic in income sectors sensitive to improvement in agricultural rent, especially the tithe-driven income from canonries which increased more than fourfold, and rural mortgages in which the tribunal actually began making additional investments from the mid-1720s.[19] By the 1780s, the tribunal's obvious prosperity had emboldened several minor officials to petition the Suprema for an increase in their salaries.[20]

The Inquisition even expanded its jurisdiction after the publication of the bull *In eminenti*, which condemned Freemasonry in Spain on October 11, 1738.[21] In 1748, Masonry was added to an Edict of Faith for the first time and was included in edicts on a regular basis from 1755.[22] From 1738 to the outbreak of the French

Revolution, the Spanish Inquisition, with strong encouragement from the crown, kept up a desultory pursuit of masons, who were primarily foreigners or Spanish military officers who had been initiated into the Masonic order during sojourns in foreign countries. To the Valencia tribunal belongs the unique distinction of having received a denunciation for Masonry against Sor María de Santa Escolastica, a French Ursuline living in Sagunto and the only nun ever accused of that offense.[23]

In spite of the Valencia tribunal's fervent loyalty and a general recovery in the prestige of the Holy Office under the leadership of Inquisitor-General Juan de Camargo (1720–1733), however, the general trend of Bourbon policy was to emphasize royal perquisites (regalias) and reduce the power and independence of the Holy Office. Melchor de Macanaz's reform proposal, which was presented to the Council of Castile on November 3, 1714, went far beyond the Junta Magna report of 1696 in advocating the conversion of the Inquisition into a purely ecclesiastical tribunal and restricting its censorship function by preventing it from prohibiting any books without first submitting the case to the crown for a final decision.[24] While some of the more daring elements in this proposal were never put into effect (subordination of the Suprema to a royal secretary or direct royal nomination of calificadores), it did serve as the basis for royal policy toward the Holy Office during much of the eighteenth century.

At the consulta of February 28, 1769, the fiscales of the Council of Castile asserted that the crown had complete authority over the Inquisition, including the right to "direct it, limit it and even suppress it."[25] The royal cedula of February 5, 1770, significantly weakened the Inquisition's claim (never fully validated) to exclusive cognizance of bigamy cases by formally dividing such cases among royal courts, ecclesiastical tribunals, and the Holy Office.[26] At the same time, the Inquisition lost jurisdiction over blasphemy and sodomy, which went entirely to the ordinary courts. In 1784, moreover, the Holy Office was prohibited from arresting any royal official, titled noble, or military officer without first submitting the particulars of the case to the crown.[27]

Even more significant and far-reaching in reducing the independence and freedom of action of the Holy Office was the royal cedula of June 16, 1768, whose provisions were clearly inspired by the

Macanaz memorial of the early part of the century. In the future, according to the cedula, the Holy Office was to see that "Catholic authors" were given a chance to defend their works before they could be condemned, while inquisitorial edicts of prohibition were not to be published before being presented to the king for approval through the appropriate secretaries of the Council of Justice or Council of State. Moreover, in a clause that would have gladdened the heart of the old fiscal had he been alive to read it, the Spanish Inquisition was prohibited from publishing any papal bull without first obtaining permission from the Council of State.[28]

Late in the century, the Valencia tribunal experienced for itself the Bourbon regime's willingness to intervene directly in inquisitorial trials even after they had been decided. In May 1790, Fray Agustín de Cabades, a 51-year-old Mercedarian who had made a distinguished career for himself as a professor at the university and also served as a calificador of the Holy Office, was convicted of solicitation. The accusation against Cabades was based on repeated offenses with both male and female penitents going back twenty years as well as on several spontaneous but incomplete and mendacious confessions. He had also blatantly abused his position with the Holy Office by assuring one of his victims that she had fully carried out her new confessor's requirement that she recount her experiences with him to the Holy Office by reporting it to him since he himself was "a part of the tribunal." Confronted by such overwhelming evidence, the tribunal sentenced Cabades to abjure in the chambers of the Holy Office before the twenty oldest monks of his monastery, suspended him from his office as calificador, and exiled him for eight years from the royal court and the city of Valencia, with the first four years to be spent in reclusion in the monastery of Játiva.

Even though the Valencia tribunal's sentence appears to have been fully justified, Cabades's intellectual attainments, especially his knowledge of foreign languages (English, French, Italian), made him an exceptional individual. As a result, instead of reclusion in Játiva, Cabades was permitted to travel to El Escorial on the express order of royal first secretary Floridablanca to consult with the government about its ambitious educational reform program. In September 1790, Cabades was given special permission to return to Valencia by Inquisitor-General Agustín Rubín de Cevallos and was permitted to take up his chair of theology at the University of Valencia with his sentence of reclusion and exile entirely removed.[29]

The timidity and subservience with which the Suprema and successive inquisitors-general reacted in the face of pressure from the Council of Castile and its aggressive prosecuting attorneys were communicated to the provincial inquisitors through royal ordinances that had the effect of greatly inhibiting their response to denunciations. In 1746, Ferdinand VI replied to a request for financial assistance from the Suprema by rather contemptuously suggesting that costs could best be controlled by not making every "willful slander" an excuse for undertaking a formal investigation and that even when a denunciation was signed by a known individual, a judge did not have to be dispatched to investigate each case but that some less expensive way ought to be found.[30] On January 1 of the following year, another royal pronouncement was issued which declared that before inquisitorial tribunals undertook to follow up on charges contained in a denunciation, they would have to make a preliminary investigation to determine the veracity of the charges.[31]

That the crown's lukewarm support for the judicial activity of the Holy Office succeeded in inducing an attitude of extreme caution among Valencia's inquisitors and their agents can be seen from several cases involving perfectly ordinary citizens. In late spring 1746, for example, Dr. Diego Forner, the commissioner of Benicarló, received four separate denunciations against Patricio White for heretical propositions. In previous years, a commissioner would have immediately called in witnesses and carried out his own preliminary investigation. That this was expected is indicated by the sharp rebuke he received from Valencia's inquisitor, Dr. Manuel Xaramillo de Contreras, for his slowness in doing so. The letter from Xaramillo de Contreras was followed by another from the tribunal's prosecuting attorney ordering Forner to carry out an investigation so as to make sure the witnesses were not acting out of personal animosity toward White. Several months later, White, who had probably gotten wind of the investigation, came to see the commissioner, confessed, and was duly reconciled. There the case rested until the following year, when another denunciation for the same offense reached the tribunal. This time it took until July 11, 1766, for the tribunal to respond by ordering a new investigation. Finally, more than twenty-one years after the original denunciation, White was called to the tribunal not to be arrested and placed in the dreaded secret prison but simply for an audiencia de cargos, where the accused was presented with a summary of the charges against him and invited to reply instead of being subjected to the ignominy of arrest and trial. Four days after White presented himself in Valencia, he was notified of the evidence against him. In response, he promised to behave better in the future and was released.[32]

Another inevitable result of the atmosphere in which the tribunals were forced to operate during the eighteenth century was the suspension of cases even when the evidence against the accused was all but overwhelming. A good example of this was the case of Salvadora Cabrera, who was accused by more than 50 witnesses of a variety of offenses including blasphemy, irreverence toward holy images, and superstition. In spite of the conclusive evidence against her, the tribunal chose to suspend proceedings even after the Suprema had written to specifically approve any action it might have wished to take.[33]

Quite apart from the negative atmosphere created by royal legislation, the tribunal's wavering and unwillingness to follow through on denunciations and actually punish offenders is hardly surprising given the timorous attitude displayed by the Suprema in even the most ordinary cases. Salvadora Cabrera, a poor woman with few friends, would hardly seem like the sort of subject whose honor and reputation would stir very much concern within exalted government circles. In spite of this, the Suprema operated with an extreme, even absurd, degree of caution. After the initial suspension of her case in November 1773, the tribunal had set various of its minions to report on her activities. Since these reports indicated continual blasphemies as well as such superstitious practices as predicting the future and pretending to work miracles, the prosecuting attorney demanded her arrest. Given the by now overwhelming evidence, the fiscal won his point, and the tribunal ordered her detention subject to obtaining permission from the Suprema. After receiving a summary of the case from the tribunal, the Suprema decided, inexplicably, to submit the evidence to the calificadores of the Corte tribunal (Madrid) for their opinion. It was only after their judgment (which merely confirmed what had already been determined by the tribunal) had been received that the

Suprema dictated a sentence of a reprimand and two years of exile from Valencia city, Mislata, and Manranara.[34] The extreme punctiliousness displayed by the Suprema in the case of a poor and friendless individual—an ideal victim—is striking to the observer with some knowledge of the early history of the Spanish Inquisition. It is highly unlikely that the high conviction rates and harsh sentences of the fifteenth and sixteenth centuries would have been achieved with such an attitude. Centralization, which had now progressed to the point that the Suprema was intervening in every phase of a provincial tribunal's proceedings, must have undermined the self-confidence of provincial inquisitors, making them extremely chary of displeasing their masters in Madrid by taking any action that was not approved in advance. For its part, the Suprema was well aware that unusual displays of activity by provincial tribunals would be poorly received at court and consequently was always on the side of caution. As a result, during the last half of the eighteenth century, the Valencia tribunal continued receiving denunciations, carrying out investigations, and initiating prosecutions but with few concrete results.

If fears of the Suprema's disapproval had a chilling effect on a provincial tribunal's operations against religious and moral offenders, the Suprema's lack of support in disputes with royal courts over its civil and criminal jurisdiction continued to have a negative impact on its ability to protect it from decay. Perhaps the most glaring example of the Suprema's lack of support for the Valencia tribunal's civil jurisdiction concerned the Colegio de Villena, which had been established in 1637 by a former physician to the Holy Office.[35] When he founded the college, Dr. Villena received permission from the Suprema to place it under the official protection of the inquisitors of the Valencia tribunal who would exercise full jurisdiction over the legal enforcement of all aspects of its constitution. In July 1739, a dispute arose over the awarding of a college scholarship, and the unsuccessful candidate appealed to the civil chamber of the Audiencia, which intervened to prevent the college rector from conferring the scholarship. The successful candidate, who happened to be a descendant of the founder, then appealed to the tribunal's civil chamber, and the battle was joined when the Audiencia subpoenaed the records in the case and demanded that the notary in charge of the Inquisition's civil court appear before it to testify. Of course,

Valencia's inquisitors refused to allow this on the grounds that the Audiencia had no jurisdiction in the case since the Inquisition had always exercised control over all aspects of the college through its civil court. When the Suprema was notified about the tribunal's strong stand, however, it responded by urging the tribunal to drop the matter entirely. From the Suprema's point of view, even this humiliating form of self-effacement was preferable to challenging the Audiencia. In fact, the Suprema even suggested that if this matter could not be settled quietly, the tribunal should give up its patronage entirely so as to avoid possible censure.[36]

Even though Valencia's inquisitors were proud of their role as patrons of the Colegio de Villena, it was the maintenance of the tribunal's civil and criminal jurisdiction over the members of the "corporation" of officials and familiares that was vital to the tribunal's future as a political and social force in the kingdom. The changed atmosphere at court, however, made it almost impossible for the Suprema to effectively support the local tribunals in disputes over the fuero.

Early in the reign of Philip V, the Suprema made its position on these disputes perfectly clear in a carta acordada dispatched to the provincial tribunals. According to this letter, the widespread belief that the Inquisition was abusing its privileges stemmed entirely from the overhasty defense of officials by the provincial tribunals even in dubious cases. Instead of an aggressive defense of official privilege, tribunals were enjoined to settle disputes with the royal courts in a friendly manner, and unless there was a clear-cut case in favor of the Holy Office, local tribunals were advised to make no move without first consulting the Suprema.[37] In another carta acordada issued on December 22, 1747, Inquisitor-General Pérez de Prado further curtailed provincial tribunals' freedom of action in jurisdictional disputes with the royal courts and removed their most effective weapon by prohibiting the use of ecclesiastical censures in such cases.[38]

As we have already seen in the case of the Colegio de Villena, even when the Inquisition's jurisdiction was well established, local tribunals could not count on support from the Suprema, so that it is hardly surprising that the eighteenth century saw the gradual disappearance of official tax exemptions and personal privileges. Perhaps the most valuable of all the privileges enjoyed by officials of the inquisitorial court was the freedom from paying royal taxes. As we have seen above, this privilege was violated during the crisis years of the reign of Philip IV, but it was later restored after the fall of the count duke of Olivares. During the eighteenth century, however, all the inquisitorial tribunals gradually lost this exemption, with the Valencia tribunal's turn coming in 1743.[39]

The same process of attrition affected exemptions from local taxation enjoyed by familiares in different parts of the district. In 1752, for example, the Valencia tribunal received a complaint from the familiares of Teruel to the effect that their long-standing exemption from local taxation had now been broken and that they paid taxes like any other members of the nonprivileged orders.[40] Similarly, a letter to the Suprema from the three secretaries of the tribunal in 1785 records their loss of exemptions from sales and property taxes levied by the city of Valencia.[41]

The Valencia tribunal found out for itself just how far the Suprema was prepared to go in enforcing the new prohibition on the use of ecclesiastical censures when it sought to employ them to defend the right of Gaspar Morate, a familiar of Játiva, to refuse to serve on the village council. Such exemptions from municipal service had been customarily granted to familiares in certain places including Játiva, but this time, the town fathers defied the tribunal and refused to allow Morate to withdraw his name. Frustrated in its effort to negotiate with the town authorities, the tribunal requested permission to employ ecclesiastical censures, but its request was denied. The tribunal's defeat on this occasion sounded the death knell of yet another privilege that had been enjoyed by Valencia's familiares.[42]

The privilege that appeared to have best stood the test of time was the exemption from quartering of royal troops and officials. Customarily, familiares were classed with caballeros and hidalgos in the matter of quartering so that troops would be lodged with them only as a last resort after the homes of the nonprivileged had all been filled. Along with this important privilege came the equally valuable one of exemption from the special (and frequently heavy) charges levied on towns along the route of a marching regiment to pay the costs of transporting its supplies and equipment. During the War of Succession, of course, the frequent passage of large bodies of soldiers through the impoverished kingdom made it impossible for the exemption to be observed, and a memorial to the tribunal from the association of familiares written just after the conclusion of the war tells of many violations by hard-pressed quartering officers.[43] In August 1729, the familiares' rights suffered another setback when the government of Philip V declared flatly that familiares were not to be exempt from quartering royal troops and contributing to their transportation expenses. In obedience to this order, the Suprema ordered the tribunal to suspend the legal proceedings it had initiated against Játiva, San Mateo, and several other towns for violating the familiares' exemption.[44]

The privilege seemed dead, but the relative calm of the reign of Charles III led to a revival. In 1760, we are informed that the ranks of the familiares of Játiva were always filled because they enjoyed an exemption from quartering and from the transportation levy.[45] In Castellón de la Plana, familiares had been placed in an intermediate category, ahead of ordinary pecheros but not quite in the same class as hidalgos or employees of the royal salt monopoly. In 1781, however, the captain-general himself intervened with the city council in support of the tribunal's contention that the familiares should be classed with the nobles and hidalgos of the town with regard to quartering his majesty's soldiers.

The 1780s were a relatively tranquil period for Spain, but the outbreak of war with the French Republic in 1793 meant that large bodies of troops would be moving toward the Spanish border. The familiares' quartering exemption once again came under heavy pressure, and it is highly likely that an 1806 circular issued by the governor-general of Catalonia to the village of Ulldecona and other towns in the Catalan part of the inquisitorial district sounded the death knell of the familiares' last privilege. In this document, the captain-general declared categorically that familiares were no longer exempt from providing lodgings for soldiers passing through the territory or from contributing to their expenses. That the tribunal was now prepared to abandon the long struggle to maintain the exemption from quartering is shown by the fact that it immediately wrote to the familiares of the towns mentioned in the order telling them to obey it.[46]

It is to be expected that the gradual but inexorable loss of the privileges and exemptions formerly enjoyed by officials and familiares led to a decline in the number of persons applying for official positions. This certainly happened in some tribunals, with the Inquisition of Barcelona complaining of difficulties in filling official posts as early as 1719.[47] That this gloomy picture was not the general rule can be seen from the case of the Valencia tribunal, in which, in spite of the loss of official privilege and the stagnation in official salaries, vacancies continued to attract numerous excellent candidates and in which the network of familiares diminished but remained viable and important throughout the century.

Certainly, the conservatism of Valencian society made family traditions of service to the Holy Office a powerful incentive for individuals to apply for official positions. The note of family tradition was sounded very strongly by all parties during the struggle to succeed Manuel Fernández de Marmanillo as alguacil mayor in 1788. The candidates were Antonio María Adell y de Bie and Antonio Esplugues de Palavecino y Gamir. The former was a cavaller and the eldest son of the baron of Choza, whose family had held official positions with the tribunal since 1583 when his ancestor, Benito Sanguino, came from Castile to assume the post of receiver. Moreover, the family had been in continuous possession of the office of alguacil mayor from 1586 when Benito Sanguino assumed it until 1787 when Fernández de Marmanillo took it over. In letters to the tribunal, both Antonio María and his father stressed the importance of family tradition with the baron, who had himself been a candidate for the position in previous years, assuring Inquisitor-General Rubin de Cevellos of the great honor it would be for his son to maintain the house of Sanguino's traditions of service to the Holy Office.[48]

The other candidate, Antonio Esplugues de Palavecino y Gamir, is an example of the way in which the Valencia tribunal could still attract new blood into official ranks during the eighteenth century. He came from an old family of Genoese nobles whose ancestor, Ambrosio Palavecino, had fled the Turkish invasion of one of the Genoese-held islands in the Mediterranean (where his father was governor) and settled in Valencia. The family's service to the tribunal began with Antonio's great-grandfather, José Palavecino y Esplugues, who became secretary in 1705. His son, Joaquín Palavecino, succeeded him in 1733 and in 1757 was appointed alguacil mayor to serve during the rather frequent absences and illnesses of the incumbent Marmanillo. In his memorial, Antonio

Esplugues de Palavecino also stressed his desire to carry on his family's traditions of service to the Holy Office as well as his own urge to "affirm still more his loyalty and reverence for this tribunal of our holy faith."[49]

For men like these, who were both independently wealthy, the inadequate salaries and bonuses that came with official rank were of little importance. Over the years, a close relationship to the Holy Office had helped both families achieve an enviable reputation for purity of blood and loyalty to the Catholic faith, and both continued to regard occupation of an official post as a valuable symbol of their position in Valencian society.

Recruitment to the familiatura is also a useful indication of the tribunal's ability to attract worthy candidates to apply for official status in the eighteenth century in spite of the declining importance of special privileges and exemptions. Given the increasing endogamy that characterized the Spanish ruling elite at all levels during the seventeenth and eighteenth centuries, it is to be expected that the majority of Valencia's eighteenth-century familiares would be drawn from the ranks of those with strong family traditions of service to the Holy Office. Such candidates included Joaquín Albuixech, a ciutadà of Almusafes with some 6,000 lliures annual income who was able to present a total of seven actos positivos and whose father and uncle were then serving as familiares of the village.[50]

At the same time as it could retain the interest of families long associated with the Holy Office, the tribunal also demonstrated an impressive capacity to attract new blood. More than 37 percent of my sample of those applying to enter the corps of familiares during the century were from families who had never held any sort of official rank. Included in this group of "new" families were solid labradores like Agustín Barrachina from Benimamet, who was described by one witness as possessing the best land in the village.[51] For families such as these, like their predecessors of the sixteenth and seventeenth centuries, membership in the corps of familiares with its obvious connotations of purity of blood and fervent Catholicism was the first rung in the ladder of social advancement in a status-conscious society.

Even French merchants who in general were notorious for ignoring the censorship laws and had a reputation for holding advanced ideas were not at all averse to seeking membership in the corps of familiares. Witnesses during the genealogical investigation of Pedro Juan Barber, who applied in 1732, included three familiares, all of whom were French merchants long resident in the kingdom. One of these men, Enrique Platet, a familiar in Sagunto who had immigrated from Lyon, was succeeded by his nephew, Juan Berchere, after his death in 1773.[52]

Interestingly, especially in light of the Spanish Inquisition's reputation as the enemy of all forms of enlightenment, the Valencia tribunal had litte trouble recruiting individuals who were closely connected with or openly allied to the most advanced intellectual circles of the period. Juan Bautista Esplugues de Palavecino, for example, who was secretary of the Valencian society of Amigos del Pais, which had been founded by the Count of Floridablanca in 1777, saw nothing amiss in encouraging his son Antonio to apply for the position of alguacil mayor in 1788.[53]

Even more indicative of the tribunal's ability to attract distinguished members of Valencia's intellectual elite were the candidates who presented themselves for the position of physician to the Holy Office in 1796. Among the candidates were two distinguished professors of medicine at the University of Valencia, Pedro Barracina and Joaquín Lambart. Dr. Barracina had been a leading participant in the reform of the medical curriculum at the university and could boast of holding the first chair of practical medicine in Spain.[54] Dr. Joaquín Lambart, who was eventually selected for the post, had an even more brilliant career and was one of the leaders of the upsurge in modern anatomical studies that made the University of Valencia into the leading Spanish medical school of the late eighteenth century. It was precisely because of his superior knowledge of modern anatomy that the three Valencian inquisitors unanimously favored him for the position.[55]

Finally, two of Valencia's most distinguished intellectual leaders were Holy Office officials. Francisco Javier Borrull, who was professor at the University of Valencia between 1774 and 1779, and Joaquín Lorenzo Villanueva served as commissioner and calificador of the Valencia tribunal, respectively, and were both closely connected with the brilliant circle that surrounded Pérez Bayer, the future director of the royal library, and Gregorio Mayans y Siscar, scion of a family long associated with the Holy Office.[56] Both of these men were elected as delegates to the Cortes of Cádiz where they took opposite positions on the question of abolishing the Holy Office. Borrull emerged as one of its strongest defenders and explicitly denied that the Cortes had the power to abolish it.[57] For his part, Villanueva, who had once defended the Inquisition in his famous reply to Bishop Gregoire, became one of its strongest opponents at the Cortes, where he insisted on the incompatibility of its procedures with the rights guaranteed under the new constitution and demanded that bishops be allowed to reassume their jurisdiction over crimes against religion.[58]

Regardless of the stand they later took on the abolition of the Holy Office, the fact that the Valencia tribunal could attract such outstanding members of what might be called the "modernizing" sector of the intellectual elite, such as Villanueva or Lambart, is an indication that it was not regarded as an implacable enemy of all intellectual change. In fact, the judges of Valencia's inquisitorial tribunal, like several eighteenth-century inquisitors-general and members of the Suprema, were ambivalent about the advent of liberalism.[59] On the one hand, the tribunal ordered the arrest of one Juan González, a cavalry captain who had been overheard denouncing priests and monks for fattening themselves at the expense of the poor.[60] On the other, the tribunal took no action after Andrés Piquer, the famous anatomist and theoretician, publicly rejected the idea that angels could transport bodies through the air. It also tolerated the rather daring intellectual career of Gregorio Mayans y Síscar, whose private library contained many prohibited books including Cipriano de Valera's Castilian Bible and works by Voltaire and Puffendorf.[61] The fact that Mayans y Síscar could flout the censorship laws with impunity, take a strong public stance against the excessive privileges of the clergy, and even criticize the Holy Office itself without suffering anything more than the temporary loss of his license to read prohibited books must be attributed to the fact that many late-eighteenth-century inquisitors were tolerant of some limited forms of enlightenment.[62]

The young inquisitor, Andrés Ignacio Orbe, for example, was one of Mayans y Síscar's disciples and regularly corresponded with him during the period in which he strongly criticized the Inquisition for placing the works of Cardinal Henry Noris on the Spanish Index. Instead of denouncing him, the inquisitor made it clear that he supported his position and criticized Inquisitor-General Pérez de Prado for his role in the Noris affair.[63] Certainly, Agustín de Argüelles, one of the leading liberals at the Cortes of Cádiz and a strong supporter of the move to abolish the Holy Office, had kind words for the inquisitors of his day, whom he described as "just, enlightened and beneficent."[64]

That eighteenth-century intellectual life in Valencia developed within the context of a quasi-tolerant Holy Office was demonstrated by the fact that the leading figures of the Valencian cultural scene were never bothered by the Inquisition and also by the fact that the university library was given an inquisitorial license to purchase all manner of prohibited books. The Inquisition's complaisance in this area went so far that Francisco Pérez Bayer was given specific permission from the inquisitor-general to present his entire collection of prohibited books to the university library where it was to be made available to those holding licenses.[65] When the climate for intellectual expression began to darken after the French Revolution, the reaction was spearheaded not by the tribunal but by Valencia's Archbishop Francisco Fabián y Fuero, who, on May 6, 1792, ordered the university library's entire collection of prohibited books to be moved to a special bookcase where they were placed behind iron bars and concealed with a sheet of linen. Naturally, since the library operated under the protection of licenses issued by the Holy Office, the rector and librarians of the university appealed to the tribunal and Inquisitor-General Agustín Rubin de Cevallos, a known liberal, for protection against the overzealous prelate. The tribunal promptly sent one of its secretaries to investigate the matter and dispatched a report to Madrid, but the weakened political condition of the Holy Office did not permit it to take decisive action, and on October 23, 1793, we find the rector writing to the inquisitor-general to complain that the books remained exactly where they had been seventeen months earlier.[66] Archbishop Fabián y Fuero's victory over the university and Holy Office was destined to be short-lived, however, since just a few months after rector Blasco's despairing letter to the Inquisitor-General, the archbishop was forced to flee the city disguised as a simple priest after an acrimonious conflict with the captain-general.[67]

This incident, perhaps more than any other, illustrates the nature of the crisis that the Spanish Inquisition found itself confronting by the end of the eighteenth century. Quasi-tolerance of the intellectual tendencies of the enlightenment through a policy of issuing licenses to read prohibited books to a select and presumably trustworthy educated elite exasperated reactionaries like Archbishop Fabián y Fuero while displeasing liberals who demanded even greater freedom of expression. At the same time, the Inquisition's manifest and growing political weakness made it incapable of defending even the limited freedom of expression that could be secured through the system of licenses. Meanwhile, late in the century, when the French Revolution had produced a grave crisis for Spain's moderate reformism, the Holy Office was so weakened and demoralized that it was incapable of placing effective controls on the influx of potentially dangerous works even when called on to do so by the crown.[68] This, in turn, opened it to charges that it was an ineffective and anachronistic institution whose calificadores were described by Jovellanos in a famous phrase as "a bunch of ignorant monks who only took the job to escape from choir duty and secure their ration of stew."[69]

Nevertheless, in spite of growing frustration with the Inquisition by both liberals and conservatives and in spite of the fact that it was becoming the whipping boy of the European press, the Holy Office would probably never have been abolished if it had not been for the grave economic and fiscal crisis brought about by the Franco-Spanish conflict of 1793–1795 and the Anglo-Spanish wars of 1796–1802 and 1804–1808.

The Spanish monarchy attempted to meet the costs of war through a variety of expedients including a forced loan of 4 percent of all official salaries and the creation of the vales, interest-bearing government notes circulating as legal tender. These notes, which were to be redeemed through a special sinking fund established by the government, began to depreciate rapidly, especially after the British blockade of Cádiz in 1797 had cut off the flow of American silver.

It was to cope with this situation that the government adopted a policy of selling off the entailed property belonging to a number of public institutions including hospitals, poor houses, Colegios Mayores, and the Inquisition.[70] The royal order authorizing the sale at public auction of the real property in the possession of the tribunals of the Spanish Inquisition was issued on February 27, 1799, and had been preceded by a series of emergency measures such as forcing public institutions to invest their funds in censos to help pay for the war effort.[71] The Suprema moved quickly to put this new policy into effect, and on March 12, 1799, it sent orders to all provincial tribunals telling them to inventory their real property, have it appraised, and auction it off at a price no less than two-thirds of the appraised value. The proceeds of this auction were then to be turned over to the provincial commissioner of the Real Caja de Amortización.[72]

During the rest of 1799 and throughout the following year, the Valencia tribunal liquidated some of its most valuable rural properties to a variety of bidders, including Cristóbal Francisco de Valdés, Marquis of Valparaiso, who purchased a large farm in the huerta zone near Valencia for the sum of 8,560 lliures.[73] By February 23, 1802, the tribunal had realized some 62,584 lliures from the sale of the agricultural property.[74]

In a very real sense, the application of desamortización to the tribunal was the beginning of the process that would lead inevitably to abolition. With the sale of its real property, the tribunal was losing irretrievably an essential part of the fiscal independence that it had so painfully acquired in the sixteenth century.

In August 1805, moreover, the tribunal began to lose its actual physical possessions when the Suprema demanded an inventory of all the paintings that could be found on the premises. This inventory was carried out at the behest of Manuel Godoy, the royal favorite, who was building up a collection of fine paintings.[75] Undoubtedly aware of what was to come, the tribunal tried to stall by ignoring the Suprema's request for a complete inventory and sending a letter that described its holdings only in general terms, but it was eventually forced to comply.[76] Godoy chose the six most valuable of the tribunal's paintings for his collection, including four by Jacinto Espinosa, and a doleful letter to the Suprema dated November 5, 1808, records that the walls of the inquisitor's own rooms had to be partially demolished so that they could be removed and that far from compensating the tribunal for its loss, Godoy had insisted that the tribunal pay the cost of building special packing cases for the paintings out of its own funds. In 1808, after Godoy's fall from power, his property was confiscated and ordered sold at public auction by the new regime of Ferdinand VII. On the assumption that its paintings would be among the items in Godoy's possession, the tribunal wrote the Suprema to demand their return. In its reply, the Suprema promised merely to find an "opportune moment" to reclaim the pictures, and since those described did not form part of the general inventory that was drawn up just after the abolition of 1820, we may be sure that on this occasion, as on so many others, the Suprema was unable to offer effective assistance.[77] In the end, this despoilment turned out to be an evil portent of the eventual fate of the tribunal's furnishings and physical possessions compared to which the loss of a few paintings would seem relatively minor.

The year 1808 proved as fateful for the Spanish Inquisition as it was to be for the Spanish nation as a whole. After Charles IV abdicated in favor of his son Ferdinand on March 19, 1808, and then protested to Napoleon that his abdication had been coerced, both he and Ferdinand were brought to Bayonne and induced to renounce the Spanish crown to Napoleon. On May 2, 1808, there occurred the famous "dos de Mayo" in which the population of Madrid rose against the French occupation force under the command of Field Marshal Murat. Shortly thereafter, Napoleon summoned his brother Joseph from Naples and awarded him the Spanish throne, but although acknowledged by an assembly of leading Spaniards called at Bayonne, he was rejected by the overwhelming majority of the population. This was the beginning of that great and heroic but also quixotic resistance against the French that eventually resulted in their withdrawal, leaving Spain in ruins.

Throughout this early phase of the Spanish catastrophe, the attitude of the Suprema was resolutely pro-French. Several members, including its dean, were members of the Bayonne assembly, which later constituted itself a Cortes and adopted Spain's first constitution. In it, nothing was said about abolishing the Inquisition, but it declared that Catholicism should be the only religion in Spain and her empire.[78]

After the suppression of the May 2 rising, the Suprema made haste to write to the provincial tribunals condemning them as an example of insubordination and disrespect for authority and enjoining them to enlist the aid of the commissioners and familiares of their respective districts in promoting public tranquility.[79] This attitude was not shared by all of the provincial tribunals, however, and on August 26, 1808, the inquisitors of the Llerena tribunal issued a manifesto condemning the Suprema's collaboration with the French.[80]

Influenced by this pressure and also by the increasing constraints being placed on its activities by the French occupation authorities in Madrid, the Suprema began switching sides during the following month, and on September 28, it ordered that all provincial tribunals pledge their support to the Junta Central, which was attempting to coordinate national resistance to the French.[81] By the middle of the following month, both the Suprema and the Valencia tribunal were acting in concert with the Junta. On November 11, for example, it relayed the Junta's order to impede the introduction of Masonic propaganda to all provincial tribunals, and the Valencia tribunal responded by immediately alerting all port commissioners and notaries.[82] The increasing tensions between the French occupation authorities in Madrid and the Suprema and the growing disloyalty of that body to Joseph's regime may well have influenced Napoleon to issue a decree suppressing the Inquisition on December 4, 1808.[83] Inquisitor-General Arce y Reynoso immediately resigned, while the Junta Central, which appointed Pedro de Oviedo y Quintano, the Bishop of Orense, to replace him, could not obtain papal approval because communication with Pius VII had become impossible. In August 1810, the Council of Regency ordered the Suprema to resume its functions, and by the end of March 1811, the government was considering the appointment of individuals to fill the posts of prosecuting attorney and secretary.[84] With the Inquisition in this anomalous but hopeful situation, the Junta now decided to convene a national Cortes at Cádiz where it had taken refuge after Spanish forces had been defeated in a series of engagements at the hands of the Grande Armée.

The Cortes opened on September 24, 1810, and the issue of whether or not to reestablish the Inquisition immediately became the subject of acrimonious controversy in the press, giving rise to a considerable pamphlet literature, including *The Inquisition Unmasked*, which was reprinted in an English translation by William Walton in 1816. The issue was eventually referred to the Committee on the Constitution, which concluded that the Inquisition was incompatible with the new constitution, and on January 22, 1812, after lengthy debate, the Cortes approved this proposition by a vote of 90 to 60.[85] In effect, the Inquisition was not actually suppressed but superseded by the reestablishment on January 26, 1813, of the Law of the Partidas that gave bishops and their vicars full authority over matters of heresy.[86] In Valencia, of course, the tribunal had already ceased functioning after the seizure of Valencia city by Marshal Suchet on January 8, 1812. On February 22, the Cortes published a long decree, designed to be read out in the pulpits of all parish churches, that justified the actions it had taken with regard to the Holy Office. In this document, which accurately reflected the point of view taken in *The Inquisition Unmasked*, the decline of Spain and the decadence of the Catholic faith were blamed on the abuses of the Holy Office, while reestablishment of the bishop's traditional jurisdiction was presented as a way of better protecting Catholicism and public morality.[87]

The growth of opposition to the proceedings of the Cortes of Cádiz was not slow to manifest itself, however, and when Ferdinand VII returned to Spain he lost no time in pronouncing all its acts null and void on May 4, 1814. Several months later, by the decree of July 21, 1814, Ferdinand restored the Holy Office.[88] This was followed by the decrees of August 18 and September 3 which restored to the various tribunals the real estate and revenues from mortgages and prebends that had been absorbed by the treasury or had passed into the hands of the Caja de Consolidación, with the account to be paid from the date of the Inquisition's reestablishment.[89]

With the Inquisition's financial problems seemingly about to be resolved, the new inquisitor-general, Francisco Xavier de Meir y Campillo, and the provincial inquisitors immediately set about putting into motion the machinery of the Holy Office. Provincial tribunals began recruiting new calificadores and familiares, and even though certain tribunals appear to have had difficulties in finding the requisite candidates, the Valencia tribunal encountered few problems. These candidates paid substantial fees for their genealogical investigations as well as a special contribution to relieve the penury of the Suprema.[90]

During Lent 1815, moreover, a ferocious Edict of Faith was published in Madrid which not only invited the faithful to denounce all the traditional heresies but added to that list of forms of modern rationalist philosophy.[91] In the same month, the Suprema set forth a series of regulations that once again enlisted confessors in the war against heresy. Confessors were ordered to refuse absolution to their penitents unless they presented a declaration of any doctrinal errors that they might have committed. Written declarations presented by such individuals would then be sent to the Holy Office, which would have to grant permission for absolution.[92]

In spite of this feverish display of activity, however, the Valencia tribunal that was reestablished after July 1814 was a shadow of what it had been even during the late eighteenth century. Although luckier than some tribunals in the sense that it could move back to its old quarters in the palace of the Inquisition, that building was in a sad state of disrepair, and the tribunal only logged sixteen cases for the balance of the year. On October 26, 1814, the tribunal wrote the Suprema to the effect that a great deal of its furniture had been removed from the palace and that it had lost all the religious ornaments from the oratory, making the celebration of mass impossible. The tribunal had issued an edict calling on all those with knowledge of the location of any of its property to come forward to aid in its recovery and requested permission to purchase whatever it needed to resume functioning. This the Suprema reluctantly granted but reminded the tribunal to purchase only what was "absolutely necessary," given the extreme financial penury of the Holy Office.

Evidently, the Inquisition's palace had been despoiled not only by common vandals but also by distinguished members of Valencia's ecclesiastical hierarchy. In September 1814, the tribunal reported that it had given up its efforts to recover the window glass that had been taken from the palace by officials of the archdiocese because the glass had been cut down to size in order to be used for the vicar-general's apartments.[93]

To make matters worse, the serious economic depression that followed the end of hostilities made the crown's promises with regard to restoration of the Inquisition's financial position largely illusory.[94] The financial penury of the Suprema itself during those years was so great that it was forced to turn to the provincial tribunals for assistance. In November 1814, it set at 130,896 reales the annual contribution required from the Valencia tribunal and denied it permission to pay out anything for salaries without specific permission.[95] The tribunal must have found it impossible to meet this demand as the Suprema reduced it to 96,000 reales annually in the following year.[96]

In 1817 and 1818, the tribunal's financial condition continued to deteriorate. As a result of the economic crisis of the postwar period and the sharp decline in agricultural prices from 1812–13, the tribunal found it impossible to collect on many of its censos.[97] In 1818, the tribunal reported that it had been unable to pay salaries for the last four months and did not have enough funds to maintain its prisoners.[98]

Quite apart from the physical and financial difficulties experienced by the reestablished tribunal, sporadic demonstrations of royal favor were not enough to prevent royal courts and officials from continuing their guerrilla war against its jurisdiction as they had in the eighteenth century. In April 1815, a special censorship tribunal was established under the direction of the regent of the Audiencia. Local customs officials immediately recognized the authority of the new tribunal and refused to allow books to leave customs even with the permission of the Inquisition's port commissioner unless they had also been released by the officials of the censorship tribunal.[99] Shortly thereafter, the censorship tribunal expanded its jurisdiction still further by claiming the right to clear books exported from the kingdom. The Suprema meekly responded to this demand, which further reduced the authority of the Holy Office, by cautioning the tribunal to maintain its accustomed supervision over books entering or leaving the kingdom but without in any way opposing the new censorship tribunal.[100]

In 1816, there occurred an even more flagrant violation of the inquisitorial fuero when the Audiencia insisted on taking cognizance of a civil suit brought by the tribunal's secretary, Francisco Cachuno, against his nephew, José Soriano. In defense of the well-recognized rights of officials to bring suit in the tribunal's civil court, it formulated a jurisdictional brief against the Audiencia and then wrote the Suprema for permission to pursue the matter. The Suprema, true to its usual attitude in such cases, refused permission in light of a recent decision taken by Ferdinand VII in a dispute involving the Seville tribunal and the Asistente of Utrera.[101] The renewed offensive of the royal courts against the Inquisition and the Suprema's seeming inability to offer effective support simply confirmed trends already well under way before the abolition of 1813.

At the same time, the Valencia tribunal had abandoned its

former quasi-tolerance of liberal thought and thrown itself whole-heartedly into the campaign against Masonry and liberalism that was being mounted under Ferdinand VII's reactionary govern-ment. This strong identification with the radical right wing left the tribunal isolated and vulnerable when the political balance of power shifted and liberalism made a comeback after 1820.

In spite of the appointment of the reactionary Francisco Javier Elío as captain-general of Valencia in 1814, there was virtually no serious persecution of the leading Valencian liberals until the begin-ning of 1817. On January 17 of that year, liberals and Masons failed in an attempt to assassinate the captain-general and return the kingdom to a constitutional regime. Several of the leaders of this conspiracy were executed and others were forced to flee. For its part, a resurgent Valencia tribunal participated in the repression by detaining Dr. Nicolás María Garelli, a leading liberal and professor of civil law at the university. Garelli, who led a "tertulia" at which advanced liberal and constitutional ideas were freely discussed, had played a key role in drawing up the manifesto by which the university congratulated the Cortes of Cádiz for its suppression of the Inquisition.[102] Obviously, there was no love lost between Garelli and the tribunal, and on June 20, 1817, three days after the failure of the plot, he was summoned to explain a provocative lecture he had given on the subject of the defunct constitution of Cádiz.[103]

The mob that supported the January 17 plot had shouted its support for the 1814 constitution and denounced the Inquisition, which was clearly becoming identified in the public mind with extreme antiliberalism. The Valencia tribunal, however, failed to heed this warning and continued to closely collaborate with the reactionary regime of Captain-General Elío. After the failure of the Vidal conspiracy of January 1–2, 1819, repression of liberals and Masons was further intensified. Captain-General Elío, who had been personally involved in thwarting the plot, ordered the execu-tion of thirteen of its leaders, while the Valencia tribunal arrested twenty-four others who were suspected of complicity on the grounds that they were members of Valencia's outlawed Masonic lodge. Those arrested were some of the most important and influen-tial liberals in the kingdom, including Ildefonso Diaz de Ribera, Count of Almodóvar, Bernardo Falcó, Valencian delegate to the ordinary Cortes of 1813–14, and Mariano Beltrán de Lis, a member of Valencia's leading family of liberals.[104]

All of these men still languished in the prisons of the Holy Office when on March 10, 1820, the news reached Valencia that Ferdinand VII had been forced to reinstate the 1813 constitution, simultaneously abolishing the Holy Office on the grounds that it was incompatible with its provisions. On the same day, a mob invaded the precincts of the tribunal and liberated its prisoners, including the Count of Almodóvar, who was immediately made captain-general by popular acclamation. On the following day, the Inquisition's palace was again assaulted by a mob, which carried off a large quantity of books and papers. On March 17, the new captain-general responded to growing popular pressure and ordered the arrest of those most heavily compromised by their involvement with the Elío regime. This group included Francisco Javier Borrull, the calificador who had defended the Inquisition so strongly at the Cortes of Cádiz, and the four serving Valencian inquisitors, Encina, Toranzo, Montemayor, and Royo.[105]

The March 9 decree had seemingly dealt a fatal blow to the Holy Office, and to make matters worse, it was followed on March 20 by a royal order for inventories to be drawn up of all its remaining property. The Bureau of Public Credit was authorized to take over the administration of this property until its ultimate disposition should be determined by the Cortes, which was shortly to be convened. Soon thereafter, on August 9, 1820, the Cortes issued a decree that declared that confiscated property was to be auctioned off by the bureau.[106]

In Valencia, the royal order of March 20 was reflected in the activity of a small committee composed of Benito Artalejo, representing the intendant and the national treasury, and José Torres y Machi and Teodoro Royo, principal commissioner and treasurer of the local branch of the Bureau of Public Credit, respectively. On May 13, this committee proceeded to the inquisitorial palace where Artalejo formally took possession of it and immediately turned it over to the representatives of the Bureau of Public Credit.[107] On May 16, the committee decided to inventory the palace's furnishings and other property. And on June 4, obviously anticipating the Cortes' decision, it resolved to sell that property at a series of auctions beginning on June 21, 1820.[108] While these auctions were continuing, the committee took a brief trip outside the city, where on October 4 one of the tribunal's remaining farms was formally turned over to the representatives of the bureau.[109]

It would be superfluous to recount here the well-known story of the disastrous three years of liberal rule that culminated in the invasion of Spain by a French army led by the duke of Angoulême in April 1823. Unlike the French invaders of the Napoleonic period, this army was received warmly and soon had taken possession of the entire country. After the collapse of the liberals, Ferdinand VII was restored to his absolute power and signed a decree annulling all acts since March 7, 1820.[110]

This decree would seem to have automatically restored the Holy Office. Indeed, the Valencia tribunal appears to have shown some glimmerings of life, recording a few cases up to the beginning of July 1824.[111] Nevertheless, whatever his initial inclinations, Ferdinand became more and more fearful of formally reinstating the Inquisition as he had done in 1814.

For one thing, there was considerable foreign pressure on him not to reestablish the Holy Office, pressure that he was in no position to resist because of his financial and military dependence on the French. Even more important in the mind of an autocrat like Ferdinand was the fact that formal reestablishment had become part of the political program of the extreme right, a group that tended to view Ferdinand himself with grave misgivings. No matter how reactionary he was, even Ferdinand was not willing to give in to demands voiced in the right-wing press for the extermination of liberals to the fourth generation.[112] Ferdinand's relative moderation, in turn, led to increasing hostility between his government and the extreme right. In the first few years of his restoration to absolute power, there were several serious right-wing conspiracies against him which derived their strength from the paramilitary Guardias Realistas and secret societies, like the Angel Exterminador, who openly favored Ferdinand's brother Carlos. In the face of all this agitation, Ferdinand preferred to rely on his newly created police force whose superintendent-general, Juan José Rechacho, warned that the extreme right was planning to use a restored Inquisition as a weapon to exterminate all the king's loyal supporters.[113]

Ferdinand's growing fears of a revived Inquisition were reinforced by the activities of the Juntas de fé that were established in certain dioceses. In Valencia, the Junta was headed by Dr. Miguel Toranzo, one of the last inquisitors of the Valencia tribunal who had been imprisoned by the liberals. It was Toranzo who handed down the last death sentence for heresy in Spain. This case involved Cayetano Ripoll, a schoolmaster from Rusafa just outside Valencia city who had become a deist while a prisoner in France during the Peninsular War. He was arrested on September 29, 1824, and during the two years that his trial lasted, he repelled the repeated attempts by theologians to convert him and maintained his convictions to the end. After sentencing, he was turned over to the criminal chamber of the Audiencia and executed on July 26, 1826.[114] On August 6, Valencia's fanatical right-wing archbishop, Simón López, wrote to Toranzo to congratulate him on his conduct of this case and express the pious hope that it would "serve as a warning to some while increasing the devotion of others."[115]

The Ripoll case and the activities of the Juntas de fé thoroughly alarmed Ferdinand, and he notified the Audiencia that these tribunals had no official standing whatsoever. In spite of this evidence of royal disfavor, they continued a shadowy existence for at least one more year, although under increasingly difficult circumstances. Their extinction could not be long delayed, however, and on March 16, 1827, we find Inquisitor Toranzo writing to Archbishop López to tell him that he feared that the Junta's many enemies were just waiting for an opportunity to destroy it.[116]

Toranzo's fears were justified as Ferdinand's government became more and more fearful of a revived Inquisition, which his chief of police warned would be tantamount to a rightist putsch.[117] The fatal blow came from a rather unexpected source, however, as the government was able to enlist the aid of the new papal nuncio, Monsignor Tiberi. The papacy was not at all reluctant to collaborate in the destruction of inquisitorial jurisdiction in Spain, and in a papal brief of October 5, 1829, Pius VIII granted the nunciatura's tribunal of the Rota appellate jurisdiction over cases involving religious heresy.[118] This flagrant example of papal interference in Spanish affairs, which would have been bitterly resented only a few decades earlier, perfectly accorded with Ferdinand's wishes, and he confirmed the papal brief on February 6, 1830.[119]

In the meantime, the property of the Holy Office had been transferred to the collector-general of the Bureau of Espolios y

Vacantes to be administered by the general-superintendent of the property of the Inquisition.[120] In 1830, this post was held by Valentín Zorilla, an old inquisitor. In Valencia, the administrator of the tribunal's remaining property was Vicente Mora, who had been receiver in 1815–16. Mora resided in a room in the palace of the defunct tribunal, other parts of which had been rented out to a variety of individuals, including a master carpenter and an architect.[121] Mora continued to collect income owed the tribunal from its remaining urban and rural mortgages and rent as well as the income from prebends and sent 28,000 reales to the office of the collector-general of Espolios in 1834.[122] In the same year, Mora paid out more than 30,000 reales in salaries to former officials of the tribunal and their heirs.

By the early 1830s, therefore, the Spanish Inquisition had become little more than a minor subcommittee of the treasury, administering the dwindling property of a defunct institution. It still had power as a symbol, especially for the Carlist right, which was now engaged in a civil war against Isabella II's regency government. Perhaps for this reason alone, the regency decided to issue a formal decree of abolition. This document, which was careful to point out that Ferdinand himself had vested authority over matters of faith in the bishops, abolished the Inquisition and confiscated its remaining property. The final extinction of this institution, which had played such an important role in Spanish history for hundreds of years, took place against a background of an acrimonious debate about its real impact on Spanish life and thought, a debate that continues undiminished to the present day.

Conclusion

My approach here assumes that institutions created by a specific society and culture are so embedded in that society and culture as to be inseparable from it. Thus, the concepts of liberalism and toleration that emerged during the eighteenth and nineteenth centuries should not be applied uncritically to an institution that developed under certain very special late-fifteenth-century conditions. Clearly, as I have sought to demonstrate, the image of the arbitrary, omnipotent, and monolithic Inquisition handed down to us by an earlier historiography is in need of substantial modification.

Invidious comparisons between the judicial procedures of Anglo-Saxon common law courts and the Inquisition, for example, merely serve to confuse the issue of judicial fairness, one of the most difficult problems now facing Inquisition scholars. A complete lack of scientific means for evaluating physical evidence and an often uncritical dependence on the testimony of witnesses as well as a prosecutory bias may well have made it impossible for those accused of crimes to obtain a fair trial in the modern sense before any early modern criminal tribunal. The Inquisition was little different from other tribunals in this respect, although the secrecy of its proceedings and the disabilities placed on the defense were significant obstacles for anyone who wished to demonstrate his innocence.

But the law and legal institutions have their own inner dynamic, and that is just as true in Spain as in countries with a tradition of common law. As the resolution of the debate over the nature of the evidence presented in witchcraft accusations was to demonstrate, the Spanish Inquisition was perfectly capable of generating procedural safeguards internally and of imposing them on provincial judges through a process of judicial review.

The Inquisition's impact on Spanish society as a whole and on certain groups within it was ambiguous and far more complex than historians have yet imagined. In the case of the Judeo-conversos, for example, its ferocious persecution of Judaizers helped to maintain popular anti-Semitic feeling, and it was not at all averse to exploiting that anti-Semitism in its own political or financial interests. But as I have shown above, the Valencia tribunal, at least, provided a channel through which certain converso families could be more fully integrated into Old Christian society. In this sense, the tribunal reacted positively to altered public perceptions of the conversos (if not the Portuguese New Christians) reflected in the seventeenth-century debate on limpieza and the strong feelings of guilt experienced by many people when they stopped to read the captions under the sanbenitos that could still be seen in many churches.[1]

As far as the Moriscos were concerned, the tradition of "conservative dissent" from the idea that force could be legitimately used in matters of conscience was shared by at least some of Valencia's inquisitors.[2] This attitude may well have helped to prevent a repetition of the harsh measures taken against the converted Jews. Around the time of the expulsion, moreover, the Valencia tribunal seemed more than willing to accommodate the continued presence of Moriscos in spite of its earlier stand in favor of expulsion. In this instance, financial and bureaucratic considerations were allowed to outweigh concern for religious heresy.

The impact of the Holy Office on wider Old Christian society is even more difficult to assess. Here, the historian runs the risk of making the Inquisition responsible for everything that went wrong in Spain or trivializing its role in the name of fairness and balance. Of course, it would be absurd to place all the blame for Spain's drastic failure to keep pace with intellectual changes in the rest of Europe on the action of the Holy Office. But, along with the Council of Castile, the Inquisition did exercise a great deal of censorship authority over intellectual production. Even more important perhaps in determining the atmosphere in which intellectual life could develop was the Inquisition's absolute jurisdiction over propositions. In the pulpit, at academic disputations, or in the lecture halls

of the University of Valencia itself, the Inquisition was omnipres-
ent, to be invoked whenever a discussant strayed from the bounds
of orthodoxy. There can be little doubt that the intervention of the
tribunal on the side of the conservatives in the debate over peripa-
tetic philosophy helped to make the University of Valencia into a
bastion of Aristotelianism until well into the eighteenth century.

It is even more difficult to comprehend the impact that the
repression of offenses such as blasphemy and superstition had on
popular culture. Certainly, the public punishment of blasphemy by
such a feared and respected institution as the Holy Office could not
have failed to have an inhibiting effect on normal social intercourse,
as any blasphemous expression or remark might be reported. It
would be naive to assume, however, that the tribunal's attack on
the principal forms of superstition, love magic and curative magic,
had much impact on the unreasoning convictions of the popular
masses. Apart from the fact that the church's position on magic and
the supernatural was highly ambiguous, the social causes for these
practices remained unchanged. Furthermore, there is considerable
evidence to suggest that the very fact that a practitioner had been
punished by the Holy Office served to enhance her reputation
among potential clients.[3]

It might plausibly be argued that the Inquisition's growing concern over solicitation is a tribute to the feminization of the church
in general and of confession in particular. There is considerable
evidence from confessor's manuals that it was women, not men,
who heeded the call for more frequent confession and communion
voiced by such popular religious figures as Francisco de Osuña and
Tomás Carbonell.[4] By punishing soliciting confessors, the Inquisition was responding to the deep disappointment and profound disil-
lusionment suffered by many women when they found that the
sacrament they cherished was being mocked and abused even as
they confessed. Ironically, however, public awareness of the removal, reclusion, and suspension from confessing of many formerly
respected priests may well have encouraged the rising tide of anticlericalism that was to engulf Spain in the 1840s and 1850s. The
examples of superstition and solicitation should teach us that the
actions of the Inquisition, like those of any other judicial institution, may have unintended and unforeseen effects.

Finally, by choosing to emphasize the political evolution of the

Valencia tribunal and the changing character and functions of its familiares, I have sought to demonstrate that the Inquisition was far from the monolithic institution portrayed by traditional historiography. Established during a period of strong central government when it was widely believed that Spain's problems would be resolved through the imposition of religious conformity, the Valencia tribunal eventually had to reckon with the forces of regionalism. Although it remained fully committed to its role as defender of the faith, political necessity made the tribunal come to terms with the local power elite, build and maintain a network of clients, and accommodate itself to a position of diminished royal support. By the middle of the sixteenth century, the heroic period of charismatic authority was coming to an end and the long career of the Valencia tribunal as a regional bureaucratic institution was just beginning.

Notes

Introduction

1. For converso attitudes toward the Inquisition, see Haim Beinart, *Conversos on Trial: The Inquisition in Ciudad Real* (Jerusalem: The Magnus Press, 1981), 294–295. For the Spanish Protestant view, see Reginaldo González Montano, *A Discovery and Playne Declaration of Sundry Subtill Practices of the Holy Inquisition of Spain* (London: Ihon Day, 1568). For a Catholic viewpoint, see Caesare Carena, *Tractatus de Officio Santissimae Inquisitionis, et modo procedendi in causis fidie* (Cremona: Baptistam Belpierum, 1655), and D. de Simancas, *De catholicis institutionibus* (Vallisoleti: Aegidii de Colomies, 1552).

2. Denis Diderot and Jean d'Alembert, *Encyclopédie ou dictionnaire raisonné des sciences, des arts et des métiers*, 20 vols. (Neufchastel: Samuel Faulche et Compagnie, 1765), 8: 775.

3. Ibid.

4. For the controversy over Llorente's work, see J. Pérez Villanueva, "La historiografía de la Inquisición española," in J. Pérez Villanueva and Bartolomé Escandell Bonet, eds., *Historia de la Inquisición en España y América*, 4 vols. (Madrid: BAC, 1984), 1:14–16.

5. H. C. Lea, *Historia de la Inquisición española*, 3 vols. Trans. Angel Alcalá (Madrid: Fundación Universitaria Española, 1982).

6. These results were first reported in Gustav Henningsen, "El banco de datos del Santo Oficio: Las relaciones de causas de la Inquisición española," *Boletín de la Real Academia de la Historia*, CLXXIV:549–570.

7. Agostino Borromeo, "Contributo allo studio dell' Inquisizioni e dei suoi rapporti con il potere episcopale nell' Italia spagnola del Cinquecento," *Annuario dell' Instituto storico italiano per l'eta moderna e contemporanea*, vols. 29–30, 219–276. Richard Greenleaf, *The Mexican*

Inquisition of the Sixteenth Century (Albuquerque: University of New Mexico Press, 1969); B. Escandell Bonet, "El tribunal peruano en la época de Felipe II," in Pérez Villanueva and Escandell Bonet, _Historia de la Inquisición_, 1:919–937.

8. See chap. 7, 401–404.

9. Ricardo García Cárcel, _Orígenes de la Inquisición española_ (Barcelona: Peninsula, 1976), 137. García Cárcel contradicts himself in his second volume, but his assertion that the tribunal did not have commissioners until 1580 is also wrong. Ricardo García Cárcel, _Herejía y sociedad en el siglo XVI_ (Barcelona: Peninsula, 1980), 137.

10. García Cárcel, _Herejía_, 17–124.

11. Robert I. Burns, S.J. _The Crusader Kingdom of Valencia_, 2 vols. (Cambridge: Harvard University Press, 1967), 1:4–7,9.

12. The linguistic and cultural division of post-Reconquest Valencia is discussed in Joan Fuster, _Nosaltres, els Valencians_ (Barcelona: Ediciones 62, 1962), 30.

13. Thomas Glick, _Irrigation and Society in Medieval Valencia_ (Cambridge: Harvard University Press, 1970), 11–13.

14. J. H. Elliott, _Imperial Spain_ (New York: The New American Library, 1966), 28–30.

15. Teresa Canet Aparisi, _La audiencia valenciana en la época foral moderna_ (Valencia: Institució Valenciana D'Estudis I Investigació, 1986), 66, 72.

16. James Casey, _The Kingdom of Valencia in the Seventeeth Century_ (Cambridge: Cambridge University Press, 1979), 232.

17. Ibid., 225. For the medieval origins of Valencia's traditional laws, see Fuster, _Nosaltres_, 44–46.

I: Between Monarchy and Kingdom

1. Juan Antonio Llorente, _A Critical History of the Inquisition of Spain from the Time of Its Establishment to the Reign of Ferdinand VII_ (London: Geo. B. Wittaker, 1826; reprint ed., Williamstown, Mass., 1967), 11.

2. Ibid., 12.

3. Llorente, _A Critical History_, 16–17.

4. For the migration of the Albigensian "perfecti" across the Pyrenees, see chap. V in E. Le Roy Ladurie, _Montaillou: The Promised Land of Error_ (New York: George Braziller, 1978), 89–102.

5. Eymerich's _Directorium inquisitorum_ was first published in 1503 and then republished five times in Peña's edition between 1578 and 1607.

Nicolás Eymerich and Francisco Peña, *Le manuel des inquisiteurs*, ed. and trans. Louis Sala-Molins (Paris: Mouton, 1973), 15.

6. Tarsicio de Azcona, *Isabel la Católica* (Madrid: Editorial Católica, 1964), 378–379.

7. Albert A. Sicroff, *Les controverses des statutes de pureté de sang en Espagne du XV au XVII siècle* (Paris: Marcel Didier, 1960), 32–36.

8. Azcona, *Isabel la Católica*, 397–398.

9. Beinart, *Conversos on Trial*, 308–309.

10. Elliott, *Imperial Spain*, 30–31, 43–44; Jaime Vicens Vives, *An Economic History of Spain* (Princeton: Princeton University Press, 1969), 308–309.

11. Henry Charles Lea, *A History of the Inquisition of Spain*, 4 vols. (New York: Macmillan, 1906–07), 1:27–28.

12. Llorente, *A Critical History*, 17.

13. Ibid., 23.

14. Azcona, *Isabel la Católica*, 392.

15. Ibid., 396.

16. Ibid., 573–574.

17. Ferdinand and Isabella were able to gain control over the monastic reform movement during the pontificate of Alexander VI. Ibid., 591.

18. Ibid., 406.

19. García Cárcel, *Orígenes*, 44.

20. Azcona, *Isabel la Católica*, 408.

21. García Cárcel, *Orígenes*, 47–48.

22. Lea, *A History*, 1:247–249.

23. AHN, *Inquisition*, September 13, 1484, leg. 533, f. 18.

24. AHN, *Inquisition*, June 26, 1484, leg. 533, f. 18.

25. Lea, *A History*, 1:248.

26. For threats made against Lieutenant-Inquisitor Baltasar Sánchez de Oruela, see AHN, *Inquisition*, January 8, 1521, leg. 533, f. 3.

27. García Cárcel, *Orígenes*, 49–50.

28. Ibid., 52, 80.

29. Ibid., 50.

30. Ibid., 55.

31. AHN, *Inquisition*, December 8, 1497, lib. 242, ffs. 7v–8v.

32. García Cárcel, *Orígenes*, 52, 59.

33. AHN, *Inquisition*, November 21, 1498, lib. 242, ffs. 82–83.

34. AHN, *Inquisition*, March 21, 1499, lib. 252, f. 125.

35. Lea, *A History*, 1:243.

36. AHN, *Inquisition*, September 6, 1553, lib. 911, f. 76.

37. AHN, *Inquisition*, September 27, 1499, lib. 242, f. 152.

38. AHN, *Inquisition*, October 17, 1500; October 26, 1500, lib. 242, ffs. 231, 235.

39. AHN, *Inquisition*, September 12, 1520, lib. 317, ffs. 105–107.

40. AHN, *Inquisition*, May 8, 1500, lib. 242, f. 200.

41. Lea, *A History*, 1:329.

42. AHN, *Inquisition*, lib. 100, f. 133r–v. quoted in José Martínez Millán, *La hacienda de la Inquisición, 1478–1700* (Madrid: CSIC, 1984), 75.

43. Lea, *A History*, 1:355.

44. AHN, *Inquisition*, May 11, 1554, lib. 1210, ffs. 52–54. The Suprema had followed a policy of specifically encouraging the provincial tribunals to use this formidable weapon; see AHN, *Inquisition*, August 18, 1545, lib. 322, ffs. 394–395.

45. AHN, *Inquisition*, "agravios hechos por el Inquisidor Aguilera" (1565–6), leg. 1790, exp. 2, f. 90v. This important visitation really began on June 12, 1566, when Jerónimo Manrique presented his powers to the tribunal. Most of the evidence against the officials and inquisitors was presented to Manrique and not, as implied by García Cárcel, *Herejía*, 136–137, to his successor, Soto Salazar. AHN, *Inquisition*, June 12, 1566, leg. 1790, exp. 2, nf. García Cárcel seems unaware of this first phase of the visitation.

46. AHN, *Inquisition*, "Memorial de los agravios que pretenden los oficiales reales de Su Magestad en esta ciudad y reino de Valencia se hazen por los Reverendos Inquisidores de dicha ciudad y reino a la juridición y preheminencias que la dicha Real Magestad tiene," May 18, 1567, leg. 1790, exp. 2, cap. 26.

47. Eymerich and Peña, *Le manuel*, 88–90.

48. Lea, *A History*, 1:353.

49. AHN, *Inquisition*, January 11–28, 1528, leg. 533#2, f. 13.

50. Archivo del Reino de Valencia, February 10, 1525, *Generalidad*, lib. 1950, ffs. 19–103, quoted in García Cárcel, *Orígenes*, 111.

51. Casey, *The Kingdom*, 179.

52. AHN, *Inquisition*, December 5, 1565, leg. 503#1, nf.

53. AHN, *Inquisition*, (1556) procesos criminales, leg. 1781, exp. 1.

54. AHN, *Inquisition*, July 10, 1568, lib. 1210, f. 10. For the violation of the 1568 *Concordia*, see July 31, 1573, lib. 970, f. 429. For merchants who collaborated in this traffic, see the hearings held by the tribunal: AHN, *Inquisition*, July 29, 1573, lib. 960, ffs. 434–435, 454. García Cárcel's assertion that the Valencia tribunal did not have commissioners until 1580 is patently untrue since the proceedings against the commissioner of Teruel date from 1573. García Cárcel, *Herejía*, 134.

55. AHN, *Inquisition*, August 28, 1514, lib. 960, f. 64. This sweeping

exemption was extended to the officials of all tribunals in 1568, Martínez Millán, *La hacienda,* 189.

56. García Cárcel, *Herejía,* 139; AHN, *Inquisition,* August 5, 1570, lib. 960, f. 16.

57. AHN, *Inquisition,* May 11, 1554, lib. 1210, f. 54.

58. AHN, *Inquisition,* July 10, 1586, lib. 1210, f. 58.

59. AHN, *Inquisition,* July 15, 1575, lib. 960, f. 43v.

60. AHN, *Inquisition,* July 9, 1575, lib. 960, f. 37.

61. For the special fuero enjoyed by the members of the Order of Montesa, see BNM, December 16, 1593, MSS 2731, f. 18.

62. Lea, *A History,* 1:429.

63. AHN, *Inquisition,* Instrucciónes de 1498, lib. 1210, f. 1431.

64. AHN, *Inquisition,* February 26, 1551, lib. 911, f. 18.

65. AHN, *Inquisition,* July 10, 1568, lib. 1210, f. 62.

66. AHN, *Inquisition,* July 10, 1568, lib. 1210, f. 60.

67. AHN, *Inquisition,* June 9, 1589, lib. 960, f. 28.

68. AHN, *Inquisition,* "Memorial de los agravios," May 18, 1567, leg. 1790, exp. 2, cap. 26.

69. AHN, *Inquisition,* January 7, 1564, leg. 519#2, f. 23.

70. AHN, *Inquisition,* February 19, 1565, leg. 503#1, nf.

71. AHN, *Inquisition,* "Memorial de los agravios," May 18, 1567, leg. 1790, exp. 2, cap. 31.

72. AHN, *Inquisition,* December 27, 1561, lib. 911, f. 230.

73. AHN, *Inquisition,* August 1, 1579, lib. 960, f. 581.

74. AHN, *Inquisition,* September 18, 1555, lib. 911, f. 154.

75. AHN, *Inquisition,* February 26, 1551, lib. 911, f. 18.

76. AHN, *Inquisition,* May 15, 1545, lib. 1210, ffs. 815–816.

77. AHN, *Inquisition,* December 25, 1552, lib. 911, f. 23.

78. AHN, *Inquisition,* March 23, 1553, lib. 960, ffs. 2–2v.

79. AHN, *Inquisition,* April 12, 1553, lib. 960, f. 614.

80. García Cárcel, *Herejía,* 251.

81. AHN, *Inquisition,* July 29, 1553, lib. 960, nf.; August 4, 1553, lib. 911, ffs. 79–79v. Sensing the new attitude at Court, the Suprema ordered the tribunal not to proceed against the viceroy. AHN, *Inquisition,* August 5, 1553, lib. 911, ffs. 80–80v.

82. AHN, *Inquisition,* May 11, 1554, lib. 1210, f. 53.

83. AHN, *Inquisition,* May 11, 1554, lib. 1210, f. 54.

84. AHN, *Inquisition,* July 12, 1560, lib. 911, f. 353.

85. AHN, *Inquisition,* July 10, 1568, lib. 1210, ffs. 58–60, 62, 63.

86. AHN, *Inquisition,* April 21, 1567, leg. 503#1, nf.

87. AHN, *Inquisition,* July 10, 1568, lib. 1210, f. 61.

88. AHN, *Inquisition*, October 5, 1583; January 13, 1584; February 8, 1610, leg. 505#1, ffs. 16, 26, 108.

89. AHN, *Inquisition*, July 10, 1568, lib. 1210, ffs. 58, 60, 65.

90. AHN, *Inquisition*, November 14, 1560, lib. 497, f. 95.

91. AHN, *Inquisition*, February 21, 1568, lib. 911, f. 842.

92. AHN, *Inquisition*, February 9, 22, 1563, leg. 503#1, ffs. 46v, 65.

93. AHN, *Inquisition*, August 27, 1582, lib. 960, ffs. 18–23, 27.

94. AHN, *Inquisition*, February 3, 1595, lib. 960, f. 241.

95. Lea, *A History*, 2:279.

96. AHN, *Inquisition*, July 1, 1592; August 26, 1592, leg. 505, ffs. 327–328, 331; July 20, 1592, lib. 960, f. 283.

97. Jover was released on bail at the tribunal's request, but the Audiencia evidently had no intention of cooperating with the tribunal on this case since he was promptly rearrested and returned to the royal prison. AHN, *Inquisition*, (1598), procesos criminals, leg. 1780, f. 6.

98. AHN, *Inquisition*, March 10, 1608, lib. 919, ffs. 550–553. The Suprema eventually ordered Sans to resign his post with the Audiencia. AHN, *Inquisition*, September 18, 1608, lib. 919, f. 575.

99. AHN, *Inquisition*, April 10, 1589, lib. 916, f. 730.

100. AHN, *Inquisition*, March 8, 1553, lib. 960, f. 8v–9.

101. AHN, *Inquisition*, March 23, 1553, lib. 960, f. 624.

102. AHN, *Inquisition*, March 9, 1627, lib. 922, ffs. 825–826; also see January 23, 1569, lib. 912, ffs. 103–103v, for the tribunal's complaints about the stubborn attitude of the Audiencia and its refusal to attempt to settle disputes amicably.

103. AHN, *Inquisition*, April 20, 1569, leg. 503#1, nf.; August 28, 1570, leg. 503#1, nf.

104. AHN, *Inquisition*, August 1, 1579, lib. 960, ffs. 589–590.

105. AHN, *Inquisition*, October 6, 1619, lib. 960, f. 587.

106. Sebastián Garciá Martínez, "Bandolerismo, Piratería, y control de moriscos en Valencia durante el reinado de Felipe II," *Estudis* I (1972):142.

107. Ibid., 142.

108. AHN, *Inquisition*, October 20, 1597, lib. 917, f. 918.

109. J. Porcar, *Cosas evanguadas en la ciutat y regne de Valencia*, transcriber V. Castaneda Alcover (Madrid: Cuerpo Facultativo de Archiveros, Bibliotecarios y Arqueólogos, 1934), 162–163.

110. García Martínez, "Bandolerismo," 129.

111. AHN, *Inquisition*, December 2, 1601, lib. 960, ffs. 272–273.

112. AHN, *Inquisition*, January 30, 1603, lib. 960, f. 258.

113. AHN, *Inquisition*, July 23, 1603, lib. 960, f. 262.

114. AHN, *Inquisition*, September 3, 1621, leg. 804#2, ffs. 174–176.

115. AHN, *Inquisition*, April 26, 1613, leg. 508#2, f. 406.

116. BNM, December 27, 1633, MSS 844, ffs. 7–7v.

117. AHN, *Inquisition*, August 11, 1600, lib. 918, ffs. 264–265.

118. AHN, *Inquisition*, August 14–18, 1600, lib. 918, ffs. 240–240v.

119. AHN, *Inquisition*, August 17, 1600, lib. 918, ffs. 238–238v.

120. The viceroy, marquis of Caracena, resorted to similar tactics in the case of familiar Pedro Linares. AHN, *Inquisition*, April 10, 1610, leg. 803#1, ffs. 632–664.

121. AHN, *Inquisition*, August 21, 1600, lib. 918, ffs. 266–266v. Also see AHN, *Inquisition*, January 19, 1627, lib. 920, ffs. 589–589v, for the tribunal's complaints about Viceroy Enrique de Ávila y Guzmán, marquis de Povar, and the way he favored the Audiencia and attacked the tribunal's jurisdiction over familiares in violation of the "spirit of the concordia."

122. Porcar, *Cosas evanguadas*, 120.

123. AHN, *Inquisition*, August 21, 1600, lib. 918, f. 266.

124. Lea, *A History*, 3:74.

125. García Cárcel, *Herejía*, 40.

126. AHN, *Inquisition*, January 8, 1576, lib. 960, ffs. 230–232.

127. AHN, *Inquisition*, April 28, 1573, leg. 503#1, nf.; April 30, 1573, lib. 913, ffs. 42–45. Ribera was so peeved at the tribunal that he refused to attend the auto de fé of May 3, 1573.

128. AHN, *Inquisition*, October 21, 1566, leg. 503#1, nf.

129. AHN, *Inquisition*, December 21, 1568, lib. 912, f. 8v.

130. AHN, *Inquisition*, June 15, 1568, lib. 912,, ffs. 112–113v.

131. AHN, *Inquisition*, June 21, 1568, lib. 912, f. 114.

132. For the details of these negotiations, see chap 2.

133. For the tribunal's relations with Archbishop Navarra, see García Cárcel, *Herejía*, 41.

134. AHN, *Inquisition*, December 11, 1561, leg. 503#1, nf.

135. AHN, *Inquisition*, December 27, 1561, lib. 911, ffs. 229–230. For a confusing and incomplete account of this incident based on only partial knowledge of the documentation, see García Cárcel, *Herejía*, 41. García Cárcel clearly fails to appreciate or even comment on the importance of this event in the history of the tribunal.

136. AHN, *Inquisition*, December 24, 1561, leg. 324, ffs. 15v–16.

137. AHN, *Inquisition*, January 2, 1562, leg. 503#1, f. 13.

138. AHN, *Inquisition*, December 5, 1565, leg. 503#1, nf. The inquisitors had already taken refuge in the parish church of San Andrés where they had a chapel. AHN, *Inquisition*, December 5, 1565, leg. 1787, f. 2.

139. For a brief discussion of these "old taxes," see Casey, *The Kingdom*, 156. For the jurats' efforts to make the tribunal's officials pay the sises, see AHN, *Inquisition*, June 2, 1576, lib. 960, f. 62.

140. Casey, *The Kingdom*, 167, 170–171.

141. AHN, *Inquisition*, September 17, 1591, lib. 970, ffs. 330–331, 342v. Earlier in his term, Viceroy Moncada had had a bitter argument with the tribunal over the windows from which the inquisitors would watch the Corpus procession. AHN, *Inquisition*, June 16, 1582, lib. 916, ffs. 302–302v.

142. AMV, *Manuels de consells y establiments*, September 18, 20, 1591, lib. A-118, nf.

143. AHN, *Inquisition*, September 17, 1591, lib. 960, f. 342v.

144. AHN, *Inquisition*, September 23, 1591, lib. 90, ffs. 365–367v.

145. AHN, *Inquisition*, September 26, 1592, lib. 960, f. 379.

146. García Martínez, "Bandolerismo," 153. As S. N. Eisenstadt has noted, center-periphery relations in the traditional monarchies were characterized by continuity and interpenetration whereby the institutions of the "center successfully permeated the periphery in an attempt to mobilize support for the policies of the center while relatively autonomous forces of the periphery have continually impinged on the center." S. N. Eisenstadt, "Varieties of Political Development: The Theoretical Challenge," in S. N. Eisenstadt, *Building States and Nations*, I:41–752 (Beverly Hills: Sage, 1973), 56.

147. AHN, *Inquisition*, October 10, 1592, leg. 505#1, f. 339.

148. AHN, *Inquisition*, October 22, 1592, lib. 917, f. 367.

149. AHN, *Inquisition*, January 25, 1592, lib. 960, ffs. 359–361.

150. Porcar, *Cosas evanguadas*, 57.

151. AMV, *Manuels de consells y establiments*, June 11, 1603, lib. A-30, nf.

152. AHN, *Inquisition*, July 6, 1603, lib. 960, f. 283.

153. AHN, *Inquisition*, May 16, 1609, lib. 960, ffs. 400–404.

154. AHN, *Inquisition*, March 23, 1553, lib. 960, ffs. 2–2v.

155. AHN, *Inquisition*, June 18, 1603, lib. 960, f. 295. It was Gaspar Daqui who acted as city council notary during the 1603 crisis. AMV, *Manuels de consells y establiments*, June 13, 1603, lib. A-130, nf.

156. AHN, *Inquisition*, December 11, 1561, leg. 503#1, ffs. 7–8v.

157. AHN, *Inquisition*, July 20, 1573, lib. 913, ffs. 3–4v.

158. AHN, *Inquisition*, April 1, 1619, leg. 1784#1, f. 42.

159. AHN, *Inquisition*, May 19, 1612, leg. 804#2, nf.

160. AHN, *Inquisition*, April 1, 1619, leg. 1784#1, f. 42v.

161. Porcar, *Cosas evanguadas*, 128.

162. Ibid., 129.

163. Ibid., 159.

164. Ibid., 196.

165. AHN, *Inquisition*, April 1, 1619, leg. 1784#1, f. 53v.

166. Porcar, *Cosas evanguadas*, 179, 184.

167. AHN, *Inquisition*, June 13, 1614, leg. 506#1, f. 410.

168. Porcar, *Cosas evanguadas*, 189.

169. Ibid., 210.

170. AHN, *Inquisition*, July 12, 1618, leg. 506#2, f. 1797. Rome was already signaling its displeasure with the cult. AHN, *Inquisition*, April 28, 1618, leg. 506#2, f. 158.

171. Porcar, *Cosas evanguadas*, 309–312.

172. AHN, *Inquisition*, April 1, 1619, leg. 1784#1, f. 37v. Also see Cabezas's letter attacking the cult: AHN, *Inquisition*, February 16, 1619, leg. 506#2, ffs. 70, 70v.

173. Porcar, *Cosas evanguadas*, 213.

174. AHN, *Inquisition*, May 27, 1619, leg. 506#2, f. 304.

175. AHN, *Inquisition*, June 12, 1619, leg. 506#2, f. 314.

176. AHN, *Inquisition*, July 22, 1619, leg. 506#2, f. 328.

177. AHN, *Inquisition*, August 28, 1619, leg. 506#2, f. 350.

178. AHN, *Inquisition*, March 9, 1620, leg. 506#2, f. 422.

179. AHN, *Inquisition*, June 26, 1634, leg. 507#1, f. 286.

180. AHN, *Inquisition*, September 3, 1621, leg. 804#2, ffs. 179–180. Also see the case of familiar Alejandro Portell who was turned over to the tribunal after being arrested on criminal charges by agents of the Audiencia: September 15, 1705, leg. 503#3, exp. 7.

181. AHN, *Inquisition*, March 29, 1661, leg. 503#2, exp. 5, ffs. 131–131v.

182. AHN, *Inquisition*, December 22, 1659, leg. 503#2, exp. 5, ffs. 93–95.

183. García Cárcel, *Herejía*, 65; AHN, *Inquisition*, December 9, 1571, leg. 503#1, nf.

184. Lea, *A History*, 4:356; Porcar, *Cosas evanguadas*, 310–311.

II: Judicial Procedures and Financial Structure

1. Lea, *A History*, 2:457–458; García Cárcel, *Orígenes*, 180, notes that the period of grace in Valencia could be as long as six months.

2. García Cárcel, *Orígenes*, 180.

3. Ibid., 180.

4. Henry Kamen, *Inquisition and Society in Spain in the Sixteenth and Seventeenth Centuries* (Bloomington: Indiana University Press, 1985), 162. The edicts of grace were experimented with later in the sixteenth century as part of royal policy toward the Moriscos; Lea, *A History*, 3:340.

5. Lea, *A History*, 2:92–93.

6. Ibid., 94–96.

7. AHN, *Inquisition*, December 5, 1589, lib. 916, ffs. 670–671.

8. Michel Foucault, *Surveiller et punir: Naissance de la prison* (Paris: Gallimard, 1975), 62.

9. AHN, *Inquisition*, March 16, 1642, leg. 210, ffs. 311–313.

10. AHN, *Inquisition*, (1506), leg. 597#1, exp. 8.

11. AHN, *Inquisition*, September 23, 1568, leg. 802#1, nf.

12. Lea, *A History*, 2:93–94.

13. AHN, *Inquisition*, April 17, 1654, leg. 523#1, f. 7.

14. AHN, *Inquisition*, January 20, 1570, leg. 518#1, f. 9.

15. Lea, *A History*, 1:238.

16. AHN, *Inquisition*, October 18, 1517, lib. 497, ffs. 55–56.

17. AHN, *Inquisition*, July 31, 1560, leg. 1792, nf.

18. AHN, *Inquisition*, May 18, 1590, lib. 917, f. 61.

19. Alonso de Villadiego y Montoya, *Instrucción política y práctica judicial* (Madrid: B. Cano, 1788), 87.

20. AHN, *Inquisition*, leg. 508#2, nf., "memoria de las personas testificadas por Francisco Caffor."

21. AHN, *Inquisition*, November 20, 1582, lib. 915, f. 376.

22. AHN, *Inquisition*, January 9, 13, 1687, leg. 803#1, ffs. 237v–238v.

23. AHN, *Inquisition*, November 22, 1680, leg. 804#2, nf.

24. AHN, *Inquisition*, March 4, 1790, leg. 562#1, f. 6.

25. AHN, *Inquisition*, December 17, 1764, leg. 562#2, f. 8.

26. AHN, *Inquisition*, January 24, 1612, leg. 804#2, f. 235v.

27. AHN, *Inquisition*, November 4, 1678, leg. 800#1, nf.

28. AHN, *Inquisition*, November 8, 1691, leg. 803#2, nf.

29. AHN, *Inquisition*, April 8, 1671, leg. 800#1, nf.

30. John H. Langbein, *Prosecuting Crime in the Renaissance* (Cambridge: Harvard University Press, 1974), 135–136.

31. Ibid., 130–132.

32. Ibid., 137.

33. Eymerich and Peña, *Le manuel*, 47.

34. Ibid., 48.

35. Virgilio Pinto Crespo, *Inquisición y control ideológico en la España del siglo XVI* (Madrid: Taurus, 1983), 242.

36. Eymerich and Peña, *Le manuel*, 214–215.

37. AHN, *Inquisition*, May 30, 1565, leg. 503#1, nf.

38. AHN, *Inquisition*, August 3, 1566, leg. 1790, exp. 2, nf., charge #88.

39. AHN, *Inquisition*, (1566), leg. 1790, exp. 2, nf. "el lic. Bernardino de Aguilera Inquisidor de Valencia respondiendo a los cargos y capítulos que el lic. D. Jerónimo Manrique me ha puesto."

40. Langbein, *Prosecuting Crime*, 181.

41. Foucault, *Surveiller*, 46.

42. Lea, *A History*, 2:548–550. For a detailed defense of the need to conceal the names of witnesses, see AHN, *Inquisition*, October 8, 1528, lib. 320, ffs. 98v–99.

43. Villadiego y Montoya, *Instrucción política*, 64.

44. BNM, MSS 718, ffs. 84–86.

45. García Cárcel, *Orígines*, 183. For the acquisition of property that later became the inquisitorial compound, see ARV, *Clero*, "Instrumentos pertenecientes a la compra de casas en que se fábrica el real palacio de la Inquisición," lib. 1404. García Cárcel, *Herejía*, 204.

46. AHN, *Inquisition*, February 2, 1542, leg. 536#1, f. 3.

47. AHN, *Inquisition*, October 12, 1564, leg. 530#1, f. 8.

48. For complaints about the "ruinous state" of the prison, see AHN, *Inquisition*, August 16, 1563, leg. 503, f. 57v. The letter that may have prompted the Inquisitor-General's investigation came from Alcalde Benito Sanguino; AHN, *Inquisition*, January 22, 1582, lib. 915, ffs. 147–147v. García Cárcel, *Herejía*, 205–206.

49. AHN, *Inquisition*, March 11, 1583, lib. 915, ffs. 488–488v.

50. AHN, *Inquisition*, March 19, 1582, lib. 915, ffs. 331–334; García Cárcel, *Herejía*, 206–207, reproduces only one-half of the map drawn by the visitor which he mistakenly calls the "plan proposed," when as the text of the accompanying letter makes quite clear, it was a map of the Inquisition compound as it then existed.

51. Lea, *A History*, 2:513.

52. AHN, *Inquisition*, May 26, 1528, leg. 1790, exp. 1, ffs. 7v, 12v.

53. AHN, *Inquisition*, June 18, 1566, leg. 1790, exp. 2, f. 34.

54. AHN, *Inquisition*, lib. 918, f. 728, quoted in García Cárcel, *Herejía*, 204–205.

55. AHN, *Inquisition*, July 4, 1575, lib. 913, f. 495.

56. Tomás Cerdan de Tallada, *Visita de la cárcel y de los presos* (Valencia: Pedro de Huete, 1574); Lea, *A History*, 2:534.

57. AHN, *Inquisition*, July 18, 1566, leg. 1790, exp. 2, ffs. 158v–165.

58. García Cárcel, *Orígenes*, 183.

59. AHN, *Inquisition*, December 12, 1623, leg. 507#1, ffs. 195–196.

60. AHN, *Inquisition*, March 27, 1564, leg. 519#1, f. 2. More than 20 percent of the accused confessed either during these early hearings or just after the accusation was presented.

61. Eymerich and Peña, *Le manuel*, 123.

62. AHN, *Inquisition*, January 24, 1659, leg. 518#2, f. 14.

63. AHN, *Inquisition*, June 18, 1565, leg. 530#1, f. 8.

64. Lea, *A History*, 2:479.

65. Langbein, *Prosecuting Crime*, 147–148.

66. Lea, *A History*, 2:563–564.

67. AHN, *Inquisition*, October 26, 1537, leg. 536#3.

68. Lea, *A History*, 3:42.

69. Ibid., 3:4.

70. Ibid., 2:545–546.

71. See the cases of Vezquey "Moro" in AHN, *Inquisition*, November 13, 1508, leg. 548#1, exp. 25; Esperanza Madrit, June 12, 1495, leg. 551#3, exp. 38; and Francisco Bairi, January 31, 1537, leg. 549#1, exp. 9.

72. BNM, "Instrucciones de Torquemada" (1484), MSS 935, f. 6v.

73. AHN, *Inquisition*, August 22, 1573, leg. 559#3, f. 11.

74. AHN, *Inquisition*, October 8, 1576, leg. 548#1, f. 1.

75. AHN, *Inquisition*, January 4, 1521, leg. 559#2, f. 12.

76. Lea, *A History*, 2:538. Spanish jurisprudence in general tended in the direction of increasing the number of crimes in which the testimony of less desirable witnesses could be accepted. Tomás y Valiente, *El derecho penal de la monarquía absoluta* Madrid: Tecnos, 1969. 176–177.

77. Lea, *A History*, 2:543.

78. AHN, *Inquisition*, January 4, 1521, leg. 559#1, f. 12.

79. H. J. Berman, a noted authority on Roman law goes so far as to refer to "a virtual presumption of guilt" in criminal cases. Harold J. Berman, *Law and Revolution* (Cambridge: Harvard University Press, 1983), 610, n. 35.

80. See Langbein, *Prosecuting Crime*, 235–236, for the denial of defense counsel in France. AHN, *Inquisition*, October 8, 1528, lib. 320, ffs. 98v–99v.

81. Lea, *A History*, 3:71–72.

82. AHN, *Inquisition*, December 23, 1654, leg. 523#1, f. 7.

83. Lea, *A History*, 3:74–75.

84. Langbein, *Prosecuting Crime*, 157. See Foucault, *Surveiller*, 41, for a description of the elaborate "arithmetic" of proofs.

85. Eymerich and Peña, *Le manuel*, 209.

86. Kamen, *Inquisition and Society*, 174–175. For complaints about the indiscriminate use of torture in the secular courts, see Tomás y Valiente, *El derecho penal*, 153–154.

87. Torture was administered to 693 persons, or 19.4 percent, in the period after 1540. The relative leniency of the Valencia tribunal would seem to belie the impression given by Lea, who at one point asserts that "the regular practice was to repeat the torture." Lea, *A History*, 3:28–29. My figure is considerably lower than that given by García Cárcel, *Herejía*, 199, but it is based on a much larger number of cases extended over a longer period.

88. Lea, *A History*, 2:562; Langbein, *Prosecuting Crime*, 157. On the Valencia tribunal, about 30 percent were convicted with only one witness.

89. Foucault, *Surveiller,* 42–43.

90. García Cárcel, *Orígines,* 174.

91. From 1554 to 1820, the Valencia tribunal suspended 58 percent of its cases. In contrast, from 1530 to 1609, it suspended only 9 percent. García Cárcel, *Herejía,* 212.

92. Kamen, *Inquisition and Society,* 186.

93. Exile was imposed in 8.4 percent of the cases from 1554 to 1820.

94. AHN, *Inquisition,* January 18, 1567, leg. 503#1.

95. Some form of religious instruction was imposed on 8.3 percent of the cases. Reclusion affected 1.3 percent of the tribunal's victims.

96. AHN, *Inquisition,* December 17, 1764, leg. 562#2, f. 8.

97. The scourging was imposed on 7.3 percent of cases.

98. Lea, *A History,* 3:138. Public shaming affected 0.8 percent of cases.

99. Ibid., 142. Altogether, the Valencia tribunal imposed galley service on 8.2 percent of its victims, with slightly less than half (3.9%) being given the three-year minimum.

100. Tomás y Valiente, *El derecho penal,* 252.

101. Lea, *A History,* 3:143.

102. AHN, *Inquisition,* (1593), leg. 505#2, f. 121.

103. Francisco Tomás y Valiente, "Las carceles y sistema penitenciario bajo los borbones," *Historia* 16, 7 (October 1978): 74. The tribunal sentenced a little over one-tenth of its victims to forced labor.

104. Lea, *A History,* 3:151.

105. AHN, *Inquisition,* June 21, 1566, leg. 1790, exp. 2, f. 48.

106. Eymerich and Peña, *Le manuel,* 207–208; García Cárcel, *Herejía,* 203.

107. Lea, *A History,* 3:162–166.

108. Lea, *A History,* 3:172–179.

109. Tomás y Valiente, *El derecho penal,* 394.

110. Lea, *A History,* 3:183–185.

111. Ibid., 195–199.

112. García Cárcel, *Orígines,* 191.

113. Ibid., 174.

114. These figures came from my own calculations.

115. AHN, *Inquisition,* May 24, 1699, leg. 510#1, ffs. 136–137.

116. Lea, *A History,* 3:209–210.

117. See Foucault, *Surveiller,* 51–58, for a brilliant discussion of the political role of public executions under the Old Regime.

118. García Cárcel, *Orígines,* 191–192.

119. Ibid., 167, García Cárcel, *Herejía,* 206. Jaime Contreras and Gustav Henningsen, "Forty-four Thousand Cases of the Spanish Inquisition (1540–1700)," in Gustav Henningsen and John Tedeschi, eds., *The Inquisi-*

tion in Early Modern Europe (DeKalb: Northern Illinois University Press, 1986), 118–119.

120. AHN, *Inquisition*, May 12, 1512, lib. 960, f. 122.

121. Lea, *A History*, 2:180.

122. AHN, *Inquisition*, June 4, 1557, lib. 911, f. 237.

123. Lea, *A History*, 2:185.

124. AHN, *Inquisition*, May 2, 1562; November 21, 1562; December 2, 1562, leg. 503#1, ffs. 27, 41v.

125. AHN, *Inquisition*, August 17, September 16, 1572, leg. 503#1.

126. Lea, *A History*, 2:181. The 1566 visitation resulted in a number of charges of judicial irregularities being lodged against the two inquisitors. AHN, *Inquisition*, August 3, 1566, leg. 1790, exp. 2, f. 151. For Philip II's respect for the law and judicial system, see Geoffrey Parker, *Philip II* (London: Hutchinson, 1979), 58–60.

127. Lea, *A History*, 2:181.

128. AHN, *Inquisition*, April 30, 1568, leg. 503#1, nf.

129. AHN, *Inquisition*, August 2, 1625, leg. 507#1, f. 498.

130. Villadiego y Montoya, *Instrucción política*, 66.

131. Robert Mandrou, *Magistrats et sorciers en France au XVII siècle* (Paris: Plon, 1968), 345.

132. Gustav Henningsen, "El 'banco de datos' del Santo Oficio: Las relaciones de causas de la Inquisición española," *Boletín de la Real Academia de la Historia*, 174 (1977): 564.

133. AHN, *Inquisition*, November 23, 1632, leg. 508#2, f. 233.

134. Works such as Simancas, *De catholicis institutionibus*, were extremely influential. Lea, *A History*, 2:476. Also see Mario L. Oncaña Torres, "El corpus jurídico de la Inquisición española" in Pérez Villanueva, *La Inquisición española*, 912–916.

135. AHN, *Inquisition*, "Memoria de las causas despachadas en la inquisition de Valencia en los años de 1647 y 1648 y lo resuelto a ellas por el Illmo. Señor Obispo de Palencia Inquisidor-General y Señores del Consejo de Su Magestad," leg. 509#3, ffs. 243–244. The Suprema reviewed 3.7 percent of the sentences handed down by the tribunal, mitigating the penalty in 1.5 percent and increasing it in 0.6 percent.

136. AHN, *Inquisition*, June 17, 1658, leg. 510#3, ffs. 49–50.

137. AHN, *Inquisition*, February 3, 1683, lib. 932, f. 226.

138. See Chap. VIII. Valencian law prescribed automatic death sentences for sodomites; Cerdan de Tallada, *Visita*, 197–198.

139. García Cárcel, *Orígenes*, 135.

140. Martínez Millán, *La hacienda*, 277–278, notes that salaries paid to inquisitors rose from 60,000 maravedís in 1498 to 250,000 in 1603 and for

fiscales, from 30,000 to 170,000 in the same period. Salaries always comprised the largest part of the tribunal's budget.

141. AHN, *Inquisition*, (1553), lib. 911, ffs. 102–103.

142. Lea, *A History*, 2:210. The third inquisitor was removed after 1677. Martínez Millán, *La hacienda*, 258.

143. Llorente, *A Critical History*, 24.

144. AHN, *Inquisition*, January 12, 1561, lib. 324, f. 2v.

145. Lea, *A History*, 2:453.

146. Ibid., 453–454; AHN, *Inquisition*, September 10, 1569, lib. 497, f. 111v.

147. AHN, *Inquisition*, November 6, 1623, leg. 507#1, f. 165.

148. Lea, *A History*, 2:193.

149. AHN, *Inquisition*, August 3, 1520, lib. 317, f. 66v; April 10, 1671, lib. 498, ffs. 190v–191.

150. AHN, *Inquisition*, September 19, 1806; November 14, 1806; February 28, 1807; April 15, 1807, leg. 517#1, ffs. 20, 24, 34, 39.

151. AHN, *Inquisition*, August 3, 1606, lib. 332, ff. 9v–10.

152. Lea, *A History*, 2:455.

153. AHN, *Inquisition*, September 16, 1801, leg. 517#1, f. 89. Of course, Polop was given more time; December 15, 1801, leg. 517#1, f. 97.

154. AHN, *Inquisition*, October 6, 1498, lib. 242, nf.

155. In 1499, the original provision of September 10, 1495, was renewed and extended to those who had not originally come forward; AHN, *Inquisition*, April 25, 1499, lib. 242, nf.

156. AHN, *Inquisition*, April 25, 1499, lib. 242.

157. García Cárcel, *Orígines*, 144.

158. Burns, *The Crusader Kingdom*, 1:124.

159. AHN, *Inquisition*, October 14, 1575, lib. 497, ffs. 166v–178.

160. AHN, *Inquisition*, June 11, 1531; April 24, 1533, leg. 800#1, ffs. 1–2. Lea, *A History*, 2:330.

161. García Cárcel, *Orígines*, 154–157.

162. García Cárcel, *Herejía*, 159, 162.

163. AHN, *Inquisition*, April 19, 1570, lib. 497, f. 156v.

164. AHN, *Inquisition*, May 23, 1556, lib. 911, f. 188.

165. AHN, *Inquisition*, August 23, 1556, lib. 911, ffs. 203–205.

166. AHN, *Inquisition*, June 8, 1562, lib. 911, ffs. 497–500.

167. AHN, *Inquisition*, June 9, 1562, leg. 503#1, nf.

168. In his letter detailing the properties in Centelles's estate, the receiver noted the "mucha necesidad" in which the tribunal found itself at that time. AHN, *Inquisition*, July 4, 1566, leg. 503#1, exp. 1, nf.

169. García Cárcel, *Orígines*, 159–160.
170. Martínez Millán, *La hacienda*, 94–95.
171. Ibid., 316.
172. Ibid., 103, 106–107.
173. AHN, *Inquisition*, November 6, 1556, leg. 503#1, nf. For the tribunal's struggles to take over benefices in Gandía and Mora, see AHN, *Inquisition*, February 28, 1567, and May 12, 1570, leg. 503#1.
174. AHN, *Inquisition*, February 9, March 3, 1563, leg. 503#1, ffs. 47v, 48v.
175. Henry Kamen, "Confiscations in the Economy of the Spanish Inquisition," *Economic History Review* 17 (1965): 514–517.
176. AHN, *Inquisition*, July 7, 1588, lib. 916, ffs. 638–639.
177. See Chap. VI, below, for the tribunal's shifting attitude toward the Moriscos.
178. AHN, *Inquisition*, October 26, 1615, leg. 506#1, ffs. 507–510.
179. García Cárcel, *Herejía*, 147.
180. AHN, *Inquisition*, June 27, 1615; July 1, 1615, leg. 506, lib. 88, nf., ffs. 478–479. Quoted in Martínez Millán, *La hacienda*, 293–297. The Suprema also sent aid to the tribunal in the form of an emergency grant of 2,000 ducats to help cover salary payments.
181. García Cárcel, *Herejía*, 175. The original royal order dates from May 30, 1623. By March 5, 1624, the tribunal had received 5,211 lliures in principal from the duke, and the Suprema ordered it immediately reinvested in the new censals situated in the city of Valencia. AHN, *Inquisition*, March 5, 1624, leg. 507#1, f. 277.
182. Martínez Millán, *La hacienda*, 369–370.
183. Ibid., 370.
184. AHN, *Inquisition*, February 23, 1706, leg. 2308, nf.

III: Inquisitors and Officials

1. Julio Caro Baroja, *El Señor Inquisidor y otras vidas por oficio* (Madrid: Alianza, 1968), 18.
2. Lea, *A History*, 2:233–237.
3. Caro Baroja, *El Señor*, 16.
4. Richard L. Kagan, *Students and Society in Early Modern Spain* (Baltimore: Johns Hopkins University Press, 1976), 90. For a more detailed study of this reform, see Stephen Haliczer, *The Comuneros of Castile: The Forging of a Revolution, 1475–1521* (Madison: University of Wisconsin Press, 1981), 207–220.
5. See chap. 1 for the attitude of the Audiencia and jurats.

6. For the importance of the post, see Casey, *The Kingdom*, 169.

7. AHN, *Inquisition*, 1592, leg. 1336, exp. 5.

8. Bernardo Boyl was married to Melchor Figuerola's daughter, Luciana, and applied for a familiatura in 1612; AHN, *Inquisition*, 1612, leg. 6232, exp. 7. In 1634, Boyl and Gaspar Figuerola appear as signatories to a petition signed by all the familiares of Valencia city and its immediate environs; AHN, *Inquisition*, May 13, 1634, leg. 1788#1, exp. 5.

9. AHN, *Inquisition*, 1620, leg. 1257, exp. 1.

10. AHN, *Inquisition*, April 18, 1715, leg. 503#3, exp. 7, ff. 209v–210.

11. Ibid.

12. AHN, *Inquisition*, 1637, leg. 1188, exp. 7.

13. For the difficulties of the Inquisition in Teruel, see chap. 1.

14. AHN, *Inquisition*, 1753, leg. 1288, exp. 27.

15. AHN, *Inquisition*, 1755, leg. 1236, exp. 22. In this genealogy, it was noted that "el Inquisitor-General le ha confiado los principales negocios de la mitra."

16. Kamen, *Inquisition and Society*, 61.

17. AHN, *Inquisition*, 1592, leg. 1242, exp. 12.

18. Antonio Domínguez Ortíz, *Sociedad y estado en el siglo XVIII español* (Barcelona: Ariel, 1976), 403.

19. Ibid., 403–404.

20. Ibid., 413–414.

21. AHN, *Inquisition*, 1780, leg. 1324, exp. 16.

22. Annie Molinié-Bertrand, "Les 'Hidalgos' dans le royaume de Castille à la fin du XVIe siècle: Approche cartographique," *Revue d'histoire économique et sociale*, t. 52, no. 1 (1974), 66–68.

23. Janine Fayard, *Les Membres du conseil de Castille à l'époque moderne* (Geneva: Droz, 1979), 342–343.

24. Richard L. Kagan, *Lawsuits and Litigants in Castile, 1500-1700* (Chapel Hill: University of North Carolina Press, 1981), 120.

25. Antonio Domínguez Ortíz, *Las clases privilegiadas en la España del Antiguo Régimen* (Madrid: Ediciones Istmo, 1973), 75.

26. Ibid., 72.

27. Ibid., 78.

28. J. H. Elliott, *The Count-Duke of Olivares* (New Haven: Yale University Press, 1986), 184; Domínguez Ortíz, *Las clases*, 82.

29. Domínguez Ortíz, *Sociedad y Estado*, 349–350, for a discussion of the wholesale creation of titulos by the Bourbons.

30. AHN, *Inquisition*, 1597, leg. 1429, exp. 8.

31. AHN, *Inquisition*, 1597, leg. 1542, exp. 26, leg. 1549, exp. 26.

32. Marie Claude Gerbet, *La noblesse dans le royaume de Castille* (Paris: Publications de la Sorbonne, 1979), 137–138.

33. L. P. Wright, "The Military Orders in Sixteenth and Seventeenth Century Spanish Society," *Past and Present* 43 (1969), 45, 51, 52.

34. Ibid., 55.

35. AHN, *Inquisition*, 1743, leg. 1503, exp. 13.

36. AHN, *Inquisition*, 1601, leg. 1372, exp. 10; Ernesto Schäfer, *El Consejo Real y Supremo de las Indias*, 2 vols. (Seville: Universidad de Sevilla, 1935–1947), I:359.

37. AHN, *Inquisition*, 1575, leg. 1572, exp. 1. For a description of Seville's judicial system, see Francisco Morales Padrón, *La ciudad del quinientos: Historia de Sevilla III* (Seville: Universidad de Sevilla, 1977), 226–231.

38. AHN, *Inquisition*, 1589, leg. 1370, exp. 22.

39. For this distinguished family, see above.

40. See the discussion of this term in Henry Kamen, *European Society: 1500–1700* (London: Hutchinson, 1984), 120–124.

41. AHN, *Inquisition*, 1627, leg. 1415, exp. 8.

42. Kamen, *European Society*, 125.

43. See Elliott, *The Count-Duke*, 298, for the opposition to Olivares's proposal to modify the purity of blood statutes and reward those with a distinguished career in trade.

44. Langbein, 206.

45. Diego de Simancas, *De catholicis institutionibus* (Valladolid, 1552), quoted in Caro Baroja, *El señor Inquisidor*, 20.

46. Kagan, *Students and Society*, 97.

47. AHN, *Inquisition*, "Relación de los individuos de cada tribunal de la Inquisición," 1666, lib. 1323.

48. Kagan, *Students and Society*, 197.

49. Ibid., 98.

50. Ibid., 220–222.

51. AHN, *Inquisition*, "Relación de los individuos," lib. 1323, ffs. 24, 89–90. Some individuals simply could not afford the expense and time necessary to obtain advanced degrees. An extreme but perhaps not so unusual instance is that of Córdoba's inquisitor, Pedro de Villaviciencia Ferrer, who spent a total of 26 years at the University of Salamanca, 7 of which were at the Colegio Mayor de Cuenca. In contrast, licentiate Antonio de Ayala y Verganza, who had served on the Valencia tribunal some years earlier, took his graduate degree at the University of Ávila in just one year. "Relación de los individuos," ffs. 64–65, 24.

52. Kagan, *Students and Society*, 66, 109.

53. For the foundation of San Bartolomé, see Kagan, *Students and Society*, 66. None of the inquisitors of 1666 had attended San Bartolomé.

54. Kagan, *Students and Society*, 136.

55. Fayard, *Les membres*, 60.

56. For a breakdown of cases being heard by the Valladolid chancillería, see Kagan, *Lawsuits and Litigants*, 110–111. For a description of the matters that came before the Council of Castile, see Fayard, *Les membres*, 14–18.

57. Ibid., 74, 78.

58. Ibid., 80.

59. Ibid., 61. Fayard points out that acceptance of such posts declined from the reign of Philip IV when graduates would rather remain in residence at the university than accept a position they considered unworthy of them.

60. Antonio Domínguez Ortíz, "Regalismo y relaciones iglesia estado en el siglo XVII," in *Historia de la Iglesia en España*, 5 vols., ed. Ricardo García-Villoslada (Madrid: Biblioteca de Autores Cristianos, 1979), 4:96-97.

61. AHN, *Inquisition*, "Relación de los individuos," 1666, lib. 1323, ffs. 18–19.

62. R. Olaechea, *Anotaciones sobre la inmunidad*, 299, as cited in Teófanes Egido, "El regalismo y las relaciones Iglesia-Estado en el siglo XVIII," in García-Villoslada, *Historia*, 4:134.

63. Domínguez Ortíz, "Regalismo," 103.

64. Ibid., 100.

65. The condemnation and exile of the royal advocate general, Melchor de Macanaz, for his violently regalist *Pedimento fiscal* is a case in point. See chap. 9.

66. Out of 249, there were only two councillors of the Indies who were former inquisitors. One of these was a former inquisitor of Valencia, Pedro Gutiérrez Flores. Schäfer, *El consejo*, 1:353–366.

67. Examples of this among the inquisitors of Valencia include Francisco Alarcón Covarrubias, Bishop of Ciudad Rodrigo; Pedro Cifontes de Loarte, Bishop of Avila; and Fernando de Loazes, later bishop of Tarragona and Valencia.

68. Kagan, *Students and Society*, 80, points out that priests holding university degrees dominated benefices after the early sixteenth century.

69. Lea, *A History*, 2:416–418.

70. AHN, *Inquisition*, "Relación de los individuos," lib. 1323, f. 23. For the income of the Inquisitor-General around the same time, see Lea, *A History*, 2:196.

71. AHN, *Inquisition*, "Relación de los individuos," lib. 1323, f. 23.

72. Marcel Couturier, *Recherches sur les structures sociales de Chateaudun* (Paris: SEVPEN, 1969), 138–142, 228.

73. AHN, *Inquisition*, 1650, leg. 1342, f. 2. Both of Ochagavia's grandfathers as well as his father and brother served as familiares.
74. AHN, *Inquisition*, 1642, leg. 1189, f. 5, lib. 1323, "Relación de los individuos," ffs. 23–24.
75. Fayard, *Les membres*, 266.
76. AHN, *Inquisition*, 1713, leg. 1570, f. 23; Fayard, *Les membres*, 245.
77. Wright, "The Military Orders," 52; Domínguez Ortíz, *Las clases*, 23.
78. Ibid., 23–24.
79. Wright, "The Military Orders," 61.
80. See chap. 5.
81. For an excellent edition of this work complete with revealing notes, see Sebastián de Horozco, *Cancionero*, ed. Jack Weiner (Berne: Herbert Lang, 1976).
82. Jack Weiner, "Sobre el linaje de los Horozco," *Actas del primer congreso internacional sobre la picaresca* (Madrid: Fundación Universitaria Española, 1975), 793.
83. Ibid., 799.
84. Ibid., 797.
85. Ibid.; AHN, *Inquisition*, 1624, leg. 1431, f. 18.
86. Weiner, "Sobre el linaje," 794–795.
87. AHN, *Inquisition*, 1616–20, leg. 1515, f. 2.
88. Weiner, "Sobre el linaje," 803.
89. For the financial difficulties of the members of the Council of Castile in the seventeenth century, see Fayard, *Les membres*, 426–427.
90. Lea, *A History*, 2:223–233.
91. AHN, *Inquisition*, March 12, 1600, lib. 918, f. 173.
92. Azcona, *Isabel la Católica*, 324–326, 333–336, 346.
93. AHN, *Inquisition*, November 15, 1504, lib. 1210, ff. 1431–1432.
94. AHN, *Inquisition*, March 12, 1600, lib. 918, ffs. 173–174.
95. AHN, *Inquisition*, May 25, 1610, lib. 497, f. 284.
96. AHN, *Inquisition*, November, 20, 1484, lib. 1210, f. 1405.
97. AHN, *Inquisition*, 1560, leg. 1790, exp. 2, f. 10v.
98. Some of the early provincial inquisitors and Inquisitor-General Jiménez de Cisneros were associated with the rather puritanical monastic reform movement. Azcona, *Isabel la Católica*, 396, 594.
99. AHN, *Inquisition*, September 28; October 2, 1566, leg. 1790, exp. 2. Inquisitor Bernardino de Aguilera was praised for his fairness by witnesses during the visitation of 1566.
100. AHN, *Inquisition*, May 29, 1528, leg. 1790, exp. 1, ffs. 28, 31.
101. Aguilera's health problems were probably the product of over-

work since his colleague, Gregorio de Miranda, had a nervous disorder and was absent for long periods.

102. AHN, *Inquisition*, October 3, 1566, leg. 1790, exp. 2.

103. AHN, *Inquisition*, August 3, 1566, leg. 1790, exp. 2, list of charges against licentiate Bernardino de Aguilera, charge #5.

104. AHN, *Inquisition*, April 24, 1566, leg. 1790, exp. 2, additional charges against licentiate Bernardino de Aguilera, charge #11.

105. See chap. 1.

106. AHN, *Inquisition*, September 6, 1566, leg. 1790, exp. 2, nf.

107. AHN, *Inquisition*, August 30, 1566, leg. 1790, exp. 2, nf.

108. AHN, *Inquisition*, "Agravios hechos por el inquisidor Aguilera ansi a la cuidad y reino de Valencia como a los particulares de dicha ciudad reino y districto," April 8, 1566, leg. 1790, exp. 2, nf.

109. AHN, *Inquisition*, December 5, 1565, leg. 1790, exp. 2, nf.

110. AHN, *Inquisition*, June 27, 1566, leg. 1790, exp. 2, f. 120v.

111. AHN, *Inquisition*, June 30, 1566, leg. 1790, exp. 2, f. 125.

112. AHN, *Inquisition*, July 10, 1568, leg. 1210. Items included in the Concordia that appear to have been derived from accusations lodged against Aguilera during the visitation of 1566 include #6 and #51, which modified the use of ecclesiastical censures and provided mechanisms for resolving jurisdictional conflicts without employing them, #11, which prohibited artisans from placing the Inquisition's shield over their doors, and #24, which denied the newly created commissioners the right to issue export licenses.

113. AHN, *Inquisition*, 1648, leg. 1487, exp. 3.

114. For the details of the recovery of Catalonia, see Elliott, *Imperial Spain*, 349. For Chacón y Narvaez's early career and his success with the Valencian estates, see AHN, *Inquisition*, November 27, 1666, lib. 1323, f. 50.

115. For the career of licentiate Alonso de Salazar Frías, see AHN, *Inquisition*, leg. 2220, exp. 21b. Salazar Frías played a key role in the Basque witchcraft trials of the early seventeenth century. Gustav Henningsen, *The Witches' Advocate: Basque Witchcraft and the Spanish Inquisition* (Reno: University of Nevada Press, 1980). In 1619, he was sent to the Valencia tribunal to restore morale after the Padre Simón affair.

116. AHN, *Inquisition*, December 23, 1653, leg. 1784#2, f.

117. AHN, *Inquisition*, July 28, 1653, leg. 1784#2, f. 3.

118. AHN, *Inquisition*, January 20, 1653, leg. 1784#2, f. 4.

119. AHN, *Inquisition*, January 20, 1653, leg. 1784#2, f. 11.

120. AHN, *Inquisition*, January 20, 1653, leg. 1784#2, ff. 27–28.

121. AHN, *Inquisition*, December 23, 1653, leg. 1784#2, f. 229.

122. AHN, *Inquisition*, November 27, 1666, lib. 1323, f. 59.

123. Magali Safatti, *Spanish Bureaucratic Patrimonialism in America* (Berkeley: Institute of International Studies, University of California, 1966), 38.

124. Even though Roche was born in Macaranbros, a village in the archbishopric of Toledo, he was descended from a distinguished Valencian family that was firmly entrenched in Valencia's municipal oligarchy. AHN, *Inquisition*, 1601, leg. 1372, exp. 6.

125. AHN, *Inquisition*, January 9, 1620, leg. 3707#1, ffs. 87v–88.

126. AHN, *Inquisition*, March 9, 1620, leg. 3707#1, f. 92v.

127. AHN, *Inquisition*, July 16, 1620, lib. 923, f. 114.

128. See below.

129. AHN, *Inquisition*, October 24, 1628, lib. 922, f. 937.

130. AHN, *Inquisition*, November 26, 1630, leg. 2317, nf.

131. AHN, *Inquisition*, July 19, 1636, leg. 509#1, f. 121.

132. AHN, *Inquisition*, September 30, 1636, leg. 509#1, ffs. 15–15v.

133. AHN, *Inquisition*, September 30, 1636, leg. 509#1, ffs. 14–14v.

134. AHN, *Inquisition*, February 8, 1636, lib. 926, f. 614.

135. AHN, *Inquisition*, January 11, 1638, lib. 926, ffs. 286–287.

136. AHN, *Inquisition*, May 11, 1627, lib. 922, f. 845.

137. AHN, *Inquisition*, January 28, 1631, lib. 923, ffs. 22–23.

138. AHN, *Inquisition*, January 13, 1638, leg. 509#1, f. 321.

139. AHN, *Inquisition*, April 3, 1639, leg. 1788#2, exp. 8.

140. AHN, *Inquisition*, September 2, 1636, leg. 509#1, f. 130; September 30, 1636, leg. 509#1, ffs. 7–7v. The prisoners had keys to their cells and an outside door was left open for them to enter and leave as they wished.

141. AHN, *Inquisition*, August 12, 1659, leg. 503#2, ffs. 76–77.

142. For the details of Roche's will, see ARV, *Clero*, September 6, 1647, lib. 11217, ffs. 1–5.

143. AHN, *Inquisition*, 1636, leg. 1506, exp. 9.

144. AHN, *Inquisition*, 1652, leg. 1265, exp. 2.

145. AHN, *Inquisition*, 1733, leg. 1284, exp. 1, f. 5.

146. AHN, *Inquisition*, October 25, 1529, leg. 1790#1, f. 47v.

147. AHN, *Inquisition*, lib. 1210, f. 1412.

148. AHN, *Inquisition*, April 29, 1558, lib. 911, ffs. 261, 269–270.

149. AHN, *Inquisition*, March 28, 1554, lib. 911, f. 126; September 27, 1556, f. 176v.

150. See Lea's incomplete account of the family; Lea, *A History*, 2:221.

151. Apparently this was not difficult for someone with basic skills, especially when many books of written formularies existed to help the uninitiated. One of these books, which may well have been available to

Juan del Olmo was Bartolomé de Albornoz, *Arte de los contratos* (Valencia, 1573), reference in Kagan, *Lawsuits and Litigants in Castile*, 140.

152. AHN, *Inquisition*, September 30, 1636, leg. 1784#2, f. 19. José Vicente del Olmo, *Relación histórica del Auto de fé que se celebró en Madrid: Este año de 1680* (Madrid: Roque Rico de Miranda, 1680).

153. AHN, *Inquisition*, August 14, 1696, lib. 933, nf.

154. AHN, *Inquisition*, 1750, leg. 2317, nf.

155. AHN, *Inquisition*, 1719, leg. 1281#1, exp. 1.

156. AHN, *Inquisition*, June 26, 1659, leg. 503#2, f. 74.

157. The Suprema clearly anticipated that Palomares would have to be given the opportunity to perform "algunas informaciones de limpieza" in its letter of appointment. AHN, *Inquisition*, December 2, 1623, leg. 507#2, f. 16. Regarding Palomares's finances, see AHN, *Inquisition*, November 9, 1627, lib. 922, f. 723v.

158. AHN, *Inquisition*, September 28, 1627, lib. 922, f. 724.

159. AHN, *Inquisition*, September 30, 1636, leg. 509#1, f. 14v.

160. AHN, *Inquisition*, September 30, 1636, leg. 1784#2, f. 11v.

161. AHN, *Inquisition*, September 30, 1636, leg. 1784#2, f. 12.

162. AHN, *Inquisition*, November 18, 1636, leg. 509#1, nf.

163. AHN, *Inquisition*, Sept. 30, 1636, leg. 1784#2, f. 2.

164. AHN, *Inquisition*, April 20, March 10, 1638, ffs. 219, 238.

165. Lea, *A History*, 2:189.

166. AHN, *Inquisition*, November 27, 1687, lib. 498, f. 211. This carta acordada prohibiting the notarios from carrying out genealogical investigations confirms those of August 21, 1606, and April 8, 1624.

167. I. A. A. Thompson, *War and Government in Habsburg Spain, 1560–1620* (London: Athlone Press, 1976), 200, 275.

168. AHN, *Inquisition*, January 23, 1638, lib. 926, f. 353.

IV: Familiares and Unsalaried Officials

1. Lea, *A History*, 2:273.

2. Jaime Contreras, *El Santo Oficio de la Inquisición de Galicia, 1560–1700* (Madrid: Akal, 1982), 67.

3. Ibid., 86.

4. AHN, *Inquisition*, April 22, 1630, lib. 923, ffs. 405–406.

5. AHN, *Inquisition*, February 26, 1551, lib. 911, f. 18.

6. Lea, *A History*, 2:276.

7. AHN, *Inquisition*, April 14, 1551, lib. 911, f. 6.

8. Lea, *A History*, 2:276–277.

9. AHN, *Inquisition*, June 13, 1552, leg. 503#2, f. 45.

10. AHN, *Inquisition*, July 29, 1552, leg. 503#2, f. 57.

11. See chap. 1, 27.

12. AHN, *Inquisition*, July 10, 1568, lib. 1210, ffs. 56, 58.

13. García Cárcel, *Herejía*, 147.

14. AHN, *Inquisition*, "Libre dels familiares del sanctoffici del any 1575", leg. 628#1, exp. 1

15. AHN, *Inquisition*, June 1603, lib. 960, f. 211.

16. Numbers of familiares for the district have been arrived at by combining the list of 1602 with the names of familiares drawn from genealogies.

17. García Cárcel, *Herejía*, 149.

18. AHN, *Inquisition*, March 4, 1597, leg. 505#2, ffs. 89–90v.

19. AHN, *Inquisition*, December 24, 1619, leg. 502#1; February 26, 1623, nf.

20. AHN, *Inquisition*, June 14, 1661, leg. 503#2, exp. 5, ffs. 137–137v; October 1, 1697, leg. 2306#1, nf.

21. For the number in 1748 and 1806, see J. Martínez Millán, "La burocracia del Santo Oficio en Valencia durante el siglo XVIII," *Miscelanea Comillas*, XL, no. 77 (1982), 155. Numbers were beginning to recover as early as 1720; AHN, *Inquisition*, June 18, 1720, leg. 503#3, exp. 7, ff. 350–356.

22. For an early reference to the appointment of an excessive number of notaries, see AHN, *Inquisition*, October 22, 1610, leg. 498, f. 286. In 1720, there were 60 serving notaries and only 5 commissioners. AHN, *Inquisition*, June 18, 1720, leg. 503#3, exp. 7, ff. 356–356v.

23. Contreras, *El Santo Oficio*, 72.

24. For references to the economy of Morella, see Casey, *The Kingdom*, 65, 75–76.

25. Ibid., 58.

26. See Casey, *The Kingdom*, esp. chaps. 1 and 3.

27. Ibid., table 5, 38–39, 40.

28. AHN, *Inquisition*, August 18, 1560, leg. 1792, nf. In 1560, the town was reputed to have over 40 familiares, but it could boast no more than 16 for the entire seventeenth century.

29. AHN, *Inquisition*, 1601–1602, leg. 806#1, nf.

30. AHN, *Inquisition*, March 27, 1553, lib. 960, ffs. 5–6v.

31. AHN, *Inquisition*, 1588, leg. 1781, exp. 7.

32. AHN, *Inquisition*, 1590, lib. 960, f. 52v.

33. Contreras, *El Santo Oficio*, 77, notes the opposition of many Galician lords to the establishment of familiares on their estates. This potential opposition may have been one of the reasons the tribunal of Valencia fought so hard to evade the provisions of the Concordia of 1568 which stipulated the appointment of "ordinary persons" without titles or power. AHN, *Inquisition*, July 10, 1568, lib. 1210, f. 56.

34. Lea, *A History*, 2:279.

35. The tribunal promised to obey this provision of the Concordia in a letter to the Suprema: AHN, *Inquisition*, December 7, 1568, lib. 960, f. 45. Of course, it had no intention of abiding by this.

36. For a reference to the procedures used in an early genealogical investigation, see AHN, *Inquisition*, November 20, 1551, lib. 911, f. 26; also see AHN, *Inquisition*, July 29, 1566, leg. 1790, exp. 2, ffs. 142v–143.

37. AHN, *Inquisition*, January 20, 1567, lib. 911, f. 803. Also see the testimony of licentiate Félix de Olmedo: AHN, *Inquisition*, July 29, 1566, leg. 1790, exp. 2, ffs. 142v–143.

38. AHN, *Inquisition*, July 10, 1568, lib. 1210, ffs. 58–59.

39. AHN, *Inquisition*, December 24, 1568, leg. 503#1, nf.; December 23, 1568, lib. 912, f. 8.

40. AHN, *Inquisition*, May 7, 1569, leg. 503#1, nf.; May 10, 1569, lib. 916, f. 62; August 2, 1571, leg. 503#1, nf.

41. Lea, AHN, *A History*, 2:301.

42. AHN, *Inquisition*, January 30, 1591, leg. 505#1, f. 358.

43. AHN, *Inquisition*, October 22, 1630, lib. 923, ffs. 694–695.

44. AHN, *Inquisition*, September 12, 1607, leg. 608, exp. 12.

45. AHN, *Inquisition*, February 3, 1591, lib. 917, f. 247.

46. AHN, *Inquisition*, March 2, 1663, leg. 634#1.

47. On December 2, 1653, commissioner Miguel Giner explained his failure to interview more than three witnesses over 60 years of age during a genealogical investigation in Burriana by reporting that the village had suffered so badly from the epidemic of 1648 that those were the only elderly persons left in the village. AHN, *Inquisition*, December 2, 1653, leg. 619#1, exp. 2.

48. AHN, *Inquisition*, September 5, 1614, leg. 609#1, exp. 3.

49. AHN, *Inquisition*, March 15, 1620, leg. 614#1, exp. 5.

50. Sicroff, *Pureté de sang*, 203.

51. AHN, *Inquisition*, November 28, 1726, leg. 603#1, exp. 5.

52. AHN, *Inquisition*, September 2, 1761, leg. 601#1, exp. 5. Abadia's application was helped by the fact that his wife, Mariana Mulet, came from a family with a long tradition of membership in the corps of familiares.

53. AHN, *Inquisition*, January 14, 1743, leg. 603#1, exp. 2.

54. AHN, *Inquisition*, November 24, 1612, leg. 604#1, exp. 3.

55. AHN, *Inquisition*, November 10, 1639, leg. 654#1, exp. 6.

56. Felipe Gaspar Capero and his wife, Jerónima Capero, were cousins; therefore, Felipe was related to the suspect Vidal family of his mother-in-law. AHN, *Inquisition*, August 13, 1603, leg. 633#1, exp. 1. Also see July 18, 1675, leg. 633#1, exp. 3, for Nicolás Capero notary;

December 7, 1680, leg. 633#1, exp. 2, licentiate Juan Bautista Capero, notary of Traiguera.

57. AHN, *Inquisition*, March 3, 1649, leg. 605#1, exp. 18; January 10, 1596, leg. 633#3, exp. 19.

58. AHN, *Inquisition*, February 23, 1639, leg. 642#1, exp. 2.

59. AHN, *Inquisition*, October 11, 1698, leg. 637#1, exp. 6.

60. AHN, *Inquisition*, March 5, 1740, leg. 653#1, exp. 6.

61. AHN, *Inquisition*, September 15, 1615, leg. 653#2, exp. 8.

62. AHN, *Inquisition*, November 12, 1766, leg. 653#1, exp. 7.

63. AHN, *Inquisition*, March 16, 1682, leg. 627#1, exp. 5. Félix Breva's uncle, Dr. José Breva, had served as commissioner in Castellón, then as calificador, and finally as calificador of the Suprema. AHN, *Inquisition*, September 20, 1773, leg. 627#1, exp. 6.

64. AHN, *Inquisition*, June 2, 1769, leg. 627#3, exp. 3.

65. AHN, *Inquisition*, September 16, 1645, leg. 613#2, exp. 17.

66. AHN, *Inquisition*, October 18, 1575, lib. 497, f. 178.

67. AHN, *Inquisition*, October 6, 1590, lib. 916, ffs. 16, 18; September 2, 1761, leg. 601#1, exp. 5.

68. Bennassar, *L'Inquisition espagnole, XV–XVI* (Paris: Hatchette, 1979), 98.

69. García Cárcel, *Herejía*, 150.

70. García Cárcel, Las Germanías, 164–169.

71. For Charles V's policy of conciliating Castile's urban elite, which had played a leading role in the Comunero Revolution, see Haliczer, *The Comuneros*, 223–227.

72. Ibid., 222.

73. AHN, *Inquisition*, July 15–16, 1566, leg. 1790, exp. 2, ffs. 842–885.

74. AHN, *Inquisition*, May 9, 1604, lib. 497, f. 255.

75. AHN, *Inquisition*, January 2, 1668, leg. 619#1, exp. 4.

76. AHN, *Inquisition*, May 12, 1643, leg. 652#2, exp. 10.

77. AHN, *Inquisition*, May 26, 1528, leg. 1790, f. 9. García Cárcel, *Orígenes*, 97.

78. The figures are drawn from Gandía in 1725. Casey, *The Kingdom*, 43.

79. AHN, *Inquisition*, May 8, 1600, leg. 505, f. 231.

80. AHN, *Inquisition*, August 28, 1587, lib. 916, ffs. 437–438.

81. AHN, *Inquisition*, March 4, 1590, lib. 960, ffs. 58–60.

82. AHN, *Inquisition*, August 25, 1607, lib. 918, ffs. 812–814.

83. AHN, *Inquisition*, January 27, 1660, leg. 503#2, exp. 5, ffs. 103–105.

84. AHN, *Inquisition*, October 11, 1698, leg. 637, exp. 6.

85. AHN, *Inquisition*, June 6, 1639, leg. 633#1, exp. 3.

86. AHN, *Inquisition*, November 10, 1723, leg. 623#2, exp. 3.

87. AHN, *Inquisition*, August 25, 1607, lib. 918, ffs. 812, 813.

88. Casey, *The Kingdom*, 102–105.

89. AHN, *Inquisition*, August 12, 1624, leg. 630#1, exp. 1.

90. Casey, *The Kingdom*, 45.

91. Ibid., 167–169.

92. AHN, *Inquisition*, September 26, 1585; November 8, 1632; July 8, 1628, leg. 616#3, exps. 17–19.

93. Contreras, *El Santo Oficio*, 12.

94. AHN, *Inquisition*, March 29, 1653, leg. 614#1, exp. 4.

95. AHN, *Inquisition*, April 16, 1761, leg. 604#3, exp. 13.

96. AHN, *Inquisition*, October 16, 1767, leg. 624#1, exp. 5.

97. AHN, *Inquisition*, March 13, 1590, leg. 633#1, exp. 8.

98. AHN, *Inquisition*, September 4, 1631, leg. 633#2, exp. 12.

99. AHN, *Inquisition*, March 2, 1648; April 12, 1658, leg. 655#1, exps. 6, 7.

100. AHN, *Inquisition*, March 10, 1752, leg. 655#2, exp. 9; leg. 655#1, exp. 5.

101. AMV, *Insaculación*, 1661, Tomo 4, f. 32.

102. AMV, *Insaculación*, 1686, Tomo 6, f. 171.

103. AMV, *Insaculación*, 1686, Tomo 6, f. 171.

104. Casey, *The Kingdom*, 46.

105. AHN, *Inquisition*, 1610, leg. 1783#2, exp. 11.

106. AHN, *Inquisition*, September 5, 1639, leg. 608#1, exp. 6.

107. AHN, *Inquisition*, September 26, 1596, lib. 960, f. 241. The precarious nature of mercantile wealth in the kingdom made the tribunal insist on enrolling only the best established merchants; March 16, 1660, leg. 503#2, ff. 110v–111.

108. Contreras, *El Santo Oficio*, 125–126.

109. It was not unusual for an applicant to boast that he lived off the income from the agricultural land he rented out. AHN, *Inquisition*, September 15, 1641, leg. 645#1, exp. 14. Others were more adventurous. Miguel Barbera, who was described as possessing the best agricultural land in the village of Adzaneta, also engaged in the manufacture of wax. AHN, *Inquisition*, October 23, 1780, leg. 616#1, exp. 5.

110. AHN, *Inquisition*, March 9, 1754, leg. 614#1, exp. 6.

111. AHN, *Inquisition*, November 20, 1771, leg. 609#1, exp. 5.

112. AHN, *Inquisition*, July 12, 1782, leg. 603#1, exp. 1.

113. AHN, *Inquisition*, November 14, 1575, leg. 617#3, exp. 16.

114. The Suprema permitted an important part of the investigation of Miguel Dalp to be waived because his son was serving as a familiar. AHN, *Inquisition*, June 28, 1616, leg. 503#1, nf.

115. AHN, *Inquisition*, November 8, 1632, leg. 616#3, exp. 18.

116. AHN, *Inquisition*, September 28, 1640, leg. 620#2, exp. 11.

117. AHN, *Inquisition*, November 12, 1717, leg. 602#2, exp. 12.

118. When they married, Miguel Feliu and Jacinta Gavila were related to a total of thirteen familiares. AHN, *Inquisition*, December 3, 1648; January 10, 1658, leg. 655#1, exps. 6, 7.

119. AHN, *Inquisition*, June 4, 1641, leg. 623#2, exp. 7.

120. AHN, *Inquisition*, March 29, 1653, leg. 614#1, exp. 4.

121. AHN, *Inquisition*, January 11, 1655, leg. 625#1, exp. 2.

122. AHN, *Inquisition*, January 19, 1690, leg. 640#1, exp. 7.

123. AHN, *Inquisition*, May 17, 1747, leg. 617#1, exp. 5.

124. AHN, *Inquisition*, September 13, 1633, leg. 644#1, exp. 19.

125. Contreras, *El Santo Oficio*, 104–106.

126. AHN, *Inquisition*, September 5, 1583, lib. 915, ffs. 448–448v.

127. Enrique Cock, *Relación del viaje hecho por Felipe II en 1595 a Zaragoza, Barcelona, y Valencia*, eds. A. Morel-Fatio and A. Rodríguez Villa (Madrid: 1876), 208. When Philip II visited Valencia in 1585, Enrique Cock reported that everyone had to house members of the royal guard "except those who belonged to the Holy Office." Cock, *Viage*, 208.

128. AHN, *Inquisition*, July 27, 1638, leg. 509#1, nf.

129. AHN, *Inquisition*, July 27, 1640, leg. 509#1, nf.

130. AHN, *Inquisition*, July 10, 1658, lib. 1210, f. 64.

131. Lea, *A History*, 1:378.

132. AHN, *Inquisition*, October 17, 1626, lib. 922, f. 372.

133. AHN, *Inquisition*, July 5, 1639, lib. 498, f. 54.

134. Lea, *A History*, 1:378.

135. Contreras, *El Santo Oficio*, 139. This was confirmed later in the century: AHN, *Inquisition*, January 12, 1668, lib. 498, f. 186.

136. Kagan, *Lawsuits and Litigants*, 29–30.

137. BNM, December 16, 1593, MSS. 2731, fss. 18–19.

138. See the tribunal's decision against the Count of Benavente in the criminal case that he brought against Pedro Polo, one of the familiares from his village of Villamarchante. Polo was absolved of the obviously trumped up charges. AHN, *Inquisition*, December 23, 1760, leg. 2320#1, nf.

139. AHN, *Inquisition*, October 12, 1576, leg. 1781, exp. 2.

140. AHN, *Inquisition*, "procesos criminales," leg. 1781#1, exp. 9.

141. AHN, *Inquisition*, February 26, 1551, lib. 911, f. 18.

142. Lea, *A History*, 1:446.

143. AHN, *Inquisition*, July 28, 1632, leg. 508#2, ffs. 171–174.

144. Lea, *A History*, 1:447–448.

145. Kamen, "Public Authority," 661, 665, 667–669.

146. Ibid., 679.

147. Ibid., 660–663.

148. AHN, *Inquisition*, July 28, 1632, "Memoria de algunos perdones hechos por el Marquis de los Vélez," leg. 1788#2, exp. 24.

149. Kamen, "Public Authority," 680.

150. AHN, *Inquisition*, July 14, 1631, lib. 923, ffs. 75–76.

151. AHN, *Inquisition*, March 2, 1633, leg. 508#2, f. 282.

152. AHN, *Inquisition*, July 28, 1632, leg. 1788#2, exp. 24, ffs. 15–16. The Audiencia and the viceroy had been authorized to commute penalties (including the death penalty) to monetary payments in several cedulas: Canet Aparisi, *La Audiencia*, 99.

153. AHN, *Inquisition*, June 20, 1628, lib. 922, f. 909.

154. AHN, *Inquisition*, October 31, 1628, lib. 922, f. 910.

155. AHN, *Inquisition*, July 28, 1632, leg. 1788#2, exp. 24, f. 3v.

156. Lea, *A History*, 1:448.

157. Ibid., 2:273.

158. Kamen, *Inquisition and Society*, 148.

159. AHN, *Inquisition*, September 1, 1589, lib. 916, f. 713.

160. AHN, *Inquisition*, April 17, 1566; July 25, 1567; May 31, 1567, lib. 911, ffs. 666, 705, 764.

161. AHN, *Inquisition*, January 21, 1603, leg. 804#2, f. 4.

162. AHN, *Inquisition*, June 27, 1672, leg. 802#2, f. 55.

163. AHN, *Inquisition*, May 29, 1672, leg. 802#2, f. 16.

164. Contreras, *El Santo Oficio*, 75–76.

165. AHN, *Inquisition*, February 6, 1606, leg. 803#1, ffs. 303–304.

166. Carlo Ginzburg, "The Dovecoate Has Opened Its Eyes: Popular Conspiracy in Seventeenth-Century Italy," in Gustav Henningsen and John Tedeschi, eds. *The Inquisition in Early Modern Europe: Studies on Sources and Methods* (DeKalb: Northern Illinois University Press, 1986), 190.

167. Ibid.

168. Kamen, *Inquisition and Society*, 148.

169. AHN, *Inquisition*, February 8, 1575, lib. 913, f. 439.

170. AHN, *Inquisition*, January 14, 1566, lib. 911, ffs. 657–660.

171. AHN, *Inquisition*, June 27, 1566, leg. 1790, f. 29.

172. AHN, *Inquisition*, March 29, 1553, lib. 960, ffs. 6–6v.

173. AHN, *Inquisition*, November 12, 1610, lib. 960, ffs. 257–258.

174. AHN, *Inquisition*, October 24, 1642, leg. 803#1, nf.

175. See chap. 1.

176. For an account of a typical genealogical investigation, see "derechos de las informaciones de Jaime Fos y Anna Capella," AHN, *Inquisition*, April 1, 1632, leg. 662#1, exp. 8. In this investigation, which cost 1,006 reales, Fos paid 44 reales to the fábrica de Sevilla.

177. AHN, *Inquisition*, December 9, 1631, lib. 923, f. 148.
178. AHN, *Inquisition*, June 3, 1637, leg. 509#1, f. 228.
179. Lea, *A History*, 2:282.
180. This fee was 60 reales during the early seventeenth century, and it was collected by the tribunal's secretaries as part of the applicant's deposit. At times, the confraternity's receiver had great difficulty in obtaining these funds from the secretaries. AHN, *Inquisition*, March 13, 1618, leg. 509#2, f. 149.
181. Lea, *A History*, 2:283.
182. AHN, *Inquisition*, 1749, leg. 1746#1.
183. AHN, *Inquisition*, May 28, 1630, leg. 508#1, ffs. 270–271v; July 30, 1630, f. 302.
184. AHN, *Inquisition*, "Data y descargo dado por el Dr. Salvador Sales, depositario de pretendientes de familiares del Santo Oficio de la Inquisición de Valencia de lo que pago por cuenta de la cofradía de familiares desde enero de 1701 hasta ultimos de diciembre," leg. 4667#1, ffs. 14–15.
185. AHN, *Inquisition*, July 24, 1645, leg. 509#2, f. 323.
186. AHN, *Inquisition*, April 25, 1632, leg. 807#2, nf.
187. AHN, *Inquisition*, April 25, 1632, leg. 807#2, nf.
188. AHN, *Inquisition*, April 1, 1632, leg. 807#1, nf.
189. AHN, *Inquisition*, April 14–18, 1632, leg. 807#2, nf.
190. AHN, *Inquisition*, April 22, 1632; June 14, 1645, leg. 807#2, nf.
191. AHN, *Inquisition*, May 2, 1649, leg. 807#2, nf.
192. AHN, *Inquisition*, April 22, 1632, leg. 807#2.
193. AHN, *Inquisition*, April 26, 1632, leg. 807#2, nf.
194. The 1649 visitation, for example, only yielded six denunciations or confessions, three of which were sent to the Zaragoza tribunal since the accused lived in that district, and only one resulted in prosecution by the Valencia tribunal.
195. AHN, *Inquisition*, February 19, 1565, leg. 503#1, nf.
196. AHN, *Inquisition*, May 4, 1774, leg. 640#2, exp. 11.
197. AHN, *Inquisition*, July 10, 1568, lib. 1210, f. 61.
198. This figure is drawn from a sample of 72 individuals who carried out genealogical investigations and whose ecclesiastical status was given in the document.
199. AHN, *Inquisition*, March 5, 1794, leg. 2388, nf.
200. This evidence is derived from a sample of 106 notaries whose ecclesiastical office is mentioned in genealogical investigations. The tribunal had the services of 50 notaries in the early 1740s, but by 1798, this had been reduced to 11. Martínez Millán, "La burocracia," 153.
201. AHN, *Inquisition*, June 25, 26, 1672, leg. 802#2, f. 48.

202. AHN, *Inquisition*, April 2, 1570, leg. 557#7.

203. AHN, *Inquisition*, February 1, 1649, leg. 529#2, f. 5.

204. AHN, *Inquisition*, March 2, 1613, leg. 559#1, f. 7.

205. AHN, *Inquisition*, June 5, 1616, leg. 653#1.

206. AHN, *Inquisition*, March 11, 1647, leg. 631#1, exp. 4.

207. AHN, *Inquisition*, May 13, 1752, leg. 605#2, exp. 17.

208. Kamen, *Inquisition and Society*, 61, 254. For an example of the popularity of the Holy Office among seventeenth-century intellectuals, see Luis Diez de Aux, *Compendio de la fiestas que ha celebrado la Imperial ciudad de Zaragoza* (Zaragoza: Ivan de Lanuja y Quartanet, 1619), 81–82.

V: The Converted Jews: From Persecution to Assimilation

1. García Cárcel, *Orígenes*, 195. For the expansion of Jewish communities in medieval Valencia, see Robert I. Burns, *Muslims, Christians and Jews in the Crusader Kingdom of Valencia* (Cambridge: Cambridge University Press, 1984), 137–138. For the Jews of medieval Valencia, see Leopoldo Piles Ros, "La judería de Alcira (notas para su estudio)," *Sefarad* XX (1960): 363–767; "La judería de Burriana: Apuntes para su estudio," *Sefarad* XII (1952): 105–124; and "Los judíos en la Valencia del siglo XV: El pago de deudas," *Sefarad* VII (1947): 151–156.

2. Philippe Wolff, "The 1391 Pogrom in Spain: Social Crisis or Not," *Past and Present* 50 (Feb. 1971): 9–10.

3. Ibid., 18.

4. Azcona, *Isabel la Católica*, 371.

5. Francisco Márquez Villanueva, "Conversos y cargos concejiles en el siglo XV," *Revista de Archivos, Museos y Bibliotecas* 63 (1957): 505.

6. Angus Mackay, "Popular Movements and Pogroms in Fifteenth-Century Castile," *Past and Present* 55 (May 1972): 59–60. In Valencia, as in Castile, social pressure on the Jews appears to have decreased during the fifteenth century. Piles Ros, "Los judíos en la Valencia," 152, 154.

7. "Sentencia-Estatuto de Pero Sarmiento," June 5, 1449, quoted in Eloy Benito Ruano, *Toledo en el siglo XV* (Madrid: CSIC, 1961), 191–196.

8. Andrés Bernáldes, *Historia de los Reyes Católicos*, 599 et seq., cited by Haim Beinart, *Conversos on Trial*, 21.

9. Vatican Archives, Reg. Vat. 394, 410 Nicolas V, September 24, 1449, quoted in Benito Ruano, *Toledo*, 198.

10. Alonso de Oropesa, *Lumen ad revelationem gentium*, cited in Albert Sicroff, *Les controverses des statutes de pureté de sang*, 72.

11. Beinart, *Conversos*, 23.

12. Benzion Netanyahu, *The Marranos of Spain from the Late XVth to the Early XVIth Century* (New York: American Academy for Jewish Research, 1966), 3.

13. Julio Caro Baroja, *Los Judíos en la España moderna y contemporánea,* 3 vols. (Madrid: Arión, 1962), 1:298.

14. AHN, *Inquisition,* August 1, 1487, leg. 534#1, exp. 6.

15. AHN, *Inquisition,* January 24, 1486, leg. 535#1, exp. 13.

16. Ordering meat from Jewish butchers was extremely common among Teruel's devout converso community. See the case of Manuel de Puixmija: AHN, *Inquisition,* January 11, 1486, leg. 542#2, exp. 39.

17. AHN, *Inquisition,* February 10, 1489, leg. 539#3, exp. 16.

18. Beinart, *Conversos,* 286–293, 297.

19. AHN, *Inquisition,* January 20, 1486, leg. 535#1, exp. 14.

20. AHN, *Inquisition,* July 7, 1490; August 17, 1496, leg. 543, exp. 11.

21. AHN, *Inquisition,* May 29, 1518, leg. 534#1, exp. 10.

22. See Chap. VIII for oaths sworn by the Old Christians charged with blasphemy.

23. AHN, *Inquisition,* June 8, 1519, leg. 559#3, exp. 12.

24. AHN, *Inquisition,* September 24, 1520, leg. 535#1, exp. 5.

25. Archivo General de Simancas, *Patronato Real,* March 31, 1492, leg. 28, f. 6. Quoted in Luis Suárez Fernández, *Documentos acerca de la expulsión de los judíos* (Valladolid: CSIC, 1964), 391–395. As I have argued elsewhere, see Stephen Haliczer, "The Castilian Urban Patriciate and the Jewish Expulsions of 1480–92," *The American Historical Review* 78 (February 1973): 49. The ideas expressed in the decree reflect the view of Jewish iniquity expressed in the writings of certain converso intellectuals rather than the reality of converso/Jewish social relations. Certainly, the portrait of Spain's Jews as eager to make converts among Christians is not in accord with Jewish traditions, while the outright hostility expressed toward the conversos (who would have been the only logical object of such a campaign) by Jewish rabbis and other Jewish observers during the fifteenth century makes it highly unlikely that it would have been seriously contemplated. Netanyahu, *The Marranos,* 135–201.

26. AHN, *Inquisition,* January 20, 1488, leg. 536#2, exp. 19.

27. AHN, *Inquisition,* August 22, 1486, leg. 534#1, exp. 2.

28. AHN, *Inquisition,* September 3, 1485, leg. 542#2, exp. 40; May 10, 1485, leg. 535#1, exp. 4; August 9, 10, 1485, leg. 542#2, exp. 25.

29. AHN, *Inquisition,* April 23, 1485, leg. 542#2, exp. 25.

30. Netanyahu, *The Marranos,* 175.

31. AHN, *Inquisition,* August 22, 1504, leg. 542#1, exp. 7.

32. AHN, *Inquisition,* October 9, 1501, leg. 542#1, exp. 15.

33. See the testimony of Francisca Janaloyas, AHN, *Inquisition*, May 10, 1485, leg. 135#1, exp. 14.

34. AHN, *Inquisition*, July 22, 1485, leg. 542#2, exp. 39.

35. AHN, *Inquisition*, September 15, 1493, leg. 801#2, exp. 4, ff. 312–314.

36. In Pedro Besant's case, the man noticed that he refused to eat any meat they purchased from Christian butchers and insisted on slaughtering chickens himself. AHN, *Inquisition*, February 26, 1486, leg. 535#1, exp. 14.

37. AHN, *Inquisition*, January 11, 1486, leg. 542#2, exp. 39.

38. AHN, *Inquisition*, January 25, 1492, leg. 540#1, exp. 6.

39. AHN, *Inquisition*, May 11, 1519, leg. 539#3, exp. 14.

40. AHN, *Inquisition*, May 19, 1519, leg. 539#3, exp. 14.

41. AHN, *Inquisition*, November 16, 1503; September 19, 1505, leg. 542#1, exp. 7. For a listing of additional trials involving these families, see García Cárcel, *Orígines*, 273, 301. García Cárcel is, of course, unaware of the way in which these trials first developed.

42. García Cárcel, *Orígenes*, 167, 171–174. The analysis of the social composition of Judaizers after 1540 comes from my own material.

43. Beinart, *Conversos on Trial*, 12–13.

44. This "demonizing" process was a product of mid-century and may be seen in the text of *Sentencia-Estatuto* as well as in satires like the apocryphal correspondence between Yussuf, head of the Jewish community in Constantinople, and Chamorro, head of that in Toledo. Beinart, *Conversos on Trial*, 7–8. For the link between demonic practices and religious heresy made by the medieval church, see Norman Cohn, *Europe's Inner Demons* (New York: New American Library, 1977), 16–59.

45. Eymerich and Peña, *Le manuel*, 138–139; Beinart, *Conversos on Trial*, 13.

46. AHN, *Inquisition*, May 10, 1491, leg. 598#2, nf.

47. See Chap. II for a discussion of the period of grace.

48. García Cárcel, *Orígines*, 180. In all too many cases, trials stemmed from trifling omissions in the original confession. The major charges levied against Jofre Belcayre, for example, were that he had not mentioned the names of all the persons who had participated in celebrating Judaic ceremonies with him and that he had once, some forty years earlier, discussed leaving Spain for Naples where he proposed to live as a Jew. For this, he was sentenced to die at the stake. AHN, *Inquisition*, August 26, 1516, leg. 539#1.

49. AHN, *Inquisition*, 1506, leg. 597#1, exp. 8, ffs. 28–40.

50. Juan Anton, one of these immigrants, had converted in Naples some years earlier and now lived in Teruel. Ibid., f. 56. In several cases,

the individuals listed on the census were later tried and penanced by the Holy Office. García Cárcel, *Orígenes*, 256, 300.

51. AHN, *Inquisition*, May 28, 1528, leg. 1790, exp. 1, ff. 15, 18–19.

52. AHN, *Inquisition*, May 28, 1528; June 21, 1528, leg. 1790#1, ffs. 17, 38–39.

53. AHN, *Inquisition*, May 29, 1528, leg. 1790#1, f. 27.

54. AHN, *Inquisition*, February 18, 1540, leg. 542#1, exp. 26.

55. This according to the testimony of Ausias Cardona, a familiar of the Holy Office who had known Almenara for twenty-five years.

56. Direct evidence that Munibrega actually made that statement comes from the testimony of Nuncio Bartolomé de Brezianos.

57. AHN, *Inquisition*, February 25, 1542, leg. 534#2, exp. 12. The admiral's intervention in favor of the conversos is recorded in his trial record. AHN, *Inquisition*, January 30, 1569, leg. 550#1, exp. 4, ff. 328–332.

58. AHN, *Inquisition*, October 16, 1543; May 12, 1544, leg. 542#1, exp. 26.

59. Lea, *A History*, 3:433.

60. AHN, *Inquisition*, November 27, 1551, lib. 911, ffs. 6–6v.

61. James Boyajian, *Portuguese Bankers at the Court of Spain* (New Brunswick, N.J.: Rutgers University Press, 1983), 2–3.

62. Ibid., 8, 11.

63. Vicente da Costa Mattos, *Discursio contra los Judíos*, Fr. Diego Gavilan Vega, trans. (Madrid: Viuda Melchor Alegre, 1680). The first Spanish edition was in 1633.

64. AHN, *Inquisition*, April 15, 1586, lib. 916, f. 516.

65. AHN, *Inquisition*, May 16, 1586, leg. 539#1, exp. 5.

66. AHN, *Inquisition*, June 16, 1586, leg. 539#1, exp. 5.

67. AHN, *Inquisition*, March 24, 1638, leg. 804#2, ffs. 464–466.

68. For tax reform in the kingdom, see Henry Kamen, *The War of Succession in Spain 1700–15* (London: Weidenfeld and Nicolson, 1969), 323–327.

69. Lea, *A History*, 3:309. For a complete list of New Christians tried in Valencia between 1718 and 1726, see AHN, *Inquisition*, leg. 503#2, exp. 6.

70. Isabel de los Ríos was tried twice by the Holy Office. The first time, she was sentenced to reconciliation and perpetual imprisonment by the Logroño tribunal, and the second time, the Valencia tribunal handed down the death sentence. AHN, *Inquisition*, May 2, 1693; February 24, 1723, leg. 543#2, exp. 10.

71. For the testimony of María de Tudela, see AHN, *Inquisition*, 1718–19, leg. 160#2, exp. 11. For the trials of the leading Valencia tobacco

monopolists and their families, see AHN, *Inquisition*, leg. 3725#3, exps. 196, 197, 198, 199, 202, 214, 221. For the coordination of the efforts of several tribunals on these cases, see AHN, *Inquisition*, May 16, 1719, leg. 503#3, exp. 7, ffs. 317v–318; September 19, 1719, ffs. 329–330. The tribunal discussed its disappointment with the meager financial results of the case against Felipe de Paz in AHN, *Inquisition*, June 30, 1722; June 22, 1723, leg. 513#3, ffs. 398–399, 417–418v. The author would like to thank Rafael de Leca García for pointing out some of this material.

72. Sicroff, *Les controverses*, 88–93, 270–281.

73. Ibid., 93.

74. AHN, *Inquisition*, October 13, 1569, lib. 912, ffs. 150–150v.

75. AHN, *Inquisition*, August, 3, 1520, lib. 317, f. 68v.

76. AHN, *Inquisition*, February 6, 1531, lib. 320, f. 386.

77. AHN, *Inquisition*, June 20, 1682, leg. 807#1, nf.

78. Lea, *A History*, 3:169.

79. AHN, *Inquisition*, November 8, 1567, leg. 503#1, nf.

80. AHN, *Inquisition*, March 8, 21, 1644, leg. 807#1, ffs. 5–6.

81. AHN, *Inquisition*, June 18, 1613, lib. 919, ffs. 848–849.

82. For the Suprema's insistence on maintaining the sanbenitos, see Lea, *A History*, 3:170.

83. AHN, *Inquisition*, May 11, 1627, lib. 922, f. 845; see also above.

84. AHN, *Inquisition*, June 22, 1627, lib. 922, f. 842.

85. AHN, *Inquisition*, August 23, 1628. This is contained in the tribunal's letter of September 12, 1628, lib. 922, ffs. 882–882v. This letter gives the text of the Suprema's letter of August 31, 1628.

86. AHN, *Inquisition*, August 31, 1628, lib. 922, f. 865.

87. This had occurred on January 28, 1628, according to an official document issued by Gregorio de Tapia, secretary of the Council of the Military Orders. AHN, *Inquisition*, August 30, 1628, lib. 922, f. 857.

88. AHN, *Inquisition*, May 12, 1628, lib. 922, ffs. 858–859.

89. The actos positivos were affirmative decisions made by authorized institutions, including the Inquisition and the Council of the Military Orders, regarding the purity of blood of an applicant. Three were enough for a family to be considered of pure blood so that a family member presenting that number of actos would not have to undergo a formal genealogical investigation when he applied for a position covered by the "purity" statutes. Lea, *A History*, 2:306–308. Vicente boasted of his family's accumulation of actos positivos in AHN, *Inquisition*, May 11, 1629, lib. 922, f. 844.

90. AHN, *Inquisition*, October 17, 1629, leg. 508#1, f. 176.

91. AHN, *Inquisition*, September 26, 1630, leg. 508#1, ff. 347–348.

92. AHN, *Inquisition*, October 10, 1647, leg. 509#3, f. 97.

93. AHN, *Inquisition*, August 11, 1699, leg. 1361#1, nf.

94. AHN, *Inquisition*, July 12, 1700, leg. 1361#1, ffs. 75–76.

95. This letter was brought into evidence by the fiscal as one of many reasons for rejecting Tomás Ginart y March's application. AHN, *Inquisition*, June 6, 1701, leg. 1361#1, ff. 225–226.

96. AHN, *Inquisition*, January 26, 1700, leg. 1361#1, nf.

97. This according to expert testimony furnished by the court archivist. AHN, *Inquisition*, March 4, 1704, leg. 1361#1, f. 361.

98. AHN, *Inquisition*, May 31, 1704, leg. 1361#1, ffs. 394–398.

99. AHN, *Inquisition*, June 25, 1704, leg. 1361#1, f. 400.

100. AHN, *Inquisition*, July 9, 1704, leg. 1361#1, ff. 401–402.

101. AHN, *Inquisition*, September 7, 1700, leg. 1361#1, f. 24.

102. Sicroff, *Les controverses*, 212–216.

103. AHN, *Inquisition*, October 23, 1777, leg. 607#1, exp. 1. That conversos from less influential families could still be rejected is proven by the case of Mateo Cebrian: AHN, *Inquisition*, June 21, 1718, leg. 503#3, exp. 7, f. 300.

104. AHN, *Inquisition*, September 14, 1792, leg. 542, exp. 34; May 6, 1815, leg. 535, exp. 12.

105. AHN, *Inquisition*, May 31, 1707, leg. 2308, nf.

106. AHN, *Inquisition*, November 20, 1643, leg. 509#2, ffs. 224–226. Jacob Cansino, who was official interpreter for the Spanish crown in Oran, actually made several trips to Madrid and dedicated a book to the Count Duke of Olivares. Yosef Hayim Yerushalmi, *From Spanish Court to Italian Ghetto* (New York: Columbia University Press, 1971), 167–168.

VI: The Moriscos

1. Robert Burns includes a detailed analysis of the treaties signed with Eslida and Alfandech in Robert I. Burns, *Muslims, Christians and Jews*, 60–79.

2. Henry Charles Lea, *The Moriscos of Spain: Their Conversion and Expulsion* (Philadelphia: Lea Brothers and Co., 1901), reprint ed. (New York: Greenwood Press, 1966), 58.

3. Henri Lapeyre, *La Geógraphie de l'Espagne morisque* (Paris: SEVPEN, 1959), 27–28.

4. Tulio Halperin Donghi notes that in 1565, only several hundred of the more than 20,000 Morisco families were tenants of the realengo: Tulio Halperin Donghi, *Un conflicto nacional: Moriscos y cristianos viejos en Valencia* (Valencia: Institución Alfonso el Magnánimo, 1980), 58.

5. Ibid., 138. Even before the period of the Germanías, certain Old Christians were taking it on themselves to bully Valencia's mudéjares into

conversion. This campaign was supported by the tribunal. AHN, *Inquisition*, November 13, 1508, leg. 548#1, exp. 25.

6. A description of the conversion in Játiva is given in testimony in the case of Jerónimo Catala who declared that the Agermanats threatened to sack the Moorish quarter and massacre its inhabitants. AHN, *Inquisition*, December 9, 1524, leg. 550#1, exp. 10. Also see Ricardo García Cárcel and E. Císcar Pallares, *Moriscos i agermanats* (Valencia: L'Estel, 1974), 122–125; Antonio Domínguez Ortíz and Bernard Vincent, *Historia de los Moriscos: Vida y tragedia de una minoría* (Madrid: Revista de Occidente, 1978), 23.

7. Lea, *The Moriscos*, 69.

8. Ibid., 70.

9. AGS, *Estado*, January 30, 1589, leg. 212, as quoted in P. Boronat y Barrachina, *Los Moriscos españoles y su expulsión* (Valencia: Francisco Vives y Mora, 1901), 2:460–461.

10. Lea, *The Moriscos*, 68.

11. AHN, *Inquisition*, September 14, 1532, lib. 319, f. 123.

12. Lea, *The Moriscos*, 75–76.

13. Ibid., 78.

14. AHN, *Inquisition*, April 22, 1525, lib. 319, 180; Lea, *The Moriscos*, 79.

15. Ibid., 87.

16. AHN, *Inquisition*, April 3, 1530, leg. 558#2, exp. 15.

17. Lea, *The Moriscos*, 86.

18. Domínguez Ortíz and Vincent, *Historia*, 24; AHN, *Inquisition*, January 6, 1526, lib. 319, f. 261v.

19. Domínguez Ortíz and Vincent, *Historia*, 96.

20. Ibid., 96–97.

21. Louis Cardaillac, *Moriscos y cristianos: Un enfrentamiento polémico*, trans. Mercedes García Arenal (Madrid: Fondo de Cultura Económica, 1979), 45.

22. Ibid., 47.

23. AHN, *Inquisition*, July 5, 1560, leg. 1792, nf.

24. AHN, *Inquisition*, May 25, 1568, lib. 911, f. 964.

25. AHN, *Inquisition*, December 5, 1567, leg. 548#1, exp. 2.

26. Cardaillac quotes approvingly the comment made by the profoundly anti-Morisco archbishop of Valencia, Juan de Ribera, to the effect that all of the expelled Moriscos were "infidels." Cardaillac, *Moriscos*, 94. But see the case of Baltasar de Alaque, a leading Morisco religious teacher, who was strongly impelled toward genuine conversion to Christianity by a missionary campaign. AHN, *Inquisition*, testimony of Juan Pastor, rector of Yátova, March 13, 1573, leg. 548#1, exp. 7.

27. Andrew Hess, "The Moriscos: An Ottoman Fifth Column in

Sixteenth-Century Spain," *The American Historical Review* 74 (October 1968).

28. In a recent work that sums up current scholarship on the linguistic history of Valencia before 1609, María del Carmen Barceló Torres concludes that the region was characterized by a duality in the use of Arabic and Catalan until the end of the sixteenth century. María del Carmen Barceló Torres, *Minorías islámicas en el país valenciano: Historia y dialecto* (Valencia: Universidad de Valencia, 1984), 151.

29. AHN, *Inquisition*, August 28, 1587, leg. 1791, nf.

30. Jaime Bleda, the violently anti-Morisco and anti-Semitic memorialist of the early seventeenth century, speaks bitterly of those who "defended" the Moriscos at court and in the universities. Jaime Bleda, *Coronica de los moros de España* (Valencia: Felipe Mey, 1618), 884–886.

31. Cardaillac, *Moriscos y cristianos*, 148.

32. Ibid., 147–148.

33. Cardaillac, *Moriscos y cristianos*, 193, admits that "if the aljamiada manuscripts are the sign of cultural degradation, those written in Castilian testify to a certain assimilation."

34. Ibid., 186–187.

35. Domínguez Ortíz and Vincent, *Historia*, 240.

36. AHN, *Inquisition*, May 23, 1568, leg. 1791, nf.

37. Domínguez Ortíz and Vincent, *Historia*, 135.

38. AHN, *Inquisition*, September 22, 1573, lib. 915, ff. 415–415v.

39. García Cárcel, *Orígines*, 220; *Heregía*, 223.

40. AHN, *Inquisition*, October 15, 1584; March 23, 1586, leg. 548#1, exp. 8. Also see the case of Pedro Crespi, the nearly blind and illiterate Morisco who carried an amulet with Islamic religious writings in the hope that it would help restore his eyesight. AHN, *Inquisition*, January 10, 1583, leg. 550#2, exp. 18.

41. AHN, *Inquisition*, June 30, 1602, leg. 939, f. 167. In 1603, the bishop of Segorbe wrote to the Holy See boasting of the 300 Moriscos who regularly attended mass and received the sacraments in his diocese. Barceló Torres, *Minorías islámicas*, 144.

42. Boronat y Barrachina, *Los moriscos*, 2:555.

43. AHN, *Inquisition*, March 8, 1612, leg. 803#1, nf.

44. See the increased level of religious knowledge and observance between the two trials of Miguel Aquem (1592, 1602). AHN, *Inquisition*, November 15, 1591; May 29, 1602, leg. 548#2, exps. 17, 18. The assimilation of Christian practices is astonishing even in an obdurate Morisco like Juan Cavero who lived in the strongly Islamic Vall de Uxó. He went to mass regularly, confessed, and knew all the basic prayers. AHN, *Inquisition*, September 25, 1590, leg. 549#2.

45. Cardaillac, *Moriscos y cristianos*, 244–249. I am aware that Cardaillac asserts (248) that the Moriscos of Valencia had different and more traditional views, but there is evidence to the contrary in trial records. See AHN, *Inquisition*, November 8, 1604, leg. 548#1, exp. 10.

46. AHN, *Inquisition*, September 5, 1604, lib. 938, ffs. 219, 229v, 235.

47. Domínguez Ortíz and Vincent, *Historia*, 95.

48. AGS, *Estado*, December 4, 1581, leg. 212, as quoted in Boronat y Barrachina, *Los moriscos*, 1:292.

49. Domínguez Ortíz and Vincent, *Historia*, 95.

50. Archivo del Real Colegio de Corpus Christi, 1595, Asignatura I, 7, 8, as quoted in Boronat y Barrachina, *Los moriscos*, 2:713–714.

51. AHN, *Inquisition*, March 7, 1582, leg. 806#2. The testimony was especially reliable since it came from a local Old Christian hidalgo and was later confirmed by a Morisco villager, Jaime Gibet.

52. See Aznar de Cardona's response to a Morisco's question about confession. Pedro Aznar de Cardona, *Expulsión justificada de los moriscos de España* (Huesca: Pedro Cabarte, 1612), ffs. 50v, 51.

53. AHN, *Inquisition*, December 12, 1564, leg. 1790.

54. AHN, *Inquisition*, March 16, 1558, lib. 911, ffs. 974–976v.

55. Boronat y Barrachina, *Los moriscos*, 1:285–286.

56. The crown eventually acceded and forgave them their contributions to the fund. BNM, 1601–1604, sig. ff. 9, as quoted in Boronat y Barrachina, *Los moriscos*, 2:431–243.

57. In the discussion that preceded his vote, the count conceded that "even now they have not even begun the rectories." AGS, *Estado*, n.d., as quoted in Boronat y Barrachina, *Los Moriscos*, 2:466. For a different and far more optimistic view of the rectories that was not shared by any other observer, see Bleda, *Coronica*, 887.

58. AHN, *Inquisition*, May 23, 1565, leg. 548#1, exp. 2; September 5, 1605, lib. 938, ffs. 236–237.

59. AHN, *Inquisition*, October 27, 1605, leg. 803#1, ffs. 279–280.

60. AHN, *Inquisition*, February 28, 1569, leg. 550#1, exp. 4. Of course, the admiral benefited financially from his tolerant policies. Moriscos who went through his territories paid 1 to 3 ducats for a pass. See the testimony of Miguel Zaragoza: March 7, 1542, f. 332v.

61. AHN, *Inquisition*, March 15, 1563, lib. 911, f. 515.

62. AHN, *Inquisition*, May 5, 1573, leg. 548#1, exp. 12.

63. Mercedes García-Arenal, *Los moriscos* (Madrid: Editora Nacional, 1975), 155.

64. AHN, *Inquisition*, July 7, 1553, lib. 911, f. 516.

65. AHN, *Inquisition*, April 22, 1575, lib. 913, ffs. 459–460.

66. Damián Fonseca's warning that any state with a population divided

along religious lines ran a grave risk of destruction was typical of this highly negative attitude. Damián Fonseca, *Justa expulsión de los moriscos de España* (Rome: Jacomo Mascardo, 1612), 170.

67. AHN, *Inquisition*, September 5, 1587, leg. 505, nf. These fears were fed by the alarming reports of redemptionist friars like Juan de Rojas who warned in 1576 that Valencia's Moriscos would rise at the first opportunity: AHN, *Inquisition*, March 31, 1576, leg. 548#1, exp. 1.

68. Ellen G. Friedman, *Spanish Captives in North Africa in the Early Modern Age* (Madison: University of Wisconsin Press, 1983), 12. Bleda, *Coronica*, 890.

69. Friedman, *Spanish Captives*, 38–42, 191.

70. Ibid., 11.

71. AHN, *Inquisition*, November 4, 1576, leg. 548#1, exp. 1.

72. Friedman, *Spanish Captives*, 12.

73. Ibid., 7.

74. AGS, *Estado*, February 2, 1599, leg. 165, as quoted in Boronat y Barrachina, *Los moriscos*, 1:388–389.

75. Domínguez Ortíz and Vincent, *Historia*, 116–117.

76. García-Arenal, *Los moriscos*, 220–221.

77. Bleda discusses the hatred expressed by the militia forces that had been mobilized to combat the Morisco rebellion that broke out just after the expulsion order became known. The Moriscos who surrendered had to be brought to the coast under escort by regular troops, Jaime Bleda, *Defenso fidei in causa neophytorum, sive Morischorum*, as Appendix, *Breve relación de la expulsión de los moriscos de Valencia* (Valentiae: Ioannem Chrusostomum Garriz, 1610), 592–594.

78. AGS, *Inquisition*, July 17, 1528, lib. 15, f. 468, quoted in Boronat y Barrachina, *Los moriscos*, 1:423–428.

79. AHN, *Inquisition*, July 7, 1568, lib. 911, ffs. 926–931.

80. AGS, *Estado*, February 16, 1565, leg. 329, quoted in Boronat y Barrachina, *Los moriscos*, 1:534–535.

81. Miranda is referred to as commissioner in Philip's letter of February 19, 1566. AHN, *Inquisition*, February 19, 1566, leg. 1791, nf.

82. Ibid., 525–526.

83. Ibid., 532–540.

84. AHN, *Inquisition*, February 19, 1566, leg. 1791, nf.

85. AHN, *Inquisition*, February 26, 1583, leg. 1791, nf.

86. García Cárcel, *Herejía*, 27–28.

87. Lea, *The Moriscos*, 98.

88. AHN, *Inquisition*, March 2, 1532, lib. 321, ffs. 34–34v.

89. Lea, *The Moriscos*, 99.

90. García Cárcel, *Herejía*, 53.

91. AHN, *Inquisition*, March 14, 1557, lib. 911, ffs. 245–248.

92. García-Arenal, *Los moriscos*, 135. For the tribunal's demand that its jurisdiction be fully restored on the grounds that the Moriscos "live like Moors," see AHN, *Inquisition*, February 9, 1563, leg. 503#1, f. 47v.

93. García Cárcel, *Herejía*, 57, 60.

94. AHN, *Inquisition*, July 6, 1568, lib. 911, f. 929v.

95. AHN, *Inquisition*, July 6, 1568, lib. 911, ffs. 909–909v; June 25, 1568, leg. 549#1, exps. 7, 11.

96. AHN, *Inquisition*, January 12, 1568; December 24, 1577, leg. 548#1, exp. 2.

97. AHN, *Inquisition*, March 4, 1568, lib. 911, f. 886; García Cárcel, *Herejía*, 79.

98. AHN, *Inquisition*, April 8, 1566, leg. 1791, exp. 2, nf.

99. AHN, *Inquisition*, June 23, 1568, leg. 503#1, nf.

100. For the Concordia between the Moriscos and the tribunal, see AHN, *Inquisition*, October 12, 1571, lib. 917, ffs. 808–813. For a detailed discussion of the Inquisition's obligations under the agreement and the frank admission by Valencia's inquisitors that the tribunal had always kept any money it earned from fines, see AHN, *Inquisition*, July 14, 1595, lib. 917, ffs. 770–773.

101. García Cárcel, *Herejía*, 81–83, 98–99; Domínguez Ortíz and Vincent, *Historia*, 56.

102. García Cárcel, *Herejía*, 99.

103. Ibid., 99–102. For the tribunal's initially positive view of Polo's evidence against the alleged plot, see AHN, *Inquisition*, April 19, 1587, lib. 937, ffs. 1–3. García Cárcel, *Herejía*, 102, seems rather confused as to the real outcome of this case, but the heavy punishment given at the auto de fé of April 19, 1587 (200 lashes and perpetual galley service), and the details of the sentence against the two men makes it clear that the tribunal had concluded that the entire plot was a fabrication and that the men had perjured themselves. AHN, *Inquisition*, April 19, 1587, lib. 937, ffs. 1–3.

104. Jaime Contreras, "Las causas de fé en la Inquisición española (1500–1700): Análisis de una estadística," unpublished report presented at the Simposium Interdisciplinario de la Inquisición Medieval y Moderna (Copenhagen, 1978), 37.

105. Information about the life-style of these families comes from hearings held before the royal captain of the city and community of Teruel. The royal order to investigate the truth of their claim that they should be considered Old Christians is in AHN, *Inquisition*, September 21, 1575, lib. 916, ffs. 224–225. Also see October 13, 1575, lib. 916, ffs. 226–227, 228, 229, 230–232v.

106. See the trial of Diego de Arcos, AHN, *Inquisition*, March 23, 1582, leg. 549#1, exp. 4, and Francisco López Royz, November 26, 1581, leg. 552#2, exp. 20.

107. AHN, *Inquisition*, May 22, 1581, lib. 913, ffs. 121–121v, 139. García Cárcel, *Herejía*, 104, implies wrongly that this suggestion was first put forward in 1582.

108. AHN, *Inquisition*, July 30, 1587, leg. 1791, nf. Also see Boronat y Barrachina, *Los moriscos*, 1:625, 630. García Cárcel, *Herejía*, cites only Boronat's summary of this document and not the document itself.

109. Friedman, *Spanish Captives*, 6–7.

110. Contreras, "Las causas de fé," 37.

111. AGS, *Estado*, January 30, 1608, leg. 212, as quoted in Boronat y Barrachina, *Los moriscos*, 2:457–474.

112. Boronat y Barrachina, *Los moriscos*, 2:150–151; García Cárcel, *Herejía*, 124.

113. Bleda, *Defensio fidei*, 597–601, prints the expulsion decree.

114. For the revelation told to the Valencian noble, Juan Boil de Arenos, by his confessor, Fray Luis Bertrán, in an effort to get him to ask the king to expel the Moriscos, see Fonseca, *Justa expulsión*, 163. For heavenly attempts to warn Spain of impending doom if the Moriscos were allowed to remain, see ibid., 166–169.

115. Halperin Donghi, *Un conflicto*, 183.

116. Archivo General Central, *Inquisición de Valencia*, leg. 604, as quoted in Boronat y Barrachina, *Los moriscos*, 2:657–665.

117. García Cárcel, *Herejía*, 92.

118. Archivo del Real Colegio de Corpus Christi, January 31, 1608, Sig. I, 7, 8, 63, as quoted in Boronat y Barrachina, *Los moriscos*, 2:142–143; García Cárcel, *Herejía*, 123.

119. AHN, *Inquisition*, June 13, 1606, lib. 918, ffs. 761–768. García Cárcel, *Herejía*, 122, discusses this memorial but glosses over this aspect of the proposal.

120. AHN, *Inquisition*, January 30, 1609, lib. 933, ffs. 127–127v. Also see the tribunal's letter suggesting several cases of Moriscos who had been condemned to the galleys for release in a payment that could be used "para que se pudiese fabricar la casa y cárcel de la penitencia." AHN, *Inquisition*, lib. 935, ffs. 125–126. Also see AHN, *Inquisition*, August 21, 1608, lib. 332, ff. 184–185, for additional commutations.

121. These statistics are based on 1,681 Moriscos tried by the tribunal from 1580 to 1615.

122. Contreras, "Las causas de fé," 37.

123. AHN, *Inquisition*, March 7, 1615, leg. 506, f. 460. For a detailed account of these rebellions, see Bleda, *Defenso fidei*, 590–591.

124. Lapeyre, *La géographie*, 64, 66.

125. Friedman, *Spanish Captives*, 210–221.

126. Ibid., 24; AHN, *Inquisition*, October 16, 1612, lib. 919, ff. 514–514v; March 26, 1613, leg. 553#2, exp. 18; October 30, 1624, leg. 548#2, exp. 21.

127. AHN, *Inquisition*, February 3, 1615, leg. 506#1, f. 454.

128. AHN, *Inquisition*, October 29, 1624, leg. 548#1, exp. 21.

129. AHN, *Inquisition*, August 27, 1625, leg. 507#1, f. 514.

130. Between 1615 and 1700, there were 204 cases, but they were heavily concentrated in the first years after the expulsion. Contreras, "Las causas de fé," 37.

131. The figures on the eighteenth and nineteenth centuries are my own.

132. Domínguez Ortíz and Vincent, *Historia*, 109.

133. AHN, *Inquisition*, January 26, 1568, leg. 548#1, exp. 2, f. 30v.

134. Domínguez Ortíz and Vincent, *Historia*, 109. The so-called alfaquis (Islamic religious teachers) were usually just private individuals with some religious learning. AHN, *Inquisition*, October 22, 1591, leg. 550#2, exp. 20.

135. AHN, *Inquisition*, October, 1965; January 6, 1566, lib. 911, ff. 598, 603.

136. Domínguez Ortíz and Vincent, *Historia*, 121–124. See the case of the famous Morisco physician, Jerónimo Pachet, who was tried in 1567 and 1580 and deprived of the right to practice medicine in his second sentence: AHN, *Inquisition*, October 23, 1580, lib. 936, ff. 275v, 276. Also see the case of Gaspar Capdal, the brilliant young Morisco physician (24) who was deprived of the right to practice medicine: AHN, *Inquisition*, January 7, 1607, leg. 549#2, exp. 19.

137. This conclusion is based on the 677 Moriscos tried by the Holy Office whose occupations are stated in the relaciones de causas.

138. For example, 4.3 percent of those tried for Protestantism were professionals.

139. Casey, *The Kingdom*, 84.

140. Ibid., 33.

141. Domínguez Ortíz and Vincent, *Historia*, 120.

142. Halperin Donghi cautions us not to exaggerate the wealth and importance of these petty traders. Halperin Donghi, *Un conflicto*, 73–75.

143. Casey, *The Kingdom*, 40, points out that 3 percent of the landless Moriscos of Játiva had workshops.

144. Casey, *The Kingdom*, 43–44, compares the farms held by Moriscos with the requirements of the Old Christian settlers after the expulsion.

145. Ibid., 38–39; Halperin Donghi, *Un conflicto*, 86.

146. AHN, *Inquisition*, July 1, 1596, lib. 917, ffs. 1007–1010. Also see the inventory of the possessions of Beatriz Gamir, AHN, *Inquisition*, September 5, 1583, leg. 551#2, exp. 19.

147. Women comprised 28.5 percent of the Morisco offenders and a remarkably similar 30 percent of the Judaizers. This is a very high percentage compared to such "male" offenses as propositions, where they only made up 6.1 percent of the offenders.

148. AHN, *Inquisition*, June 13, 1606, lib. 918, f. 766.

VII: Illuminism, Erasmianism, and Protestantism:
The Problem of Religious Dissent

1. Lea, *A History*, 3:411.

2. Kamen, *Inquisition and Society*, 198–199.

3. Ibid., 203.

4. García Cárcel, *Herejía*, 343, mentions this in general terms. The statistic comes from my own survey of the relaciónes de causas. More than 89 percent of the accused were Old Christians.

5. Kamen, *Inquisition and Society*, 202. J. Martínez de Bujanda, "Literatura y Inquisición en España en el siglo XVI," in Joaquín Pérez Villanueva, ed., *La Inquisición española: Nueva visión, nuevos horizontes* (Madrid: Siglo Veintiuno, 1980), 587, discusses the anticlerical humor in Lazarillo de Tormes which remained even after it had been expurgated by order of the Holy Office.

6. Lea, *A History*, 4:139, 328.

7. AHN, *Inquisition*, September 17, 1564, leg. 519#1, exp. 2.

8. Kamen, *Inquisition and Society*, 202.

9. For an account of the official support for the reform of the clergy, see Azcona, *Isabel la Católica*, 469–484, 565–608.

10. Antonio Márquez, *Los alumbrados: Orígines y filosofía* (Madrid: Taurus, 1972), 127–136.

11. Lea, *A History*, 4:6–7.

12. Márquez, *Los alumbrados*, 125–126. Melquiades Andrés Martín, "Pensamiento teológico y vivencia religiosa en la reforma española," in José Luis González Novalín, ed., *Historia de la Iglesia*, 3, pt. 2:346–350.

13. Marcel Bataillon, *Erasmo y España*, trans. Antonio Alatorre, 2d ed. (Madrid: Fondo de Cultura Económica, 1979), 183–184.

14. Lea, *A History*, 4:3.

15. Ibid., 9.

16. Andrés Martín, "Pensamiento teológico," 279–282.

17. Bataillon, *Erasmo*, 180–182.

18. Márquez, *Los alumbrados*, 64–69; Lea, *A History*, 4:7–14.

19. Márquez, *Los alumbrados*, 25.

20. For the Illuminists of Extremadura, see Alvaro Huerga, *Historia de los alumbrados*, 2 vols. (Madrid: Fundación Universitaria Española, 1978). For later manifestations, see Lea, *A History*, 4:41–42.

21. Huerga, *Historia*, 1:382.

22. AHN, *Inquisition*, January 14, 1538, leg. 533#1, exp. 5.

23. Contreras, "Las causas de fé," 28, 50, fails to list any Alumbrado cases for the tribunal for the period 1560–1700. While it is true that most of the cases I place under this heading were not called Alumbrado by the tribunal, I have preferred to read the record and classify them in accordance with the generally accepted definitions of Illuminism. The case of Fray Vicente Oriente was definitely called Alumbrado. AHN, *Inquisition*, June 22, 1649, leg. 529#2, exp. 5.

24. These were the words of one of her chief devotees, Remigio Choza, the vicar of the parish church of San Miguel in Valencia city. AHN, *Inquisition*, April 8, 1669, lib. 944, f. 54v.

25. AHN, *Inquisition*, June 9, 1672, lib. 944, f. 48v.

26. Ibid., f. 44.

27. Ibid., April 8, 1669 (Choza), f. 36; June 9, 1672 (Torres), f. 46.

28. Ibid., July 10, 1668, f. 36.

29. Ibid., June 9, 1672, f. 46.

30. Ibid., June 9, 1672, f. 48v.

31. Ibid., January 14, 1669, f. 66.

32. AHN, *Inquisition*, February 18, 1675, lib. 944, f. 64.

33. For the trials and sentences of the priests, see AHN, *Inquisition*, February 13, 1675, lib. 944, f. 52v; August 26, 1676, leg. 529#2, exp. 3, and March 27, 1675, leg. 529#2, exp. 4. José Navarro went mad in his cell and died in Valencia's general hospital without regaining his sanity; Choza died in the general hospital of Alicante while still serving his sentence.

34. See chap. 1.

35. Josefa Clement was not imprisoned until July 19, 1674, even though testimony against her had been received as early as May 8, 1668, and her general confession on June 9, 1668.

36. For a discussion of the spirituali, see Dermont Fenlon, *Heresy and Obedience in Tridentine Italy* (Cambridge: Cambridge University Press, 1972).

37. Márquez, *Los alumbrados*, 172–175.

38. This bull merely reinforced earlier papal support even though it was far from the full protection hoped for by Erasmians like Alfonso de Valdés. Bataillon, *Erasmo*, 264.

39. Ibid., 262–263.

40. Ibid., 265.

41. Ibid., 309–310.

42. AHN, *Inquisition*, January 19, 1536, leg. 531#1, exp. 38. Mezquita was only held for a total of ten days. He was released on January 29, 1529.

43. Bataillon, *Erasmo*, 975–981.

44. Pinto Crespo, *Inquisición y control*, 155–156.

45. Ibid., 157.

46. Bataillon, *Erasmo*, 702.

47. Jean-Pierre Dedieu, "Le modèle religieuse: Le refus de la Réforme et le contrôle de la pensée," in B. Bennassar, ed., *L'Inquisition espagnole*, 279–281.

48. These were essentially the views of Dr. Constantino, one of the leading Erasmians of Seville. Bataillon, *Erasmo*, 536.

49. González Martínez, "Bandolerismo," 85.

50. Bataillon, *Erasmo*, 607, 728.

51. González Martínez, "Bandolerismo," 86–87. AHN, *Inquisition*, December 9, 1562, leg. 503#1, exp. 1, f. 43v.

52. AHN, *Inquisition*, Letter from Arquer, October 22, 1551, leg. 109#1, exp. 1, ffs. 89–91v.

53. AHN, *Inquisition*, March 20, 1573, leg. 109#1, exp. 1, nf.

54. Bataillon, *Erasmo*, 730–731.

55. For this incident, see chap. 1.

56. Bataillon, *Erasmo*, 732. For the sentence itself, see Manuel Ardit Lucas, *La Inquisició al país València* (Valencia: Sanchis i Cardona, 1970), 73.

57. AHN, *Inquisition*, May 2, 1562, leg. 503#1, exp. 1, f. 26. For the tribunal's complaint about its poverty, see June 9, 1562, ffs. 29–30.

58. Lea, *A History*, 3:453. García Cárcel, *Herejía*, 336, asserts mistakenly that the trial lasted "scarcely a year" when it actually took more than 17 months.

59. AHN, *Inquisition*, September 22, 1564, leg. 503#1, exp. 1, nf.

60. AHN, *Inquisition*, 1526, leg. 800#3, exp. 11.

61. AHN, *Inquisition*, June 23, 1751, leg. 530#2, exp. 15; Lea, *A History*, 3:477–479.

62. Abel Poitrineau, "La inmigración francesa en el reino de Valencia," *Moneda y Crédito* 137 (June 1976): 106–107, 112–113.

63. AHN, *Inquisition*, November 6, 1574, lib. 913, f. 232.

64. AHN, *Inquisition*, April 17, 1566, lib. 911, ffs. 666–666v.

65. AHN, *Inquisition*, June 19, 1568, lib. 497, ffs. 105–106.

66. AHN, *Inquisition*, April 19, 1587, lib. 937, ffs. 42v–43v.

67. AHN, *Inquisition*, September 9, 1583, leg. 531#1, exp. 6.

68. AHN, *Inquisition*, October 12, 1564, leg. 530#1, exp. 8.

69. AHN, *Inquisition*, June 26, 1612, leg. 811#2, f. 283. For a similar case, see AHN, *Inquisition*, August 1, 1634, leg. 803#1, ffs. 32–33.

70. AHN, *Inquisition*, May 17, 1597, leg. 505#2, f. 104; Lea, *A History*, 3:463.

71. Lea, *A History*, 3:464.

72. AHN, *Inquisition*, October 8, 1605, lib. 497, ffs. 264–265.

73. AHN, *Inquisition*, April 22, 1605, lib. 497, ffs. 265–266.

74. Lea, *A History*, 3:465.

75. BNM, June 10, 1609; MSS. 287, f. 13; Lea, *A History*, 3:465.

76. AHN, *Inquisition*, May 19, 1620, ffs. 309v–310v.

77. AHN, *Inquisition*, October 24, 1647, lib. 497, ffs. 113v–114.

78. AHN, *Inquisition*, September 15, December 16, 1651, leg. 503#3, ffs. 413, 414; Lea, *A History*, 3:469.

79. AHN, *Inquisition*, October 27, 1664, leg. 551#1, f. 278.

80. Kamen, *The War of Succession*, 292.

81. Dedeiu, "Le modèle," 291.

82. Ibid., 289.

83. AHN, *Inquisition*, May 23, 1565, leg. 548#1, exp. 2.

VIII: The Inquisition in the Post-Tridentine Era

1. Hubert Jedin, *A History of the Council of Trent*, 2 vols. (New York: B. Herder, 1961), 2:10, 29.

2. Jedin, *A History*, 2:331.

3. Peter Burke, *Popular Culture in Early Modern Europe* (London: Temple Smith, 1978), 220–221. For a discussion of the relative role of reforming bishops and the Inquisition in imposing Tridentine reforms in Cuenca, see Sara Nalle, *Religion and Reform in a Spanish Diocese: Cuenca, 1645–1650* (Ph.D. dissertation, Johns Hopkins University, 1983), 54.

4. Burke, *Popular Culture*, 211–212.

5. Lea, *A History*, 4:328.

6. Tomás y Valiente, *El derecho penal*, 224.

7. Lea, *A History*, 4:329.

8. Eymerich and Peña, *Le manuel*, 63–64.

9. Lea, *A History*, 4:331–332.

10. Ibid., 4:329–330.

11. García Cárcel, *Orígenes*, 204.

12. García Cárcel, *Herejía*, 343. The overall figures are my own, as Contreras fails to differentiate between blasphemy and propositions.

13. AHN, *Inquisition*, January 14, 1612, leg. 804#2, f. 235v.

14. AHN, *Inquisition*, May 3, 1647, lib. 941, ffs. 295–298.

15. AHN, *Inquisition*, July 23, 1643, leg. 803#1, nf.

16. Antonio Maravall, *La Cultura del Barroco: Análisis de una estructura histórica* (Barcelona: Ariel, 1975), 138–139.

17. Burke, *Popular Culture*, 212–213.

18. AHN, *Inquisition*, December 14, 1742, leg. 522#6.

19. AHN, *Consejos*, December 20, 1701, leg. 4759, as quoted in Tomás y Valiente, *El derecho penal*, 424–426.

20. Jean Pierre Dedieu, "Le modèle sexual: La défense du mariage chrétien," in Bennassar, *L'Inquisition espagnole*, 326–327.

21. AHN, *Inquisition*, December 14, 1474, lib. 713, f. 335.

22. For the tribunals of Toledo and Logroño, see Dedieu, "Le modèle." The figures on Valencia are my own.

23. Lea, *A History*, 4:316.

24. Dedieu, "Le modèle sexuel," 315–316.

25. AHN, *Inquisition*, September 15, 1563, leg. 503, f. 58.

26. AHN, *Inquisition*, July 7, 1567, leg. 518#1, exp. 11.

27. AHN, *Inquisition*, October 1, 1746, leg. 518#2, exp. 21.

28. Lea, *A History*, 4:319.

29. Dedieu, "Le modèle sexuel," 319.

30. Lea, *A History*, 4:322–323.

31. AHN, *Inquisition*, December 11, 1765, leg. 518#2, exp. 15.

32. AHN, *Inquisition*, October 26, 1569, leg. 518#1, exp. 9.

33. AHN, *Inquisition*, September 17, 1564, leg. 518#1, exp. 13.

34. Tomás y Valiente, *El derecho penal*, 226–227.

35. Bartolomé Bennassar, "Le modèle sexuel: L'Inquisition d'Aragon et le répression des péchés 'abominables,'" in Bennassar, *L'Inquisition espagnole*, 342; AHN, *Inquisition*, September 30, 1687, lib. 932, f. 337v; Cerdan de Tallada, *Visita*, 198.

36. Lea, *A History*, 4:363. García Cárcel, *Herejía*, 288, seems unaware that Clement VII's Brief of February 24, 1524, gave jurisdiction over sodomy only to the tribunals of Aragon.

37. Bennassar, "Le modèle," 346–347.

38. García Cárcel, *Orígenes*, 211.

39. García Cárcel, *Herejía*, 288, follows Contreras when he asserts that the tribunal tried 379 cases of sodomy and bestiality between 1540 and 1700, but these figures are unreliable because Contreras lumped these offenses with several others so that the figure of 379 must include many offenses unconnected with the "crimes against nature." Contreras, "Las causas de fé," 18. Rafael Carrasco, *Inquisición y represión sexual en Valencia* (Barcelona: Laertes, 1985), 38, counts 347 cases between 1566 and 1775, 259 of which referred to male homosexuality, but Carrasco is not aware of the existence of ARV, *Clero*, leg. 161, and has therefore left out many eighteenth-century cases.

40. AHN, *Inquisition*, November 7, 1572, leg. 503#1, nf.

41. AHN, *Inquisition*, January 28, 1573, leg. 503#1, nf.

42. Lea, *A History*, 4:371.

43. AHN, *Inquisition*, January 2, 1572, leg. 503#1, nf.; Lea, *A History*, 4:370; AHN, *Inquisition*, December 12, 1573, lib. 913, f. 163.

44. AHN, *Inquisition*, November 7, 1572, leg. 503#1.

45. AHN, *Inquisition*, August 22, 1616, leg. 559#1, exp. 7.

46. Lea, *A History*, 4:369.

47. AHN, *Inquisition*, November 14, 1624, leg. 507#1, f. 392.

48. García Martínez, 86–87.

49. AHN, *Inquisition*, April 23, 1573, leg. 503#1, nf. The tribunal warned the Suprema in this letter that Francisco Tallada and Miguel Centelles were in extreme personal danger as a result of their testimony.

50. AHN, *Inquisition*, June 18, 1573, leg. 503#1, nf.; February 21, 1575, leg. 503#1, nf.

51. AHN, *Inquisition*, November 20, 1572, leg. 503#1, nf.

52. AHN, *Inquisition*, October 14, 1574, leg. 503, nf.

53. AHN, *Inquisition*, November 18, 1575, lib. 913, ffs. 571, 575.

54. AHN, *Inquisition*, April 23, 1571, leg. 503#1, nf., for a list of ten leading Valencian nobles already punished or under suspicion for aiding their Morisco vassals.

55. García Cárcel, *Herejía*, 293. In his brief comment on this case, García Cárcel makes no mention of the original sentence, which was noted in Lea, *A History*, 4:370, and leaves the mistaken impression that he was not punished at all.

56. AHN, *Inquisition*, July 19, 1613–August 22, 1616, leg. 559#1, exp. 7.

57. AHN, *Inquisition*, August 9, 1581, leg. 559#1, exp. 2.

58. AHN, *Inquisition*, March 25, 1621, leg. 518#1, exp. 5.

59. Tomás y Valiente, *El derecho penal*, 229.

60. Carrasco, *Inquisición y represión*, 31.

61. AHN, *Inquisition*, February 9, 1609, leg. 803#1, f. 429v.

62. AHN, *Inquisition*, July 24, 1666, leg. 802#1, f. 346.

63. Carrasco, *Inquisición y represión*, 120–121.

64. AHN, *Inquisition*, April 23, 1574, leg. 559#3, exp. 16.

65. AHN, *Inquisition*, May 15, 1758, leg. 560#1, exp. 7; Carrasco, *Inquisición y represión*, 25, discusses this case.

66. AHN, *Inquisition*, May 16, 1796, leg. 560#1, exp. 3. A similar easy-going attitude toward homosexuality may be seen in Bouchard's *Confessions* written in the seventeenth century which contains an account of casual homosexuality among schoolmates at a Jesuit academy. Aldous Huxley, *The Devils of Loudun* (New York: Harper, 1952), 10. All this is a far

cry from the "massive societal rejection" of homosexual behavior seen among the popular classes by Carrasco, *Inquisición y represión*, 22.

67. AHN, *Inquisition*, February 5, 1573, lib. 913, ffs. 13–14.

68. See above.

69. AHN, *Inquisition*, September 30, 1687, lib. 932,, ffs. 337–338. Carrasco, *Inquisición y represión*, 63–65, presents ten cases in which the Suprema intervened to alter sentences. In some cases, the Suprema made the penalty somewhat harsher, but it never imposed the death penalty and, in three cases, reduced it to galley service.

70. Carrasco, *Inquisición y represión*, 69, has a considerably higher figure for those relaxed for sodomy, but the additional cases I draw from the eighteenth century tend to reduce the percentage of executions and other heavier penalties.

71. E. P. Thompson, *Whigs and Hunters: The Origins of the Black Act* (New York: Pantheon, 1975), 260.

72. Alfred Soman, "Les Procès de Sorcellerie au Parlement de Paris (1565–1640)," *Annales* ESC (July–August 1977): 810–811.

73. Tomás y Valiente, *El derecho penal*, 230–231.

74. H. C. Erik Midlefort, *Witch-hunting in Southwestern Germany* (Stanford: Stanford University Press, 1972), 18.

75. Mary O'Neil, "Magical Healing, Love Magic, and the Inquisition in Late-Sixteenth-Century Modena," in Stephen Haliczer, ed., *Inquisition and Society in Early Modern Europe* (London: Croom-Helm, 1986), 91.

76. Gaspar Navarro, *Tribunal de superstición ladina* (Huesca: Pedro Bluson, 1631), 1631, ffs. 52–55v. Navarro cites the *Malleus Maleficarium* quite frequently; see ffs. 56v–57, 61–62.

77. Lea, *A History*, 4:217.

78. Henningsen, *The Witches' Advocate*, 176.

79. Lea, *A History*, 4:212–213.

80. Henningsen, *The Witches' Advocate*, 371–373.

81. AHN, *Inquisition*, June 19, 1588, lib. 937, ffs. 74–75v. For the child witches of Germany, see Midlefort, *Witch-hunting*, 144–145, 159, 179.

82. AHN, *Inquisition*, December 15, 1642, lib. 941, ffs. 209–210.

83. AHN, *Inquisition*, March 14, 1640, January 9, 1648, lib. 941, ffs. 324v–326.

84. Porcar, *Cosas evanguadas*, 69, 78, 79, 101, 114, 121.

85. Keith Thomas, *Religion and the Decline of Magic* (London: Weidenfeld and Nicolson, 1971), 25.

86. Ibid., 29.

87. Ibid., 49–50.

88. Lea, *A History*, 4:198–199.

89. AHN, *Inquisition*, October 7, 1732, leg. 514, f. 60.

90. AHN, *Inquisition*, March 18, 1680, leg. 804#2, nf.

91. AHN, *Inquisition*, January 9, 1648, lib. 941, f. 326.

92. AHN, *Inquisition*, January 28, 1651, lib. 941, ffs. 346–347.

93. AHN, *Inquisition*, October 3, 1642, lib. 941, ffs. 213–214.

94. AHN, *Inquisition*, November 26, 1653, leg. 523#1, exp. 7.

95. Ibid.

96. Midlefort, *Witch-hunting*, 183–185.

97. Jedin, *A History*, 25; T. M. Parker, "The Papacy, Catholic Reform and Christian Missions," in R. B. Wernham, ed., *New Cambridge Modern History* 3 (Cambridge: Cambridge University Press, 1960), 45.

98. Jedin, *A History*, 355.

99. Bossy, "The Counter-Reformation and the People of Catholic Europe," *Past and Present*, no. 47 (May 1970): 52–53.

100. Jedin, *A History*, 99.

101. Antonio Mestre, *Ilustración y reforma de la Iglesia: Pensamiento político-religioso de D. Gregorio Mayans y Síscar* (Valencia: Ayuntamiento de Oliva, 1968), 223–224.

102. Pinto Crespo, *Inquisición y control*, 253; Lea, *A History*, 4:99.

103. Kamen, *Inquisition and Society*, 205.

104. Burke, *Popular Culture*, 211.

105. See Lea, *A History*, 4:139, for definitions of propositions.

106. AHN, *Inquisition*, March 13, 1691, leg. 558#5, exp. 5.

107. AHN, *Inquisition*, August 3, 1638, "méritos de la causa de fé contra Fray Jerónimo Navarro," lib. 926, ffs. 7–12; June 3, 1630, lib. 923, f. 600.

108. AHN, *Inquisition*, November 10, 1629, lib. 923, f. 574.

109. AHN, *Inquisition*, September 18, 1638, lib. 923, f. 573.

110. For a discussion of the role of the religious orders in education, see Francisco Martín Hernández, "La formación del clero en los siglos XVII y XVIII," in Antonio Mestre, ed., *Historia de la Iglesia*, 4:524–581.

111. AHN, *Inquisition*, November 22, 1680, leg. 804#2, nf.

112. AHN, *Inquisition*, November 18, 1698, leg. 1786#1, exp. 6.

113. Pinto Crespo, *Inquisición y control*, 197–233; J. M. López Piñero, *Ciencia y técnica en la sociedad española de los siglos XVI y XVII* (Barcelona: Labor Universitaria, 1979), 197–204, 373–374.

114. AHN, *Inquisition*, April 26, 1638, leg. 804#2, ffs. 483–484.

115. López Piñero, *Ciencia y técnica*, 316–317, 389–393, 415.

116. AHN, *Inquisition*, June 7, 1691, leg. 803#2, f. 382.

117. AHN, *Inquisition*, November 8, 1691, leg. 803#2, nf.

118. Jedin, *A History*, 371–372, 388.

119. The bishop of Sinigaglia voiced the concerns of many of his col-

leagues when he demanded "greater care and reverence in the administration of the sacraments." Jedin, *A History*, 384.

120. Lea, *A History*, 4:100.

121. Ibid., 4:96; AHN, *Inquisition*, September 17, 1625, leg. 507#1, f. 549.

122. Lea, *A History*, 4:99.

123. AHN, *Inquisition*, March 20, 1563, lib. 324, ffs. 39–40.

124. Juan Machado de Chaves, *Perfecto confessor y cura de almas*, 2 vols. (Barcelona: Pedro de la Cavalleria, 1641), 2:776.

125. See the case of Fray Lorenzo de Santissima Trinidad, a friar obsessed with masturbation who constantly brought it up while confessing Josefa de Jesús María. AHN, *Inquisition*, May 21, 1710, leg. 564#3, exp. 13.

126. AHN, *Inquisition*, August 24, 1764, leg. 564#1, exp. 13.

127. AHN, *Inquisition*, May 4, 1691, leg. 803#1, nf.

128. Lea, *A History*, 4:123–124.

129. AHN, *Inquisition*, April 14, 1750, leg. 2317#1, nf.

130. AHN, *Inquisition*, May 13, 1764, leg. 562#2, exp. 8.

131. AHN, *Inquisition*, December 12, 1577, lib. 497, ffs. 183–184.

132. Lea, *A History*, 4:126. See the case of Pascual Giner who lost his benefice and could no longer support his aged mother and sisters. AHN, *Inquisition*, July 4, 1713, leg. 2309, nf.

IX: Decline and Abolition of the Holy Office in Valencia

1. Kamen, *The War of Succession*, 284–286.

2. AHN, *Inquisition*, December 16, 1710, leg. 2308, nf.

3. AHN, *Inquisition*, May 11, 1707, leg. 2308#1, nf.

4. Játiva was sacked and practically destroyed after being captured on May 24. Kamen, *The War of Succession*, 296–297.

5. AHN, *Inquisition*, May 19, 1707, leg. 2308#1, nf.

6. Lea, *A History*, 4:225.

7. AHN, *Inquisition*, July 26, 1707, leg. 2308#1, nf.

8. Lea, *A History*, 4:276. On this occasion, Balmaseda signed himself "Inquisidor y juez apostólico contra los eclesiásticos disidentes."

9. AHN, *Inquisition*, January 14, 1710, leg. 503#3, exp. 7, ffs. 127v–129.

10. AHN, *Inquisition*, June 19, 1708, leg. 2308#1, nf. For Macanaz's role in supervising the confiscation of rebel property, see Kamen, *The War of Succession*, 321. Later, when the tribunal attempted to take advantage of an ambiguous clause in its grant to take actual possession of the

village, the Council of Castile acted to stop it. AHN, *Inquisition*, January 29, 1709, leg. 503#3, exp. 7, ffs. 97–98v.

11. Lea, *A History*, 1:315, 319.

12. AHN, *Inquisition*, February 10, 1725, leg. 514#1; Kamen, *The War of Succession*, 320.

13. AHN, *Inquisition*, March 10, 1745, leg. 2315, nf.

14. AHN, *Inquisition*, July 29, 1760, lib. 922, nf.

15. Domínguez Ortíz, *Sociedad y estado*, 265.

16. AHN, *Inquisition*, February 23, 1706, leg. 2308, nf.

17. Vicente Martínez Santos, "La Sedería de Valencia 1750–1800," *Moneda y Crédito* 134 (1975):116.

18. Manuel Ardit Lucas, *Revolución liberal y revuelta campesina* (Barcelona: Ariel, 1977), 22. Also see Fernando Andrés Robres, *Crédito y propiedad de la tierra en el país Valenciano* (Valencia: Edicions Alfons el Magnànim, 1987), 240–251.

19. Ricardo García Cárcel, "Las rentas de la Inquisición de Valencia en el siglo XVIII," *Estudis* 4 (1975): 236–237; AHN, *Inquisition*, December 9, 1724, leg. 514#1, f. 69.

20. AHN, *Inquisition*, December 12, 1780, leg. 2324, nf.; November 30, 1784, leg. 3303, nf.

21. José Antonio Ferrer Benimeli, "Inquisición y Masonería," in *Historia de la Inquisición en España y América*, 4 vols., J. Pérez Villanueva and B. Escandell Bonet, eds. (Madrid: Biblioteca de Autores Cristianos, 1984), I:1288.

22. Ibid., 1298.

23. Ibid., 1303.

24. Teófanes Egido, "La Inquisición de una España en guerra," in *Historia de la Inquisición*, 1243.

25. Marcelin Defourneaux, *L'Inquisition espagnole et les livres français au XVIII siècle* (Paris: Presses Universitaires de France, 1963), 62.

26. This cedula is attached to several bigamy cases tried by the Valencia tribunal. See AHN, *Inquisition*, January 16, 1776, leg. 516#1, f. 2; December 12, 1782, leg. 516#1, f. 50.

27. Francisco Martí Gilabert, *La abolición de la Inquisición en España* (Pamplona: Universidad de Navarra, 1975), 38.

28. Teófanes Egido, "La Inquisición," 1244–1246.

29. AHN, *Inquisition*, May 4, 1790; September 24, 1790, leg. 562#1, exp. 6.

30. AHN, *Inquisition*, lib. 503, f. 122, quoted in J. Martínez Millán, "Los cambios en el Santo Oficio español," in *Historia de la Inquisición*, I:1372.

31. AHN, *Inquisition*, January 27, 1747, leg. 2316, nf.

32. AHN, *Inquisition*, June 4, 1756; February 25, 1767, leg. 558#3, exp. 33.

33. AHN, *Inquisition*, November 10, 1773, leg. 534, exp. 24.

34. AHN, *Inquisition*, January 17, 1775, leg. 534, exp. 24.

35. AHN, *Inquisition*, February 3, 1637, leg. 509#1, nf.

36. AHN, *Inquisition*, July 18, 1739; August 7, 1739, leg. 2351#1, nf.

37. AHN, *Inquisition*, June 22, 1705, lib. 498, ffs. 237–237v.

38. Martínez Millán, "Los cambios," 1378.

39. Ibid., 1277.

40. AHN, *Inquisition*, June 28, 1752, leg. 2317, nf.

41. AHN, *Inquisition*, June 25, 1785, leg. 3303, nf.

42. AHN, *Inquisition*, March 12, 1749, leg. 2316, nf.

43. AHN, *Inquisition*, August 13, 1715, leg. 2309, nf.

44. AHN, *Inquisition*, August 17, 26, 1729, leg. 514#1, ffs. 9–9v.

45. AHN, *Inquisition*, September 23, 1760, lib. 932, f. 2309.

46. H. C. Lea Library, University of Pennsylvania, *Manuscripts*, April 24, 1806, leg. 64, nf.

47. Lea, *A History*, 4:388.

48. AHN, *Inquisition*, November 29, 1788, leg. 2326, nf.

49. AHN, *Inquisition*, December 5, 1788, leg. 2326, nf.

50. AHN, *Inquisition*, July 27, 1762, leg. 604#3, exp. 13.

51. AHN, *Inquisition*, October 23, 1747, leg. 617#1, exp. 6.

52. AHN, *Inquisition*, February 29, 1774, leg. 615#3, exp. 12; August 7, 1773, leg. 621#1, exp. 2.

53. AHN, *Inquisition*, December 5, 1788, leg. 2326, nf.

54. AHN, *Inquisition*, May 2, 1796, leg. 2389, nf. For a discussion of educational reform at Valencia University, see Richard Herr, *The Eighteenth-Century Revolution in Spain* (Princeton: Princeton University Press, 1969), 166, 169.

55. AHN, *Inquisition*, May 6, 1815, leg. 2321, nf.

56. Mestre, *Ilustración*, 448.

57. Gilabert, *La abolición*, 178–183.

58. Ibid., 186–189.

59. In 1782, for example, Inquisitor-General Felipe Beltrán seriously considered issuing a new and more liberal index of prohibited books: Gaspar Gómez de la Serna, *Jovellanos o el español perdido* (Madrid: Sala, 1975), 157.

60. AHN, *Inquisition*, September 9, 1715, leg. 2309, ffs. 15–20.

61. AHN, *Inquisition*, December 20, 1803, leg. 2330#1, nf. Gregorio Mayans y Síscar was even used as a calificador by the Valencian tribunal. Manuel Mayans y Síscar, his brother, served the tribunal as secretary during the 1730s and 1740s. Mestre, *Ilustración*, 203, 423. See AHN,

Inquisition, March 15, 1735, leg. 1322, exp. 8, for the genealogy of Manuel Mayans y Síscar.

62. Mestre, *Ilustración*, 371.

63. *Biblioteca Archivo Hispano Mayansiana*, Andrés Orbe to J. A. Mayans, Valladolid, September 25, 1748, as quoted in Mestre, *Ilustración*, 423.

64. Gilabert, *La abolición*, 151.

65. The number of persons holding inquisitorial licenses to read prohibited books increased dramatically during the century; Defourneaux, *L'Inquisition espagnole*, 135. Pablo de Olavide's papal license to read prohibited books was confirmed by the Inquisitor-General.

66. AHN, *Inquisition*, May 7, 12, 1792, leg. 2327#1, nf.

67. Ardit Lucas, *Revolución liberal*, 97.

68. Defourneaux, *L'Inquisition espagnole*, 86–88, 99. Jean Sarrailh, *La España ilustrada de la segunda mitad del siglo XVIII* (México: Fondo de Cultura Económica, 1957), 311–312.

69. Gaspar Melchor de Jovellanos, *Representación a Carlos IV sobre lo que era el tribunal de la Inquisición*, cited by Gilabert, *La Inquisición*, 45.

70. Herr, *The Eighteenth-Century Revolution*, 282, 391–394.

71. AHN, *Inquisition*, January 7, 1794, leg. 516#3, f. 20.

72. AHN, *Inquisition*, March 12, 1799, leg. 517#1, ffs. 19–27.

73. AHN, *Inquisition*, June 26, 1800, leg. 517#1, f. 32.

74. H. C. Lea Library, University of Pennsylvania, *Manuscripts*, February 23, 1802, leg. 43, nf.; also see AHN, *Inquisition*, June 11, 1801, leg. 517#1, ffs. 78, 95, for correspondence with the Suprema regarding the transfer of funds realized from the sale of farms by the tribunal.

75. AHN, *Inquisition*, August 6, 1805, leg. 2331#1, nf.

76. AHN, *Inquisition*, August 9, 28, 1805, leg. 2331#1, nf.

77. AHN, *Inquisition*, November 5, 1808, leg. 2331#1, nf.

78. Lea, *A History*, 4:400.

79. AHN, *Inquisition*, May 11, 1808, "cartas del consejo," leg. 517#3, f. 31, as quoted in Lea, *A History*, 4:539–540; AHN, *Inquisition*, March 6, 1808, leg. 517#3, f. 31.

80. AHN, *Inquisition*, August 26, 1808, leg. 517#1, f. 31.

81. AHN, *Inquisition*, September 28, 1808, leg. 517#1, f. 33.

82. AHN, *Inquisition*, November 11, 1808, leg. 517#1, f. 34.

83. Lea, *A History*, 4:412, 414.

84. Gilabert, *La abolición*, 90.

85. Ibid., 194.

86. Lea, *A History*, 4:412, 414.

87. Ibid., 414.

88. Ibid., 424.

89. Ibid., 426–427.

90. AHN, *Inquisition*, March 28, 1817, leg. 5667#2, nf. This document is the account of Sernan Noguera from which forty reales was paid "al consejo por el nuevo impuesto."

91. Marcelin Defourneaux, "Les dernières années de L'Inquisition espagnole," *Annales Historiques de la Révolution Française* (1963):164–165.

92. AHN, *Inquisition*, February 1, 1815, leg. 517#1, nf.

93. AHN, *Inquisition*, October 26, 1814, leg. 2331#1, nf.

94. Lea, *A History*, 4:427.

95. Ibid., 4:428.

96. AHN, *Inquisition*, November 21, 1816, leg. 517#1, nf.

97. Ardit Lucas, *Revolución liberal*, 232–33; AHN, *Inquisition*, July 30, 1817, leg. 4671#2, nf.

98. AHN, *Inquisition*, December 16, 1818, leg. 4671#2, nf.

99. AHN, *Inquisition*, April 24, 1816, leg. 2331, nf.

100. AHN, *Inquisition*, June 4, 1815, leg. 517#2, nf.

101. AHN, *Inquisition*, January 26, March 1, 1816, leg. 2331#1, nf.

102. Ardit Lucas, *Revolución liberal*, 226.

103. AHN, *Inquisition*, January 20, 1817, leg. 2331#1, nf.

104. AHN, *Inquisition*, June 25, 1819, leg. 517#2, nf.

105. Ardit Lucas, *Revolución liberal*, 226.

106. Lea, *A History*, 4:437.

107. ARV, May 13, 1820, ffs. 326v–327.

108. ARV, May 13, 1820, leg. 1887, ffs. 354v–355, 356v–357; October 12, 1820, ffs. 366–367; October 13, 1820, ffs. 367v–368; October 17, 1820, f. 368; November 7, 1820, ffs. 369v–372.

109. Ibid., October 4, 1820, f. 365.

110. Lea, *A History*, 4:449.

111. Ibid., 458.

112. Luis Alonso Tejeda, *Ocaso de la Inquisición en los últimos años del reinado de Fernando VII* (Madrid: Zero, 1969), 90.

113. Ibid., 123,

114. Lea, *A History*, 4:461.

115. AHN, *Inquisition*, August 6, 1826, leg. 517#2, nf.

116. AHN, *Inquisition*, March 16, 1827, leg. 517#2.

117. Tejeda, *Ocaso de la Inquisición*, 160, 173–174.

118. Ibid., 220.

119. Lea, *A History*, 4:462.

120. Ibid., 459.

121. ARV, *Clero*, leg. 161, ffs. 63, 70, 75, 81.

122. Ibid., f. 81.

Conclusion

1. Pedro Galindo, *Parte Segundo del directorio de penitentes y práctica de una buena y prudente confesion* (Madrid: Antonio de Zafra, 1680), 450.

2. Henry Kamen, "Toleration and Dissent in Sixteenth-Century Spain: The Alternative Tradition," *The Sixteenth-Century Journal* (Spring 1988):4.

3. See chap. 8.

4. Fidèle de Ros, *Un maître de sainte Thérèse: Le père François de Osuna* (Paris: Gabriel Beauchesne, 1936), 221–226; Tomás Réluz, *Vida y virtudes del Fray Tomás Carbonell* (Madrid: Viuda de D. Francisco Nieto, 1695), 306, 325.

Glossary

actos positivos:	A decree of Philip IV in 1621 established that anyone who had obtained three positive results from genealogical investigations would be considered of "pure" lineage from then on.
auto de fé:	Ceremony at which the sentences of those convicted of offenses by the Holy Office would be read out to the public.
carta acordada:	Administrative regulation issued to the provincial tribunals by Madrid.
Bailía General:	The main royal treasury in the Kingdom of Valencia.
censals:	Long-term loans made on real estate.
ciutadà:	Distinguished citizens enjoying rentier status.
Diputació:	Standing committee of the Valencian Cortes responsible for collecting the subsidies granted the crown.
Estament Militar:	The Noble estate of the Valencian Cortes.
familiar:	Unpaid lay assistant to the Holy Office.
furs:	The traditional constitutional law of the Kingdom of Valencia.
insaculació:	Drawing for municipal offices from a list of names of persons previously approved for office holding.

jurat:	Chief municipal magistrate. In the city of Valencia, six jurats would form the city council.
lliura:	Valencian coin: 20 sous = 1 lliura, 21 sous = 1 Castilian ducat.
Peatge and Quema:	Royal customs duties belonging to the crown and free of any parliamentary grant.
relaciones de causas:	Summaries of completed cases sent to Madrid by the provincial tribunals.
Sanbenitos:	Penitential garments worn in public by the condemned.
taqiyya:	An attitude of external conformity adopted by many Moriscos to mask their continued belief in Islam.

Selected Bibliography

Archives

Archivo Histórico Nacional: Cartas acordadas
Cartas al Consejo
Cartas del Consejo
Expedientes de competencias
Expedientes de visitas
Informaciones genealógicas
Juntas de Hacienda
Libros de concordias
Libros de depósitos de pretendientes
Libros de testificaciones
Procesos criminales
Procesos de fé
Relaciones de fé
Varios

Archivo Municipal de Valencia: Manuels de consells y establiments
Libres de insaculació

Archivo del Reino de Valencia: Clero
Biblioteca Nacional de Madrid: Raros
Henry Charles Lea Library, The University of Pennsylvania:
Manuscripts

Printed Sources

Arguëllo, G. *Instrucciones del Santo Oficio de la Inquisición sumariamente, antiguas y modernas.* Madrid: Imprenta real, 1630.

Bleda, Jaime. *Defensio fidei in causa neophytorum, sive Morischorum.* Valentiae: Ioannem Chrusostomum Garriz, 1610.

————. *Coronica de los moros de España.* Valencia: Felipe Mey, 1618.

Castro, A. *Adversus omnes haereses.* Coloniae: Melchior Novesanus, 1539.

Carena, Caesare. *Tractatus de Officio Santissimae Inquisitionis.* Cremona: Baptistam Belpierum, 1655.

Eymerich, N., and Peña, F. *Le manuel des inquisiteurs.* Translated and edited by Louis Sala-Molins. Paris: Mouton, 1973.

Escolano, Gaspar. *Décadas de la insigne y coronada ciudad y Reyno de Valencia.* 2d ed. 2. vols. Edited by J. B. Perales. Valencia: Terraza Aliena, 1878–1880; reprint, Valencia: Librerias Paris-Valencia, 1980.

Fonseca, Damián. *Justa expulsión de los moriscos de España.* Rome: Jacomo Mascardo, 1612.

González Montano, Reginaldo. *A Discovery and Playne Declaration of Sundry Subtill Practices of the Holy Inquisition of Spain.* London: John Day, 1568.

Machado de Chaves, Juan. *Perfecto confessor y cura de almas,* 2 vols. Barcelona: Pedro de la Cavalleria, 1641.

Navarro, Gaspar. *Tribunal de la superstición ladina.* Huesca: Pedro Bluson, 1631.

Paramo, L. *De origine et progressu officii Santae Inquisitionis.* Madriti: Typographia regia, 1598.

Porcar, J. *Cosas evanguadas en la ciutat y regne de Valencia.* V. Castaneda Alcover, transcriber. Madrid: Cuerpo Facultativo de Archiveros, Bibliotecarios y Arqueólogos, 1934.

Simancas, Diego de. *De catholicis institutionibus.* Vallisoleti: Aegidii de Colomies, 1552.

Villadiego y Montoya, Alonso de. *Instrucción política y práctica judicial.* Madrid: B. Cano, 1788.

Secondary Sources

Ardit Lucas, Manuel. *Revolución liberal y revuelta campesina.* Barcelona: Ariel, 1977.

Azcona, Tarsicio de. *Isabel la Católica.* Madrid: Editorial Católica, 1964.

Baer, Yitzak. *A History of the Jews in Christian Spain.* 2 vols. Philadelphia: Jewish Publication Society, 1966.

Barceló Torres, María del Carmen. *Minorías islámicas en el país valenciano: Historia y dialecto.* Valencia: Universidad de Valencia, 1984.

Bataillon, Marcel. *Erasmo y España.* Translated by Antonio Alatorre. 2d ed. Madrid: Fondo de Cultura Económica, 1979.

Beinart, Haim. *Conversos on Trial: The Inquisition in Ciudad Real.* Jerusalem: The Magnus Press, 1981.

Bennassar, Bartolomé, ed. *L'Inquisition espagnole, XV–XVI siècle.* Paris: Hachette, 1979.

Boronat y Barrachina, P. *Los moriscos españoles y su expulsión.* Valencia: Francisco Vives y Mora, 1901.

Boyajian, James. *Portuguese Bankers at the Court of Spain.* New Brunswick, N.J.: Rutgers University Press, 1983.

Burns, Robert. *The Crusader Kingdom of Valencia.* 2 vols. Cambridge: Harvard University Press, 1967.

———. *Muslims, Christians, and Jews in the Crusader Kingdom of Valencia.* Cambridge: Cambridge University Press, 1984.

Canet Aparisi, Teresa. *La audiencia valenciana en la época foral moderna.* Valencia: Institució Valenciana D'Estudis I Investigació, 1986.

Cardaillac, Louis. *Moriscos y cristianos: Un enfrentamiento polémico.* Translated by Mercedes García Arenal. Madrid: Fondo de Cultura Económica, 1979.

Caro Baroja, Julio. *El señor inquisidor y otras vidas por oficio.* Madrid: Alianza, 1968.

———. *Los Judíos en la España moderna y contemporànea.* 3 vols. Madrid: Arión, 1962.

———. *The World of the Witches.* Translated by O. N. V. Glendinning. London: Weidenfeld and Nicolson, 1965; Chicago: University of Chicago Press, The Nature of Human Society Series, 1975.

Carrasco, Rafael. *Inquisición y represión sexual en Valencia.* Barcelona: Laertes, 1985.

Casey, James. *The Kingdom of Valencia in the Seventeenth Century.* Cambridge: Cambridge University Press, 1979.

Contreras, Jaime. *El Santo Oficio de la Inquisición de Galicia 1560–1700.* Madrid: Akal, 1982.

Couturier, Marcel. *Recherches sur les structures sociales de Chateaudun.* Paris, SEVPEN, 1969.

Defourneaux, Marcelin. *L'Inquisition espagnole et les livres français au XVIII siècle.* Paris: PUF, 1963.

———. *Annales Historiques de la Révolution Française* 2 (1963): 161–184.

Domínguez Ortíz, Antonio. *Sociedad y estado en el siglo XVIII español.* Barcelona: Ariel, 1979.

Elliott, J. H. *The Count-Duke of Olivares.* New Haven: Yale University Press, 1986.

Fayard, Janine. *Les membres du conseil de Castille a l'époque moderne.* Geneva: Droz, 1979.

Foucault, Michel. *Surveiller et punir: Naissance de la prison.* Paris: Gallimard, 1975.

Friedman, Ellen. *Spanish Captives in North America in the Early Modern Age.* Madison: University of Wisconsin Press, 1983.

Fuster, Joan. *Nosaltres, els Valencians.* Barcelona: Ediciones 62, 1962.

García Cárcel, Ricardo. *Orígenes de la Inquisición española.* Barcelona: Peninsula, 1976.

———. *Herejía y sociedad en el siglo XVI.* Barcelona: Peninsula, 1980.

———. "Las rentas de la Inquisición de Valencia en el siglo XVIII," *Estudis* 4 (1975): 231–240.

García Cárcel, Ricardo, and Ciscar Pallares, E. *Moriscos i agermants.* Valencia: L'Estel, 1974.

Gerbet, Marie Claude. *La noblesse dans le royaume de Castille.* Paris: Publications de la Sorbonne, 1979.

Greenleaf, Richard. *The Mexican Inquisition of the Sixteenth Century.* Albuquerque: University of New Mexico Press, 1969.

Halperin Donghi, Tulio. *Un conflicto nacional: Moriscos y cristianos viejos en Valencia.* Valencia: Institución Alfonso el Magnánimo, 1980.

Haliczer, Stephen. "The Castilian Urban Patriciate and the Jewish Expulsions of 1480–92," *The American Historical Review* 78 (February 1973): 35–58.

———. *The Comuneros of Castile: The Forging of a Revolution, 1475–1521.* Madison: University of Wisconsin Press, 1981.

Haliczer, Stephen, ed. *Inquisition and Society in Early Modern Europe.* London: Croom-Helm, 1986.

Hamilton, Earl J. *Money, Prices, and Wages in Valencia, Aragon, and Navarre, 1351–1500.* Cambridge: Harvard University Press, 1936.

Henningsen, Gustav. *The Witches' Advocate: Basque Witchcraft and the Spanish Inquisition.* Reno: University of Nevada Press, 1980.

———. "El 'banco de datos' del Santo Oficio: Las relaciones de causas de la Inquisición española," *Boletín de la Real Academia de la Historia* CLXXIV (1977): 549–570.

Henningsen, Gustav, and John Tedeschi, eds. *The Inquisition in Early Modern Europe.* DeKalb: Northern Illinois University Press, 1986.

Huerga, Alvaro. *Historia de los alumbrados.* 2 vols. Madrid: Fundación Universitaria Española, 1978.

Kagan, Richard L. *Students and Society in Early Modern Spain.* Baltimore: Johns Hopkins University Press, 1976.

———. *Lawsuits and Litigants in Castile: 1500–1700.* Chapel Hill: University of North Carolina Press, 1981.

Kamen, Henry. *The War of Succession in Spain.* London: Weidenfeld and Nicolson, 1969.

———. *Inquisition and Society in Spain, 1700–15.* Bloomington: Indiana University Press, 1985.

———. "Confiscations in the Economy of the Spanish Inquisition," *Economic History* Review 17 (1979): 514–517.

Ladurie, Le Roy. *Montaillou: The Promised Land of Error.* New York: Braziller, 1978.

Langbein, John. *Prosecuting Crime in the Renaissance.* Cambridge: Harvard University Press, 1974.

———. *Torture and the Law of Proof.* Chicago: University of Chicago Press, 1977.

Lapeyre, Henri. *La Géographie de l'Espagne morisque.* Paris: SEVPEN, 1959.

Lea, Henry Charles. *A History of the Inquisition of Spain.* 4. vols. New York: Macmillan, 1906–07.

———. *The Moriscos of Spain: Their Conversion and Expulsion.* Philadelphia: Lea Brothers, 1901; reprint, New York: Greenwood Press, 1966.

Llorente, Juan Antonio. *The History of the Inquisition of Spain.* London: G. B. Wittaker, 1827.

Mandrou, Robert, *Magistrats et sorciers en France au XVII siècle.* Paris: Plon, 1968.

Márquez, Antonio. *Los Alumbrados: Orígines y filosofía.* Madrid: Taurus, 1972.

Martínez Millán, José. *La hacienda de la Inquisición, 1478–1700.* Madrid: CSIC, 1984.

Mestre, Antonio. *Ilustración y reforma de la Iglesia: Pensamiento político-religioso de D. Gregorio Mayans y Síscar.* Valencia: Ayuntamiento de Oliva, 1968.

Molinié-Bertrand, Annie. "Les 'Hidalgos' dans le royaume de Castille à la fin du XVIe siècle," *Revue d'histoire économique et sociale* 52 (1974): 62–78.

Netanyahu, Benzion. *The Marranos of Spain from the Late XVth to the Early XVI Century.* New York: American Academy for Jewish Research, 1966.

Parker, Geoffrey. *Phillip II.* London: Hutchinson, 1979.

Pérez Villanueva, Joaquín, ed. *La Inquisición española: Nueva visión, nuevos horizontes.* Madrid: Siglo Veintiuno, 1980.

Pérez Villanueva, J., and Escandell Bonet, Bartolomé, eds. *Historia de la Inquisición en España y América.* 4 vols. Madrid: Editorial Católica, 1984.

Pinto Crespo, Virgilio. *Inquisición y control ideológico en la España del siglo XVI.* Madrid: Taurus, 1983.

Reglá, Joan, ed. *Historia del país Valencià.* 4 vols. Barcelona: Ediciones 62, 1975.

Sicroff, Albert. *Les controverses des statutes de pureté de sang en Espagne du XV au XVIII siècle.* Paris: Marcel Didier, 1960.

Tejeda, Luis Alonso. *Ocaso de la Inquisición en los últimos años del reinado de Fernando VII.* Madrid: Zero, 1969.

Tomás y Valiente, Francisco. *El derecho penal de la monarquía absoluta.* Madrid: Tecnos, 1969.

Wolff, Philippe. "The 1391 Pogrom in Spain: Social Crisis or Not," *Past and Present* 50 (February 1971): 5–18.

Yerushalmi, Yosef Hayim. *From Spanish Court to Italian Ghetto.* New York: Columbia University Press, 1971.

Index